REALITY AND FAITH

By the same author:

Theology and Preaching, a translation by Harold Knight of *Dogmatik und Verkündigung*

REALITY AND FAITH

THE THEOLOGICAL LEGACY OF
DIETRICH BONHOEFFER

by

HEINRICH OTT

FORTRESS PRESS · PHILADELPHIA

Printed in Great Britain

CONTENTS

CONTENTS

Part Three

THE FUTURE

ABBREVIATIONS,
ACKNOWLEDGMENTS, ETC.

Works of Bonhoeffer:

LPP   *Letters and Papers from Prison*, 3rd. rev. edn., tr. Fuller, rev. Clarke, etc., S.C.M. Press, 1967 (E.T. of *Widerstand und Ergebung*, Munich, 1951, 12th edn., 1964). (Note:—Earlier editions of E.T. gave too free a translation to meet Ott's almost exegetical purposes).

E   *Ethics*, tr. Horton Smith, S.C.M. Press, 1955 (E.T. of *Ethik*, Munich, 1949).

Ch.   *Christology*, tr. Bowden, Collins, 1966 (from *Ges. Sch.* III, pp. 166–242—Lectures from students' notes).

SC   *Sanctorum Communio*, tr. Gregor Smith, Collins, 1963 (E.T. of Ibid., Berlin, 1930, 3rd. edn., Munich, 1960—Doctoral Dissertation).

AB   *Act and Being*, tr. Noble, Collins, 1962 (E.T. of *Akt und Sein*, Gütersloh, 1931, and Munich, 1956—Inaugural Dissertation).

CD   *The Cost of Discipleship*, tr. Fuller, S.C.M. Press, 6th. (complete) edn., 1959 (E.T. of *Nachfolge*, Munich, 1937).

Creation and Fall, tr. Fletcher, 1959; in *Creation and Temptation*, S.C.M. Press, 1966 (E.T. of *Schopfung und Fall*, Munich, 1937).

Ges. Sch.   *Gesammelte Schriften*, I–IV, Munich, 1958–61.

No Rusty Swords, tr. Robertson and Bowden, Collins, 1965.

The Way to Freedom, tr. Robertson and Bowden, Collins, 1966. (Both selections from *Ges. Sch.*).

American publishers are as follows:

LPP, E, CD, and *Creation and Fall*: The Macmillan Co.

AB   *No Rusty Swords*, and *The Way to Freedom*: Harper & Row

Ch.   under the title *Christ the Center*: Harper & Row

SC   under the title *Communion of Saints*: Harper & Row

A*   9

Others:

Die mündige Welt (Collected Essays on Bonhoeffer), I–IV, Munich, 1959–63.

Zeit und Geschichte. Zeit und Geschichte. Dankesgabe an Rudolf Bultmann zum 80. Geburtstag, Tübingen, 1964.

English readers may also require:

RGG *Die Religion in Geschichte und Gegenwart,* Tübingen, 3rd edn., 1957–65 (Encyclopaedia of Religion).

WA *Weimarer Ausgabe* (Standard Edition of Luther's Works).

ThZs *Theologische Zeitschrift,* Basel.

ZThK *Zeitschrift für Theologie und Kirche,* Tübingen.

rowohlts deutsche enzyklöpadie (a library of scientific paperbacks).

Denzinger. Enchiridion symbolorum definitionum et declarationum de rebus fidei et morum, ed. Heinrich Denzinger. (Standard collection of authoritative Roman documents).

Thanks are extended to the publishers of English translations of many of the works quoted for allowing borrowings to be made.

PREFACE

TODAY (on February 4, 1966, to be exact) Dietrich Bonhoeffer would be sixty years old and doubtless the recipient of a *Festschrift* both massive and important in content, as the honoured teacher of several generations of students, and at the same time a man at the height of his intellectual creative power, our teacher and contemporary. But the witness of his life as Christian and theologian in fact found fulfilment in another way more than twenty years ago—and for that reason has speedily and widely won the attention of Christendom both in Europe and in America.

But Bonhoeffer is not merely of historical significance. Up till now he has not become a landmark in the history of theological ideas; more than twenty years after his death he still belongs in the history of the Christian Church and of theology more to the future than to the past. However great the impression left by his life and work already in the years immediately after the War, the time has only gradually become ripe for the understanding of him. But today the situation would seem so to have developed that he *must* be understood in the essence and in the whole power of his thought. For the present situation of Christendom is determined by the certainty of our need for renewal in the Church. This is why in our day the Roman Catholic Church has set out on the way of *aggiornamento* with its Second Vatican Council.

But what has become of the Protestant *aggiornamento*? For after all, this is a problem for all Christendom! Often one gets the impression that in the Protestant world the awareness which it would require of the problem is still suppressed by a widespread attitude of clericalism or traditionalism. And yet it is this awareness of the problem which in the Protestant martyr Dietrich Bonhoeffer meets us with a distinctness which cannot but be noticed. On the other side it would seem to me that things are made too easy in the Protestant movement called the "Death of God Theology", in that while it certainly sees clearly the problem set to Christians through their confrontation by an era of implicit atheism, it does not solve the problem but rather gets rid of it by hasty concessions to the spirit of the age.

Dietrich Bonhoeffer saw clearly that the necessary renewal of the Church of Jesus Christ could not easily be carried out, that it required a spiritual foundation which could bear its weight, and a transformation in the awareness of faith. That is to say, theology is summoned to an exceptionally taxing effort of thought. This was the road on which Bonhoeffer was to be found, and accordingly his theology could be said to have an eminently practical significance, belonging to "Church politics" in the widest sense.

My own theological preoccupation with Bonhoeffer goes back a considerable time. My introduction to him was made through his *Ethik* ("Ethics"), and the impressions gained from the study of it were then confirmed by *Widerstand und Ergebung* ("Letters and Papers from Prison") and the earlier writings. In the Preface to *Dogmatik und Verkündigung* (1961— E.T., "Theology and Preaching", tr. Knight, Lutterworth, 1965) I first mentioned Bonhoeffer in a similar context, even then beside Rudolf Bultmann and Karl Barth. What in these two teachers seemed to be normative, without the possibility of really bringing the two together, I found united in Bonhoeffer. And in the interim the theological factual position has for me become still further clarified.

Usually we are led along a path of thought and do not arbitrarily go as we please. This has been my experience with Bonhoeffer and the problem of reality. The problems, because of which Bonhoeffer became important, gradually, but inevitably, took a clearer shape and in the same measure my interest in him also grew, until finally it became clear to me that my next step would have to be to deal with him. And this I have attempted to do in this book.

Although the discussions which follow concentrate to a large extent on the thought of Bonhoeffer, and are often even quite explicitly devoted to the exegetical questions of the interpretation of his relevant passages, yet the claim cannot be made that a comprehensive historical and general interpretation of his work is here being offered. There is not the necessary completeness for that. Nevertheless the purpose is throughout a systematic one, though not in the sense that Bonhoeffer is to serve merely as a source-book and confirmation for my own thoughts, but rather in the sense of a dialogue, and a dialogue in which one speaker as teacher has the first and most important word. (But not necessarily the last word also—that no good human teacher would claim!) In the last resort we probably only discover truth by coming together in dialogue. And it has been my experience, which has stood the test, that it is precisely when we recognize some fact and wish to speak about it that we do well to maintain discussion with those thinkers who have heard the call of the same subject. God be thanked that we are seldom alone when essential subjects lay their spell upon us. But conversely we surely do most justice to a thinker when we speak, not primarily *about* him, but *with* him about his *subject*. And this again we can only do when his subject is important to ourselves also.

This book contains many extended quotations from Bonhoeffer himself. This should be the expression of the fact that the partner in discussion gets his opportunity to speak. On the other side the reader should be put in the position where he can the more easily test the correctness of my interpretation of Bonhoeffer as an affirmation which I myself make on the same subject and for which I take responsibility. The numerous footnotes in the book are not to be understood as a scholarly apparatus, but equally as systematic statements on the subject itself. That much is said in a supplementary way in footnotes is due to the fact that the manuscript of considerable parts served first as the basis for lectures.

As the book took form it became obvious to me that the road it travelled led yet further. The next two steps which are forced upon one by the subject itself are (1) a theological demonstration of the personal nature of God in conjunction with the personal and existential nature of human life, and (2) the working out of a Christologically determined, non-casuistic ethic. This, *sub conditione Iacobea*, will be the continuation of the quest on the subject of "Reality and Faith".

Finally, there remains to me the pleasant duty of expressing thanks. I thank the *Schweizerische Nationalfond zur Forderung der wissenschaftlichen Forschung* for its generous support in the form of a credit for the publication of the book, Frau E. Gebus-Jundt for unwearied help in the preparation of the manuscript, and my assistant, Dr. Klaus Otte, D.Theol., for his conscientious checking of quotations and revision of printer's proofs. Finally I thank my friend, Dr. Ervin Vályi Nagy. Our unforgettable discussions on the bank of the Plattensee, in Budapest and in Basel, conversations in which it was often impossible to say to whom a thought had originally come, remain indissolubly bound up with the coming into being of this book.

At, Drew University
  Madison, N.J., U.S.A.
    February 22, 1966   HEINRICH OTT

PROLOGUE — JEREMIAH 45

IN THE LAST YEAR and a half of his life, during the time of his imprisonment, one word of Holy Scripture above all others occupied the mind of Dietrich Bonhoeffer. It was the short chapter Jeremiah 45, the word of Jahweh through Jeremiah to Baruch, who was lamenting his own fate and that of his people:

> "Behold what I have built I am breaking down, and what I have planted I am plucking up, even this whole land. And do you seek great things for yourself? Seek them not. For behold I am bringing evil upon all flesh, says the Lord; but I will give you your life as a prize of war in all places to which you may go." (Jeremiah 45; 4, 5; trans. as in LPP quotations following).

Of the one phrase above all, ". . . I will give you your life as a prize of war . . .", Bonhoeffer confesses that he would never get away from it any more, and he quotes it on the most varied occasions and from the most varied points of view. We can confirm this by reading his letters from prison (LPP). The Bible text seems to have made itself something like a keyword for what was axiomatic in his Christian and theological life in this last significant period. There seems to ring out in it what was most elemental in his life, in its experience and in its meaning.

In it he found that sense, so important for Bonhoeffer precisely in his last months, of solidarity with certain men, without whom he could not live, a solidarity unbroken even by walls or by distance. This sense of being united with his fellowmen, which even then in his late thought breaks through with great power, presses in upon him in the word from Jeremiah,

> ". . . It is only then that we feel how closely our lives are bound up with other people's, and in fact how the centre of our own lives is outside ourselves and how little we are separate

entities. The 'as though it were a part of me' is perfectly true, as I have often felt after hearing that one of my colleagues or pupils has been killed. I think it is a literal fact of Nature that human life extends far beyond our physical existence. Probably a mother feels this more strongly then anyone else. There are two passages in the Bible which always seem to me to sum the thing up. One is from Jeremiah 45, 'Behold, what I have built I am breaking down, and what I have planted I am plucking up . . . And do you seek great things for yourself? Seek them not . . . But I will give you your life as a prize of war . . .'' (LPP, p. 65).

Again, in it he found the consciousness of the fragmentary character of his own life, a knowledge of himself on Bonhoeffer's part which will gain pre-eminent importance methodologically as we come to deal with his thought. The days of neatly rounded, inwardly complete, records of lives and their works seem to be over.

If our life is but the remotest reflection of such a fragment, if we accumulate, at least for a short time, a wealth of themes and weld them together into a harmony in which the great counter-point is maintained from start to finish, so that at last, when it breaks off abruptly, we can sing no more than the chorale, *Vor deinen Thron tret' ich allhier*, we will not bemoan the frag-mentariness of our life, but rather rejoice in it. I can never get away from Jeremiah 45 . . . Here, too, is a necessary fragment of life—"but I will give you your life as a prize of war" (LPP, pp. 135ff.).

He also reflects upon the exceptional time in which he is fated to live, and on one occasion says,

"I think that God is about to accomplish something that, even if we take part in it either outwardly or inwardly, we can only receive with the greatest wonder and awe" (LPP, p. 151).

This letter is written on April 30, 1944, and without doubt Bonhoeffer is here thinking of the impending attempt on Hitler, and the hoped-for revolution, the end of the National Socialist rule of terror. And he remarks on the subject, ". . .and we shall have to repeat Jeremiah 45: 5 to ourselves every day" (LPP, p. 151).

The same is true of his "Thoughts on the Baptism of D.W.R." of May, 1944, where he writes:

"But we have learnt by experience that we cannot plan even for the coming day, that what we have built up is being destroyed overnight, and that our life, in contrast to that of our parents, has become formless or even fragmentary. In spite of that I can only say that I have no wish to live in any other time than our own, even though it is so inconsiderate of our outward well-being. We realize more clearly than formerly that the world lies under the wrath and grace of God (... here follows the quotation from Jeremiah 45 ...). If we can save our souls unscathed out of the wreckage of our material possessions, let us be satisfied with that. If the Creator destroys his own handiwork, what right have we to lament the destruction of ours? It will be the task of our generation, not to 'seek great things', but to save and preserve our souls out of the chaos, and to realize that it is the only thing we can carry as a 'prize' from the burning building" (LPP, p. 169).

And finally, in autumn 1944 Bonhoeffer sounds the note, so important to him, of "this-worldliness":

"I discovered later, and I am still discovering right up to this moment, that it is only by living completely in this world that one learns to have faith. One must completely abandon every attempt to make something of oneself ... By this-worldliness I mean living unreservedly in life's duties, problems, successes and failures, experiences and perplexities. In so doing we throw ourselves completely into the arms of God, taking seriously, not our own sufferings but those of God in the world—watching with Christ in Gethsemane. That, I think, is faith, that is *metanoia*; and that is how one becomes a man and a Christian (cp. Jeremiah 45!)" (LPP, pp. 201f.).

This is how Bonhoeffer speaks of his concrete situation in prison and of his human experiences, how he reflects on his life, how he gives meaning to the age in which he lives, and how he thinks of his great theological theme. It is always with the same text emblazoned before him, a text whose very sound and rhythm, as bearers of a promise, had surely laid their spell upon him, "but I will give you your life as a prize of war". What is the common factor in all these sides to his life, the common purport behind all these thoughts, so unconnected to all seeming with one another? It is surely no return, as one might perhaps think at a superficial glance, to an imperishable individual possession of salvation. Bonhoeffer's whole thought is orientated too strongly against individualism for that.

It is difficult to speak about what Bonhoeffer felt in the unextinguishable ring of this saying, what led him, what clarified and inspired his life and thought—and what he yet manifestly never expressed directly himself. Yet to put what was obviously an unspeakable comfort for him into a single rough concept, was not the common factor in these so seemingly disparate contexts for the text from Jeremiah a call to existential concreteness which could not be avoided? "But I will give you your life as a prize of war"; "life" here means the life of each man in his own unalterable concrete context, that one is *hic und nunc* in the given situation and context of the course of one's life. For Bonhoeffer it was his living in imprisonment with that quite palpable sense of solidarity with men outside, with whom one is bound together "as though it were a part of me" (LPP, p. 65).

> "I think it is a literal fact of Nature that human life extends far beyond our physical existence" (LPP, p. 65).

It was living in that storm-tossed time in which, for the eye of faith, God was quite palpably preparing to act. It was living in the fragmented course of life which was his fate, the life which was ordained for this individual. It was living in the "this-worldliness" of life, with all "its duties, problems, successes and failures, experiences and perplexities". In accepting such a this-worldliness, such a concreteness, a man becomes a Christian and, properly speaking, a "man" for the first time! Such acceptance is faith and conversion.

"But I will give you your life as a prize of war . . .", that is to say, God shows to man in this concreteness of his existence, that he is forcing it upon him and yet at the same time presenting it to him as his, as his "prize of war" which is and will remain his own. "I will give you your life as a prize of war" means that "this life of yours as it is I give you as a possession which cannot be lost and a place where you are to find me, your Lord". In prison, in the fragmentary course of one's own life, in the irresistible tempest of the time, in the ambiguity and complexity, and yet primitiveness and banality, of the being of everyman dwells God. Here and nowhere else will he be found. What a man experiences, whether it be in brutal unalterable harshness, or in the brooding of a scarcely noticeable feeling or question, the many things which befall him, "the silent things, the good and the evil, the things endured, in which you walk..." Gottfried Benn, *Epilogue IV*), these are the dwelling-place of God.

"Behold, what I have built I am breaking down and what I have planted I am plucking up ... but I will give you your life as a prize of war in all places to which you go." Whatever else may happen, God is genuinely there in your life! You will find the invisible only and precisely in what you see and experience! This entangled life of delight and sorrow which is yours is the one thing which remains to you, which you save out of the catastrophe. It is your prize of war and in it you possess all that you need.

Obviously this "life", this "living soul", is no individualistic category which permits the individual to appear alone before God. The individuality includes and will not relinquish the concrete involvement of our destinies with those of our fellows.

It would be said that in this late experience of Bonhoeffer with a Bible text, in the fascination which it has for him and which it gains for the reader through him, we have illuminated for us the *one* theme of his life's history and life's work. For this seems to me to run through his thought from beginning to end, the uncompromisingly honest endeavour to look in the face the concreteness of the reality lived and to be lived by us, to stand by it without subtraction, without speculative addition, without self-deception, without allowing himself to be misled by artificial theories and mere words which lack equivalent value in the experience of reality. We are challenged by our time, by our own existential situation. If we still can speak about God we must do so within the compass of this existential situation. The reality of our life, the reality of our experiences, is inescapable. We cannot flee from it, we cannot flee from the era in which we are placed, from the convictions of this era or from its historical entanglements. On one thing Bonhoeffer was quite clear, that he must stand firm through a demonic age, but he found his place in this very age and did not hanker after living in any other. Again one cannot escape from the entanglements of one's own personal life, nor from the men one is confronted with here and now, whether or not this is what one has already conceived and wished. Reality is called reality because its effects are inescapable. This is its fundamental mark.

But if God lives and if Jesus Christ is his final word, then this must be as inescapable as life itself. To fail to see or to deny the inescapability of the situation, to seek to break out of it, would have been for Bonhoeffer a flight into insincerity. It would have been insincere to speak about God, and to seek to find him elsewhere than strictly in this place, in the military prison at Tegel, in a National Socialist Germany which, already bearing the marks of collapse, was unleashing its last demons, in the anxiety and fragmentariness of a life of insecurity, a life claimed at all times by the duties of the moment, a life highly endowed with talents which secretly bore in themselves the consciousness that they were not to reach their fulfilment, in coming face to face with the nobility or banality of this man or that, and this in the midst of an age which was largely convinced that man by himself was able to be quit of most problems and had no more need of the "working hypothesis of God". If God lives anywhere, Bonhoeffer deduced, he lives here. It was the enlightenment given to Jacob, "Surely the Lord is in this place and I knew it not" (Gen. 28: 16). And so for Bonhoeffer the two inescapabilities, the inescapability of God and the inescapability of the situation, converged. So reality became his keyword, his motto, the word which stood for his problems. The problems he thus sensed appears in varied forms in the course of his pilgrimage, but in the last resort it is always the same.

PART ONE

Situation and Method

CHAPTER ONE

DIETRICH BONHOEFFER AND THE PRESENT THEOLOGICAL SITUATION

I. *General Characteristics of the Situation*

AFTER thinking about a Bible text in this way in order to bring before ourselves Bonhoeffer's basic experiences and questions, we ask in the second place about his possible significance for the present theological (and ecclesiastical) situation. For it is no mere historical interest which causes our desire to concern ourselves with him, but the fact that we look for certain insights arising out of our discussion with him, in other words because we believe that what he felt and thought is as topical in our own situation as it was in his, indeed it may be that it is only now beginning to gain its proper relevance.

Bonhoeffer as a martyr has become to a wide public a kind of Protestant saint of our own time, and surely not unjustly so. But to make sure that the result will not be a sentimental Bonhoeffer cult without clear lineaments we must give thought to *what* this Christian witness stands for, and what is exemplary and of especial importance in his testimony.

The situation in our own day of Protestant Christendom is marked on the one side by a hardening into fronts within and on the other by mighty challenges without. To put it very crudely and without discrimination, an objectivism orientated towards tradition is faced by a subjectivism orientated towards the present. This position has lasted since at least the end of the Second World War, and since then men have often in the end had little more to say than polemic and votes of no confidence. The challenges from without come on the one side from a humanity which, more or less consciously, has not ceased to expect the word of truth from the Church of Jesus

Christ, a humanity which asks for bread and not stones, and on the other side from Christian Churches of another stamp, in particular the Church of Rome which is setting out to satisfy this challenge of modern humanity, and seeks the co-operation and solidarity of Protestant Christians to that end, knowing that only one unified witness of the Church will appeal to a humanity which is one. Now it would seem that in the last years of the war Bonhoeffer saw—or foresaw— a situation very like this and judged accordingly, except of course that he could not have foreknown the astonishing ecumenical developments of the last few years. He saw the fronts harden, he saw the unfruitfulness of certain approaches and emphases, and for this reason he refused every party allegiance, and made himself all the more resolutely open to the challenge of men because he recognized in it the challenge of God himself. For this reason Bonhoeffer must appear to us one of the most hope-inspiring figures, perhaps the most hope-inspiring figure, of modern Protestantism. For we look to him, not merely for some solution of the problems hanging over us, but for directions for the fulfilment of our own important tasks. He will prove himself helpful in three respects: (1) as regards the challenge of ecumenical discussion, especially with his conception of the Church as *Communio Sanctorum*, (2) as regards the authenticity of the Church's word to the world, especially with the question which was engaging his attention most of all at the end, his postulate of a non-religious interpretation of Biblical concepts, and also with the especial theme of his *Ethics*, his main work which he had just begun, his concept of responsible activity in the world, and (3) finally, as regards the reformulation of the central points of our faith in keeping with our task of today, especially with his Christological "vision", the foundation supporting his *Ethics* and the specific kernel of his thought.

2. *Bonhoeffer and the Atheism-Debate in Theology*

There has been given to Protestant theology the task of keeping alive and expounding the theological legacy of Dietrich Bonhoeffer, perhaps the most radical Protestant thinker of our era. Twenty years have now passed since the untimely death of this Christian witness, but what he thought and sensed is today more relevant, belongs more to the present and future, than much that is only now being written.

The work which he left behind him justly demands our strictest attention. His legacy must be carefully administered and made fruitful. For we can find in this theologian the approach to a solution of almost every essential problem which is the concern of theology today.

Thus, for example, Bishop John A. T. Robinson in his *Honest to God* (S.C.M., 1963) quotes Bonhoeffer at the decisive point where, under the heading "The End of Theism?", he speaks of the necessity of a transformation in the Christian understanding of God. He cites his words about "having to live in the world *etsi Deus non daretur*", about God himself "who makes us live in this world without using him as a working hypothesis", who compels us to "live without God" before him and with him (cp. Robinson, pp. 37ff.), and passes very quickly from this point to the conclusion, "We shall eventually be no more able to convince men of a God 'out there' whom they must call in to order their lives than persuade them to take seriously the gods of Olympus. If Christianity is to survive, let alone to recapture 'secular' man, there is no time to lose in detaching it from this scheme of thought, from this particular theology or *logos* about *theos*, and thinking hard about what we should put in its place" (p. 43). Robinson gave this question a wide popularity, without however completely thinking it through, and in the end it remains somewhat uncertain what precisely he seeks to include under the heading, "a theistic scheme of thought". It is not only what is to take the place of the old which is uncertain, and Robinson is careful to leave that question open, but also what in any case is this "old" which is to disappear as soon as possible. Robinson may speak of the antiquated and in the last resort mythological "theistic" picture of a God "out there", but it remains a question if, purely as a matter of phenomenology, his grasp of the "theistic" faith in one God has been adequate. Is the essential point of this faith really to be found in the definition of God as one "out there"? Surely traditional Christian doctrine has rather always been aware that God is not only "without" the world, but also at the same time in a most real sense *in* the world as the God who is near, who surrounds me at all times here and now in my concrete reality, "in whom we live and move and have our being", and who is therefore not only the distant ruler of a world above and beyond. Robinson then has already missed the essence of "theism" in his description of it. Its true essence could be described in this way, that in my here and now I am confronted by a person, greater than myself and inescapable. Again, when Robinson, says, "Classical Christian theology has not in fact spoken of God as 'a person' . . . and the Church's best theologians have not laid themselves open to such attack . . . Yet popular Christianity has always posited such a supreme personality" (pp. 39f.), he overlooks something essential. For in the fundamental facts of prayer to God, but also in the fundamental facts of theology in general,[1] the personality, the confrontation, the independence and freedom of God are already implicitly present as part of what is said, even if we grant that the common understanding of person and personality is not adequate for this subject, nor indeed sufficiently clear in itself.

It is these fundamental facts for example, and not any "theistic" otherworldliness, which are what is properly the meaning of the authoritative statement of Roman doctrine in Vatican I, which maintains the existence of God with the utmost binding force, though we must add at the same time, in a way which demands unending interpretation, with this formulation:

> "*Sancta catholica apostolica Romana Ecclesia credit et confitetur, unum esse Deum verum et vivum, creatorem ac Dominum coeli et terrae, omnipotentem, aeternum, immensum, incomprehensibilem, intellectu ac voluntate omnique perfectione infinitum; qui cum sit una singularis, simplex omnino et incommutabilis substantia spiritualis, praedicandus est et re et essentia a mundo distinctus, in se et ex se beatissimus, et super omnia, quae praeter ipsum sunt et concipi possunt, ineffabiliter excelsus*" (Denzinger, 1782).

(E.T. as in New. Cath. Encycl. (Cath. Univ. Amer.), Vol. VI, 1967, p. 542, in Art. "God")—"The Holy Catholic Apostolic Roman Church believes and confesses that there is one true living God, Creator and Lord of heaven and earth, almighty,

---

[1] I have already spoken of this in rather more detail in *Theologie als Gebet und als Wissenschaft*, ThZ Jg. 14, 1958, pp. 120–132, the article also appearing in *Kirche und Verkündigung. Aufsätze zum Kerygma der Gegenwart*, Evangelische Verlagsanstalt, Berlin, 1960, pp. 57ff.

eternal, immense, incomprehensible, infinite in intelligence, in will and in all perfection, who as being one, sole, absolutely simple and immutable spiritual substance, is to be declared as really and essentially distinct from the world, in supreme beatitude in and from Himself, and ineffably exalted above all things beside Himself which exist or are conceivable".)

Everything, quite everything, in this statement of doctrine is open to question and stands in need of interpretation. Almost every concept employed would today surely have to be replaced by others. Questionable, for instance, and scarcely tenable is the concept here used of substantiality. Questionable is the ontological category of perfection, the dualism of intellect and will, and in need of interpretation through and through are such concepts as *unus, vivus, omnipotens, aeternus*, etc. And yet when all has been said the fundamental position, the declaration which is intended here, remains clear, and in my belief it so belongs to the Christian faith and confession that it could not be surrendered. This remarkable discrepancy, this collocation, at first sight so astonishing, of essential clarity on the one side, and deep-seated openness to question and need of interpretation on the other, can only be understood by one who has made himself at home in one fundamental problem of theology, the problem of hermeneutics, and who has the courage to venture into the still unlit deeps of this problem. There is much here which still awaits a first working-out. We can perhaps discern a certain approach to the consideration of this just-mentioned element of discrepancy, in Luther's thoughts on the outward and inward clarity of Holy Scripture, as he expounds them in *De Servo Arbitrio*.[2]

---

[2] Cp. W.A. 18, p. 609; "*Et ut breviter dicam, Duplex est claritas scripturae, sicut et duplex obscuritas. Una externa in verbi ministerio posita, altera in cordis cognitione sita. Si de interna claritate dixeris, nullus homo unum iota in scripturis videt, nisi qui spiritum Dei habet. ... Si de externa dixeris, Nihil prorsus relictum est obscurum aut ambiguum, sed omnis per verbum in lucem producta certissimam, et declarata toto orbi, quaecunque sunt in scripturis.*"
(E.T., *The Bondage of the Will*, tr. Packer and Johnston, James Clarke & Co., 1957, pp. 73f.: "In a word: The perspicuity of Scripture is twofold, just as there is a double lack of light. The first is external, and relates to the ministry of the Word; the second concerns the knowledge of the heart. If you speak of *internal* perspicuity, the truth is that nobody who has not the Spirit of God sees a jot of what is in the Scriptures ... If on the other hand you speak of *external* perspicuity, the position is that nothing whatsoever is left obscure

And yet the very posing of the problem could surely bring its own light—that I say something and have a picture of what I say, and that at the same time there yet remains an immense, unending amount to say, and that accordingly there enters a certain discrepancy between the unequivocality of the fact meant and the unavoidable variety and ambiguity of its exposition. And this is what we mean when we say that the fundamental facts, the God who confronts us, must always remain the same in theology and in confession of faith, and that yet all concepts in terms of which we have to speak of it must remain in the balance inviting question.

It follows that, while one may have reasons for being reserved or negative in one's attitude to "theism" as an "-ism", it is impossible to set aside these fundamental facts, if one is not to lose sight of the content of theology itself. To do Bishop Robinson justice on this point, it is important to note that he is cautious here. "We may not yet have a name with which to replace 'theism': indeed it may not prove necessary or possible to dispense with the term (hence the query in the title of this chapter)" (p. 43). This really brings us to the central question of *Honest to God* and *God is Other*. Of course God is always "other", a fact which has already been proclaimed with explosive power and effectiveness by the dialectical theology, and what is demanded from man is "honesty", unconditional and unreserved sincere openness in face of this fact—and is what we call "faith" really anything other than just this? But there remains then the question, "Who is this 'other' God?" But, and this is *our thesis*, if Robinson brings into question, not only "theism" as an "-ism" over-burdened in concept and portrayal, but also what we have called the fundamental facts themselves, then he has *no right whatever to quote Bonhoeffer* as an authority.

And it is interesting to note that this is precisely what he

---

or ambiguous, but all that is in Scripture is through the word brought forth into the clearest light and proclaimed to the whole world").

It is true that in this Luther did not yet have in view in any systematic way the general subject-matter of hermeneutics as we are concerned with it here. But in his concern with the Word of God in Holy Scripture he has nevertheless sensed something of the dialectic between the unequivocality of the fact meant, and the ambiguity, historical conditioning and openness to question of our understanding of it.

does at this point, and does with emphasis. Here is the decisive passage in Bonhoeffer which Robinson quotes under the title *"The End of Theism?"*:

> "And we cannot be honest unless we recognize that we have to live in the world *etsi deus non daretur*. And this is just what we do recognize—before God! God himself compels us to recognize it ... God would have us know that we must live as men who manage our lives without him. The God who is with us is the God who forsakes us ... The God who lets us live in the world without the working hypothesis of God is the God before whom we stand continually. Before God and with God we live without God ..." (LPP, p. 196).

There can be no doubt that we have here a kinship in the facts with Robinson. It was not for nothing that Eberhard Bethge, the friend of Bonhoeffer and editor of his works, edited and gave an introduction to the German translation of Robinson's book. The fact is that Bonhoeffer and Robinson are both facing the same stupefying phenomenon and problem, the "implicit atheism" of Christians and non-Christians in a technological age. But the question here at stake is that of the solution, or of the road to be taken in quest of a solution. Is it possible, in the endeavour to proclaim God to these contemporaries and to speak responsibly about God in theology, to seek to "end theism" as far as the fundamental facts are concerned? Or would one in the process "end" the Gospel itself? Possibly its essence is precisely "theism". If we follow this train of thought we could ask how these statements of Bonhoeffer with the phrase *etsi deus non daretur* are to be understood. Is it a case of the word *deus* here meaning a theist idea of God, while the word "God" points to another understanding of him which is no longer theist, perhaps to a concept of God as "the Ground of our being"? Then this real God today would be compelling us to live *etsi deus non daretur*, that is to say, the better understanding of God would be freeing us from the other, poorer, theist one. This solution, which could be that of Robinson, is too naïve and does not do justice to the characteristic dialectic of what Bonhoeffer seeks to say. For him the *"deus"* of the short Latin phrase is exactly identical with the "God" who "compels" us so to live before him. By both it is the one God who is meant, the one God always the same, confronting man in freedom, the God of those "fundamental facts", and whether or not the words "theism" or "theist" could or should be used with reference to him is throughout an irrelevance. And the mystery is precisely this, that *the same* God is present to man and acts upon him, *in the act of* his withdrawing himself from him and letting him live without God.

Bonhoeffer himself has not resolved or even adequately interpreted this dialectic, if I may so call it with the proviso that the word "dialectic" of course still does nothing to bring us a solution. But many, and among them perhaps Robinson, influenced and inspired by Bonhoeffer, have got rid of the problem in an all too naïve and undialectical way. Robinson's book doubtless gives voice to many justified trends of thought and raises many problems which are now really timely,[3] so that its immense effect is surely no accident, but its decisive weakness is to be found at this point. He has perhaps himself told the truth when he says in his Preface that "in retrospect, it will be seen to have erred in being", not too radical, but rather "not nearly radical enough" (p. 10). But possibly it is true in a different sense from that intended by Robinson himself.

Bonhoeffer himself is more radical than these followers of his who are all too ready to get rid of his dialectic, create a manageable solution of the embarrassing problem, and settle down comfortably in it. He thinks of the root of the problem without allowing himself to be forced into a simplification. The characteristic mark of this is when such followers quote him and then precisely at the decisive turn find that they can quote him no longer. This sets him at the starting-point and at the same time at the turning-point of a monstrous and inescapable ambiguity, as yet unsolved, one which he was perhaps the first among more recent theologians to see clearly. In him there finds expression, but still only as an intuition, what others are too ready to explain away doctrinally—and doctrinairely!

We see then Bonhoeffer already in the centre of one of the

---

[3] What seems to me a particularly discriminating and just criticism of Robinson's book is the essay by Robert Leuenberger, *Ehrlich vor Gott*, in *Reformatio*, No. 8, 1964. It deserves this description both for its valuation of Robinson's justified criticism of the outward forms of the Church, and for its decisive rejection of the theological foreshortening of which the book is guilty.

great battlefields of present-day theological controversy. The atheism-debate in theology is today making its waves burst upon the Protestant theological scene, among other reasons as a consequence of the great influence of Robinson's book. But it would be very mistaken to regard it as a mere passing fashion in Protestantism, and as such as really of third-rate importance. It has completely laid hold of Roman Catholic theology also, among other reasons as a result of the Council, proving thereby that it is a problem set for theology by our era.[4]

In this chapter we are endeavouring to find Bonhoeffer's place in theological discussion as it is today. And here we see him already at one of its centres. We shall have to show still other connecting lines between him and the theology of the present, but we shall pause for a moment at the "atheism problem". In German-speaking Protestant theology this has above all been a live issue in the debate between Herbert Braun, and Manfred Mezger, on the one side, and on the other Helmut Gollwitzer.[5] We shall seek here, with the help of a few characteristic quotations, to come to grips with the situation, because by these quotations the startling relevance of Bonhoeffer's thought will come still more clearly to light. We shall see in the course of this examination that there is in Herbert Braun, who presents his thesis with a lucid simplicity and with intellectual power, a clearly recognizable framework of premises which make it easy to sketch the counter-possibility and to show the obvious limitations of his conception. And we shall recognize on the other side that Helmut Gollwitzer emphasizes with complete justice the dangerous narrowness of Braun's conception and as against it seeks to give due place to the content of theology, its fundamental facts, but that while he does so there is a way in which he does not think radically enough, and that he sometimes remains bogged down in mere affirmations, a fact which gives his opponents the chance to

---

[4] One could think here of the recent appointment of a special "Secretariat for Unbelievers" under the leadership of Cardinal König of Vienna.

[5] Cp. esp. Herbert Braun, *Gesammelte Studien zum Neuen Testament und seiner Umwelt*, Tübingen, 1962, pp. 243–309, and *Gottes Existenz und meine Geschichtlichkeit im Neuen Testament. Eine Antwort an Helmut Gollwitzer*, in *Zeit und Geschichte*, 1964, pp. 399ff.; Helmut Gollwitzer, *The Existence of God as Confessed by Faith*, tr. Leitch, S.C.M., 1965; Manfred Mezger, *Redliche Predigt*, in *Zeit und Geschichte*, pp. 423f.

overlook and misunderstand his concern. And then it will be seen that it is precisely from Bonhoeffer that Gollwitzer's great concern, to think adequately of the personal reality of God as *the* fact of the Gospel, can be articulated as a precise problem, and surely then brought to a real, and not merely an asserted, alternative solution. And we shall see that it is from Bonhoeffer in the same way that the possibility which we are to sketch as a counter to Braun's conception, a concept of reality which is differentiated with the personal confrontation of God as a constant with remains firm, can be carried beyond a sketch to something of greater intellectual clarity.

Our thesis is that Bonhoeffer stands at the focal point of all the important questions discussed today by theology, or at least by systematic theology, and that he does so in such a way that his contribution is sometimes still something to be awaited, a contribution to which expression and relevant pointedness would have to be given by interpretation of his work, a contribution which in the matter in hand would still surpass in depth and illuminating power those already given. In this sense we believe that we can see in him the most radical and modern Protestant thinker of our time.

We have cast in the first place a glance at the atheism-debate in theology, a debate round which revolves, not only Protestant, but also Roman Catholic theology, though the latter naturally does so in a different way, since Catholics begin by being precluded by their doctrinal authorities from certain approaches. That this problem must obtrude itself upon us, and that this debate must be fought through, are facts founded upon developments in the history of the human spirit, in particular founded upon an epochal transformation in the human situation and in human awareness. It would not be correct, it is true, to say about this that man had completely lost the direct awareness of God, for sinful man has never possessed an unbroken relation to him. But surely the "collective premise" of Western humanity that there is a God, the presupposition which was universally understood and widely accepted without question, has become unstable. Of this factual situation Christian theology must take account, and Bonhoeffer was the first to recognize it. This is why he stands at the starting-point of the atheism-debate, but also at its crucial point, and is out ahead of those who have already made their contribution on this question, sometimes with quotations from him. The critical point of this debate is that point where the decision has to be made whether or not, in order to preserve the Christian *Kerygma*, we have to hold on to the fundamental facts of theology, our personal response to God, or rather our personal confrontation by God himself. To be unwilling to do this means that on this we can no longer quote Bonhoeffer. But the proper *articulation* of the fundamental facts, the credible articulation in our situation, is itself a question at stake. And in this the conceptual label "theism" plays only a secondary role.

How we are further to explain the historical revolution which led to the atheism-debate is of less importance and perhaps a question not to be answered with certainty. Theology must concentrate all its powers on speaking credibly in the situation as it has actually developed and now is.

We turn to examine the crucial point of the debate between Herbert Braun and Helmut Gollwitzer, where Gollwitzer puts up a fight for the fundamental facts while Braun seems ready to surrender them. Our surmise leads us to expect that Bonhoeffer is in advance of both, of Braun in the facts and of both in his methods.

But before we take up Braun and Gollwitzer critically with the aim of a more concrete understanding of Bonhoeffer's significance, I want to make the preliminary point that in my opinion we only have the right to approach Braun, Mezger and Gollwitzer critically when we really understand the actual problem which lies behind the atheism-debate in theology. For Gollwitzer it has to be said that with his great skill in theological understanding he has throughout realized this problem and this situation, and that therefore he is speaking to the point throughout. His protest is surely justified as necessary in the situation which the discussion had reached. It must be granted of his work, *The Existence of God as Confirmed by Faith*, that, as is obvious, it is a polemical work determined by the situation, and that therefore it still lacks that final precision which comes when the subject has really been thought out. But such publications, too, have in certain situations their good purpose.

We begin with Braun and refer to one of his most recent statements, *Gottes Existenz und meine Geschichtlichkeit im Neuen Testament. Eine Antwort an Helmut Gollwitzer.* In doing so we cannot deal with Braun's whole position, with its two constitutive concepts, "I ought" and "I can", which he uses to interpret what in his opinion is the determinative and truly unique and irrelinquishable element in the New Testament and the Christian *Kerygma* in general, but merely refer to what in him is essential for the salient point in the debate between atheism and theism. Braun formulates the problem as he sees it as follows:

"It is at this point rather that disagreement begins; does the event in which there comes to me the 'I can' and 'I ought' which saves me imply the confession of a *deus per se* and the confession of another world breaking into this" (p. 411).

The event to which Braun first refers is that of the *Kerygma*, in so far as it becomes effective in me and verifies itself as reality. "I ought" and "I can" mean that I become a participant in grace and in significance, at the disposal of none but set free for the doing of what I ought to do and of myself am unable to do, set free for the event of true human fellowship. By the latter half, *"deus per se"* and "breaking into this world", he means theism. His problem then is, "Does the *Kerygma* imply theism?" This is a very real problem which it is necessary to understand and to know how to value rightly, and to do so from our own experience also. In fact all Christian words as such, even the highest, the name "God", are here of no further help to us. To this extent Manfred Mezger is absolutely right when, in complete agreement with Braun, he gives a warning in his article, *Redliche Predigt* (pp. 423ff. in the same *Festschrift*), against a too frequent and unconsidered use in our preaching of the word "God" as a mere name, a use of it which really says nothing:

"All that can be said, then, of 'God' can be said of our human reality or not at all. Of course in addition to this there are ventures in metaphysical thinking. But they hover in the air and are dumb. One cannot interrogate dumb things. Sincere preaching does not send the questioning hearer from one mathematical unknown to another. It answers with the hearer's own reality.

There it must take its stand; there alone, too, it can prove itself real". (p. 425).

The mere name "God" does not help us at all. It must permit itself to be interpreted and to this extent verified in terms of our reality, the reality of the hearer and that of the speaker himself. But is the appropriate interpretation a formula, as for example the "I ought" and "I can", in which the meaning of the name "God" vanishes, and beyond which nothing more can be said about God? Can we only speak responsibly and credibly about God to our contemporaries, who no longer take for granted as a presupposition the existence of God, by explicitly *no longer* speaking about God? And, an important point which raises the question of subjective sincerity, we must always number ourselves among these contemporaries. The problem must be taken seriously at this crucial point. Of course in so doing we must also understand that formulae like "I ought" and "I can" are still not unexceptionable interpretations with which we can regard the task as finished, but that in their turn they, too, begin by being names which, to prove their employability, require interpretation in terms of reality as lived by men. Once again, does the word "God" say anything more than, for example in Braun's language, the formulae "I ought" and "I can", or does it, saying just that and nothing else, then vanish into these formulae to become quite superfluous as an independent expression? Has the "Person" God, and speech about him any concrete significance at all for me?

Braun, in polemic against Gollwitzer, formulates his own answer very clearly:

> "Gollwitzer rightly begins with the Word, but, in contrast to my experience, he passes beyond the Word to a person 'God' who must first of all qualify what is done by the Word. This underlining of the person of God brings Gollwitzer into conflict with the New Testament itself, where it is not Christian love, but love which has never once thought of Jesus, that is demanded (Matt. 25: 35-40)" (p. 412).

In other words, the meaning of speech about God does not at all demand the type of theological interpretation which assumes his personal nature, but it vanishes completely and entirely into "I ought" and "I can" in the event of human fellowship. This is admittedly not something of which we can be masters; the grace of being able to live in human fellowship is in the true meaning of the words something which comes to us and has nothing to do with any projection of subjective possibilities. In this event God is real, but to go beyond it and to speak of a "personal God" has no meaning at all.

As the Biblical foundation for this position of his Braun gives the following. There is certainly a Word of God, that is to say, a Word in which what cannot be claimed by us is promised as a gift. But this Word is always mediated. "There is no Word of God which does not meet us as a word of man, and which therefore is not shaped *secundum hominem recipientem*" (p. 416). Thus far our agreement with Braun may be taken for granted. There is no point in making polemic against the modern description of the Word of God as the almighty event of the Word, for it is correct! The Word *is* truly an event, otherwise it would not be the Word of God. We should then come into conflict with at least the whole Reformation! And the Word of God always encounters us through the medium of human words, and therefore through the medium of quite definite human concepts and pictures which are subject to the changing times. To say this is to say that the Word of God is shaped *secundum hominem recipientem*.

But Braun establishes exegetically that there is already within the Biblical canon a quite definite change in the concepts and pictures of the receiving man, speaking generally, a change from the Old Testament to the New. The Old Testament has its quite definite and bodily objective pictures of the personal God JHWH living outside the world; JHWH dwells in heaven and comes down occasionally to earth, etc. In the New Testament, as also in its environment in the history of religions, this objective transcendence of God is still something presupposed as a matter of course. And yet "the picture of God, as we pass from the Old to the New Testament, is unmistakably moving from the objective to the spiritualized" (p. 403). Braun established statistically for the New Testament "a disappearance of the personal name". "The living God", too, is only seldom mentioned.

36

"There is a clear exaggeration in his (sc. Gollwitzer's) assertion, that this Old Testament expression, which is limited in the New to a missionary term to combat polytheism, represents a bracket uniting the two Testaments ... And like the name of God, the manner of his behaviour is altered in passing from the Old to the New. In the Old Jahweh comes down; in the New coming down is something for angels or for the gnostically understood Redeemer ...", etc. (*ibid*.).

"This transformation is one in the spiritual outlook of man of the time, a transformation *secundum hominem recipientem*", —and Braun continues, "The interpreter of today only requires to avail himself of this and carry it further" (p. 404).

In this connection Braun speaks of an "interpretative correction" (p. 416) already appearing in the Bible itself. The parallel in this to certain well-known arguments in Bultmann's demythologizing is unmistakable. And yet it seems to us to be fundamentally wrong to go on from this to speak of finding in Braun a "necessary consequence" of Bultmann's approach, as both opponents and adherents of Braun's trend of thought often do.[6] There is too much speaking in theology about so-called "necessary consequences" of any given position, instead of allowing the facts to speak for themselves, and measuring the position against the facts which are its goal.

If we are dealing with an "interpretative correction" which is already being carried out in the New Testament itself, and which the present-day interpreter only requires to continue to its conclusion, the question arises about this process of correction and especially about its criterion. What is being corrected? With what better final position in view is it being corrected? And where do we find the criterion for judging that this final position is better or more "correct"? Braun finds a starting-point for his process of correction in a very corporeal Old Testament picture of the anthropomorphic personality and objective transcendence of God. For him the two of these characteristically go together, two closely connected features of one and the

---

[6] Rudolf Bultmann, as is said in repeated published and unpublished statements, has never thought of regarding as theologically abolished the confrontation of God as a "person" whom we can address. The *extra nos* of the reality of God has certainly for him the place of its appearance and verification in the realm of human relations, but it does not vanish behind the discharge of these.

same phenomenon! In the New Testament this corporeal objectivity is now being gradually corrected, though of course by no means as yet abolished. The Old Testament name for God, JHWH, (*Kyrios* as applied to God), yields place to *Theos*.

"The trend is clear; as far as the designation of God is concerned, one part of the New Testament lays no value whatever, and the other part a very unemphatic value, on any special underlining of the identity of the God proclaimed there with the Jahweh of the Old Testament" (Footnote added, Against Gollwitzer, p. 117 (E.T.)) (p. 402).

Or,

"God is a related concept, but the relation is to the Word, not to an objective person. For this reason the atheist misses the mark, misses indeed the purpose of his life, not *qua* atheist, but when the "I ought" and "I can" in the Gospel and in human relations are lost to him" (p. 413).

And further,

"It is this rigid localization of the *extra nos* which prevents me from saying that God intervenes concretely in the course of events, that our God can do this. I agree that this is the presumption of the Biblical texts. But in them it is not, as in Gollwitzer, something emphasized, and made obligatory with raised index-finger; it is taken for granted in passing, since it is shared by the Biblical texts with wide areas of ancient religious literature" (p. 415).

These quotations make clear the answer to our questions about the "interpretative correction" asserted by Braun; we begin from a bodily objective, personally anthropomorphic and objectively transcendent understanding of God. The goal of the process is already there in the Bible, an understanding of the *Kerygma* which has not yet, it is true, eliminated the implications of this understanding of God, but clearly attenuates them and shows them as peripheral. The criterion of this asserted corrective trend, or rather one side of the criterion and the negative one, is the assumption that the personality, or personal confrontation, of God can be completely eliminated, since it is not to be assigned to the essential structure of the *Kerygma*, or "Word", but to the unimportant matter of the form it takes, to the changing content of the pictures supplied by the *homines recipientes.*

Braun would surely recognize as his own these premises which we have laid down. It can further be shown quite beautifully from Braun's own example how even the purely "historical-critical" conclusions of the exegete, even when these are supported by compelling statistical evidence, are dominated by an admixture from systematic theology which is no longer under the control of historical criticism, which would now have to be the historical self-criticism of the exegete himself. It can be demonstrated time and again that we are dealing with premises from systematics, and now in our case with Braun it can be really convincingly demonstrated, by showing that there are counter-possibilities, different premises on the same level of systematics, which make possible a completely different exegetical understanding, and which from the viewpoint of the phenomena of the text make just as good sense.

That the New Testament does not "make obligatory with raised index-finger" that moment in its presuppositions which Braun has in mind, namely the transcendence and personality of God, can theoretically be due, as Braun thinks, to the fact that this moment is peripheral for these presuppositions. But it can quite as easily be due to the fact that it belongs to them so necessarily and by its very nature as a central and unalterable moment that it does not require to be made explicit at all except when need arises. For Gollwitzer on the other hand this need has arisen, and this is why he believes that he must bring out "with raised index-finger" the importance of precisely this element. It is a difficult hermeneutical problem which arises here, that of the explicit and the implicit in the historical form given to a meaning. It is a problem which, far from being thought out, has surely as yet been scarcely adequately posed.

A framework of systematic theology is conceivable according to which the personal confrontation of God appears as the kernel of the *Kerygma* which must not be surrendered, its basic element. And then from this point of view we could no longer speak of an "interpretative correction", or at most it could mean that the all too corporeal anthropomorphism of the picture of God was replaced by a more "spiritualized" understanding of his personal nature. Certainly Braun can justly claim to establish such a development in the Bible. But the personal nature of the fundamental facts is only brought in question by such a change if one begins by assuming that it is unessential and belongs to the *homo recipiens* and not to the *verbum*.

We called the framework we have just sketched a "conceivable systematic framework". In fact its only purpose *in this context* is to weigh in the balance Braun's exegetical thesis and to show how it depends in itself upon a systematic presupposition and so make clear that such an "autarchic exegesis" as Braun appears to strive after is impossible. The belief, widespread today, in the autarchy of Biblical exegesis is a superstition. However much systematic thought must look towards exegesis, it is equally true on the other side that exegesis requires the clarification given by systematics, by systematic reflection on the premises which may sometimes be implicitly asserted along with an exegetical affirmation. That is to say, systematic and exegetical thought embrace one another reciprocally.[7] In actual fact my own opinion is that this systematic counter-possibility, just sketched in opposition to Braun's thesis, is not merely "conceivable" but really appropriate to the facts of Holy Scripture. In saying this I am by no means denying the process of correction established by Braun. But this process is not to be interpreted as a preparation for a gradual departure from "theism", but as a gradual universalizing, a coming into view ever more clearly of the universal range, appropriate to every man, of these fundamental facts of personal encounter with God. That Jahweh comes down from heaven is, when portrayed in this corporeal way, which in any case does not touch the heart of the matter, a

[7] This basic factual position is in need of further comprehensive clarification. To the best of my knowledge, up till now very little work has been done on this. It must also be taken into consideration at this point that we cannot naïvely measure the understanding of reality in a text from the past against our own, usually unconsidered, understanding, but that to complete the exegesis the two understandings, that of the text and that of the exegete, must be worked out far enough ontologically to allow them really to confront one another. For all speech implies an understanding of speech and therefore a certain understanding of reality. See as a monograph on this, Klaus Otte, *Das Sprachverständnis bei Philo von Alexandrien*, in *Beiträge zur Geschichte der biblischen Exegese*, Vol. 7, Tübingen, 1968.

particular factual position belonging to the history of religion; it can be understood as a religious phenomenon, but has nothing to do with me today. It is only an existential interpretation of this Old Testament picture, and one which goes better to the heart of the matter, which is able to make clear how far this is my concern. This existential interpretation is prepared for in the New Testament by this process of spiritualizing and making less corporeal the picture of God. The goal then of the Biblical process of correction is not a "departure from theism", but an existential interpretation which can show the personal confrontation of man and God as a universal reality in which every human being is concerned. Does this make human existence into the criterion, to quote what is today widely a theological commonplace? No! Rather man has to obey the Word of God not only in his life but also in his theology, which after all is also part of the *vita christiana*. But the criterion of our *obedience (Gehorsam)* is whether *we have heard (gehört)*! Otherwise our supposed obedience is simply an insincerity.

But further Braun's reference to the fact that there was also something like "theism" and "monotheism" in the religious environment of Christianity carries no weight as an argument. For, once again from the viewpoint of systematics, we make a thoroughly questionable assumption if we will only allow as essentially valid for Christianity what is peculiar to it. Thus, for example, Braun also holds the prayer of petition to be nothing essentially and specifically Christian, because it is also found in other religions (cp. p. 418). Fundamentally we have here a manner of thinking which compares ideologies with one another, and picks out what is peculiar in one as against others.

That the "counter-possibility", which seeks to understand the *Kerygma* itself precisely in terms of personality in its fundamental factual nature, has not yet been adequately worked out is no argument against either its possibility or its necessity. There is no single text in the Bible which could be quoted against such a framework; much rather one could count as evidence in its favour every passage where *God* or *God's speaking* is the subject. In addition there is need for further clarification about, for example, the "I can" and "I ought" which Braun has to offer in its place as his view of the essence of the *Kerygma*.

But it is precisely here that one meets the problem on which further work requires to be done. Who in this case is able to say beforehand if the further clarification of the two interpretations of the *Kerygma*, for the sake of brevity that of Braun and that of Gollwitzer, will not in the last resort show them to be convergent. And then possibly Braun and Mezger are just as truly correct in their positive statements, their "I can" and "I ought" and their setting free for human relations, as they are astray from the facts of the Gospel on their negative side, their disputing of what they label "theism". In that case the two interpretations, instead of competing with one another, rather need and include one another structurally. But here again Bonhoeffer comes into the controversy. The fact that Braun can find in Bonhoeffer an emphatically strong support for his *positive* statement, but on the contrary none at all for his *negative* statement, in so far as it is directed not only against a metaphysical theism but against the personally acting God, is a certain indication, though of course not so much as a material argument, in favour of the mutual inclusiveness of the two interpretations. And the two are united most intimately in Bonhoeffer. God is a person ("he", not "it") who hears prayers and acts concretely in history. But the transcendence of God encounters us in our neighbour. The manner and the significance of this interpenetration admittedly requires to be still further thought out.

We see then already in this first point how Bonhoeffer is in advance of the formalism of Braun's arguments in the atheism-debate in theology. We find given in him that "counter-possibility" to Braun's systematic premises. He puts, in the lectures on *Christology* of 1933 for example, the question about the *personality* of the present Lord as an ontological one about the structure of the "Who". And in him are found clearly in juxtaposition and involvement with one another these two interpretations which are competitive in Braun and Mezger, and possibly also in Robinson. And so he carries further, precisely at the decisive point, this "atheism-debate" in theology to which he himself in his lifetime had given the impulse.

Another point at which Bonhoeffer pushes forward in advance of Braun is to be found in Braun's apperception of the Biblical representations of God. On Braun's side, it is obviously a matter of "objectifying" these representations with the greatest possible bodily objectivity.

> "Such texts (sc. on God's dwelling in Heaven, the return of Jesus from Heaven, etc.) . . . are no analogical manner of speaking, that is to say, not like the representation of forgiveness in Luke 15: 11ff. as the father receiving back the son who had gone off. The texts rather imply realities which take place or will take place in the realm of worldly experience. That is, they in fact speak of an objectivity which is factually objective reality" (p. 400).

In other words, this can only mean that the texts speak in precisely the same objectifying way of God's dwelling in Heaven, as does for example a modern engineer about the wings of an aeroplane. But Braun surely in saying so lays claim to an all too naïve and unquestioned ability to review the understanding of reality and relation to it of a bygone age, its understanding and use of language. He seems to overlook the ambiguities which arise in this very respect because of the different times and the different worlds. And this is surely in very close keeping with the assured and simple concept of reality which he regards as binding upon himself. He has himself this firm and settled understanding of reality which seems to be for him no longer something to be questioned, and he presupposes a similarly firm and settled understanding, no longer requiring further query, for the Biblical witnesses, though now it is a supernaturalist and objectivist one.

> "I am brought out of my imprisonment within myself, I learn to know myself as a liar, I experience love and am made capable of love. Thus I learn to say 'God' correctly, without thereby branding as error a 'Yes' to the unbrokenness of immanence. For this relearning which is mediated through encounter does not refer to one's theory of knowledge, nor does the breaking through my imprisonment within myself by the without mean a without which comes from beyond immanence. I do not learn thereby to speak of God's own being outside the world. That 'I can' and 'I ought' do not come from me but happen to me is not questioned in this. This is how I can think of God *in* this experience, and precisely how the name of God becomes something I can concretely pronounce" (p. 416).

This *"unbrokenness of immanence"* in which Braun will profess faith, without thereby ceasing to be a theologian and to speak of "God", is in the last resort the criterion by which the "interpretative correction" which he sees already there in the Bible and carries himself to its logical conclusion finds its full meaning. This presupposed criterion then determines the nature of his theological result:

> "So I do not require to commit the inconsistency of giving up the all too corporeal objectivity of the New Testament, where for instance Heaven is a place ... and yet holding to the non-immanence and aseity of God. It does not help at all to explain that this inconsistency is intentional; the locality of God's dwelling-place and his spatial intervention belong just as much to the presuppositions of the New Testament texts as does his transcendent aseity. Such an intentional inconsistency, it may be on the part of an interpreter, is therefore not vouched for by the New Testament itself ..." (*ibid.*).

It certainly is not if we begin by making the concept of an "unbroken immanence" into a canon of reality, on the basis of which we accept the New Testament. From such a viewpoint it is true that as well as many concrete traits portraying the Biblical understanding of God, the dwelling in Heaven and the like, the thought also of a personally confronting God belongs to exactly the same category of objectifying and mythological representations. But this is precisely a question of the criterion. It is a well-known logical rule that, according to the viewpoint one adopts, A and B together can be contrasted with C, or A and C together with B, or B and C with A. Now the criterion of "unbroken immanence" is so conceived from the very start that it is no longer possible to distinguish between personality as a component of our understanding of God and certain concrete representations of its content. In addition, Braun is enabled by this canon to declare that such details of representation as God's dwelling in Heaven, etc., are not to be understood in any analogical way, but in a bodily objective manner. But it may be that both understandings are false! It may be that the concept "analogical" is also still not sufficiently discriminating to describe the true state of the facts.

But the statement about the unbrokenness of immanence is a metaphysical statement, and one which is metaphysically disputable. It is true that it has become the custom in many theological circles today to regard the word "metaphysics" as taboo.[8] In this, with some inclination towards Bonhoeffer's use of the word but with a certain fundamental vagueness, "metaphysics" is taken to mean a dualist concept of "world" and "world beyond". But, as has been said, the concept of the unbrokenness of immanence, which has been given currency in opposition to this, must on its side be described as metaphysical. Instead, therefore, of making the word "metaphysics" taboo, and persisting in an antithesis, which in its turn is metaphysical and somewhat undiscriminating as well, between "unbroken immanence" on the one side and "supernaturalist, or metaphysical, dualism" on the other, one would surely do better to refrain from imposing taboos, lay the basis of a differentiated concept of "metaphysics", and consciously embark upon the "metaphysical", as we must admit, consideration of the reality of the real, so necessary today even for theologians.[9]

[8] More unprejudiced is the attitude to the problem of metaphysics widely found in present-day American Protestant theology, as for example in Schubert M. Ogden, one of the most important of the more recent American theologians. As against the anti-metaphysical philosophy of pure "linguistic analysis" he tends to a new integral metaphysic which he seeks to develop as a metaphysic of *becoming*, in contrast to the "classical" metaphysic of being. He builds here on the thoughts of A. N. Whitehead and C. Hartshorne, and directs theology towards the exposition of such a metaphysic. Cp., *inter alia*, Ogden, *The Temporality of God*, in *Zeit und Geschichte*, pp. 381ff., and also, to appear shortly, Vol. IV of the series, *New Frontiers in Theology*, ed. J. M. Robinson and J. B. Cobb, jnr., with contributions from S. M. Ogden, G. Ebeling, E. Fuchs, V. Pannenberg, H. Ott. I myself endeavour there to develop my own criticism of Ogden's undertaking. ("*The Temporality of God*" is also included in Ogden, *The Reality of God*, S.C.M., 1967, pp. 144ff.—Tr.).

[9] It would be in place to say something about the specific concept of "metaphysics" as we find it in the later Heidegger. He departs step by step on his own way from traditional Western metaphysics, but, we must add, keeps close to the text of this tradition, which he queries and interprets in the light of its unconscious premises. He seeks less to "terminate (*überwinden*)" than to "redirect (*verwinden*)" Western metaphysics. In this he has a very pregnant and precise conception of "metaphysics"; and one of the main purposes of my *Denken und Sein*, 1959, was to show the especial area covered by this concept in Heidegger and to bring evidence that his interpretation could not be quoted in support of that vague, undifferentiated "dualist" conception of "metaphysics".

Again the thesis advocated by, among others, Friedrich Gogarten (cp. e.g., *Demythologizing and History*, tr. Horton Smith, S.C.M., 1955, pp. 21–39), that formerly men thought in terms of a dualist "metaphysics", but that today this way of thinking must give way to a radically historical one, though assumed by many today without examination as an axiom, would still require in my

There is of course in Bonhoeffer a certain parallel to these speculations in the philosophy of history (or theology of history), when he speaks of the development towards a world come of age. But on this point he is only feeling his way forward, thinking experimentally and seeking a path for himself. And what is essential is not that he attempts to give this way of mankind to maturity a framework within the philosophy of history, but the genuine experience which in his case lies behind the attempt, the experience with men of the present day to whom one can no longer simply "come with God". (This is treated more fully in Chapter Three.)

If in one quite specific sense Bonhoeffer rejected the "metaphysical" or the "otherworldly" as a mark of the religious, yet it is nevertheless a fact *that the question of the knowledge of the reality of the real, into which he flung himself so wholeheartedly, is in a wider sense "metaphysical" or "ontological"*, and that in his wrestling with it he maintained unreservedly the "personal nature of the fundamental facts" of all theology. Indeed, the question "What is reality?" could be called the peculiar theme of all his theological thinking. He does not begin, as does Braun for example, by sheltering himself against the difficulties which come with discrimination by presupposing as an axiom some too naïve and secure concept of reality, such as that of "unbroken immanence".

Since Bonhoeffer really engages himself with this question of reality, he gains as he does so a differentiated concept of it, and is as a result in advance of those who with only a very partial justification quote him in the theological "atheism-debate". We have made Herbert Braun our concern for so long because he supports a trend in the "atheism-debate" which shows particularly clearly by contrast the topicality and the greater radicality of Bonhoeffer on this question.

This problem of atheism, very much an existential problem,

---

opinion to be tested with particular care. However much this outlook may contain that is right in details, yet it seems to me that in its construction as a philosophy of history it sets in opposition to one another roughly sketched and oversimplified positions in the history of thought, that it poses insufficiently differentiated antitheses, and in this way remains too much cut off from the wrestling with the concept of reality which is so live today in theological and philosophical thought—and surely in still wider fields. A more detailed debate on this subject would be worthwhile!

does in fact exist today for the Church and for theology. Gerhard Ebeling, for instance, has outlined it with the striking statement that for many men today the name God has lost not only its self-evident character (*Selbstverständlichkeit*) but largely also its intelligibility (*Verständlichkeit*)![10] And we cannot avoid it, we must face it in our theology. Of that fact Bonhoeffer had an exemplarily clear vision. But neither must theology, as I see it, take the easy way out when faced by this problem and surrender lightly what since its origins has been the subject of faith for millenia. This is unfortunately what Braun does, if we have rightly understood him. But Bonhoeffer does not do it. For this reason it is also true that he has reached no settled conclusion. But the thought-pictures which are not completed, which deliberately have not attained to ultimate clarity, the thought-pictures which are still on the way there, have the greater appeal. As Teilhard de Chardin says on one occasion, "I ascribe no final and absolute value to the various systems of thought in natural science. What I love in them is not the concrete form in which they appear, but the task which they have undertaken . . ." Relative incompleteness in thought and caution in making claims for it is as a rule an indirect pointer to a greater nearness to the facts.

Before we pass on to a short critical examination of Gollwitzer's counter-thesis to Braun, there should be noted another *exegetical matter of fact* which meets us in the New Testament, but to which Braun, because of his rigid axiomatic antithesis between theist "transcendence" and "unbroken immanence" can scarcely give due attention. It is the thought of a Christological universalism, as we find it especially in the so-called *Deutero-Pauline* literature, Colossians and Ephesians, but also in Hebrews, the thought of the indwelling of the whole of created reality in Christ, and of Christ in the whole of created reality. We could think here of passages like Col. 1: 15ff., "He is the image of the invisible God; his is the primacy over all created things. In him everything in heaven and earth was created, not only things visible but also the invisible orders . . . ; the whole universe has been created through him and for him. And he exists before everything and all things are

[10] Cp. *Theology and Reality*, in *Word and Faith*, tr. Leitch, S.C.M., 1963, p. 194.

held together in him". Or of Ephes. 1: 10, the *anakephalaiosis* "that the universe, all in heaven and in earth, might be brought to a unity in Christ". Or of Hebrews 1: 2f., "whom he has made heir to the whole universe, and through whom he created all orders of existence: the Son who is the effulgence of God's splendour and the stamp of God's very being, and sustains the universe by his word of power" (All quoted from N.E.B.— Tr.). Bonhoeffer was struck by this matter of fact, as on his presuppositions he *could* be struck, and he referred, as we shall yet see, in crucial passages to texts from the Deutero-Paulines.

This insight and this witness could in fact well be a new element in the New Testament, and it could be of exceptional importance for us as light on the New Testament understanding of reality. As far as the phenomena of the text go, Braun should really have paid attention to this line of thought, but on what are obviously systematic grounds he can have nothing to do with it. For this insight completely contradicts his bringing together under the heading "theism" God's personal nature on the one side and God's objective transcendence on the other. Here once for all the personally objective, present Lord is no longer experienced as the "transcendent" but as the "immanent", personally present in all created reality. Does then this perspective from quite specifically New Testament evidence open a way towards an exposition of reality which is still, or possibly for the first time, relevant for us today? Or is there here again only a further fact for the history of religion, another mere "religious representation" which remains without significance for our present problem of reality? *Probandum et experiendum est!* We must have our experiences with the Word of God. And in them much, if not everything will depend on whether theologians are prepared to enter into such new perspectives of the Biblical understanding of reality.

This same perspective in one's wrestling with reality, which Bonhoeffer accepted, is also given a further powerful statement and expounded with his own peculiar stamp by Bonhoeffer's contemporary who outlived him by about ten years, Father Teilhard de Chardin. Granted that Teilhard's existentialist context is the researcher's gaze over millions of years and over the unheard-of perspectives of our time, while that of Bonhoeffer is human relationships and human steadfastness in a narrowly limited area, in an acute situation of crisis. Yet, each in his own way, both have entered upon and truly passed through the specifically "modern" experience of our epoch. Typical also of both could be the fact that their most important and visionary works have to some extent a fragmentary character, and have only posthumously gained the place which sets their mark upon history. And from their "modern" experience as Christians, each according to the context of his life, both have succeeded in displaying and proclaiming the *universal* Christ as he is testified to in the Deutero-Paulines. My personal opinion is that Teilhard's thought of the universal Christ, although its place for him is in the context of his cosmological visions and speculations, yet has a meaning quite independent of these, as an attempt to base his expression of the essence of reality both on the Christian faith and on the experience of modern man. And as such it is an ontological venture! And can we say that it is just this picture of Christ, still the same yesterday, today and for ever even if each time the manner and form of his encounter is new, that it is this aspect of the Divine reality which impresses itself on the Christian faith in a way fitting our epoch as a result of the experience of our time? Just as, for example, a particular picture of Christ impressed itself on Luther in a way fitting his epoch as a result of the experience of his time.

In any event, there is an astonishing correspondence of approach and outlook between Bonhoeffer and Teilhard. It is rewarding to investigate the material relation existing between the two, although they can scarcely have known of one another.[11]

As against the trend in Braun, Helmut Gollwitzer brings into its own what he himself describes most powerfully by his quotation from Luther, WA, 43, p. 481; *"Persona Dei loquentis et verbum significant nos tales creaturas esse, cum quibus velit loqui Deus usque in aeternum et immortaliter"* (p. 150 in Gollwitzer; E.T. there, "The person and the word of God who speaks signify that we are such creatures as God wishes to speak with, to eternity and immortality"). Immediately thereafter he turns to oppose very directly Karl Jaspers, and in so doing comes in

[11] A more detailed treatment of this in the last chapter.

49

conflict with Braun's systematic premises, as we have worked them out above.

"The reproach that here a human picture of the Absolute is made absolute, instead of being recognized as a picture and constantly transcended, arises from a resolve not to take the ground of the origin of personal talk with God as seriously as it is taken by the Christian faith itself . . ." (*ibid.*).

In this Gollwitzer is expressing exactly what we meant by Braun's systematic premises, for Braun does in fact seem to have made this resolve not to take so seriously the ground of the origin of personal talk with God. Now it is not, of course, enough here to do what Gollwitzer does and lay down the opposite affirmation. Gollwitzer strongly registers his protest in a certain theological situation. But he, of course, seeks to do more, and it is to be asked how far he succeeds in this, how far he has succeeded in really showing *why* the ground of the origin of personal talk with God is to be taken seriously, and why in consequence so speaking with God is a point not to be surrendered.

It would now be material to show, and at this point it would be the real task of the "atheism-debate" in theology to show, how far the personally confronting God is not merely a certain religious or metaphysical representation, which can be united with the essential kernel of the *Kerygma* or disunited from it as is appropriate, but how far it is itself an indispensable *component of the Kerygma.* But how can such a thing be shown? Surely it can only be done by showing that *the personal confrontation of God is a component which essentially determines the situation of my existence,* the situation, that is to say, which is met, and in a certain respect first of all created, by the *Kerygma.* There is no other way of showing this, for the *Kerygma* cannot be taken by itself in isolation and examined in its components, for it is essentially, in fact *per definitionem,* an event affecting my existence. The *Kerygma* can only be thought of as *Kerygma* in connection with human existence, precisely what we would call an existential interpretation. In any other way than this, in any other way than by pointing to the connection with my present existence, the *Kerygma* is not *Kerygma,* the Biblical texts remain mere information about a bygone religiousness.

Only by the road leading through present existence can one show that the personal nature of God belongs to the essential structure of the *Kerygma* and dare never be surrendered. To formulate it again in yet another way, the task set us consists in showing that surrendering "theism" or the personal nature of God means, not only renouncing a certain religious or metaphysical representation, but becoming blind to an active element or dimension of existence.

We find in Bonhoeffer astonishingly relevant beginnings to this demonstration of how our present existence gains its structure from personal confrontation by God. We meet with equally astonishing beginnings in Teilhard de Chardin. The Christological universalism of both, the universalism of the "present Lord", is more radical and to that extent more "modern" than the "a-theistic" theological attempts to solve the pressing problem of atheism. On the other hand it seems to me questionable whether in his polemical work Gollwitzer has brought in this necessary demonstration. It already seems questionable for this reason, that Braun, in his answer to Gollwitzer with which we have dealt, can maintain his position completely unbroken, unassailed by the fear that he might possibly have overlooked an essential dimension of existence. Gollwitzer, too, seems to have sensed the limits of his own attempt when he writes:

> "In the same way we shall not now speak of all the dimensions and aspects of the concepts of existence and reality. The task of expounding a view of reality which arises from the encounter with God is a vast and ever new one, to which we shall here make only a very partial contribution, though certainly one that belongs at the start, by considering . . . what could be meant, or rather to Christian eyes must be meant, by 'non-objective' talk of God and by speaking of the existence and non-existence of God" (p. 202).

But again it is even questionable if Gollwitzer can carry through his protest against the danger of a "theological atheism", if indeed anyone at all can carry through the whole purpose convincingly without expounding a complete "view of reality which arises from the encounter with God". As a theological task this is immense, a task to which one will not be able at all to do justice without embarking upon the whole range of problems connected with reality and existence. And then one will only lay oneself open to the suspicion and misunderstanding of having merely clung to a religious representation which has won our affections, without noticing the signs of the times and the real nature of the problem.

But it is also completely pertinent when Gollwitzer (p. 201) writes of the task of a Christian doctrine of the Holy Spirit, that it has the aim of "not letting the *extra nos* of the divine acts and words become one which excludes every *in nobis* and which is thus a 'bad' outerness". Gollwitzer obviously here sees clearly that to oppose all attempts to reduce the reality of God to the reality of human understanding of life it is not enough simply to assert and give value to the *extra nos* of this Divine reality, *that rather it is necessary to show that this "without" is at the same time the true "within"*, in so far as such concepts are at all applicable here, *that it is the basic component of man's real existential situation.* But this does not mean that *"in nobis"* is simply to be added to *"extra nos"*, a merely additive, merely "assertive" and therefore not "enlightening" type of thinking frequently met with in theological thought. The task here is to *demonstrate* the *"in nobis"* as the true" *extra nos"* and the *"extra nos"* as the true *"in nobis"*! Hence the God who confronts me is not simply the "transcendent One", he is the constitutive factor of my "immanent" existence, of immanent reality, indeed, in general, in the "concrete unity of nature and grace", to use Teilhard de Chardin's expression. But this does not mean, say, that the living God is now reduced in value to a mere "component of existence", rather speaking of a component of existence means that it is a necessary element in the essential knowledge of the human situation, the real and concrete *"condition humaine"*, to recognize also that man does not exist without the confrontation of the living God.[12] Then for example, to become still more concrete, it must be shown that the phenomena of human relations, towards which the theologians of Braun's trend of thought would completely orientate

---

[12] A classical text for this factual position is also to be found in Calvin, Inst. I, 1, *Dei notitiam et nostri res esse coniunctas, et quomodo inter se cohaereant* (E.T., Battles, S.C.M., 1960, I, p. 35; "The knowledge of God and that of ourselves, are connected. How they are inter-related").

the *Kerygma*, can also only be understood in their whole depth from the personal confrontation of God.[13]

The position then could well be that the reality of the God who confronts us can only be preserved and made credible within the horizon of human relations and through their fulfilment. To this extent it is both legitimate and necessary to insist upon human relations as the true place of encounter with the reality of God, and this much the theologians of Braun's alignment have in common with Bonhoeffer. But this insight into existence as the place of encountering and verifying must not and dare not lead to a theoretical assertion of its exclusiveness, that is, to a denial of the personal nature of God in favour of personal relations as exclusively between men. In the encounter with contemporaries, with atheistic contemporaries— and in that description we always to a certain extent include ourselves—the believer and the Church will always bear their testimony to the reality of God by maintaining simple responsibility and faithfulness in human relations, and will do so without demanding from the receivers of the testimony the previous recognition of the "existence of God", the so-called "theistic presumption". But this includes and does not exclude the Church's firm grasp on faith in the "existence of God" as the subject of the testimony. *It is precisely at the point where one thinks of the existential fulfilment of human relations that one will come against the personal confrontation of God as their final grounds and content.* And where this factual position does not stand out clearly, it is the phenomena of human relations themselves which have not been sufficiently thought through. But of course this in its turn does not mean that the personal confrontation of God is simply our appropriate theoretical principle for interpreting a practical and existential reality, namely human relations. Rather our interpretation of human relations on its side finds its existential fulfilment through faith in the existence of a personal and suprapersonal God. It finds it in prayer and trust in the promises of God. But again this

---

[13] I have formulated this challenge systematically in pp. 378f. of my article, *Existentiale Interpretation und anonyme Christlichkeit*, in *Zeit und Geschichte*, pp. 367ff. There are further thoughts on the theme, thoughts which however have perhaps only the character of an attack and an approach, in my book, *Theology and Preaching*, tr. Knight, Lutterworth, 1965 (See Chapter Seven, "God's Judgement and Wrath").

fulfilment is not a separate one accompanying the human fulfilments and, as it were, merely "attached" to them; it is a fulfilment which in its "embracing concreteness" integrates all concrete human relations within itself. When a believer prays for his fellowmen, this prayer is in its essence no substitute for unfulfilled acts of human responsibility and faithfulness, nor yet something going on independently alongside these; rather, intercessory prayer integrates all human relations in activity and suffering, encloses them, gathers them together and brings them to God. "In, with and amidst" the openness of the believer in activity and suffering there takes place intercession as openness for one's fellowman and openness for God in one. And where the concrete possibility of being for others in action ceases, there still remains openness for one's fellowmen mediated through openness for God and gaining concrete expression in intercession. On this very phenomenon of intercession much could surely be learned from Bonhoeffer, especially in his last period, in his letters from prison. And if Braun in other respects had thought through in a truly phenomenological way and followed into their depths the phenomena of human relations on which he lays such stress, surely he would have himself been led with a relevant necessity to the point at which the untenability of his position, his theological a-theism, would be evident.

To sum up, in his protest against the danger of a "Christian atheism" which he perceived, in his polemical writing against the corresponding theological tendency, Helmut Gollwitzer has established that speaking of the *a se* of God is not to be exchanged for an "in itself" of immanent objectivity. Words about the existence and the *a se* of God are legitimate and indispensable for the Christian, and must not be placed in inverted commas as a naïve objective way of speaking, or given up for such unconsidered reasons. When "God is" is said in the confession of faith this "is" is certainly something completely different from "is" as said of what is within the world. If "is" were only to be used in this latter sense, then it would have to be said of God that "he is not". But yet it is always better to say "God is" in the uncharacteristic or peculiar sense which "is" must then assume than to reduce him to a mere function of a significance, to an "expression for . . .", and therefore to speak no more of his reality. The alternatives, "objective reality" or "expression of a significance", are false alternatives. We must beware of adjusting theological speech about God to any such previously conceived system of thought.

This, roughly sketched, is the position advocated by Gollwitzer. I agree with him materially in the essentials, my methodological reservations being directed towards the limits in his undertaking which he himself has recognized and indicated. He himself demands both an understanding of reality which arises out of encounter with God and a doctrine of the Holy Spirit which has the task of showing that the confrontation and "without" of God is no "bad outerness" which excludes every *in nobis*. Certainly he *names* this very task, but he does not set about it. We have sought to demonstrate by the phenomena and problems of faith connected with intercession that human relations as the horizon of the encounter of faith, the principle so strongly emphasized by Braun's trend in theology, and personal confrontation by God *himself* are not in mutual competition or mutually exclusive, but may, and this is a matter for question and necessary examination, include and depend upon one another. We find fruitful approaches in Bonhoeffer to further thought on such questions, to a solution of the unavoidable problem of a total and radical understanding of reality based upon personal encounter with God, of an understanding of the earthly phenomena of human relations based upon the confrontation of the Divine Thou, and the Thou of the present Lord Jesus Christ. For he saw and felt that problem.

Yet all this would have to be demonstrated and verified in our thinking by the consistent working out of a "theology of the Holy Spirit" which showed us the *"extra nos"* of God as at the same time the true *"in nobis"*, which showed that the personal and suprapersonal God is in no way some transcendent anthropomorphic "object", but that, as he who is nearer to us than we are ourselves, he is the constitutive moment giving form to our real existential situation. Not to *think through* this thought would be to incur the suspicion that one still advocated a "bad outerness", and indeed Gollwitzer's protest against the danger of a "Christian atheism" is in point of fact often misunderstood in this way today.

In his book, *Gottes Sein ist im Werden*, Tübingen, 1965, Eberhard Jüngel has recently expressed an interesting opinion on the controversy between Braun and Gollwitzer, seeking to bring a new point of view to the discussion and to relax the rigidity of the fronts while giving its value to the subject of the controversy, the being of God, in its Trinitarian form. This he does in close dependence upon Karl Barth, of whose exposition of the Trinity in *Church Dogmatics*, I, 1, his thoughts are and are meant to be a paraphrase. The subject-matter of his contribution is as follows. The conception in Gollwitzer of the being of God as being "in and for himself" is insufficient for a suitable consideration of the fact of revelation. Rather the "being for us" of God which appears in revelation is already founded upon the eternal being of God, and yet not in any such way as if God *must* be for us in his eternal being. Jüngel comes to this conclusion, "God's being for us, as relational being, is the recapitulation of his relation to himself as Father, Son and Holy Spirit ... In the recapitulation what is repeated can be recognized. In his being for us God's being for himself can be recognized as a being which establishes and makes possible being for us ... God's being is self-consistent (a) in the event of God's relation with himself as the relation of Father, Son and Holy Spirit, and (b) in the event of revelation, as the relation of God's being for us to his being in the event of his relation to himself ... The 'establishing' referred to is to be thought of as the power adequate for the relation of correspondence marked (a), the power in which God is *in secret* the same as he *reveals* himself to be. God's being hidden and his being revealed as relational being is being in the power of becoming" (pp. 117f.).

Jüngel, then, sets against Gollwitzer's rightly intended but not wholly adequate concept of "being in and for itself" a more differentiated concept of the being of God as relation to himself, as eternal becoming. He seems to me to have rightly recognized the weakness of Gollwitzer's attempt. His paraphrase of Barth is both subtle and correct, and to bring the doctrine of the Trinity into the discussion at this point is a move of great promise. Yet his subtle book remains an example of "revelational positivism", in the sense in which that expression is interpreted in Chapter Three, Section 5 below. And for this reason Jüngel still does not achieve all that he might have by his reference to the doctrine of the Trinity. He does not succeed in an existential interpretation of the Trinity, the demonstration of the Trinitarian composition of the encounter which takes place in the revelation of the free personal God, and therefore of human existence confronted by God. And hence

Jüngel's expositions remain in a conceptual Heaven, that of the concepts of dogmatic tradition, in which he knows how to move about with agility, but they scarcely reach the earth, there to become illuminating and to show for preaching and all responsible speech about God in our time what it means that the reality of God dwells among men without its thereby becoming a mere human function. Yet his attempt seems promising. It is a fact that one *should* speak here of the Trinity, and Gollwitzer's justified concern would obtain a necessary reinforcement and differentiation from it. Jüngel seems to me to have himself recognized where the gaps in his attempt are and in what direction further progress must be made when he writes, "But the recapitulation is nothing without that which is to be recapitulated (sc. the recapitulation of God's Trinitarian relation to himself taking place in his being-for-us in the revelation in Christ). In Gollwitzer's words, God's being-for-us is nothing without his being-for-himself. The *ratio essendi* of recapitulation is that which has to be recapitulated. The problem whose subject-matter is dealt with in this context would have to be considered as an equivalent to the doctrine of *En-* and *Anhypostasia* within a doctrine of the recapitulation of the being of God. If God's being for us is the recapitulation of his being for himself, such a doctrine of recapitulation would have to give value from the point of view of the relationships to what *En-* and *Anhypostasia* made valid Christologically for the *relata*, God and man" (pp. 115f.). The doctrine of the recapitulation of the being of God would then be precisely the doctrine of the Trinitarian composition of encounter with God and of existence confronted with God. Trinitarian composition is in the last resort none other than Christological composition, because it is in Christ that God discloses his eternal secret. There seems to me to be a promising approach to this doctrine of the Trinitarian composition of encounter with God and of existence in Augustine, in *De Trinitate*, Books VIII and IX. Essentially I agree with Jüngel's conclusion, "But at the same time, if the statement really holds good that the being of God is recapitulated in the correspondence of the relations *ad extra* and *ad intra*, then the statement that 'God is in and for himself' is *in concreto* just as false as the statement 'God is God only as the God of men' " (p. 116). The basis for this Trinitarian end to the one-sided formulations about the being of God which we find both in Braun and in Gollwitzer is to be found in the specific *unique* character of the personal being of God, and this has been all along within the sights of the Church doctrine of the Trinity.

3. *Bonhoeffer's Position between Karl Barth and Rudolf Bultmann*

We have tarried a long time by the problem of atheism in theology, on the one hand because of the especial importance of this question in present-day theological discussion, and on the other hand because of Bonhoeffer's especial affinity with this subject, earnest thought on which he really aroused himself through his late theological insights. But in addition there are still at least two other crucial points in the theological research and controversy of today, in regard to which the radicality, topicality and fruitfulness of Bonhoeffer's thought can be shown.

First, he could prove himself one who carried us further in the controversy between the "Barthian" and the "Bultmannian" streams of thought in Protestant theology. He himself was strongly influenced by the theology of Karl Barth. On the other hand, he knew very well how to value the theological importance and the legitimacy of Bultmann's theological concern and the challenges which come from it,[14] although in his time the debate on demythologizing was still entirely at its beginnings. But none the less Bonhoeffer has clearly dissociated himself from both of his older contemporaries, although without denying what they were really seeking to achieve. It

---

[14] Cp. the following passages from two of Bonhoeffer's letters:—". . . I find great joy in Bultmann's new volume (*Neues Testament und Mythologie*, in R. Bultmann, *Offenbarung und Heilsgeschehen*; *Beiträge zur Evangelischen Theologie*, Vol. 7, ed. E. Wolf, Munich, 1941). I am impressed again and again by the intellectual honesty of his works. Here D. is shortly to be taken to task in a somewhat stupid way at the Berlin Convention on the subject of Bultmann . . . I should like to know if any of them have worked through the commentary on St. John. The obscurantism which flourishes here, I believe under the influence of a few self-important individuals, is a real scandal for the Confessional Church . . ." March 24, 1942; *Ges. Schr.* III pp. 45f.).

"Now as to Bultmann, I belong to those who welcomed his work, not because I agreed with it; I deplore the double approach in it (the arguments from John 1: 14 and from the Radio should be kept separate . . .). He (Bultmann) ventured to say what many (and I include myself) repressed in themselves without deciding. In so doing he rendered a service to intellectual purity and honesty. The Pharisaism of faith to which we are summoned against him by many brothers to me is fatal. Nowadays both speech and answer must be frank. I should be glad to speak with Bultmann on the subject and should like to expose myself to the breath of fresh air which comes from him" (March 25, 1942. *Bonhoeffer Auswahl*, Munich, 1964, p. 537).

was from the methods by which they fulfilled their purpose that he dissociated himself, not what he recognized as their justified concerns.

He believed that he could detect in Bultmann a certain narrowing in the subject-matter of theology, the same reproach which above all has been made against Bultmann in all polemic. Whether in this he was just or unjust may remain for the moment undecided.[15]

In any event Bonhoeffer detected a danger here and called for another way of interpreting the Biblical concepts than that of Bultmann, a more radical way in his opinion, the "non-religious interpretation", which satisfied the clearly recognized need for interpretation and yet at the same time avoided every danger of an individualistic narrowing.

As regards the theology of Karl Barth, Bonhoeffer emphasized vigorously both its strength and its weakness as he saw them. He saw in Barth the epoch-making theologian who was the first to recognize the need to expound a "non-religious" theology. In this he confessed allegiance to what since the *Epistle to the Romans* has remained the fundamental *motif* of Barth's theological thinking, that theology has to begin from God's free act and not from "religious" possibilities in man. But at the same time he parted company from Barth when he reproached him with "revelational positivism", a reproach which, as we shall

---

[15] I myself, at the time of that work, made a similar assertion in *Geschichte und Heilsgeschichte in der Theologie Rudolf Bultmanns*, Tübingen, 1955. Today, without taking back the methodological and ontological criticism which I there expressed, I incline rather in my general judgement to regard the lack of breadth in subject-matter, which at first sight seems to be a mark of Bultmann, as at least virtually made up for by implication in his thought. But it is very significant and impressive in this connection to note how the Catholic theologian Gotthold Häsenhuttl, in *Der Glaubens Vollzug*, Essen, 1963, in an account of Bultmann approved by Bultmann himself as relevant, can accept his thought in such a completely positive way, although as a Catholic the obligations of his official post preclude him from the outset from embarking on any narrowing at all of the subject-matter of theology. I feel Häsenhuttl's conclusion (p. 358) to be particularly appropriate: "Perhaps I may close with the following thought. If a Catholic theologian takes up a book of Bultmann's a superficial look will see a desert staring back. One accustomed to gather beautiful flowers finds perhaps only a blade of grass here and there on the *superficies historica*. But if he looks further and makes a search on the arid ground, then he must suddenly discover that there is an abundance of underground water here. And as soon as he digs into the 'third dimension' there bubbles up a rich spring which converts the whole desert into the richest land".

show in greater detail below, was methodological and not concerned with the facts. In this he was fighting against a tendency, surely encouraged by Barth's dogmatic method, of a Barthianism to become a neo-orthodoxy which, in the security of its self-consistent dogmatic system would renounce real dialogue with contemporaries and controversy with inescapable problems.

In discussions between the "Barthian" and the "Bultmannian" trends in theological thought the difficulty lies in the fact that in Bultmann's school on the one side there is a readiness, whether justly or unjustly depends on the particular discussion, to retreat into the complaint that the man on the other side has not understood the hermeneutical problem, while on the Barthian side, again whether justly or unjustly depends on the particular discussion, the retreat tends to be into the suspicion that the other is simply "anthropologizing" the content of theology. If carried out in this way the discussion is very liable to run into a blind alley which gives scarcely any more hope of an exit.

One could not reproach Bonhoeffer with anthropologizing in any way the subject-matter of theology. His subject is expressly and emphatically what God does, the act of salvation in Jesus Christ, and his question, "Who Christ really is, for us today?" (LPP, p. 152). And if he is also continually endeavouring to define and refine his thought and his theological language towards a strictness in his use of categories, yet he never relates this categorial side to any given anthropology or ontology. It can be shown from examples both from the earlier and from the later period of his work that in this sense Bonhoeffer is a "dialectical" theologian (a "modern theologian" —LPP, p. 208) in the tradition of Karl Barth. But just as little can one reproach him with not having sensed the "hermeneutical problem". Sufficient evidence for this are the attempts which we already find in his early works to gain from the subject-matter of theology a fitting and inclusive theological doctrine of perception and ontology. In *Act and Being*, for example, and in his lectures on *Christology* of 1933, hermeneutics and ontology are closely related. But the same becomes completely clear when we look at his late plea for a "non-religious interpretation". Here Bonhoeffer sensed even more intensely and radically than any other theologian the problem of "translation" into a form appropriate for a modern man who no longer understands the Christian Biblical concepts in their traditional "religious" dress, a problem which is at the same time one of the whole real and genuine understanding of the facts. He sensed this problem not merely with reference to a so-called "modern view of life", which has a very questionable authoritarianism about it in any case, he sensed it also in the encounter with man of today, to whom the Gospel has to be directed and who in his turn has to pass it on further. It is not legitimate to draw the conclusion that, because Bonhoeffer speaks in a different language from Bultmann and with a different placing of the emphasis, we are therefore in the two dealing with two fundamentally different levels of hermeneutical concern. There may still be sensed in very differently coloured worlds of thought and experience the same fact, that the *Kerygma* of Jesus Christ, if it is to show itself living, requires today a new interpretation, a new statement. And this new statement is not something which we add, its power springs from the nature of the *Kerygma* itself.

Thus in an original way, and not merely as some disciple, Bonhoeffer unites in his theological thinking the best and most essential elements in the Barthian and the Bultmannian trends of thought, what for both of them is the one necessary point. He is influenced in the same strong way by the two *motives*; indeed he unites them in such a way that they appear in him as a single *motif*, and no longer as two which could come into conflict and between which a concealed tension rules. Theological discussion about these necessary *desiderata* could come out of its blind alley and its misunderstandings if in controversy it held to this way of thinking in which the hermeneutical sense is in such a unique way linked with that of being overpowered by the presence of the living God.

4. *Bonhoeffer and the Ecumenical Dialogue*

In the sketch of his last greater work about non-religious interpretation, of which fragments are to be found in LPP, Bonhoeffer writes:

" 'What must I believe?' is the wrong question; antiquated controversies, especially those between the different sects; the Lutheran *versus* Reformed and to some extent the Roman Catholic *versus* Protestant, are now unreal. They may at any time be revived with passion, but they no longer carry conviction. There is no proof of this, and we must simply take it that it is so. All that we can prove is that the faith of the Bible and Christianity does not stand or fall by these issues" (LPP, p. 210).

Thus Bonhoeffer expresses in one terse note what constitutes today the hope of the inter-confessional ecumenical dialogue and the power of conviction behind it. This dialogue is not concerned with frantically denying and concealing the existing serious and convincing differences, but with discovering and formulating anew the one "fact" and the one task which dawns upon us as absolutely common to all, discovering and formulating them in such a way that there gradually of itself becomes manifest the irrelevance and lack of convincing power, the lack of timeliness of very many differences traditionally regarded as serious. This statement of his was also in keeping with his practical ecumenical behaviour, his taking part in the ecumenical "Life and Work" movement rather than that on "Faith and Order", which on the face of it would have been better suited to his theological gifts.

Bonhoeffer's perspectives prove to be fruitful in an ecumenical discussion understood and carried out in this way. On the point that he was a Protestant theologian who knew himself to be bound in free responsibility to Scripture alone there can be no doubt. But on the other hand it is striking how he pushes forward along this same road to insights which seem to be peculiarly "Catholic".

Significant above all here is the thought of the *Sanctorum Communio*, the Church as the fellowship of believers and more than the mere sum of them, the thought with which Bonhoeffer dealt in detail in his doctorate and in his inaugural dissertation (SC and AB), and which, we can add, he never recanted or essentially modified in later time, and of which we can also find such examples directly or indirectly in his late utterances. The Church is Christ himself "existing as a community", his famous formula runs. "Revelation then happens within the communion; it demands primarily a Christian sociology of its own. The distinction between thinking of revelation individualistically and thinking of it in relation to community is fundamental" (AB, p. 122). His thought is anti-individualist throughout. The thought of the *Sanctorum Communio* is for him an essential element in the understanding of revelation, as well as of faith and the knowledge of faith, an element which dare not be overlooked. But it is precisely here that lies the crystallization point of almost all important questions which must be decided today between the confessions. In Bonhoeffer we are met by a Protestant way of thinking which as we think of the future can open up very fundamental possibilities of reaching new understanding precisely in this respect.

5. *Summing Up*

Thus over and over again we have found Bonhoeffer exactly at the crucial point of the theological event. So far as I can see there is only one single complex of questions on which he has not expressed himself in considerable detail, and in a fundamental way that leads to further thought, the ontological and hermeneutical question about the nature of history, of speech, of understanding, and about the appropriate methods for historical knowledge. Of course in another way, as we shall see in our chapter on "non-religious interpretation", he had a very intense sense of the hermeneutical problem of preaching, the articulation of the Gospel in our time.

But in addition to this the insights of Bonhoeffer are already very open towards everything in theology which today is preeminently topical for the whole of Christendom. If we attempt to describe the factually common element in all this, we shall see that all lines converge towards the question of the way in which the God of the Bible, the God who has revealed himself in Jesus Christ, the God whom the Church of Christ has confessed from the beginning, is real with the reality which we sense today, real in our life which he gives to us "as a prize of war". This question, because it is eminently the theological one, is especially an ontological and hermeneutical one. How is God real for us? And how can we today speak of his reality credibly, which means comprehensibly? The two are fundamentally one and the same question. It is the question about the reality of

God for faith, and at one and the same time that of the reality of faith itself. In this question there meet the three groups of theological subjects we have dealt with, the problem of atheism, the clash of Barth and Bultmann, and the thought of the *Sanctorum Communio*. In the atheism-debate in theology the question is if our sense of reality and the understanding of reality given to us exclude personal confrontation by God or if this rather is consistent with our sense of reality and sets its mark upon it, if indeed perhaps at its deepest level it first makes it possible. It is the question then of keeping balanced in opposition the God who confronts us personally and the reality which can be experienced of the world which surrounds us.[16] In the clash between "Barthian" and "Bultmannian" thought we are concerned that we should really speak about God and not man, and that we should really *speak* about God. Finally in the thought of the *Sanctorum Communio* the concern is that faith should be seen as encounter with God in its reality, that is to say in its real form, that of fellowship.

---

[16] Is such a reciprocal balancing with one another theologically legitimate? One can foresee the objection, "But God cannot be brought before the forum of our human experience". Granted! But where this objection appears the question has been wrongly put to begin with. Where else does God encounter us than in our experience, in our reality? Even if God's word bids us believe against all experience, this very "against" is again an experience. The purpose is to take the Incarnation seriously. Bonhoeffer took it seriously at every point in his thought.

CHAPTER TWO

THE LEGACY OF DIETRICH BONHOEFFER AND ITS EXPOSITION

1. *The Fragmentary and the Experimental*

A S FAR as method is concerned, it will prove a difficult task to interpret Bonhoeffer, and it is possibly a certain weakness of analyses of his work up till now that methodologically they have taken too little account of the interpreter's peculiar situation. The difficulty lies in the fact that neither as a whole nor in its parts is Bonhoeffer's work something completed. In other words, it lies in the fragmentary nature of this life and work, a nature of which Bonhoeffer himself was quite clearly aware. His interpreter must look back to his own judgement of himself here, and as it were make it the methodological principle of his interpretation.

"... it makes us particularly aware of the fragmentary and incomplete nature of our own (life). But this very fragmentariness may, in fact, point towards a fulfilment beyond the limits of human achievement: I have to keep that in mind, particularly in view of the death of so many of the best of my former pupils. Even if the pressure of outward events may split our lives into fragments, like bombs falling on houses, we must do our best to keep in view how the whole was planned and thought out; and we shall still be able to see what material was used, or was to be used, here for building ..." (LPP, pp. 78f.; February 20, 1944).

What Bonhoeffer here says expressly about his life must also be true of his work, which was so closely bound up with that life. For interpretation of his work the basis must be to recognize "how the whole was planned and thought out", or at least "what material was used here for building".

It is true that individual works of his were completed for a certain point in time and therefore given at least an outward finish, though surely the finish was also inward in such ways as, for example, giving them a logical consistency in their train of thought. This would be true of his doctorate, *Sanctorum Communio*, and his inaugural dissertation, *Act and Being*. But, without denying them, he always travelled beyond such halting-places. The earlier positions were neither forsaken later nor did they become simply available foundation-stones on which he subsequently built. Rather what was thought in the earlier stages is taken up in a later context of thought, without any binding force being retained by the formulation and shape in which earlier expression was given. The latest, for him at the end of his short life the most urgent, and therefore in a certain sense the ripest, thoughts, the *Ethics* and the sketch of the work on non-religious interpretation, of which only notes are to be found in *Letters and Papers from Prison*, remained skeletons, completely unshaped and fragmentary. As can be clearly demonstrated, he also passed through a certain development.[1] Yet even so the thoughts of his early works remain living and appear again in later contexts in altered form but with unchanged substance. In spite then of all the external lack of unity, a clear inner "direction" is still typical of his work.

One of the methodological demands which the interpreter has laid upon him by the peculiar fragmentary and yet unified character of the man's work, and by the necessity of recognizing from the fragment how the whole was conceived, we may say "what material was used for building", is the demand that we understand the *experimental style* of his thought. One cannot take every sentence which one reads in Bonhoeffer as there and then his final thought and word, and begin to build upon it a system of thought, or insert it as a finished component into any such systematic reproduction of Bonhoeffer. On the other

---

[1] Eberhard Bethge distinguishes three periods in the life and work of Dietrich Bonhoeffer: 1. The period of academic teaching at the University (*Sanctorum Communio, Act and Being*). 2. The period of the Church struggle and teaching in the Confessional Church (*Creation and Fall, The Cost of Discipleship, Life Together*, etc.). 3. The period which was under ban on publication by the National Chamber on Literature (*Ethics, Letters and Papers from Prison*). Cp. *Dietrich Bonhoeffer, Person und Werk*, in *Die mündige Welt*, I, pp. 7ff.

hand, if one thinks that one has met with contradictions in what he has said, these do not necessarily at once indicate deep discrepancies in his thought as revealed in them. One must be clear on this point, that he experimented in his theological thought, as did many a great thinker before him. We must pay attention not only to his words, but to the fact itself about which he is thinking, to the problem with which he is wrestling, to the nature and the strength of the experience in which he senses his problem. Interpretation then must not be purely philological and logical, as though we had before us a completed work full of his last word on everything, although to tell the truth even there a purely philological and logical interpreting would not be enough. But we have set us the difficult task of a sympathetic understanding both of the man and of the facts, entering on the human side into the personal situation out of which Bonhoeffer's work grew, and on the factual into the facts themselves which pressed in upon him and constituted that situation at its deepest.

To pay attention in this way, in the first place to the broad context rather than to details which have only the appearance of being well-defined, and then in addition to the facts themselves which may be largely unspoken in the work, is not caprice. It could appear so to a manner of examining which only recognizes philological strictness, but it is the one truly exact method appropriate to the special situation which we have to interpret. And this would also be true wherever a similar situation presented itself! We shall then not only have to guard Bonhoeffer's legacy but to administer it and make it bear interest. We shall have to extend the lines and continue along the paths in which he thought. Whether we are capable of any such thing remains questionable. It will depend upon how far and with what power we ourselves are claimed by the same facts as he, not merely by the fact of the Gospel which unites us all, but by the same special experience of the claim of that Gospel in a particular situation which is ours and which it falls to us to accept.

Karl Barth certainly rightly sensed and characterized the true Bonhoeffer and our situation when faced by his thought when he wrote about him to Landessuperintendent Herren-brück on December 21, 1952:

67

"But one has always run into, and still runs into today, a peculiar difficulty in Bonhoeffer. He was—how shall I put it?—an impulsive visionary thinker on whom something would suddenly dawn, and he would then give a living form to it, only to come to a halt again after some time, and one never knew whether it was to be a final halt or one only for the time being, by some thesis which happened then to be his latest one ... Is one not always obliged to grant to him that he would have spoken more clearly and concisely on another occasion and in another context, possibly withdrawing, it may be going still further? As it is he has left us to make the best of these enigmatic utterances in his letters, and at more than one place he has quite clearly revealed that he certainly sensed but still in no way knew how the story was really going to continue ..." (*Die mündige Welt, I*, p. 121).

How Bonhoeffer thought and how we stand when dealing with him is fittingly described in this passage. And yet one could doubt whether Barth, as he wrote these words, had detected the one keynote of his thought. If he had, his characterization must surely have included something on this point.[2] It is true that Bonhoeffer has left us to make the best of many enigmatic utterances. That is what he has done as far as the theologically conceptual is concerned, he has given us few concepts and statements so clear in themselves that we are left with no more to do than to collect and systematize them, before going on either to dispute or to defend them. It is certainly also true that Bonhoeffer was an impulsive and visionary thinker. And what he left us as his theological legacy is his vision of his problem, probably our problem also, and the impulse he felt towards a solution of it. It is also true that Bonhoeffer certainly sensed but in no way knew what course the subject in hand would go on to take. But for this very reason, if the problem is in other respects an important one for us, we must surely allow his premonitions to engage us and follow his indications of the way. If we do this and if after long efforts we succeed, our reward may well be that in spite of rigid fronts we are better able to satisfy the mighty challenges of our time.

[2] In disagreement with this letter of Barth's cp. also Gerhard Krause, *Dietrich Bonhoeffer und Rudolf Bultmann*, in *Zeit und Geschichte*, pp. 439ff.

2. *Legacy and Contemporaneity*

We deliberately used the concept "legacy" for Bonhoeffer's theological work and our relation to him, for it is a concept pregnant with meaning in its description of how we stand today as regards him and his work. But if we use this description there then follow certain compelling consequences for the interpretation of his thought. Because of the powerful impression evoked by his work, and especially the theologizing of his last period, the theologizing which kept becoming more and more fragmentary and yet because of that all the more radical and revolutionary in its effect, so much and such contradictory things have been written about Bonhoeffer that we cannot avoid a fundamental hermeneutical consideration of how our era and our theology stand exegetically with regard to him.

The concept of a spiritual "legacy" would imply that through his work Bonhoeffer has left us something which still possesses a certain validity today, and which therefore is not purely historical and past, or if it were, which would be recognized as a necessary stage on the historical road to the present. But Bonhoeffer's thought has in no respect been outdated by the course of the history of theology since. All that has happened is that as a result of subsequent developments the urgency of what was his anxiety has become more clearly recognizable. What he began to think must be completed in theological thought today, for his thought is no mere step towards our present but projects right into it and raises a binding claim upon us. Seen factually, he is still our contemporary. His legacy is made over to Protestant theology of our day, as material which we can use in our thinking, but at the same time as a charge laid upon us to think.

The concept of legacy unites us of today with him in one contemporaneity of work and of debate about the facts. He speaks no language of the past which would raise in an acute form the general hermeneutical problem of distance in time and make insight into the facts common to both of us only attainable by an exceptional hermeneutical effort, by some special success in "translation". Throughout it is our language he speaks, but his situation also is ours, the horizons of his life are ours, and in interpreting his work we do not need to use what H. G. Gadamer in *Wahrheit und Methode* describes as the essential element in the hermeneutical event, the "fusing of horizons".[3] What was for Bonhoeffer an open question in theology is still and in the same way an open question for us also. There is nothing that has been "settled" since him, if indeed in theology there is any genuine question which can really be "settled" at all. On this it would be truer to say that in the twenty years since his death even the formulation of questions and the reference to questions have not essentially altered. What has happened since is that a number of opinions, some of them important, have been expressed on the questions which occupied him and also occupy us. As a result new possibilities and shades of thought have been revealed, and today when we read Bonhoeffer and give further thought to his problems we must bring in new associates. We might say that today, after twenty years, there is more crystallization round the kernel of his thought. For example, at the time of his life there surely had not yet come into the light of day the fundamental significance which his *motif* of the *Communio Sanctorum* was going to win for the ecumenical discussion between Protestant and Roman Catholic theology. That is, his thought has gained through historical development this additional dimension to its relevance. But the factual problem is the same now as it was then, and now as then it is both unsolved and urgent.

We essentially think, then, today within the same horizons, in the same terminology, against the same background and in face of the same facts, as Bonhoeffer. The task and the charge given to us by the direction of his thought is not yet fulfilled. And the implication of this is that his theological legacy is still

---

[3] Tübingen, 1960. On the concept "fusing of horizons" cp. e.g. pp. 289f. "The truth is that the horizon of the present is conceived as in a continual process of formation, in so far as we must be continually testing our presumptions. Not least to such testing belongs our encounter with the past and our understanding of the tradition from which we spring. The horizon of the present cannot then be formed without the past. There is no more a horizon of the present in itself than there are historical horizons which have to be discovered. *Rather understanding is always the event of fusing such horizons which had been believed to exist in themselves.* Under the rule of tradition such fusing takes place continually. For there old and new grow together again and again into a living validity, without either of them being at all expressly contrasted with the other".

present among us, as a legacy in the strict sense, both a gift and a responsibility.

In this sense a description today of the thoughts of Bonhoeffer must necessarily be given at two levels, if one may make such a formal division; on the other hand it must busy itself with the interpretation of his writings, but on the other it must be further work on them as on questions concerning us. A description of Bonhoeffer which is not at the same time the interpreter's own study of systematics is, properly speaking, scarcely possible. Such an assertion may, it is true, sound like a commonplace, for is not precisely the same thing true for every work of interpretation which is in earnest and carried out for more than a mere historical and antiquarian interest? I believe in fact that H. G. Gadamer has expressed a fundamental truth of all hermeneutics, and one which in practice is all too often forgotten or denied in present-day historical and philological interpretations, when for example he writes:

"Hence it is more than a metaphor, it is remembrance of the original, when the hermeneutical task is conceived as entering into discussion with the text. If the exposition which achieves this is linguistically successful, what it means is not some translation into a strange medium, but on the contrary the re-establishment of the original communication of meaning. What is handed down in literary form is in this way brought back from the distant thing which it has become into the living present of discussion, the first accomplishment of which is always question and answer" (*Wahrheit und Methode*, 1960, p. 350).

By this standard all true exposition is always a discussion about a common "fact", one concerning the author and the interpreter in common. And Gadamer is right to emphasize that in order to understand a text we must understand the question which the text seeks to answer, but to understand a question means to ask it oneself.[4] I cannot understand a question

---

[4] Cp. *Wahrheit und Methode*, pp. 352ff. "If we seek to understand we must also in our questions go behind what is said (sc. in a certain text). As an answer it must be understood in the light of the question to which it replies ... To this extent the meaning of a statement is relative to the question which it answers, but this is another way of saying that it necessarily goes beyond its own actual words. The logic of the Arts is, as is shown by this consideration, a logic of the question" (p. 352). The context here refers to a most remarkable

without asking it myself, in other words, unless it is also an open question for me. In this sense, if we say that in the interpretation of Bonhoeffer we stand with him before the same open question, this is only exactly what is true of any hermeneutical situation at all. But if we mean that in Bonhoeffer's case theological discussion has not passed beyond him to enter into new horizons, then this general hermeneutical situation appears with a peculiar emphasis, or, we might say, with a peculiar purity. Certainly we shall also only understand and fittingly expound theologians like J. H. Newman, or Vatican I, or Luther and the Council of Trent, or Thomas Aquinas or Augustine or the Biblical writers themselves, if we, so to speak, endeavour across the ages to enter with them as contemporaries into a discussion on a common subject. But when we do this the horizon has become a strange one. They had other partners in discussion to whom they turned explicitly or implicitly, they saw other dangers against which they sought to defend themselves or to define their position, they had other presuppositions in the history of civilization and in their current terminology. We will not expect of Thomas that he should presuppose the terminology of the *Existenz* philosophy current among us and what has been its material discoveries, and in the same way one could not demand of us today that we, for example, should commit ourselves to the scholastic terminology and its ontological implications, simply surrendering every new insight and every new expression of thought since then. In such a case compulsion would have been used on one side or the other and a discussion would not be possible. But we do not despair of a discussion being in fact possible between us and the New Testament witnesses, between us and

---

controversy with R. G. Collingwood and his thought, as expressed in *Logic of Question and Answer*, which Gadamer takes up and develops further critically. Collingwood seeks to regard the event of exposition as immanent in a text's own horizon of questions, the question before the text *itself* being exclusively authoritative for the exposition. As against this Gadamer, in my opinion rightly, defends the position that the given answer goes on working in history, and that "its trends of meaning reach out far beyond what the original author himself had in mind" (p. 354). In the progress of history "the traditional acquires new aspects of significance". "Collingwood is not right when on methodological grounds he departs from all reason to find that we have to distinguish between the question which a text is meant to answer and the question which it really answers" (p. 354).

THE LEGACY OF BONHOEFFER AND ITS EXPOSITION

Thomas, between us and Luther, etc., a discussion in fact in which throughout the partner from the past answers us by setting before us his insight into the reality at stake and teaching us of later years of a better one, if we are able to hear him! But in such a discussion there necessarily takes place that "fusing of horizons"; for the horizon, the "world", the exposition and the understanding of reality of the author concerned on the one side, and our own horizon of thought, our "world", and our understanding of reality on the other, must both be brought into play and as it were fused with one another. Certainly the strangeness of the horizon of the other must be recognized, but even with such strangeness there the search must be made for the possibilities of common speech. [5]

In the case of Dietrich Bonhoeffer, however, such a fusing of horizons is not necessary. His partners in discussion are to a large extent still alive today and have spoken since. The basis of his theological education and his terminological presuppositions are the same as those in which we also have grown up. The dangers which he recognized and combated are the same dangers of which we are not yet free. On the contrary, it could surely be said with complete truth that much which has been written since Bonhoeffer has not yet reached the horizon of present theological discussion.

So he stands beside us, our theological contemporary, as he might in fact have been. He also gives us an answer when we ask him rightly and carefully, for he does not belong to those who possibly had once something important to say but now have nothing more. He can show us and make us feel questions which it may be we had not yet seen in this way. He can point us to new paths of thought whose fruitfulness he surmised and along which he himself had perhaps only travelled a little distance. He can point us to problems and approaches at work on which he was straining every nerve when suddenly interrupted by death. Bonhoeffer reckoned to the end with the

---

[5] In this sense it is fundamentally meaningful and necessary when, for example, in a "Thomas-Renaissance" today the thought of Thomas is fitted by theologians and philosophers like Karl Rahner, Gustav Siewerth, Joh. Bapt. Lotz, etc., into the horizon of thought of a transcendental and existential philosophy, and understood and made fruitful in this context. (Cp. on this e.g. Otto Muck, *Die transzendentale Methode in der scholastischen Philosophie der Gegenwart*, Innsbruck, 1964).

c*   73

possibility of his survival. He compelled himself to resist any false surrender to his fate. And in the last weeks of the catastrophe of the Third Reich it looked to the very end as if he might escape with his life.[6] So we must reckon with the possibility that his endeavours to make progress in the solution of his great problem of non-religious interpretation continued to the very end.

3. *The Necessity for Dialogical Interpretation*

How can we interpret a text when we have this exceptional relation to it? How can we enter into discussion with a deceased contemporary who was torn away from the middle of his work and whose questions have remained without qualification our questions, having more than anything gained further urgency? If we assume that Bonhoeffer has something to say on a certain question, then exegetical discussion, the hermeneutical event, can only take place by our attempting to think out further what he had begun to think. This seems to me a compelling methodological consequence, and precisely the reason why there is nothing arbitrary about our carrying further what he has begun to think if in so doing we move away from him. We are then acting in the only possible strict accord with the hermeneutical situation itself. For what is begun is only something begun and not a completed work, not something so rounded off in itself that nothing should be added to it and nothing taken away. And what has been begun receives its orientation from its confrontation with its subject-matter itself, the confrontation which, because it is the claim of the subject of thought, is at once the question and first light on the answer. It is we ourselves who are confronted. For this reason nothing would be more inappropriate than to interpret Bonhoeffer with a purely "historical" interest, as if his situation were no more ours and his problem no more ours, than simply to seek to establish "what he did in fact say and mean" and go on to record, label and catalogue his thoughts. Such a method, seemingly strict and exact, would in fact and truth completely refuse to face the strict demands of the situation. Surely it would be quite impossible to establish

[6] Cp. Eberhard Bethge's account of "The Last Days" at the end of *Letters and Papers from Prison* (pp. 227ff.).

what he had really said and meant without oneself taking up the threads of the discussion.

We have already pointed out that in Bonhoeffer's case our "historical" interpretation of his work must at the same time inevitably be our own systematic study. That systematics are inevitably and obviously the road to interpretation arises from the specific character of the exegetical discussion, that it is discussion with a contemporary. When I carry on a serious discussion with a contemporary partner it is surely obvious that we cannot separate my endeavour to understand him and my endeavour to understand the subject-matter. If I did not to some degree understand the subject-matter which concerned us both, I would not understand him and our discussion would be no discussion at all. Without this I hear without hearing and in the end do not understand a single statement. But, on the other hand, I only understand the subject-matter through the partner in discussion, in the light of what he says, and in so far as I understand what he means, "what he is getting at". This twofold mediation, the partner in discussion through the subject-matter and the subject-matter through the partner, is the essence, the promise and at the same time the irremovable limit, of genuine dialogue, the dialogical structure of our understanding and thinking in history. It is the basis for the statement that truth can only be won by us in dialogue. If then we wish to come in sight of the truth with which Bonhoeffer was concerned, which laid its claim upon his thought, we must deliberately continue in dialogue. But since dialogue abhors a standstill, this includes precisely that further thinking out we mentioned of what he had begun. For the exegesis of Bonhoeffer, then, we can describe the special situation as follows. *All* hermeneutics surely has the character of a dialogue. But in dealing with texts out of the past it is generally a matter of taking up again one which came to a conclusion in its own time, the dialogue of the text with its contemporaries, and taking it up under new presuppositions, as befits the difference in time and in horizons. In the interpretation of Bonhoeffer, on the other hand, it is a matter of entering into a dialogue which has by no means come to a conclusion, and one, too, in which the presuppositions have scarcely altered. If we wish to hear at all we must take part in a dialogue which is still unfinished.

75

Interpretation then dare not make him someone dead. For in the most real sense he is still alive. He brings us before an open question, he asks us and also gives us an answer in so far as he knows one himself. He himself clearly recognized and plainly noted the exegetical situation of the open dialogue which we have described, when he wrote for example:

> "But it is all very much in the early stages; and, as usual (!), I am being led on more by an instinctive feeling for questions that will arise later than by any conclusions that I have already reached about them" (LPP, p. 177f.).

or,

> "If you want of your own accord to send . . . (name omitted) . . . extracts from my letters, you can, of course, do so. *I* would not do it myself as yet, because you are the only person with whom I venture to think aloud, as it were, in the hope of clarifying my thoughts" (LPP, p. 193).

Precisely this last statement issues a challenge to further thought, a challenge to take up the dialogue. Here there appears the demand for further dialogical interpretation of what has been said and thought as an explicit element in what was said and thought itself. It is true that we can no longer give Bonhoeffer personally that advice and clarification in discussion for which he wished in his lifetime as he wrestled with his problem, and of which he has now no more need. But surely we can ourselves be hearers *and* speakers at the same time, just as he as speaker wished at the same time to be hearer and learner, that in this way the dialogue in which he was involved and wished to be involved, the dialogue in which he approached nearer to his own subject-matter, might continue on its course. For the sake of this, while we learn from Bonhoeffer and allow him to guide us, and therefore become his hearers and learners from him, we can and must at the same time also ourselves be speakers, precisely because his is a subject which will only make itself known in dialogue. Our interpretation will then be not merely a matter of speaking about him, but also of speaking to him as if he were still among us, in order to give his thought in this way the dialogical completion which is inherent and demanded in that thought itself. Thus he writes on another occasion:

"All this is very crude and condensed, but there are certain things that I am anxious to say simply and clearly—things that we often like to shirk. Whether I shall succeed is another matter, especially if I cannot discuss it with you. I hope it may be of some help for the Church's future" (LPP, p. 211, at the end of the short sketch in which Bonhoeffer tried to summarize in a programme of headings the importance for the Church of the task of non-religious interpretation).

This may shed light on the question of the factual legitimacy of publishing the letters from prison which Bonhoeffer certainly did not write for publication and which in his intention were meant for the addressees and nobody else. Would it not have been better to leave unpublished these letters with their fragmentary train of thought, open as they obviously are to misunderstanding by many? Or to put the question in another way, has this publication any additional *factual* justification, apart from the natural biographical interest in an important contemporary? If it had been granted to Bonhoeffer to reach himself with the aid of discussion a greater clarity on his subject, then surely the relative obscurity of a biographical commentary on his work would be the appropriate place for these letters from prison, or at least for the expressly theological passages. But as things are, in order that the subject-matter with which he was concerned may come more clearly into sight, we must render it "the aid of discussion". And while we are challenged to discussion by the prison letters as a whole, with their rough draft of theological notes, it is not only they that so challenge us, but also the *Ethics* and in addition the earlier and more finished parts of his work. For Bonhoeffer himself in characteristic fashion says in the prison letters that here he was "*as usual*" being led on more by an instinctive feeling for the questions that would arise later than by any conclusions he had already reached. If the last sketch had remained unpublished we would have been in danger of being deprived for ever of the service which Bonhoeffer hoped to perform "for the future of the Church". Just because of this specifically dialogical orientation, the publication of the letters from prison, which he in his lifetime wished to keep private, was a *factual necessity*, and it is also a factual necessity that renewed dialogue should break out about these utterances of his.

And once again he says in his prison letters:

"Sometimes I am quite shocked by what I say, especially in the first part, which is mainly critical; and so I am looking forward to getting to the more constructive part. But the whole thing has been so little discussed that it often sounds too clumsy. In any case it can't be printed yet, and it will have to go through the 'purifier' later on" (LPP, p. 215).

What was little discussed must now pass through that necessary discussion, if the subject-matter on the one hand, and Bonhoeffer's contribution to it on the other, are in other respects worth discussing. With all these passages to support us, we are given with a rare clarity, and in a way which we seldom experience elsewhere, explicit methodological instructions for embarking upon our interpretation from our task itself. And there is no necessity at all to look first for general hermeneutical rules which could be applied to the special case.

4. Discussion as our Methodological Instruction for Interpretation—its Phenomenology

And yet for carrying out our exposition in detail it would be desirable if we could have the support of a thought-out *phenomenology of discussion*. So far as I know, no such thing exists up to the present.[7]

An important task has been left here for future hermeneutical study. A step in the right direction would be to analyse the phenomena of discussion as we get to know them again and again from our daily experience and from obtaining scientific,

[7] What are in my opinion the best approaches to this are found in Gadamer's *Wahrheit und Methode*. Essential points could also be won from an analysis of Heidegger's articles in *Unterwegs zur Sprache*. A very essential new contribution in the meantime to the question is Karl Rahner's small fragment, "On the Collective Finding of Truth", in *Theological Investigations*, VI, tr. K.H. and B. Krüger, D.L. & T., 1969, pp. 82ff. Rahner speaks of truths which have their ontological home in discussion, and are only given in discussion, and can therefore be only discovered in discussion, that is, "collectively", and he speaks about the necessity of unifying formulae as halting-places on discussion's journey, and the actual limits to them. The suggestions made by Rahner in this article call for penetrating study.

philosophical and theological knowledge. From these then we could extract the components of the dialogue.[8]

But in the absence of worked-out perspectives of this kind we can at the moment only name a few points which seem to us to belong to the nature of discussion with a present contemporary, for as such we must approach Bonhoeffer:

1. We then understand our partner in discussion, when we ourselves succeed in formulating what he has to say in words which are not his own.

2. When we disagree with our partner in discussion or vary in the importance which we attach to his statements, this is not necessarily an expression of disunity; it may be precisely the expression of our common quest for a truth which engages us in common.

3. Whether we have understood the words and intention of our partner in discussion is to be verified by reference to what was said. We have best understood our partner when we have better understood the subject-matter with which we are both concerned.

4. All statements of our partner in discussion are to be measured and interpreted against what was his *last* concern. This means that as a rule what he says *last* is authoritative.

1. *"We then understand our partner in discussion, when we ourselves succeed in formulating what he has to say in words which are not his own".*

Understanding requires a paraphrase. This may be explicit in the sense that I actually do it, or it may be implicit in the sense that I know throughout that I am in a position to do so. If I am in no position at all to paraphrase any process of thought with which I have met, then at least there is no guarantee or token at all that I have understood. It may then be that I am merely repeating the words in which the process of thought found its first expression, while its meaning, its bearing upon the subject-matter, remains beyond me. Thus an adroitness

---

[8] The art of philosophical discussion was subtly developed in mediaeval scholasticism. An exact knowledge of the methods of disputation employed there could bring us further on the way to a knowledge of the phenomena of discussion. The spirit of disputation is really beautifully dealt with in Josef Pieper, *Introduction to Thomas Aquinas*, tr. R. and C. Winston, Faber & Faber, pp. 75ff.

which simply repeats the words and moves obediently though skilfully in the terminology of a school is often yet no real understanding. And thus the teacher whose terminology is merely imitated does not gain from his disciple the type of real partner in discussion who in his turn would be capable of challenging him in his knowledge of the subject. In this sense ability to continue a discussion is an indication that it has been understood.

Descriptions and interpretations of a text often suffer from holding too close to the terminology and diction of the interpreted text itself, that is to say, from not paraphrasing.

But genuine paraphrase presupposes that I bring into play also my background, the presuppositions which are familiar to me, the conceptual tools to which I have long been accustomed or which come to my mind as employable, that I may with their help express the strange process of thought, make it my own and insert it into the context of my own search for truth, in other words, make it speak to me. If the partner in discussion then recognizes again his own thoughts in my paraphrase we have understood one another, we are travellers on the same road, or at least for one stretch of it. But then things do not just remain as they were in me either. The unfamiliar thought is not simply "accepted", that is, simply added as it is to the instruments at my disposal. That would mean exactly that it was not yet understood. But instead my concepts are transformed and their closed doors broken into, my presuppositions are modified and my horizon widened. I gain new dimensions of understanding and expression. Precisely because I brought something of my own into the encounter and "staked" it I am changed by the encounter and lifted up above what is my own, and in this way I am brought a stage nearer to the truth I am seeking and have to seek.

If we wish to enter into a discussion with Bonhoeffer, we must paraphrase him and in so doing bring our own background into play. But have we not just enlarged on the point that in interpreting him differences of background and horizon do not play a part because he is truly still our contemporary? Granted! But paraphrase is still an unavoidable task even in discussion between contemporaries, between partners in one another's presence. For even in such discussion each of us has his own personal horizon of thought determined by background and future and by personal spiritual experiences. In addition, as we have already said, certain new viewpoints have emerged since Bonhoeffer, without his ceasing to be our contemporary on that account. In discussion between present partners it is still true that each of us puts the emphasis in a different way and is inclined to use his own concepts. And this need not mean any factual disagreement, but only a lively rivalry in wrestling for clarity. In this way each one who with the tools which up till now have been available to him, his experiences and his horizons, takes part in the discussion will contribute something to the clarification of the subject-matter with which the other also is concerned. And it certainly is a mistake to think that one particular fact can only be expressed in one and the same way.

Thus, for example, Bonhoeffer does not speak of an existential interpretation, and on occasion he expressly dissociates himself from Bultmann's demythologizing. But this does not preclude the possibility that as a method the concept of existential interpretation, which of course can be defined in various ways, might be a suitable instrument to describe what was his concern, and perhaps to clarify it further beyond what he himself said in so many words. Or again, he never speaks of the "supernatural existential", but this does not make it impossible to employ meaningfully this concept from modern Catholic theology, and in particular from K. Rahner, when we seek to think further through Bonhoeffer's approaches to the understanding of human reality and to Christology. It is true that only in the course of the continuing discussion it will become apparent *which* concepts, experiences and dimensions are related to and will fit in with the subject-matter within Bonhoeffer's sights, and which are not and will not. That is, the concepts will require to be tested critically in discussion. It is, for example, a matter for proof whether the theological pair of concepts, "Law and Gospel", by the help of which Gerhard Ebeling[9] attempts to grasp Bonhoeffer's subject-matter and his purpose, will fit into the course of Bonhoeffer's thought, or whether they would be more likely to turn aside

[9] Cp. *The Non-religious Interpretation of Biblical Concepts*, in *Word and Faith*, tr. Leitch, S.C.M., pp. 98ff.

that stream in another direction.[10] In such a critical examination one dare not, of course, be too tolerant and hasty. In Bonhoeffer's case, just as in any other, interpretations could be sought by means of concepts of a very varied stamp, could be sought, it follows, in very different directions. One dare not employ here too readily the *principium contradictionis*. Indeed in the historical realm, in the realm of interpretation, of revolution or development in meaning, it is possible that we do not know anything like clearly enough what such a thing as a contradiction is. One must give then to apparent contradictions room, and above all time, to reveal their fruitfulness for winning new clarity. Further, with goodwill, an understanding and a continuing contact is still possible when we are going different ways. When, for example, in what follows we take a different road from Ebeling in the interpretation of Bonhoeffer, it will be understood in this sense.

2. *"When we disagree with our partner in discussion or vary in the importance which we attach to his statements, this is not necessarily an expression of disunity; it may be precisely the expression of our common quest for a truth which engages us in common"*.

In a living dialogue it should for instance be possible to say to one's partner in discussion, "I think I can see what your concern is. But at this point I would not use the concept you last mentioned, because I believe that it darkens our subject more than anything; I would not do my seeking in the direction you have just indicated; I consider that only one of your last two arguments can be used, and I know another different one, etc.". That to speak this way is possible and meaningful, appropriate and not capricious, is due to the fact that the concepts and thoughts which we employ in what is essentially dialogical thinking[11] have their crucial point, their sense and

[10] On my disagreement with Gerhard Ebeling and the comparison of his and Bonhoeffer's understanding of reality, see below in Chapters Three, Five and Eight.

[11] This is pre-eminently true of the thinking of faith, of theology. For faith is a dialogue with God. Or is perhaps all our thought a tacit dialogue with God, a bad dialogue, no doubt, marked throughout by our taciturnity toward our partner in discussion? But I have my faith, since faith is a personal act, only in the form of a dialogue with God, never in the sense of a firm possession

their purposiveness, not in themselves, not in their formulation as such, not in the "letter" or in their contriving, but outside themselves in what has to be thought and said, in the subject-matter which they have in view. Concepts and thoughts, then, are in their essence not closed and isolated intellectual pictures; but pictures which point to and are open to their subject-matter. To take an obvious example, the traditional onto-logical concepts like "substance" and "accidence", "actuality" and "potentiality", are not anything in themselves, but seek to describe the reality which surrounds us, or which we ourselves are, to make it clear and to understand it in its composition. They seek to lay down and to maintain common basic com-ponents for all that is real. We shall only understand them as we see them together with the reality which they describe, and measure them against this reality. It is true that a complication results from this in that our examining thought does not stand outside history, but is on its own part, in its experience of the real, partly given its stamp by the concepts which it has to examine.

It follows then that Dietrich Bonhoeffer's concepts and pro-cesses of thought are not to be taken, listed and valued, that is, either accepted or rejected, or partly accepted and partly rejected, as closed and static in their unalterable "being-what-they-are", but that, like all essential concepts and processes of

---

of my own, of a factual content undialogically known. Hence I cannot separate my faith from the dialogical situation and make of it an undialogical uncon-scious factual content, and as such make it, say, the basis for discussion with atheists. That is, I can never appeal to my faith. I can only attempt to bring the partner in discussion into my own discussion with God. Out of my duologue with God and my duologue with my human partner there must come into being a trilogue. Or to put it otherwise, two dialogues must mutually embrace one another. My dialogue with God must become concrete, must prove true and to a certain extent verify itself, in dialogue with the human partner. This is true of theological discussion in so far as the dialogue is a thinking one, really seeking to know. But it is also in the same way analogically true on another level related to this one, namely when the dialogue is one of action, founded on love. Here love to God must become concrete, prove true, and to a certain extent verify itself, in love for our neighbour. Our thinking and acting, our whole understanding existence, has for this reason a dialogical structure, because man is created in the image of God, i.e., he is placed in relation to God as partner in the covenant. The covenant is the inner foundation of creation (Karl Barth). This latter statement is a theological one, and yet that the being of man has at its deepest a dialogical structure can be shown phenomenologi-cally in the daily phenomena of life.

thought, they have their own peculiar dynamic. They are functions of a seeking movement and are open to their subject-matter, which we believe is also down to details our subject-matter, and is so without any realignment of sights worth mentioning. The consequence of this is that, moved by Bonhoeffer, we betake ourselves to the search along with him, but in so doing we remain free to make our counter-proposals. If we partly contradict him, if, for example, we hold less fruitful his attempt at a historical construction or his doctrine of the *Mandata*, and do not build these into our own process of thought, we are not in this speaking against Bonhoeffer, but for him and with him. For he is not to us the champion of his own "position" and "theory" as thought out by himself. So understood, he would be dead and a partner in discussion no longer. What he is is a thinker on the way to truth.

3. *"Whether we have understood the words and intention of our partner in discussion is to be verified by reference to the subject-matter itself, and not only by reference to what was said. We have best understood our partner when we have better understood the subject-matter with which we are both concerned".*

An opinion in a discussion is no final position, but simply a stage. The opinion itself has essentially this form and it would be a misunderstanding to understand it as a closed theory. As comes to light especially clearly in the statements of Bonhoeffer which we have quoted, the opinion demands an answer, an answer which must also be a critical one, whether positively or negatively. It is essentially an answer-demanding claim and challenge. And because of the dialogical nature of thought, this is also true even when the opinion is given as a definitive and intransigent one. It demands the answer which criticizes and examines, in order that it may come, speaking scholastically, to some degree to its own "fullness of being".

For this reason I cannot understand anyone, if I only "understand" his individual "opinion" as such without also understanding *what* he means by his opinion. As against this, when I have entered into the subject-matter with which he is concerned, and that not merely in a rough and general way, but in the specific way and from the specific viewpoint in and from which he is concerned with it, only then have I really understood him, only then has his opinion become real to me. In an interpretation, then, of Bonhoeffer which treats him not as a witness to the past but as a witness to the present, there must first of all be two critical discussions. The interpretation will meet two separate demands for verification. On the one hand, if we take up Bonhoeffer's thoughts and give them further life by interpretation, it will be demanded of us that our correctness, the adequacy of our conception of his thought, should be verified. But, on the other hand, it will be demanded of the dialogical interpreter that he should also demonstrate with reasons the truth of his own opinion on the subject, of his "own" contribution to the discussion with Bonhoeffer as he interprets him. Both demands are there by the nature of things. And they are two separate demands for verification which in some circumstances, and possibly as a rule, are directed at one and the same statement.[12] For the interpreter

[12] I have previously, in *Existentiale Interpretation und anonyme Christlichkeit*, in *Zeit und Geschichte*, pp. 367–379, employed and explained the *concept of verification* of theological statements. It is an unalterable theological postulate that kerygmatic and theological assertions must be verifiable if they are not to be nonsense, pure illusion, and therefore in the last resort impious. But we must note even as we say this that verification cannot mean exactly the same in the sphere of theology as it does, say, in the field of exact science. The verification which is the business of theology is no compelling proof which dispenses with faith. On the contrary, it sets one free for a real understanding venture of faith. Gerhard Ebeling is surely thinking along the same lines when he writes, "If we began before by asking whether the subject of which theology speaks can be verified as reality, we now ask whether the subject of which theology speaks verifies reality" (*Theology and Reality*, in *Word and Faith*, tr. Leitch, S.C.M., 1963 p. 195). In this article Ebeling is emphatic in his use of the concept of theological verification. We might perhaps compare the statement, "Theology—it seems—speaks of something which is not verifiable as reality" (p. 193). In the theory of science generally the concept of verification has the following meaning, "A 'statement of verifiability' may be defined in terms of either of two fundamental rules. They are: (1) An assertion is semantically meaningful when one can point to a method by which it is verifiable, and (2) An expression which is not an assertion is semantically meaningful when one can use it as part of a semantically meaningful, that is verifiable, assertion . . . (It) is to be noted that in the statements adduced verifiability is not more closely defined. In this connection, too, the first view to be accepted was an extremist one which would only permit one type of verifiability, the observation with the senses of the situation referred to in the assertion. Today one is much more tolerant, in particular one admits more than one method of observation. According, then, to the outlook prevailing today, the rules we have adduced demand only *some* method by means of which we can establish to some degree whether an assertion is right or wrong" (I. M. Bochenski, *Die zeitgenössischen Denkmethoden*, Bern, 2nd. edn., 1959,

of Bonhoeffer such a statement, it may be a single assertion or possibly a complex of assertions, will be on the one hand the appropriate rendering of Bonhoeffer's own opinion and intention on some particular subject, but on the other hand what in the opinion of the interpreter is an appropriate description of the subject itself. On both, of course, evidence must be brought, on both the interpreter must be able to face speech and give his reply. When for example we speak of Bonhoeffer's Christological universalism and seek to establish this as the deepest meaning both of the event of Christ and of reality in general, it becomes on the one hand a thesis of the interpretation of him, but on the other hand a systematic thesis with its own merits which we have learned by our contact.

But again I believe that the general experience of discussion teaches us that, while the two demands for verification and the two events of verification can certainly be distinguished from one another, yet in actual dialogue they must almost always be carried through in one single process of work or thought. It is certainly conceivable that I might say to my partner in discussion, "You are quite right when you think that ... !", and that he should reply to me, "You have misunderstood me, that is not what I thought". Then in principle I can still always be right in what I made my own opinion, thinking it was that of the other, though my interpretation of him was wrong. In this case the question of interpretation and that of the facts have become separated. But more often the other situation will be the rule, and my partner in discussion, if I have followed him at all, will say to me, "With your paraphrase you have more or less hit upon what I sought to say; you have even made it more precise and we have therefore again come a stage nearer the truth". Then he again on his side will possibly make my formulation more precise, etc., and so the dialogue follows its course. It can even happen, and is surely

---

p. 62). It is today a task for fundamental theological thought to describe exactly that method which, the subject-matter of theology being what it is, may be taken into account as a method for the verification of theological statements. In my opinion the method is that of existential interpretation, so long as one understands this concept widely enough, wider at least than Bultmann does. See on this, p. 53; n. 13.

very frequent, that the one partner in discussion only becomes aware after some time that the other has thought further along the lines of his own intention. It can even happen that yet a third party gains this knowledge before him. For the thought which someone has once expressed is no longer possessed by him alone as his exclusive intellectual private property, what has been *ex*-pressed is there, a line of thought available for public discussion, and free for others to draw what conclusions may follow. In this sense the well-known saying is true that another understands anyone better than he understands himself.[13] In the last resort, then, whether I have understood and interpreted someone rightly must be decided from the subject-matter itself. The factual discussion cannot be separated from the exegetical. When I learn through someone to understand better the subject we have discussed, and when I am able to commend this understanding of the subject, this is at least a very strong indication that I have also understood the other correctly, and understanding him correctly follow the import of his thoughts even where I pass beyond his concepts, formulations and arguments. The plausibility of the factual insight I have won in interpreting the thoughts of another is an argument for the plausibility of the interpretation itself.

Of course it is true that there always remains the limiting possibility that I, inspired by the thought of another, should win my way to a plausible insight, but that in the process I should miss precisely the other's meaning, the possibility, in other words, of the "fruitful misunderstanding". But who would venture to say in every case, and who possesses a yardstick to

---

[13] Gadamer has a different judgement to pass on this dictum, cp. *Wahrheit und Methode*, p. 280. "Not only occasionally, but again and again the meaning of a text goes beyond its author. Understanding then is not merely reproductive, it is always also productive behaviour. It is perhaps not right to describe this productive moment in understanding as better understanding. For this formula, as we have shown, was used by Romantic aesthetics to reverse what since the time of the Enlightenment had been a fundamental statement of factual criticism. . . . It is enough to say that one understands *otherwise if one understands at all*". But in my opinion it is possible to speak of a "better understanding" in so far as later discussion may bring to the light of day tendencies or possibilities of meaning which are there implicitly, and in so far as in some circumstances the historical consequences of a statement are only gradually disclosed.

measure, where at times the legitimate understanding which carries the thought further ceases, and the fruitful misunderstanding begins?

Hence if, beginning from Bonhoeffer, we succeed in developing an insight which solves the problems round which centre today's theological controversies, and which is illuminating for the whole theological ambiguity in which we today stand, this is at least an argument for our having understood Bonhoeffer and having followed the tenor of his thought. Conversely, when a certain interpretation of his is disputed, we are surely always dealing at one and the same time with Bonhoeffer and with the subject-matter itself. Discussion becomes rather uninteresting when we isolate Bonhoeffer's opinion from the facts with which he is and we are concerned, when both are not there to be dealt with in one single breath. But to unite in this way exegesis and factual discussion is no capricious or unconsidered mingling of things which should logically be separated. It is in keeping with the special logic of dialogue.

Thus in the last resort Bonhoeffer's interpreter finds himself faced by a single demand for verification. And this is also in keeping with what to date has actually happened in discussion on Bonhoeffer. For example, one asks at the same time, as a rule, what he properly meant by his charge of "revelational positivism" and whether the reproach is in any way factually justified. One cannot surely treat the two questions as independent and separate them from one another. But in following up the two the final result is a general picture which involves an answer to both, a general picture which involves the interpreter at the same time in an attitude to the theological thought of Bonhoeffer and one to that of Karl Barth. Without such a doubled involvement in one's actual attitude the whole undertaking of interpretation would be reduced to a paper problem.

Connected also with this interlocking of factual and exegetical considerations is the fact that it is of the nature of a good argument that I should as far as possible "make stronger", as the Platonic Socrates says, the arguments of the other, that I should endeavour to take them in earnest and to gain for them a power and a meaning of which possibly the other had not yet thought.[14] Although we all possess a dialogical sense, "good" dialogue is unfortunately somewhat rare. As a rule we theologians prefer polemic.

4. "*All statements of our partner in discussion are to be measured and interpreted against what was his last concern. This means that as a rule what he says last is authoritative*".

This rule is of course no rigid law, but rather a premise. If someone declares that there is no break in his thinking and that what he says in his last statement is what he always thought, he should be respected in this, and it must be assumed that the continuity which he asserts does in fact exist.

We often find that both we ourselves and others, after long explanations which are throughout meaningful and far from unclear or confused, finally declare, "What I really meant to say was . . . ", that is to say, after having tried various thoughts in steering towards a goal, we finally make one more effort to come somewhat nearer still to it than we have managed to do up to this point. As we have said, it would be unjust to assert that in such a case the person concerned in what had gone before had not so far spoken at all relevantly. This phenomenon of discussion can easily be understood when we take account of what has been established above, namely that concepts and thoughts are "open towards the subject-matter". It is surely then very possible that we should go on speaking to the subject, the self-same subject, approaching nearer, defining more closely, taking in viewpoints, explaining, removing misunderstandings, and that then yet another time we should speak still "nearer" to the "subject", approach still more

[14] This factual position is brought out with especial lucidity by Gadamer, cp. *Wahrheit und Methode*, p. 349. "To carry on a discussion demands, not arguing down the other party, but on the contrary really giving thought to the factual importance of the other opinion. It is an art of testing, which in its turn is the art of asking questions. For we have seen that to question means to lay bare and bring into the open. Questioning brings into the balance against the tenacity of opinions the facts with their possibilities. To possess the 'art' of questioning is to know how to protect oneself against one's questions being suppressed by the prevailing view. The possessor of this art will himself look for everything which supports an opinion. Dialectic consists, not in seeking to come upon what has been said in its weakness, but in first bringing it itself to its true strength. What is meant by this is not that art of arguing and speaking which is able to make a weak case into a strong one, but the art of thinking which knows how to make a statement stronger from its own merits".

directly the "subject itself" of our discussion. We must add of course that even such formulations still will by no means "contain" the "subject itself" in definitive clarity, for that surely is something essentially denied to our thought and our formulations.[15] Then in such a case this last effort is usually also directed *ad homines*. "If you still should not have completely understood me, and if my train of thought is not yet intelligible it may well be that I myself am most at fault; I should like to say what I mean just once more as exactly as I can at the moment". It is often the case that the speaker does not hit upon the desired formulation right away—and this is especially true when his thought is concerned with essential things—and he may even require a long time for it. One only needs here to consider that thought, the process of gaining knowledge, is a way to truth and a search for truth.

Now it is a consequence of taking this situation seriously, as well as being a simple law of human fairness, that one should not deny to anyone who speaks on a subject the precision which he finally gives to it, that one should permit to stand what has been up to the moment his last word on the situation, and that in consequence one should not seek unnecessarily for factual contradictions between what he said last, as his most precise definition, and what he said before, but that one should rather, and even where it is not obvious at first sight, seek to bring what was said before into closer harmony with that final precise definition, and to interpret it with this in mind. In this way one does the best service to the understanding of the person's train of thought. Of course one is still free to reply to the other, along the lines of rule 2 above, "If this is what you mean and seek to say, you would have expressed yourself better in such and such a way . . .". It is true that in this one must also be careful, for when someone who has taken a new step in his thought does not expressly recall or define more closely what he has said before, that is surely a strong indication that he, who in the first place surely knows his own thoughts best, sees no break but a continuity between

---

[15] At least in so far as our speaking is not purely informative. On the question of essential thought and "purely informative" thought, cp. my article, *Das Problem des nicht-objektivierenden Denkens und Redens in der Theologie*, ZThK, 1964, 3, pp. 327ff.

what was said earlier and what later, and regards the earlier as capable of straightforward interpretation in the light of the later.[16] Many a "scientific" dispute which was purely verbalistic, that is orientated towards the pure *verba*, would surely never have taken place, if one had held more closely to this simple matter of fact and had been willing to pay more attention in detail to the course which a discussion had taken.

We have exemplified the rule in the first place from a discussion of limited duration, but it follows from what we have said that it is also applicable to the interpretation of a longer journey, even to that of a whole life's work. This implies for the interpretation of Bonhoeffer that we should understand his whole work in the light of the theological position which is last to see daylight, that of his *Letters from Prison*. So far as I know he has recanted nothing of his earlier important statements.[17] What he said later then, in LPP and E, has a special importance for the interpretation of his whole work. The earlier statements do not contradict his later trend but they are to be explained in the light of it. In this sense I should like to speak of a "teleological interpretation" of Bonhoeffer's train of theological thought, perhaps in the sense of Heidegger's saying, "Thinking is limiting to a single thought, which remains thereafter for the world like a star in heaven".[18] But conversely, if one understands the earlier in the light of the later, a light from the earlier will also fall upon the later and give a pointer to the fitting understanding. So for example, while it might be important to understand the lectures on *Christology* of 1933 in the light of what was said about non-religious interpretation in the *Letters from Prison* of 1944,

[16] Thus, to quote an example from present-day philosophical discussion, it is in my opinion no good method of interpretation when one needlessly and against his own understanding of himself ascribes to Martin Heidegger a factual break between his thought before and after his so-called "conversion".

[17] In LPP p. 201 alone we find the short remark, "I thought I could acquire faith by trying to live a holy life. I suppose I wrote *The Cost of Discipleship* at the end of that path. Today I can see the dangers of that book, though I still stand by what I wrote". But this remark, though important, must not be counted a recantation. It must serve the purpose rather of fitting *The Cost of Discipleship* correctly into the whole of Bonhoeffer's train of thought, interpreting it (teleologically!) in the light of the one "subject" of this thinker, and not absolutizing the trend supported by it, as do many for whom precisely this side of Bonhoeffer will alone fit into their theological framework.

[18] *Aus der Erfahrung des Denkens*, Pfullingen, 1954, p. 7.

these last fragmentary utterances, conversely, become better understood from the earlier systematic endeavours.

It also results from the nature of discussion and is verifiable from our experience of it, that one can assume in most cases that what was articulated later was already there in embryo in the trend of the earlier. In this sense, if one keeps before one's eyes the whole journey made, one will discover already in the earlier the traces and beginnings of the later. This is particularly true of Bonhoeffer. For example, the demand for reality which breaks through in *Letters and Papers from Prison* is noticeable right from the beginning, as for instance when in his *Sanctorum Communio*, which he wrote at the age of twenty, he tried to conceive the Church of Christ as a theological and as a sociological phenomenon at one and the same time. We must not then purely and simply assert the principle of teleological interpretation as a rule and working hypothesis, we must also attempt to demonstrate step by step from the earlier work how this working hypothesis is justified.

There are two further characteristics of the phenomenon "discussion" which after these examinations no longer require to be developed in the same detail.

5. *"Discussion can be creative. A thought can gradually be transformed in the course of a discussion, so that in the end a new one is there, one, however, which was none the less already prepared for at the beginning of the discussion".*

Thus the concepts and thoughts out of which a discussion is built up possess to some extent an entelechy for a future form of assertion and knowledge, and at the end of the discussion this suddenly blazes into sight. But the transformation, the creative process, does not take place through some purely immanent conformity to law on the part of these thoughts and concepts, it does so through the encounter with the subject itself as it makes its claim upon the partners in discussion. And from this encounter the very discussion gets its life.

6. *"Because a discussion is not to be understood in itself, but always as an encounter with the subject, it is on occasion legitimate to take a thought out of its context".*

It can happen, for example, that partners in discussion with widely differing backgrounds to their thought approach one another gradually and have great difficulty in understanding one another, although the phenomenon on which they seek mutual understanding is one and the same, and that then all at once one of them says something which depends upon his own background and fits into his own system of thought, but which none the less like a lightning-flash gives to both the certainty that they have understood one another. In this case partner A will take this statement of partner B out of its context, which to him is strange and scarcely intelligible, and in the meantime simply concentrate upon it. It may be that more similar statements will follow, and that an understanding will be built up upon them. This understanding, a new knowledge which has been fought for and won, perhaps in a new terminology, will mean a new system of thought in which the original incompatibility of the systems of the two partners will be broken through and made relative.

In this sense, for example, we shall set side by side in Chapter Ten certain central thoughts of Pierre Teilhard de Chardin, without reference to their context in natural science and natural philosophy, and certain central thoughts out of the so differently formed world of Bonhoeffer's thought and establish surprising agreements.

5. Letter-writing as a Style of Thought

Since point 4 of our phenomenology of discussion means that an especial importance has been won for Bonhoeffer's imprisonment letters for the general interpretation of his work, I should like, at the close of this study of method, to add a kind of appendix and confirmation of the insights we have gained, by referring particularly to the hermeneutical peculiarity of the style of correspondence, in which these last thoughts meet us, and on this once more to quote Bonhoeffer and Gadamer. Bonhoeffer writes:

"Forgive me for writing all this in German script; normally I do this only when my writing is for my own use—and perhaps what I have written was more to clear my own mind than to edify you. I really don't want to trouble you with problems, for you may well have no time to come to grips with them" (Bethge at this time was on active service) "and they may only bother you; but I can't help sharing my thoughts with you, simply because that is the best way to make them clear to myself. If that does not suit you at present please say so" (LPP, p. 157, at the end of the important letter of May 5, 1944).

As a commentary on this I quote what Gadamer writes about *letter-writing* in the course of his study of the hermeneutical significance of discussion as the interplay of question and answer:

"The originality of discussion is also shown in derived forms in which the matching of question and answer is concealed. As an example of this, letter-writing forms an interesting transitional phenomenon, serving, as it were, the emotions of talking round the subject together and coming to an agreement with one another. The art of letter-writing consists in not permitting the written word to become a treatise, but in leaving it open to be taken up by the correspondent. But on the other hand it consists in rightly including and complying with that measure of finality which what is said in writing always possesses. The gap in time which separates the sending of a letter from the receipt of the reply is not merely an external point; it sets its stamp on correspondence as a form of communication and gives it its own peculiar nature as a special form of writing. It is significant, accordingly, that the shortening of the time taken by the post has led everywhere, not to an intensifying of this form of communication, but on the contrary to the collapse of the art of letter-writing" (*Wahrheit und Methode*, p. 351).

The method sketched by us in fact receives corroboration here. The latest and possibly most essential thoughts of Bonhoeffer, the goal of his mind's pilgrimage, meet us in this peculiar mediating form between the finality of a work and a living discussion of the present day. This permits us to discuss it on the one hand as an opinion put forward as valid for us also, but on the other makes it particularly clear that in interpreting one has to make use of a method learned from the experience of discussion.

Finally, all that now remains to be established is that our attempts to enter into the necessary dialogue with Bonhoeffer in no way claim to carry the dialogue to the full distance, or to think out the thoughts to the full extent demanded by the subject-matter of this discussion. The questions will remain open throughout. What we set down here can serve at most as the approach to a systematic study and to the revivification of the dialogue in one definite direction, we believe that of Bonhoeffer and at the same time that made necessary by the facts, in order that we may find ourselves completely engulfed by that event which Bonhoeffer himself described thus on August 10, 1944:

"It is as you say; 'knowing' is the most thrilling thing in the world, and that is why I am finding the work so fascinating" (LPP, p. 212).

PART TWO

The Contribution of Bonhoeffer

D

CHAPTER THREE

NON-RELIGIOUS INTERPRETATION

W E FIRST meet with the thought of non-religious interpretation in a letter of April 30 (cp. LPP, p. 152),
where Bonhoeffer entrusts it to his friend Bethge for
the first time like some secret, and does so with a certain
hesitation and reserve. There was then not a complete year
left to him in which to give it further thought.

The starting-point, and what was "bothering" Bonhoeffer
"incessantly", was "the question of what Christianity really
is, or indeed who Christ really is, for us today" (LPP, p. 152).

"The time when people could be told everything by words,
whether theological or pious, is over, and so is the time of inward-
ness and conscience—and that means the time of religion in
general. We are moving towards a completely religionless time;
people as they are now simply cannot be religious any more"
(*ibid*).

The *problem* then must be, "How can Christ become the Lord
of the religionless as well?" (p. 153). Or in other words, "How
do we speak . . . in a 'secular' way about God?" (*ibid*.). And the
goal is the realization that "Christ is no longer an object of
religion, but something quite different, really the Lord of the
world" (p. 180). But the *method*, the way to be followed, is
seen by Bonhoeffer thus,

"I am thinking about how we can reinterpret in a 'worldly'
sense—in the sense of the Old Testament and of John 1: 14—the
concepts of repentance, faith, justification, rebirth, and sanctification" (p. 157).

Then in another passage in the letters there appears an
additional list of other Christian concepts as well as those
named here. It is to be noted also that in this context he uses

almost as synonyms the expressions "non-religious", "religion-less", "thisworldly" and "worldly", perhaps with an occasional variation in emphasis. And for the further course of our interpretation the reference to the Old Testament on the one hand and to John 1: 14 on the other is important. On this point more remains to be said.

1. *The Definition of the Problem and its* Motives

We have now sketched our problem with a few short quotations. But the first task which it sets us is that of a definition of what Bonhoeffer means by "non-religious interpretation". Since he first laid down our postulate, but was wrestling for clarity without himself yet knowing how he was to reach it, (the letters giving us some interim results of this endeavour), definition will not come easy to us. In the meantime we shall attempt to describe *five elements* in the definition of the concept:

1. Non-religious interpretation is a problem of language. What is to be said can no longer be said in "pious words". Old concepts and old words must be thought out anew.

2. Non-religious interpretation is a postulate which arose from a regard for the special facts of the writer's own era, especially from regard for its human phenomena, that is, it arose out of confrontation with man himself. "People as they are now simply cannot be religious any more . . ."

3. The postulate of non-religious interpretation, it follows, results from the fact that preaching can today no longer reckon with certain presuppositions with which at other times it possibly could.

4. Non-religious interpretation is not merely a problem of language in the narrower sense, but *as such* (!) it contains a challenge to the conduct and presuppositions of the Church. It is in a certain sense a problem of the language of preaching which reflects back on the Church's conduct:

> "How do we speak (or perhaps we cannot now even 'speak' as we used to) in a 'secular' way about 'God'? In what way are we religionless-secular Christians, in what way are we the ἐκ-κλησία, those who are called forth, not regarding ourselves from a religious point of view as specially favoured, but rather as belonging wholly to the world?" (LPP, p. 153).

5. Non-religious interpretation is also not merely a problem of language or translation in any sense that what is to be "said" or "translated" is itself a fixed datum in every respect beyond question. We certainly do find in Bonhoeffer the subject of preaching presented as unquestionable, in a way of which we shall yet have to speak. But, this apart, non-religious interpretation's question about a new language is at the same time a question about the central point, about the subject itself. It is concerned with the question "who Christ really is, for us today". This is the point where the whole subject of non-religious interpretation is connected with our second group of themes, with Bonhoeffer's Christology.

Summing up then, we might perhaps define as follows:

"Non-religious interpretation is a problem of language which, in the encounter with concrete humanity of our day, aims at a new orientation of the language of the Church, in which the existential behaviour of the Church in the world is involved, and which reaches its final close definition of its subject in the question of Christology". And with this last statement we have already gone a step further. For we have said, not merely that the language problem of non-religious interpretation somehow involves the subject-matter of Christology at its heart, but that rather it is precisely in a new formulation of the fundamental Christological facts of all Christian theology that the burning question of non-religious interpretation, for Bonhoeffer certainly in the end *the* vital question for the Church in our time, will finally find its satisfying solution.

But this definition is no more than a prospectus of the problem itself, gathered together from various traits which can be recognized in Bonhoeffer. To become more concrete we must begin by posing three questions. 1. From what is Bonhoeffer dissociating himself? What does he understand by "religious interpretation"? 2. How does he seek to work out his programme in practice? 3. What kind of Christological insight will result in its being carried out? But before we embark upon these, let us ask about the *motives* which led Bonhoeffer to this undertaking—which he had only just begun. So far as I can see there are essentially three of these.

1. In Bonhoeffer's passionate account of the activation of

what he was pressing on with and was pressing on him, the first thing to strike us is a peculiar trait of his, an aristocratic way of thinking which we can also detect in him in other contexts. It may be connected with his background, with that *milieu* of upper middle-class breadth of culture and consciousness of tradition from which he sprang. But the matter surely goes deeper. It is rooted in a deep-seated trait in the character of this great personality and his relation to reality:

> "I therefore want to start from the premise that God should not be smuggled into some last secret place, but that we should frankly recognize that the world, and people, have come of age, that we should . . . confront him (sc. man) with God at his strongest point, that we should give up all our clerical tricks, and not regard psychotherapy and existentialist philosophy as God's pioneers. The importunity of all these people is far too unaristocratic for the Word of God to ally itself with them. The Word of God is far removed from this revolt of mistrust, this revolt from below. On the contrary, it reigns" (LPP, pp. 192ff.).

Surely one does not at all require any long search for further motivation, or any further pondering on the subject. The aristocratic side in Bonhoeffer is the certainty and uncompromising nature of the judgement, "I do not do that!". What he rejects as dishonourable, as "clerical tricks", as dishonest at the deepest level, is what he has called "sniffing-around-after-people's-sins in order to catch them out" (LPP, p. 191). What he labels "psychotherapy" and "existential philosophy" is at bottom not these areas of question and research as such in philosophical and psychological thought, but a specific theological, or rather pseudo-theological form of behaviour which seeks to "exercise religious compulsion" on man, to press in on him at the border, at the boundaries of his existence, to come upon him in his weaknesses, in order in this way to "make a religious landing" somehow, even in this so widely secularized age of ours. But he is convinced that this clerical undertaking will only have success with a small number of our contemporaries, with "a few intellectually dishonest people", "a few unfortunates" on whom "we fall in their hour of need" (LPP, p. 153), a "small number of intellectuals, of degenerates, of people who regard themselves as the most important thing in the world, and who therefore like to busy themselves with themselves". This method Bonhoeffer calls "secularized methodism" (LPP, p. 179), and at heart he himself was one of these straight-forward, healthy contemporaries who, adjusted to this world, had no interest at all in such things and refused to concern themselves with their existential despair. All this pseudo-theological sniffing-in-people's-tracks, which seeks first to catch man in his sin, his sin as demonstrable by psychology and existential analysis, in order in this way to prepare him for the Christian message— all this is for Bonhoeffer the expression of an inferior outlook and, quite apart from the fact that his contemporaries cannot believe in it and have rightly developed a resistance to it, unworthy of the Word of God and its nobility.

2. A second motive is what Bonhoeffer calls thisworldliness or *worldliness*. He loves the world as God's creation, in that fullness of its reality which surrounds us and can inspire us, in the wealth of possibilities which it gives to man. He praises the gift of the thisworldly world, earthly being, even where it is hard and bitter to man.[1] Even here it is still his "prize of war", his opportunity, riches in which he has a share. To the reality of this world one can only reply, "Yes!" Anything else would be dishonest, a flight from reality, an evasion, with the consequence that the God in whom one found a portion in such a way would also be *eo ipso* an unreal God and not the Living One. Hence we must not too readily take that oftheard statement, that the believer is in the world but not of it, to mean that the Christian has to live in the world with a certain indifference and lack of interest.

In this context we can place Bonhoeffer's predilection for a strong, simple and healthy humanity, certainly not in the sense of any vitalistic idealism, but in the sense of a simple thisworldliness, of life in the completely human and thisworldly

[1] Here also we can assign the thought of the polyphony of the Christian life, so characteristic of Bonhoeffer's whole attitude to reality. Cp. for instance, LPP, p. 163, "Only a polyphony of this kind can give life a wholeness and at the same time assure us that nothing calamitous can happen so long as the *cantus firmus* is kept going". Or LPP, p. 164, "The image of polyphony keeps pursuing me. When I was rather distressed today at not being with you, I could not help thinking that pain and joy are also part of life's polyphony, and that they can exist independently side by side ...". Here, too, belongs his enthusiasm for the thisworldliness of Ancient Greece as represented by W. F. Otto. Cp. LPP, p. 183.

"duties, problems, successes and failures, experiences and per-plexities". Here, too, his partiality for the Old Testament finds its place.

"My thoughts and feelings seem to be getting more and more like those of the Old Testament, and in recent months I have been reading the Old Testament much more than the New. It is only when one knows the unutterability of the name of God that one can utter the name of Jesus Christ; it is only when one loves life and the earth so much that without them everything seems to be over that one can believe in the resurrection and the new world ... In my opinion it is not Christian to want to take our thoughts and feelings too quickly and too directly from the New Testament ... One cannot and must not speak the last word before the last but one. We live in the last but one and believe the last, don't we? Lutherans (so-called!) and pietists would shudder at the thought, but it is true all the same.

... But the logical conclusions are far-reaching, e.g. for the problem of Catholicism, for the concept of the ministry, for the use of the Bible, etc., and above all for ethics. Why is it that in the Old Testament men tell lies vigorously and often to the glory of God (I have now collected the passages), kill, deceive, rob, divorce, and even fornicate (see the genealogy of Jesus), doubt, blaspheme, and curse, whereas in the New Testament there is nothing at all of this? 'An earlier stage' of religion? That is a very naïve way out; it is the one and the same God ..." (LPP, pp. 103ff.).

It is not at all easy to interpret this catalogue of morally questionable events in the Old Testament which ends the quotation. It must surely be understood in this way, that worldliness, the affirmation of this world by the Christian, dare not idealize this world, not even in the sense of an ideal type of healthy humanity, but that it must look in the face in genuine realism the whole complexity and questionableness of what is thisworldly, its banality, even what is mean in human life. It must do so in order to be prepared in such realism for the coming of the "New Testament" reality, for the recognition of the "last word" beyond the last but one. This type of realism and this affirmation of this world has a natural connec-tion with that motive of Bonhoeffer's which we named first; it would be dishonourable, because dishonest, to shelter oneself from the reality which is given us as it is. And on the other side this motive of thisworldliness has a connection with the third motive behind this postulate of his.

This third motive I would call the *realism of the human.* Bonhoeffer says, "We are moving towards a completely religionless time; people as they are now simply cannot be religious any more". And he resolutely seeks to reckon with the concrete reality of those with whom he finds himself face to face. He seeks to turn to them, for it is to them that the Gospel of Jesus Christ, if indeed it is the truth of God, must be capable of being made comprehensible. The *"salto mortale* (death-leap) back into the Middle Ages" can no longer be made. It could "only be a counsel of despair, and it would be at the cost of intellectual honesty". "And we cannot be honest unless we recognize that we have to live in this world— *etsi deus non daretur"* (LPP, p. 196). We must live in this world as those who have achieved in morals, politics and natural science the renunciation of the "working hypothesis of God". "And", Bonhoeffer adds, "this is just what we do recognize— before God. God himself compels us to recognize it" (*ibid.*). One could ask how he compels us, a question which Bonhoeffer did not himself ask in so many words, but which was throughout within the area of his thought. And the answer, if we follow him, would have to be that God compels us by confronting us inescapably with men who get along without the "working hypothesis of God", who manage their lives without it, and by making us aware, if we would attain to honesty, that we ourselves belong to this group of men.

What confronts us in Bonhoeffer under the titles "religion-lessness" and "world come of age" is not that thesis from the philosophy of history which is well enough known today, but in my opinion not sufficiently corroborated, of the gradual maturing of reason as a result of the appearance of the Christian Gospel and the ridding of the world of demons by its teaching; it is not that hypothesis of the legitimate secularization which has been brought about by Christianity itself. That thesis I regard as neither completely true nor completely false. The true state of affairs, in so far as it is possible at all to give a meaning in such a general way to the course of history and we have the necessary methodological presuppositions to do so, is probably in essence more differentiated.[2] What is certain is that as a serious theological argument the hypothesis will not bear the weight which is put upon it. It can also be shown that, while Bonhoeffer *did* on occasion make use of the philosophy of history for foundations or underpinnings for his postulate, it was typical of him to remain quite uncertain in his view and judgement of developments in the history of civilization. His picture of the course of the Western world and his judgement upon it are wavering and indefinite. It was a field in which he was experimenting. But by contrast in his statement of his postulate of a non-religious interpretation he seems to be completely sure of his facts. Surely it follows clearly enough from this that this postulate has been nourished at other springs, that behind it are other motives, another and much stronger foundation, than merely a certain theoretical judgement on the course of history.[3] The accent in Bonhoeffer

[2] It would be interesting some day to study the phenomena of the "history of religion in a religionless age", the secondarily religious manifestations of our present time, to portray them in all their breadth, and to give them existential meaning in their depth.

[3] Hanfried Müller believes that he can find the actual crucial point of Bonhoeffer's thought, the area which he develops, in the thought of the development of the world to maturity, a thought from the philosophy of history, or "theology of history". (On this, cp. Müller's essay, *Zur Problematik der Rezeption und Interpretation Dietrich Bonhoeffers*, in *Die mündige Welt*, IV, 1963, pp. 52ff., and also his comprehensive book, *Von der Kirche zur Welt. Ein Beitrag zu der Beziehung des Wortes Gottes auf die societas in Dietrich Bonhoeffers theologischer Entwicklung*, Hamburg, 1961).

That Müller is referring to matters which are actually found in Bonhoeffer is beyond doubt, but at the same time through his special interest in the interpretation of Bonhoeffer he seems to me in characteristic fashion to have missed Bonhoeffer's own real interest. He claims to have established a break, or at least a striking and revolutionary change, in Bonhoeffer's thought between the *Ethics* and the *Letters and Papers from Prison*. Cp. *Von der Kirche zur Welt*, pp. 357ff. and especially the above-mentioned essay. He sees the Bonhoeffer of the *Ethics* as the "last honourable Christian Westerner" (*Die mündige Welt*, *IV*, p. 60), quoting from it above all the chapter on "Inheritance and Decay", where Christ appears as the hidden centre of Western history. The conservative conception of history which we find documented there is replaced in the *Letters* by one that is modern and rationalist. "The ideology of the Christian West was reactionary, but Bonhoeffer wished to put it at the service of the future, of liberation from Fascism. And at this point there was bound to arise the question of a non-religious rational basis for resistance to Fascism. But the power of this inheritance showed itself in a double law in such a way as to shut out the future. Because Christ for Bonhoeffer had become in the West history, he was no longer the Coming One, but the figure associated with inheritance, the One who was gone.

In the ideology of the Christian West he was no longer present as the Crucified and future as the Risen One, he had become the figure of the actual, and in consequence history had become a religious law. But at the same time, and not unconnected with the previous point, the same inheritance, as a historical tie to a past and passing ordering of society, deprived natural man of the freedom to dedicate himself freely to the future of earthly life . . . The liberation from the lordship of a Christian past which now took place progressively in Bonhoeffer is nothing less than the transformation and conversion of a true reformation . . . The conversion thus achieved is at the same time the liberation of faith from the law of a Christian *Weltanschauung* and the liberation of the *Weltanschauung* from the burden of religious ties. Faith for Bonhoeffer is no longer what it must have seemed to be, being tied to a Christ who is the unity of the West—that myth so effective in history; it has become being taken in into the Messianic sufferings of Jesus Christ. Hence he who so believes, who freely shares the sufferings of God in the world, will see the world as it is, from a standpoint beyond all categories of religion and the theology of history. That is to say, the believer becomes free to see the world '*etsi deus non daretur*', as if there were no God, free for an a-theistic *Weltanschauung*" (*op. cit.*, pp. 70f.).

Müller seems to me to overlook the fact that the *Ethics* and the *Letters and Papers from Prison* must be regarded as essentially contemporary. As far as the stage reached in the essential development of his thought is concerned, the "Bonhoeffer of the prison letters" is none other than the "Bonhoeffer of the *Ethics*". "I sometimes feel . . . as if all I had to do now were to finish my Ethics" (LPP, p. 107).

Again, Müller overlooks the fact that the aristocratic upper middle-class mental attitude of Bonhoeffer in the prison letters is precisely the same as that in the *Ethics*. "Unless we have the courage to fight for a revival of wholesome reserve between man and man, we shall perish in an anarchy of human values. The impudent contempt for such reserve is the mark of the rabble, just as inward uncertainty . . ." (LPP, p. 35, in the article, *After Ten Years*, under the heading "The Sense of Quality"). This pronouncedly aristocratic way of thinking, this outlook which cherishes reserve and the outmoded (Western!) values, is characteristic of Bonhoeffer both in the *Ethics* and in the letters.

The fact is of course that this historical picture of "Inheritance and Decay", as well as being little thought over and scarcely worked out, does not appear again later. Even in the *Ethics* it essentially stands isolated, really fulfilling only the function of providing a certain illustrative material for Bonhoeffer's important thought, that the instructions of Christian ethics do not hold everywhere and at all times as abstract general laws, but are each of them at home in one definite realm of history. Müller certainly saw this clearly. But instead of his drawing conclusions about a "transformation amounting to a reformation" in Bonhoeffer's outlook on history also, for which no serious examples can be adduced to set against the great extent of continuity between *Ethics* and *Letters and Papers from Prison*, the more natural and plausible conclusion would be that his real interest obviously lies in another direction, and that by comparison the historical hypothesis has only a subordinate importance.

This last in my opinion is true, not only of the historical hypothesis of "inheritance and decay" in the *Ethics*, but also for the much more noted and discussed "development to a world come of age", in so far as this is treated as a thesis in the philosophy of history, and not in its proper place as an experience of our time.

is placed elsewhere; the driving force behind him is the purpose that encounter with men of today be achieved in uprightness and freedom from prejudice. For him this gains an almost visionary power. He looks at religious man of our time and meets him with a deep sympathy and solidarity.

> "I often ask myself why a 'Christian instinct' often draws me more to the religionless people than to the religious, by which I do not mean in the least any evangelizing intention, but, I might almost say, 'in brotherhood'. While I am often reluctant to mention God by name to religious people—because that name somehow seems to me here not to ring true, and I feel myself to be slightly dishonest (it is particularly bad when others start to talk in religious jargon; then I dry up almost completely and feel awkward and uncomfortable)—to people with no religion I can on occasion mention him by name quite calmly and as a matter of course. Religious people speak of God when human knowledge (perhaps simply because they are too lazy to think) has come to an end, or when human resources fail—in fact it is always the *deus ex machina* that they bring on the scene, either for the apparent solution of insoluble problems, or as a strength in human failure—always, that is to say, exploiting human weakness or human boundaries" (LPP, p. 154, in that same letter of April 30, 1944).

But again, this inclination towards religionless man pre-supposes nothing in the way of an illusory ideal figure, of a man in every respect "mature", autonomous, and responsible for himself. Bonhoeffer, and above all in prison, was coming in contact with very different types of contemporaries, some of them very questionable and even pitiable. All the time he was seeing and having experience of a cross-section of modern "religionless" man in his ordinariness and banality. It is of these he is thinking when, speaking of "secularized methodism", he writes:

> "The ordinary man, who spends his everyday life at work and with his family, and of course with all kinds of diversions, is not affected. He has neither the time nor the inclination to concern himself with his existential despair, or to regard his perhaps modest share of happiness as a trial, a trouble, or calamity" (LPP, p. 179).

But he knows from his very encounter in an "era come of age" with this kind of trivial side to human existence, that this is the real normal man, with whom we have to deal daily and of whom we must take account, while the "religious" form a small group of outsiders, often dishonest outsiders.

My own opinion is that if we go with open eyes and without prejudice into the world around us, we shall day after day have Bonhoeffer's experience anew. We shall have the experience that, even among those who would seek to remain true to the Christian tradition, whether it be because of their background, or because of an honest openness, or, as is probably most often the case, for both reasons together, even among those who would seek to remain true to the Church, the majority no longer think and feel in religious, and therefore not in Christian religious, categories. This is the description to which answer the many who seek still to be Christians in every way, but seldom or almost never come to religious services, because they no longer understand the language of the pastor with its orientation to the traditional language of Christian religiousness. The Catholic Church, quite apart from its Church discipline, probably does not have the same difficulty here, because in it the sermon traditionally goes into the background in Church services behind the sacramental event.

It would surely be completely unrealistic and fundamentally dishonest on our part to turn our backs on this situation, and to seek comfort with the handful of the faithful, the "inner circle", the committed Christians", the "nucleus community", who still believe that they can understand the traditional religious language. The mass of the indifferent must become a serious problem for the Church and its theology, not least for this very reason, that these so often still at bottom want to remain Christians.

Bonhoeffer saw this problem, and still found room in his heart, and in the end surely not without justice, for all those who were all too ready to give up their nominal Christianity. The super-abundant optimism of his faith knew that with all of them the Gospel of Christ, far from being in a hopeless position, was rather actually in an exceedingly hopeful one. It is true that his optimism was one of *faith*, trusting in the divine "nevertheless"! And on the strength of it Bonhoeffer promptly set out to the task of making the Gospel intelligible to these indifferent and religionless contemporaries, driven on in the last resort by the hope that it would obtain a better understanding among the "religionless" than among the "religious". Thus his third and perhaps strongest motive for non-religious interpretation again and again finds its clear confirmation in our own human encounter with our contemporaries.

These three motives of his which we have expounded are not, of course, to be understood as separate and additional to one another. Rather they form a triple chord which sounds a single unmistakable note. In this harmony of aristocratic manliness, thisworldliness and human realism we once again detect, perhaps at its purest in the latest period of his life, the keynote of Bonhoeffer's theological existence.

2. The Change to a Cross-theology

It is now time to pass beyond motives and to make our further questions about the execution. Above all, in order to avoid misunderstandings, we must know exactly what Bonhoeffer meant by "religious". We must know how he defined his own project as opposed to other theological positions and possibilities, for in this respect he himself found himself a wrestler with clarity up to the end.

But first we take note of a peculiar thought which we find in him in the same context at a late hour, the change to a Cross-theology used in judging the present generation. The thought first appears on July 16, 1944 when he writes that we have to live in this world *"etsi Deus non daretur"*—and that it is God himself who compels us so to do:

"God would have us know that we must live as men who manage our lives without him. The God who is with us is the God who forsakes us (Mark 15: 34).

God lets himself be pushed out of this world on to the Cross. He is weak and powerless in the world, and that is precisely the way, the only way, in which he is with us and helps us . . .

Here is the decisive difference between Christianity and all religions. Man's religiosity makes him look in his distress to the power of God in the world: God is the *deus ex machina*. The Bible directs man to God's powerlessness and suffering; only the suffering God can help. To this extent we can say that the development towards the world's coming of age outlined above, which has done away with a false conception of God, opens up a way of seeing the God of the Bible, who wins power and space in the world by his weakness. This probably will be the starting-point for our 'secular interpretation' " (LPP, pp. 196f.).

In the lively interpretation and criticism of Bonhoeffer which followed the publication of his prison letters, much was written about this thought, occurring as it does several times in his letters from this time on. But sometimes in the process writers have been much too hasty to repeat this by no means easy and self-evident *theologumenon* with their approval. The thought does not fit easily into Bonhoeffer's other approaches to Christology, as we know them from his later works, and especially from his *Ethics*. We are compelled, then, to ask what this late theological thought could have meant for him. When it appears and is there so abruptly and forcibly, it could scarcely be appropriate to list it at once as one of his dogmatic statements, to systematize it, that is to say, insert it into a 'system' of Bonhoeffer's dogmatics. Where does the thought find its place? It is not a step in his quiet exposition of the Christological problem, and yet it has Christ as its subject. It is, it seems to me, again a type of "thinker's vision". Bonhoeffer looked at man of his day and saw in the spirit humanity going forward to "a completely religionless time". And there came upon him, as it were, with elemental power the final meaning of what was happening, that it was the Passion of Christ himself which was taking place here in our time! God permits himself anew to be nailed to the Cross for the salvation of man; he chooses helplessness for our sakes. The Crucified makes himself present anew as the Crucified for our sakes. This thought took a strong hold upon Bonhoeffer. He sought to make it a kind of "principle"; perhaps this had to be "the starting-point for secular interpretation". And the behaviour of the Christian had to be in keeping with this behaviour of Christ. To be a Christian now meant to share in the sufferings of God in the world. It was at this time that there came into being his poem "Christians and Pagans", the second verse of which runs:

"Men go to God when he is sore bestead,
Find him poor and scorned, without shelter or bread,

III

Whelmed under weight of the wicked, the weak, the dead;
Christians stand by God in his hour of grieving" (LPP, p. 200).

Christian existence means to endure to the end with Christ in the night of Gethsemane. From this profound thought it is possible to draw many lines of connection with various strains in his thinking, for example, with the ethical principle of "conformation with Christ".[4] It would be profitable to plumb the depths intellectually and to set out the Christological, existential, ethical and linguistic relevance of the thought. And yet it would always have to be done with a necessary caution and with the clear consciousness that here we have no more theological "theory" to deal with. We might say that its basic trait is this, that Christ is present and at work in the reality of the world around us—and in reality precisely as it is. And this means that the presence of Christ, the Exalted, in the events of this world is not only to be *asserted*, as is done in so many sermons; what Bonhoeffer endeavours is to give a Christological significance to a definite, concrete element in the destiny of our era. In this sense the thought of the sufferings of God in the world fits into the general character of Bonhoeffer's thought as something completely in keeping.

3. Transition

Beginning from a provisional definition of non-religious interpretation, we then attempted to show the triple chord of its motives, and finally made reference to its peculiar change to a Cross-theology. Now we ask about the *boundaries to the undertaking*. We use that phrase in no critical spirit; rather we seek to bring out how on the one hand Bonhoeffer, wrestling for clarity, distinguished his own position from certain partly related theological endeavours. Thus he dissociated

[4] The "structural components", according to which the Christian is conformed with Christ, are, according to Bonhoeffer's *Ethics* as we shall show later in more detail, the three moments of the Christ-event itself, Incarnation, Cross and Resurrection. These three make up the totality of the reality of Christ. This turn to an emphatically Cross-theology, which is the mark of this latest trend in his thought, is to be seen in the context of this totality; the moment of conformation with the Crucified is set out by him in a quite exceptionally radical form. But it is none the less to be seen against the background of the totality defined by these three moments (Cp. E, pp. 17ff.—Tr.).

himself on the one side from Karl Barth, and on the other from liberal theology and from Rudolf Bultmann whom he regarded as after all a liberal in essentials. With both he felt himself from certain points of view akin in his own theological journey, and for precisely this reason the distinction was necessary. He himself endeavoured by these distinctions to gain clarity about his own task, and for this reason we must give them our careful attention. But the whole project of non-religious interpretation has also boundaries set to it by its own starting-point, namely Bonhoeffer's relation to God and his faith in Christ. And finally he sees his whole undertaking limited in its working out, and therefore in a way methodologically, by what he calls its "secret discipline". For non-religious interpretation is essentially a problem of language, in which it is relevant to find an appropriate form of speech. But this search for the right words is limited from the start by this same secret discipline, in that there are certain things on which it is appropriate to keep silence. And being what we might call a spoken *silence*, the secret discipline constitutes the boundaries which always, and from the very nature of the subject, surrounds speaking of non-religious interpretation.

4. *Bonhoeffer and Bultmann*

In the context of his development of this thought of non-religious interpretation, Bonhoeffer writes this about liberal theology:

"The weakness of liberal theology was that it conceded to the world the right to determine Christ's place in the world; in the conflict between the Church and the world it accepted the comparatively easy terms of peace that the world dictated. Its strength was that it did not try to put the clock back, and that it genuinely accepted the battle (Troeltsch), even though this ended with its defeat" (LPP, p. 180).

In quoting this verdict we are concerned, not with how far Bonhoeffer's judgement is historically justified, but with recognizing how there is mirrored in it his own view of the task of theology in our time, and therefore of his own task. It obviously belongs to the charge given to theology "not to try to put the clock back". But surely that implies that it must take seriously the secular experiences and the relation to reality of the epoch in which it is speaking, that it keep these always before its eyes, that it speak with reference to them, and, as it were, integrate them. But as against this it must not do what according to Bonhoeffer's verdict liberal theology did, in recognizing the *homo religiosus* and the religious *a priori* as a particular, though unalterable, aspect of humanity within the general realm of the cultural, the aspect on which it specialized. Theology must remain autonomous and retain charge of its own affairs, and must not accept standards from anywhere else but its own subject-matter, revelation. Non-religious interpretation must fulfil both of these demands. We turn to Bonhoeffer on Bultmann:

> "Bultmann seems somehow to have felt Barth's limitations, but he misconstrues them in the sense of liberal theology, and so goes off into the typical liberal process of reduction—the 'mythological' elements of Christianity are dropped, and Christianity is reduced to its 'essence'. My view is that the full content, including the 'mythological' concepts, must be kept—the New Testament is not a mythological clothing of a universal truth; this mythology (resurrection etc.) is the thing itself—but the concepts must be interpreted in such a way as not to make religion a precondition of faith" (LPP, p. 181f).

By Bonhoeffer's verdict Bultmann in the last resort belongs to the liberals. We might also compare LPP, p. 156, "Bultmann's approach is fundamentally still a liberal one (i.e. abridging the Gospel), whereas I am trying to think theologically". That is to say, Bultmann does not try to put the clock back. He commits himself to debate with the awareness of reality which is living in his own time, but he does not maintain the autonomy of theology, but allows a process of reduction to be dictated by the spirit of the age. Whether or not this verdict does justice to Bultmann remains a matter of controversy. He himself seeks to understand what he called by the unfortunate name "demythologizing", not as elimination, but strictly as interpretation. But this need not trouble us at the moment. Our interest is Bonhoeffer's own theological presuppositions. And he obviously is now seeking something different from Bultmann, although in one respect, in a certain dissociation from Karl Barth, he knows himself related to him. Bultmann appears, says Bonhoeffer, to have detected Barth's limitation, his "revelational positivism" of which Bonhoeffer makes so much. Only this difficulty must not be allowed to become the master to the extent to which Bultmann, both in his method and in his results, has allowed it. On the other hand, Bonhoeffer and Bultmann really appear to be at one on this point, that an "interpretation of these concepts", those of the New Testament as e.g. the "resurrection", is today unavoidable. It is only the *manner* of this interpretation demanded by our times which Bonhoeffer pictures in a different way. What conclusions can we draw from his sparse assertions about Bultmann with regard to the road which Bonhoeffer sought to take? Two things have to be said here. The first is that in Bonhoeffer's judgement Bultmann reduces, which means that for him himself the result at the end should have a greater breadth and fullness of content than Bultmann gives it. The second is that Bultmann in Bonhoeffer's view "did not go far enough" (LPP, p. 156), that is to say, his process of interpretation left untouched certain concepts and their contents.

> "It is not only the 'mythological' concepts, such as miracle, ascension, and so on (which are not in principle separable from the concepts of God, faith, etc.), but 'religious' concepts generally which are problematic. You cannot, as Bultmann supposes, separate God and miracle, but you must be able to interpret *both* in a 'non-religious' sense" (LPP, p. 156).

Bultmann, like Bonhoeffer, is surely adapting himself to the times, and his way, again like Bonhoeffer's, departs from any Barthian "revelational positivism", but his procedure is on the one side reductive and on the other not sufficiently radical, because even after his reduction has been carried out, he still keeps thinking in "religious" categories. Bonhoeffer, in spite of all he had substantially in common with Bultmann, was obviously strongly aware of the deepseated difference, but he possibly did not express it with a final factual precision. The difference in my opinion consists in the fact that Bultmann thinks as an individualist. What in individualistic religious thought had been striving for the salvation of one's own soul has become in him the question of the authenticity of one's own existence. But, as we shall show later, for Bonhoeffer such individualism is precisely a fundamental trait of the religious. This fact, incidentally, must make the attempt to appropriate Bonhoeffer which we find in Ebeling seem in reality not altogether beyond question.[5]

In his article, *Dietrich Bonhoeffer und Rudolf Bultmann*, in *Zeit und Geschichte*, pp. 439ff., Gerhard Krause sees the purpose of the two theologians as more closely allied. In the most valuable fashion he puts forward against many assertions which declare otherwise, which dispute this nearness, and use many of Bonhoeffer's statements as slogans against Bultmann in the demythologizing debate, the *hermeneutical* character which is the basis of Bonhoeffer's interpretation. But we must acknowledge that he still fails to express adequately the deepseated difference which in spite of the fundamental unity of hermeneutical purpose divides the two endeavours in thought.

We shall now attempt to describe this difference more closely with the aid of the criticism of Bonhoeffer given by Gerhard Ebeling, a theological thinker, that is, who thinks largely along Bultmann's lines. Ebeling's essay, *The Non-Religious Interpretation of Biblical Concepts*, in *Word and Faith*, tr. Leitch, S.C.M., 1963, pp. 98ff., is beyond doubt one of the most powerful, subtlest and most clearly sketched interpretations of the challenge raised by Bonhoeffer in his prison letters. Ebeling sees very clearly the ontological relevance of Bonhoeffer's venture in thought:

"To analyse the connection between theology and ontology in Bonhoeffer on the basis of the concept 'reality' is a task we must the more firmly deny ourselves within the very limited possibilities of this address, the more we see just here a cardinal point not only in Bonhoeffer's thought . . . but also in modern theology as a whole" (*op. cit.*, p. 112, n. 2).

---

[5] When we speak of such an "individualism" in theological thought this does not in any way imply a lack of the sense of responsibility for the world on the part of faith and the Church. The opposite could easily be exemplified in, for example, the writings of Gerhard Ebeling. What we mean is that the categories of this type of thought can take account only of the existence of the individual as the primary and essential realm of the event of salvation.

Elsewhere, too, he emphatically maintains the hermeneutical character of Bonhoeffer's undertaking.

"In a similar manner Dietrich Bonhoeffer's idea of a 'non-religious interpretation of Biblical concepts' also brings the hermeneutical problem into the context of the fundamental historical changes in the understanding of reality" (G. Ebeling, Art. *Hermeneutik*, in RGG, 3rd. edn., III, p. 257).

Ebeling's real criticism of Bonhoeffer runs somewhat as follows. At the beginning of the last section of his interpretation Ebeling puts his central question. "Is there a theological category which makes it possible for the problem of religion in its theological relevance, i.e. in its relation to the Christian faith, to be grasped and thought through in such a way as to bring to full clarity the insight into the nature of the Gospel which is at work in Bonhoeffer's conception?" And Ebeling's answer is that the appropriate category is the law. "The path which that (sc. Bonhoeffer's reference to circumcision on Paul e.g. in LPP, pp. 181f.) indicates for theological thought and the judgement it implies could be anticipated in summary form by saying: Religious interpretation is legalistic interpretation. Non-religious interpretation means interpretation that distinguishes law and Gospel . . . Only the interpretation that distinguishes law and Gospel is at one and the same time and without the possibility of separation Christological interpretation, concrete interpretation and interpretation of faith" (*Word and Faith*, pp. 141f.). The change, then, to a non-religious interpretation, demanded and in part accomplished by Bonhoeffer, is interpreted by Ebeling as a change from the preaching of the law to the preaching of the Gospel, or to a preaching which knows how to distinguish properly between law and Gospel.

But it is interesting to observe the point at which Ebeling, partly it is true with supporting quotations from Bonhoeffer's own statements, comes into conflict with him:

"It does indeed look as if Bonhoeffer directs the full sharpness of his criticisms against the religious man, whereas he is peculiarly sparing of the non-religious. That impression, however, is completely false in such general form. If he assents to the adulthood of the world, then what he means by that is naturally 'not the shallow and banal thisworldliness of the enlightened, the busy, the comfortable, or the lascivious' (LPP, p. 201·—Quotation altered to text of 3rd edn. LPP, not available at translation of *Word and Faith*—Tr.). But the problem lies deeper. The debate with modern non-religious man must not be made too easy by confining our-selves only to his degenerate aspects. What of his best possi-bilities for coping without God? Is it not really necessary after all to talk here of 'boundaries', to address this kind of man with an eye to his boundaries and at these boundaries to speak of God? Can it be seriously maintained that to talk of the boundaries of human life has become altogether questionable and even death and sin are today not genuine boundaries any longer?" (The reference here is to, *inter alia*, LPP, pp. 154f., "I have come to be doubtful of talking about any human boundaries—is even death, which people now hardly fear, and is sin, which they now hardly under-stand, still a genuine boundary today?— . . . As to the boundaries it seems to me better to be silent and leave the insoluble unsolved. . . . The Church stands, not at the boundaries where human powers give out, but in the middle of the village".) . . . "Did Bonhoeffer himself not testify to the significance for his own personal life of such boundary experiences? (sc. in LPP, pp. 96, 122)" (*Word and Faith*, pp. 151f.).

Ebeling's concern in his insistence on the "boundaries" is clear; it is for the universal application of the dialectic between law and Gospel, for the universal validity of the theological category of the law, for the unavoidability for men of being under the law, under the accusation of the law, in radical questionableness. Even in this situation, in this reality of his existing under the law, man is reached and freed by the word-event of the Gospel. Ebeling's essay closes with the words:

"... that therefore only the proclamation of the Word of God as law and Gospel creates this man by killing and making alive, that proves itself true only *ubi et quando visum est Deo* and not even 'non-religious interpretation' can compel it to happen. But that our task is to 'endure reality before God' and in doing so to let ourselves be driven back to our first principles, to spell out and work around the concrete interpretation of law and Gospel, and to let ourselves be drawn into the service of a new coming to expression of the Word of God—of that Dietrich Bonhoeffer is a solemn reminder to us, and one we are obliged to heed" (*op. cit.*, p. 161).

Three moments are characteristic of Ebeling's outlook:

1. Man lives under the law, that is to say, in radical, unavoidable questionableness. 2. The Gospel which in this situation reaches and frees him is essentially an event of the Word. 3. The essential effect of the event of the Word is that it makes the individual assured in his conscience. On this last we quote several sentences from Ebeling's *Towards a Christology*:

> "The question of certainty has its seat in the conscience. This is suggested by the relation between uncertainty and sin . . . The very fact that the question of uncertainty is so acute is a sign of the uncertainty of man's being." "For the confidence and certainty of faith is something radically different from man's self-assurance; it means that I seek the ground of my certainty *extra me*; it means the certainty and confidence in God which is first offered to us by Jesus . . ." "The question of certainty is man's basic question, because it is identical with human being as being that is questioned". "To reduce the question of the relation of faith to Jesus to a mere question in the history of ideas, would be to fail to understand the problem of the basis of faith, to fail to see that man in his uncertainty can never achieve certainty unless he is *confronted* by it. . . . An integral part of the event of such certainty is the conjunction of compulsion and freedom, law and grace" (*Towards a Christology*, in *Theology and Proclamation*, tr. Riches, Collins, 1966, pp. 85, 87, 93).

For Ebeling this theological context becomes the interpretative principle of Bonhoeffer's demand for a non-religious interpretation. But it seems to me that in one significant respect the trend of Bonhoeffer's thought departs from the direction taken by Ebeling's concepts, taken though these are from Luther. For Bonhoeffer the conscience of the individual is not the primary place where the reality of the event of salvation decisively becomes fact; for him the being of revelation has a communal character and revelation finds its life as a community of persons (Cp. on this our Chapter Five). The question of the individual about his authenticity, about assurance in his conscience, would surely appear to him as a new form of the individualist question about the salvation of one's personal soul. And further, for Bonhoeffer the being of man before he is reached by the Gospel as event of the Word does not count absolutely as being under the law, in radical questionableness; the power of the Gospel, the atoning grace of Christ, may be already secretly at work here. It is for this reason that Bonhoeffer can describe Christ as the concealed centre of human existence, of history and of nature (Cp. his *Christology*)! It is for this reason that he can even speak of an "unconscious Christianity" (LPP, pp. 204f.—cp. the whole of our Chapter Four). It is in fact really very characteristic of the trend and the witness of Bonhoeffer's thought that he can say of himself that speaking of "human boundaries" has become completely questionable to him. And Ebeling's specific view of man under the law, in radical questionableness, is not to be found in him, because the universal reality of Christ has always already overtaken man, even before the event of the Word meets him as a concrete event of preaching. Thus in all the three points which we have recognized as constitutive for Ebeling, his view departs from the fundamental tone of Bonhoeffer's thought. Our discussion in Chapter Nine will make this yet clearer.

If I may sum up by pointing to the positive agreement between Bonhoeffer and Bultmann, this lies in the concept "interpretation". Both theologians demand as indispensable an interpretation of Biblical and theological concepts. Bultmann names as the necessary interpretation the existential, but Bonhoeffer rejects as reductive what in effect is Bultmann's way. It must surely be said then that what Bonhoeffer holds as necessary and seeks to do is fundamentally an *existential interpretation*, but that in him it wears an essentially different appearance. Or can perhaps the expression "existential interpretation" be meaningfully applied only to Bultmann's way with its individualistic stamp? This is a terminological question. Personally I would deny it.[6]

5. *Bonhoeffer and Karl Barth: "Revelational Positivism"*

In one definite respect Bonhoeffer also knew himself to be allied to Karl Barth, whose theological achievement he regarded

---

[6] I have explained more fully the concept of "existential interpretation", which I here make basic, in my *Existentiale Interpretation und anonyme Christlichkeit*, in *Zeit und Geschichte*, pp. 367ff.). My understanding of it departs from that of Bultmann in the placing of the emphasis, but Bultmann would not necessarily have to feel it something foreign to his own intention.

as a work of genius and relevant to the time.[7] Barth was the first to think the thought of a religionless Christianity.

"Barth, who is the only one to have started along this line of thought, did not carry it to completion, but arrived at a positivism of revelation, which in the last analysis is essentially a restoration. For the religious working man (or any other man) nothing decisive is gained here" (LPP, p. 153).

"Barth was the first theologian to begin the criticism of religion, and that remains his really great merit; but he put in its place a positivist doctrine of revelation which says, in effect, 'Like it or lump it':[8] virgin birth, Trinity, or anything else; each is an equally significant and necessary part of the whole, which must simply be swallowed as a whole or not at all. That is not biblical. There are degrees of knowledge and degrees of significance; that means a secret discipline must be restored whereby the *mysteries* of the Christian faith are protected against profanation. The positivism of revelation makes it too easy for itself, by setting up, as it does in the last analysis, a law of faith, and so mutilates what is —by Christ's incarnation!—a gift for us. In the place of religion there now stands the Church—that is in itself biblical—but the world is made in some degree to depend upon itself and left to its own devices, and that is the mistake" (LPP, pp. 156f.).

The second of these quotations is then followed immediately

---

[7] The personal impression made upon Bonhoeffer in his youth by Barth was considerable. Cp. the letter of July 24, 1931 to Erwin Sutz, ". . . seminars, meetings, an open evening, and now yesterday a couple of hours at lunch with Barth. One hears and sees something there . . . But it is important and surprising in the best way to see how Barth stands over and beyond his books. There is with him an openness, a readiness for any objection which should hit the mark, and along with this such concentration and such impetuous insistence on the point, whether it is made arrogantly or modestly, dogmatically or completely uncertainly, and not only when it serves his own theology. I am coming to understand more and more why Barth's writings are tremendously difficult to understand. I have been impressed even more by discussions with him than by his writings and lectures. For he really is all there. I have never seen anything like it before and wouldn't have believed it possible" (*No Rusty Swords*, pp. 120f.).

The moral authority which in Bonhoeffer's eyes emanated from Karl Barth was also considerable. Cp. on this point the exchange of letters between the two in 1933 and 1936 (*No Rusty Swords*, pp. 237ff. and *The Way to Freedom*, pp. 114ff.), in which Barth urgently demands of Bonhoeffer that he return from England to Germany and the Church struggle "with the next ship but one", and fulfil his duty there, whereupon Bonhoeffer did in actual fact travel with the next ship but one.

[8] (The literal translation of the proverb is "Eat, bird, or die". Cp. below, p. 123.—Tr.).

by the passage we have already quoted about the "reinterpretation" in a worldly sense of certain concepts (faith, justification, etc.), of their interpretation in the sense of the Old Testament and John 1: 14. The interesting thing about this is that Bonhoeffer in his criticism of "revelational positivism" speaks about the incarnation of Christ. In addition we find already defined in the passage quoted the concept of "secret discipline", which typically always appears in the context of revelational positivism. But these are the two decisive passages about this revelational positivism, but there is a further passage where Bonhoeffer refers briefly to the "revelational positivism of the Confessing Church" (LPP, p. 181). This seems to me to show that these so hard sounding words of his are by no means a personal theological charge against Karl Barth, but the description of a tendency in the theology of the Church, the manner of thinking and speaking of a certain circle which certainly had a close connection with the work of Karl Barth but which Bonhoeffer was convinced could not do justice to the challenges of our time and the specific problem of preaching Christ in it.

Karl Barth is surely right in regarding as enigmatic what Bonhoeffer has to say about revelational posivitism and indeed about non-religious interpretation, for the two have the closest connection and are mutually explanatory. The fact is that what Bonhoeffer really seeks to say is not expressed with theological precision in either of the two short passages, a fact all the more regrettable in view of the severity of his criticism. But Barth and others were certainly not right in thinking that for such reasons the much-discussed prison letters would have been better left unpublished, on the grounds that what he said in them was surely nothing but the unclarified and confusing momentary fancies of a prisoner cut off from the outside world. However much may be left to be desired in theological precision, and anything else can scarcely be expected at the first stage of a thought, above all in the form of a letter, yet Bonhoeffer had sensed a decisive problem for the being of the Church, and one which could not be pushed aside; it was his purpose, and he regarded it as of the utmost urgency, to write a large theological work on the subject. And since, then, sudden violent death overtook and prevented him, it would not have been a good thing if his call had remained unheard, if the Church had had still to wait for another great man who knew how to put the problem with the same urgency and power. In view of this, the unriddling of the enigmatic and the extension of the broken lines, which is now passed over to us as our task, seems a charge which can justly be laid upon us.

Barth himself, however, felt so disconcerted at the charge of revelational positivism that he could write, in the already quoted letter to Landessuperintendent Herrenbrück of 1952:

> "... I blushed a little to think that it was at all *possible* that such an intelligent and well-meaning man as Bonhoeffer, *could* have had such a picture from memory of my books, which he certainly did not have to hand in his prison cell, as appears in this enigmatic expression. I only hope that he has not used it in Heaven in giving a report on me to *all* angels (together with fathers of the Church, etc.)" (*Die mündige Welt, I*, pp. 121f.).

Yet the factual question Barth seems to pass by with the remark that he does not know when on earth he had bidden a bird either "eat" the virgin birth or "die" (See my note 8 above—Tr.) and with the reference to his "neo-Calvinist friends and well-wishers" in Holland, who would surely be highly astonished at receiving him in his new capacity as "revelational positivist" (*op. cit.*).

But in this case also the primary question before the interpreter must not be whether or not Bonhoeffer's judgement on Barth is really factually justified, or to what extent it is, or whether it fits certain of his disciples but not Barth himself, but simply what exactly Bonhoeffer meant by it and in combating what kind of a tendency he used it. And in this we are not primarily concerned with the expression "revelational positivism", but use it to help us to understand better the purpose of non-religious interpretation generally. And here this charge against Barth gives us a welcome help.

This question about revelational positivism is surely especially fruitful for this reason that it might perhaps be called the negative opposite of that type of thought and interpretation which Bonhoeffer had in mind.

Against it he brings forward a threefold criticism: (1) Revelational positivism does not distinguish different degrees of significance within the whole area of the Christian message.

(2) It sets up a "law of faith". (3) It "tears away what is a gift for us", a gift through Christ becoming flesh. From this there follows as a negative effect: (a) "The world is to some degree made to depend upon itself and left to its own devices". (b) "Nothing decisive is gained" through it for religionless man of our day—and Bonhoeffer is speaking especially of working men. That is to say, the Gospel does not in this way become more understandable and more credible to man of our time, although it remains recognized that Barth has utterly separated the Gospel as the supreme reality established by God himself from every religious *a priori*, every religious clothing, every religious talent of man.[9]

If non-religious, or can we say existential, interpretation is, as Bonhoeffer saw it, the opposite of revelational positivism, then it obviously follows that it is an interpretation which makes the Gospel understandable to man of a religionless era, that it,

[9] Cp. for example Barth's *Epistle to the Romans*, tr. Hoskyns, O.U.P., 1933, on Romans 7: 1; " 'Brethren—I speak to men that know the law'. The possibility of religion is already familiar to the Christians in Rome. To whom indeed can it be unfamiliar? Paul knows it, men of every degree and all classes actually make use of it, for above all the occurrences of human life there hangs a smoke-screen of religion, sometimes heavy, sometimes light . . . We hear, we obey, we confess, we express ourselves with some passion in speech or in print, with negative or positive emphasis. We dispose ourselves upon our appropriate shelf in the emporium of religion and ethics, ticketed and labelled, with this or that philosophy of life, and we are what we are described to be upon our label . . ." (p. 230). And then on Romans 7: 6; " 'But now we are discharged from the law!' Kühl pronounces this to be a reference to the 'experience of baptism'. But that is precisely what it is not. We dare once again to affirm what no man can affirm of himself . . . The limitation which we have recognized and defined (7: 1) is broken through, and we stand on the other side of the last human possibility, the possibility of religion. But 'our' being under grace is not an experience, not one type of human behaviour, not a particular condition of human activity (6: 14). Not by virtue of our own freedom are we what we are; but rather we are what we are by the freedom of God. We are unencumbered by the inner contradictions of religion . . ., in spite of the relativity of its experiences and occurrences. The heaven which bounds this world of ours is rent asunder in the eternal moment of apprehension, in the light of the resurrection, in the light of God, in order that our vision may have space to perceive not what men think and will and do, but what God thinks and wills and does" (p. 237). It becomes clear from the passion and radicality of these statements that here the bounds of the humanly possible are passed and he is spoken of who is no longer a possibility of man. The religious horizon is broken through, and it becomes clear as with a lightning-flash that the Gospel of Christ is no "religion". It is understandable today that where this note has once sounded loudly, a fundamental transformation in evangelical theology *must* be the result.

inter alia, distinguishes the different degrees of significance, that it takes seriously the Word becoming flesh for us, that it does not tear away the "gift for us" which is thereby established, but makes it known and preserves it, receives it as true, and in consequence does not leave the world to its own devices. But in all this it speaks in no spirit of "legalism" but in a true evangelical manner. But how are all these moments to be brought together? It is really no wonder if one at first reading feels himself before some riddle.

Bonhoeffer, it is evident, emphasizes very strongly *the incarnational aspect* of the event of salvation. What has taken place is not merely revelation in some undefined general sense, revelation has taken place in that God has become flesh in Christ, that is to say, he has entered into our earthly, fleshly reality. It is here that there is a "gift for us", that is, God is given to us in Christ, and is present in the world as "God for us". We must actually, and I believe that this formulation of concepts is in keeping with the trend of Bonhoeffer's thought, use the terminology of the debate about the Lord's Supper and speak of a "real presence" of Christ in the world. And then the world is not in any way "made to depend upon itself and left to its own devices", but God is already present in it in Christ.

But now another question has to be asked. Has not Barth himself, and since this is not only a matter of him personally, has not all his following, whether more or less independent, and in some ways Bonhoeffer himself is surely to be numbered with these, have they not always emphasized most strongly precisely this incarnational aspect? Is it appropriate to lay a charge against this group on this count above all? Of course Barth from his early days begins precisely from the sovereign act of God in becoming man in Christ. How could Bonhoeffer, in a charge which was indeed not thought through to the *end*, but at least was beyond doubt *thought* about and considered, have fallen into such an error as regards the attitude of Barth to Christ's sacrifice? If this were the case, then the somewhat bewildered and head-shaking reaction of Barth's to the situation would be more than understandable! But the theological wisdom which we find in Bonhoeffer is too great, his glance too penetrating, for us to declare ourselves satisfied with such a reply.

If then we are to interpret Bonhoeffer meaningfully and fruitfully there remains only one possibility. Certainly in Bonhoeffer's eyes revelational positivism *did assert* God's becoming man, and further, relying on the promises it established, it showed zeal and diligence in building that fact up into a comprehensive system, but none the less it did not *methodologically* treat that incarnation seriously. It asserted that revelation from God took place in Christ, quite independently of all human religious needs and capabilities. And in freeing the concept of revelation from this phenomenon of "natural religion" it was a hundred times right! For God *is* free and cannot in any way be brought into an anthropological system. But then revelational positivism developed from this fundamental assertion, this axiom which it declared, a system of statements which, in so far as the basic presupposition, the axiomatic assertion, is right, must all be true in the same way and with the same importance. The result is a monolithic block, and one can only have the choice of swallowing the whole or none at all. This kind of representation, whether in preaching or in theological development, Bonhoeffer regards as in the last resort legalistic, a "law of faith". The one which he on his side regards as credible and necessary he pictures in this way, that everything is not deduced from one principle, but that the revealed truth is discovered, piece by piece, in the study of the Bible and the study of the world. For the truth of God in Christ does not only confront us in the Word of the Bible; as a "gift for us through Christ becoming flesh" it casts its rays upon us from the reality of the world, subject to the provision that the world is confronted with the Word of the Bible, for the world is not left to its own devices by God, who has already dwelt in it. In this concreteness of this world and this epoch, in the concreteness also of our own lives given to us by God as a "prize of war", Christ is present. While we interpret step by step and seek to cast light, never demanding legalistically, but demonstrating lovingly and following with reverence the tracks of the truth of Christ, it can happen that one point dawns upon us and another remains hidden, yes, it can happen that much remains so obscure for the moment that we can only halt before it in worshipping silence. And this is what is meant by "secret discipline".

The brief, and to that extent obscure, but extremely significant remarks of Bonhoeffer about "revelational positivism" have understandably kept the interpreters busy again and again. In the above I have endeavoured to follow step by step in their context the few relevant passages of his. By contrast, the interpretation of Helmut Gollwitzer, for example, does not seem to me wholly adequate. He believes that it was the admittedly "fundamentalist" style in which Bonhoeffer as the young disciple of Barth and his theological contemporaries expounded the Biblical texts and especially those of the Old Testament, disregarding the perspectives of historical criticism in exegesis, which became for the Bonhoeffer of later years the occasion for a verdict of revelational positivism. "Dietrich Bonhoeffer . . . in expounding the Old Testament knew how to find a proclamation for our situation, but I think that he was undoubtedly wrong in the theological basis which led him to believe that he could ignore the historical nature of, say, Ezra and Nehemiah, and take the Christian significance directly from the text. I suspect that this was the 'revelational positivism' which in his prison letters he believed that he could find in Barth. His charge surely hits the mark, not with Barth, but with his own earlier period, that is to say, with what he in the thirties had understood and adopted as the anti-liberal teaching of Barthian theology" (*Begegnung mit Dietrich Bonhoeffer. Ein Almanach*, 1965, p. 112). This surely does not treat sufficiently seriously the deep and fundamental nature of this charge of revelational positivism. In his essay on *Dietrich Bonhoeffer und Karl Barths Offenbarungspositivismus* (in *Die mündige Welt*, III, 1960, pp. 11ff.) Regin Prenter gives this meaning to the controversy between Bonhoeffer and Barth, that in Barth's thought as a whole there can be discovered a tendency to give "a cognitive significance to the whole history of revelation", and that this tendency "*might* well appear to a Bonhoeffer as 'revelational positivism' " (pp. 40f.). Since Prenter's own attitude to this cognitive tendency which he has discovered in Barth is one of reservation, he believes that this in no way sets aside Bonhoeffer's criticism of him. In another passage Prenter writes, "But is God's being opposed to the world really conceived by Barth as a negation of it? Does he really make the truths of revelation a pure assumption without any relation to secular life? I think it is outside all possibility of discussion that a revelational positivism of *this* kind cannot be ascribed to Barth. He, too, as a Church theologian seeks to proclaim the world as God's good creation and man as God's partner in the covenant" (p. 35). Here Prenter seems to me to be right. The one question which remains is whether Barth with his dogmatic method is really able to *achieve* in the measure demanded today what he *seeks* to do and what he beyond doubt stresses with great emphasis throughout the whole breadth of his thought. On the other hand, as far as the real purposes of Barth are concerned, what Prenter says about a trend towards a "cognitive significance" to revelation seems to me not unquestionable. In his *Exegesen und Meditationen zu Karl Barths Kirchlicher Dogmatik*, 1964, under the heading, "On the Meaning of 'Revelational Positivism' ", Martin Storch writes: "We understand the critical words about revelational positivism as above all the verdict of a man who from his forward post judged as backward-looking the fight of a Confessing Church which appealed above all to Barth. 'The Confessing Church has now largely forgotten all about the Barthian approach, and has lapsed from positivism into conservative restoration. The important thing about that Church is that it carries on the great concepts of Christian theology; but it seems as if doing this is gradually just about exhausting it' (LPP, p. 181). Here the charge of 'positivism' is certainly not abandoned. But already it appears to be fading behind this other one of a 'conservative restoration', from which Barth is expressly exempted. If we now observe the broader context, it becomes apparent that Bonhoeffer sees the struggle of the Confessing Church as in danger of hardening into a formal confessional fervour, without the interpretation which would link it to the world" (pp. 30f.). This, too, is not incorrect, but it is rather a description of the position in the history of theology, not meeting that essential kernel of Bonhoeffer's thought which can only be extracted by strict interpretation. In addition, Storch's analysis stresses the "Christian incognito, in which Bonhoeffer was so passionately interested" (p. 19), and he establishes a far-reaching agreement between Barth and Bonhoeffer on fundamental positions. "In the long run it is just because it (sc. the *Church Dogmatics*) is not concerned with laying hold on a man at any one point of his dilemma, but with setting up the authority of the Word and of revelation throughout the breadth of the human sphere, that its splendid non-pietism and its equally noble humanity in its address to man is possible. On this side Bonhoeffer could raise no charge. There is a fundamental agreement in theological position at this point which as such must appear again and again in their attitude to the 'world' " (p. 23). This, too, is true. But once more we must ask if Barth has a method which can realize this position in a way which is theologically adequate. If, as Bonhoeffer believes, he has not, this is where may lie the seeds of that restorative tendency in Barth's followers to which Storch refers.

The interpretation of revelational positivism as a failure methodologically to take the incarnation seriously seems to me, when made as a working hypothesis for Bonhoeffer's interpretation, to be supported by the way in which it brings clarification with regard to the concrete form of its opposite, the positive programme of non-religious interpretation. But the first thing requiring verification would seem to be the fittingness of the expression to describe those with reference to whom it has been coined.

We shall now attempt a first step in this direction. As we do so we must recognize that in the controversy between Bonhoeffer and Karl Barth we are dealing with a difference, not in *facts*, but in *method*. This, however, does not mean that the difference is "merely" methodological and for that reason in the end of little theological importance. A difference in method is often also a difference of attitude in thinking, and this in theology can have far-reaching consequences for preaching, for the language of the Church and perhaps also for its life, for the concrete fulfilment of its witness. As regards the facts Bonhoeffer could be described as a "Barthian"; his thought is Christocentric, not anthropocentric and "religious". He had joined the movement in theology which was given its decisive stamp by Barth. But as regards his style, his diction, the methodological purpose of his thought, he goes his own way from his early writings onward, a way which differs in characteristic fashion from that of Karl Barth.

Now the method used by the *Church Dogmatics* is in fact that everything is deduced from a *Christological systematic principle*. Thus in theological anthropology the being of man is derived from the being of the man Jesus. Or in the doctrine of redemption the threefold form of sin, for example, as pride, sloth and falsehood, is derived from the threefold aspect of the event of Christ. Everything follows from one axiom, *and a theological assertion can only count as verified if it can be deduced from the event of Christ*. Hence the imposing completeness in itself of this dogmatic work. And hence the declarative character of the diction which expresses his thoughts. And in point of fact whoever finds that the world of thought of this work challenges him and that its method brings it home to him will either have to "swallow everything" or nothing at all, that is to say, he will either have to accept or to reject the axiom with all the consequences which follow from it.

This general characteristic of the *Church Dogmatics* must of course be tested in detail. Here only an indication can be given, which cannot count as compelling evidence that Bonhoeffer's thesis is right, but only as a contribution to the morphology of what he calls "revelational positivism". In what follows there will be examined briefly a passage from the *Church Dogmatics* which in its subject-matter, in its *factual* assertion, points emphatically in the direction of a real Christian serious regard for the reality of the world, in the direction, that is, which is in direct accord with the trend of Bonhoeffer's thought.

In his *Church Dogmatics*, Vol. IV, 3, Pt. I (tr. Bromily and Torrance, T. and T. Clark, 1961), Barth speaks in Section 69/2, under the heading "The Light of Life", of Jesus as the "one and only light of life" (p. 86). It means no qualification of this exclusive theological statement when he goes on to say, "That Jesus Christ is the one Word of God does not mean that in the Bible, the Church and the world there are not *other* words which are quite notable in their way, other lights which are quite clear and other revelations which are quite real" (p. 97). "What we have to contest, however, is that any of such good words in itself and as such is the Word of God, or can be set beside the word spoken by God himself, i.e. Jesus Christ, either by way of supplement or even to crowd Him out and replace Him" (pp. 97f.).

That Jesus Christ is the one and only Word of God and light of life means that he is the *total and complete* word and light (p. 99), not exposed on any third side to any serious competition, any challenge to his truth, any threat to his authority (p. 100), not to be combined with any other truth (p. 101), not to be transcended by any other truth (p. 102). The grounds for us of our knowledge of this assertion is that *this* word of God shows himself to be such in the power of God (p. 103). But the content of the Word which so confirms itself is, "The light of Jesus Christ is the light of His life . . . But His life is His existence as the true Son of God, who as such is also the true Son of Man. This means, however, that, as a life lived as a particular existence and occurrence within human history, and among the many histories of all other men, it is a life in the *covenant* which *God* has not only made but in His omnipotent grace Himself fulfilled and completed with *man*. It is the life in which *God* is not only enthroned above in distant majesty above the heavens, in which He is not only the inconceivable source from which man comes and the inconceivable goal towards which he is directed, in which He is not only the Lawgiver by whose commands his actions and omissions are measured, the eternal good which consciously or unconsciously he misses, but to which consciously or unconsciously he aspires, the mystery by which he is encircled on every side. No, it is the life which even in His Godhead, and without its slightest diminution, God lives in terms of our common *humanity*" (pp. 105f.). In the very power of this its content this Word confirms itself as the *one* and only Word of God. "This is demonstrated by the fact that He is *this* Word, the Word with *this* content. For can we think of any word actually spoken, or any conceivable word which might be spoken, that says what the life of Jesus Christ says?" (p. 107).

But how can we count on there being, apart from this one Light of life, other bright lights in the world? "There is only one decisive answer. We can count on it as and because we come from the *resurrection of Jesus Christ,* from the *revelation* of the humiliation of God's own Son to human sin and perdition as this has been crowned by God the Father, from the revelation of man's exaltation to living fellowship with God as this has been achieved in the person of the Son, indeed, from the revelation of the *reconciliation of the world with God* effected in Jesus Christ. He has taken over the rulership of this world. All things are put under Him. *All* the powers and forces of the whole cosmos are subject to Him as He was and will be the One who accomplishes reconciliation and makes peace between God and man. Hence, according to the witness of His prophets and apostles grounded in His resurrection, the sphere of His dominion and word is in any case greater . . . than that of the *kerygma,* dogma, cultus, mission and life of the community which gathers and edifies itself and speaks and acts in their school. The greater sphere of His dominion and therefore His Word *enfolds* the lesser sphere of their word of ministry. If with the prophets and apostles we have our starting-point at His resurrection and therefore at His revelation as the One who was and is and will be, if we recognize and confess Him as the One who was and is and will be, then we recognize and confess that not He alone, nor the community which, following the prophets and apostles, believes in Him and loves Him and hopes in Him, but *de iure* all men and all creation derive from His Cross, from the reconciliation accomplished in Him, and are ordained to be the theatre of His glory and therefore the recipients and bearers of His Word. In the very light of this narrower and smaller sphere of the Bible and the Church, we cannot possibly think that He cannot speak, and His speech cannot be attested, outside this sphere" (pp. 116f.). And therefore it follows, "But this means that in the world reconciled by God in Jesus Christ there is no secular sphere abandoned by Him or withdrawn from His control, even where from the human standpoint it seems to approximate most dangerously to the pure and absolute form of utter godlessness. If we say that there is, we are not speaking in the light of the resurrection of Jesus Christ. But if we refrain from this inflexible attitude, we will certainly be prepared at any time for true words even from what seem to be the darkest places. Even from the mouth of Balaam the well-known voice of the Good Shepherd may sound, and it is not to be ignored in spite of its sinister origin" (p. 119).

But nothing of this is "natural theology". "We do *not leave* the sure ground [*sic!*] of Christology, but with the prophets and apostles, and the Christian community established and living by the Gospel, and making Christ the object of its faith and love and hope, we look for the *sovereignty of Jesus Christ* which is revealed in His resurrection and which we find to be attested by the Bible and the Church, but *not restricted* according to this testimony. Nothing could be farther from our minds than to attribute to the human creature as such a capacity to know God . . ." (pp. 117f.).

There results then finally from the resurrection of Christ this remarkable assertion. "In this sphere, too, we have to reckon with human pride, sloth and falsehood, with an optimism and pessimism which are terribly far from the truth, with unconscious blindness and only too conscious hypocrisy. But these are encountered *intra muros* as well. In neither case should we be too summary in our judgements. It is no fair test if we dismiss these words in advance on the grounds that we have in them only the basically and finally unilluminating insights and virtues of the natural man and therefore *splendida vitia*, or that we see in them hasty conclusions and illusions, or that they are not exempt from the open and secret fanaticism which the children of this world can also display in their best achievement. This may all be very true. But it may also be quite irrelevant if it is nevertheless given to certain children of the world to speak true words, i.e. words which, whatever their subjective presuppositions, stand objectively in a supremely direct relationship with the one true Word, which are not exhausted by what they are in themselves, which may even speak against themselves, but which are laid on their lips by the one true Word, by Jesus Christ who is their Sovereign, too. Even in Christian circles is it not grace and miracle, and the continual transcending of a whole mass of subjective ineptitude and distortion, if true words are spoken and heard? Should we not always ask with great attention and the greatest openness whether on the basis of some miracle true words may not also be spoken without, and seriously recognized as such?" (pp. 125f.).

In what follows Karl Barth enumerates the criteria for the recognition and right valuation of such true lights outside the walls of the Church. They are "agreement with the witness of Scripture" (p. 126), "the fruits which such true words . . . bear in the outside world" (p. 127), and "what they signify for the life of the community itself" (p. 128). What use is one to make in the community of such "free communications of Jesus Christ" in the outside world? They are freely to do their work for the correction and upbuilding of the community. But they are not on their side to be exalted into a kind of canon. "We may thus conclude that *no* conviction, however profound or joyous, as to the authenticity of such a free communication of Jesus Christ can authorize either the community or any of its members to give their discovery the exalted status of a *dogma* or to enforce it on others as if it were such. This is something which the community must not do under any circumstances (p. 134).[10]

Then Barth in what follows goes on to enumerate what the nature of these lights shining in creation could be. "A concept fundamental to all the lights which shine, the words which are spoken and the truths perceived in the whole process of making known and knowing is . . . the simple one of *existence*. What is meant is a specific *existence for one another*. What is quite certain is that existence belongs to the content of *time*, of *every* time, and therefore that, as we are human creatures in time, we may assume that existence in the form of existence for another of the intelligible and intelligent is a *reality* which within its limits is impregnable, unalterable and indestructible. This is not everything. It is not even a great deal. But it would be ridiculous to deny that it is something. For it is ultimately the

[10] Correct though this distinction is when rightly understood, yet it seems to me that in it the dialogical character of the Church's being is not taken sufficiently seriously. Especially is this true of that fact of ecclesiology of which theology today is becoming more and more aware, that it is precisely by its encounter with the changing events of the world that the Church is led to a deeper understanding of its own being and the truth with which it has been commissioned, that therefore the dialogue with the world is not without a legitimate influence on what is called in Catholic terminology "the development of dogma". At the basis of this is a fundamental insight into the incarnational structure and consequently the historicity of the Church of Jesus Christ! This is one of the basic thoughts which carried the weight of that revolutionary process of awareness in the Second Vatican Council. Cp. for example, E. Schillebeeckx, *Die Signatur des II Vaticanums*, 1965, and espec. the section on the Third Session. But on the Protestant side cp. the shortly to appear important study by Ervin Vályi Nagy, *Das dialogische Wesen der Kirche*, in *Kirche als Dialog*. by E. Vályi Nagy/H. Ott, Vol. 16 of the ecumenical series, *Begegnung*, Basel, Friedrich Reinhardt, 1967.

presupposition of every breath we draw, every word we hear and speak, every step we make or refrain from making. The light in which this is declared and preserved is only a created light. But it is certainly a light" (pp. 143f.). Further basic structures in the truth which shines in creation are, "the rhythm of terrestrial being" (p. 144), its contrariety and the significant contrasting of beginning and end, construction and destruction, that is, that it is a broken light (p. 145), "natural and spiritual laws" (p. 146). an invitation to men "into the active ordering and shaping of things, and therefore a step into freedom" (p. 147), and finally, "the unfathomable mystery of the cosmos" which "never reveals itself without new and true concealment" (p. 149). But what is the relation of this one light to the many lights in creation? They are on the one hand challenged and relativized by it (pp. 155ff.), but on the other integrated into it (p. 159). Thus while they certainly are not witnesses to God on their own, they are themselves made this by the Word of God. "In this sense they are taken, lifted, assumed and integrated into the action of God's self-giving and self-declaring to men and therefore to the world made by him. And in the power of this integration they are instituted, installed and ordained to the *ministerium Verbi Divini*. Nor are they unworthy of this ministry, for by the *Verbum Divinum* itself they are made worthy. Nor are they incapable of it, for by the same Word they are made capable. Nor are they unwilling to accept, for by this Word a new will is awakened within them, namely, the will to do it. In their discharge and execution of this ministry, 'their sound is gone out through all the earth, and their words to the end of the world' (Psalm 19: 4)" (p. 164).

It would certainly be false to say that a fundamental change had taken place in the theology of Karl Barth, as if this emphasis had not always before been virtually included in his theological thought. Yet this way in which it is made explicit, this emphatic serious treatment of the creaturely reality in which we live and which we are ourselves, surely would not have come about but for the influence of the theological developments which had been going on around Barth since the first volume of his *Church Dogmatics*. What he has worked out in detail in the section we have here described, lies, as far as its content is concerned, within the stream of that theological trend which has come so powerfully into its own in the work of Dietrich Bonhoeffer, the trend towards a *radical theology of the Incarnation*, that trend which makes Bonhoeffer in his *Ethics*, under the headings, "The Church and the World", "The Total and Exclusive Claim of Christ", and "Christ and Good People", say:

"... the most precious thing in Christianity is Jesus Christ Himself ... Only he who shares in Him has the power to withstand and overcome. He is the centre and the strength of the Bible, of the Church, and of theology, but also of humanity, of reason, of justice, and of culture. Everything must return to Him; it is only under His protection that it can live. There seems to be a general unconscious knowledge which, in the hour of ultimate peril, leads everything which desires not to fall a victim to the Antichrist to take refuge with Christ" (E, p. 178).

"The two sayings necessarily belong together as the two claims of Jesus Christ, the claim to exclusiveness and the claim to totality. The greater the exclusiveness the greater the freedom. But in isolation the claim to exclusiveness leads to fanaticism and to slavery; and in isolation the claim to totality leads to the secularization and self-abandonment of the Church. The more exclusively we acknowledge and confess Christ as our Lord, the more fully the wide range of His dominion will be disclosed to us ... The Cross of Christ makes both sayings true: 'He that is not with me is against me' and, 'He that is not against us is for us' " (E. pp. 180f.).

To this tendency in Bonhoeffer there corresponds today that trend in Catholic theology which speaks about an "anonymous Christendom", which presses on into dialogue with the world in the insight that the Church also is confronted by the truth of God through the world, and is so without departing in the least from the "sure grounds of Christology". But as regards the facts this whole theological movement would scarcely have to take exception to a word of the details which Barth has worked out in this section we have treated. Rather one could find in his thought a powerful confirmation of this necessary theological concern.

We find a difference only when we look at Barth's peculiar method of theological exposition. A statement is set down, the thesis of the one Light of life and the many lights, and of the relativization and the integration of the latter by the former. It is a thesis deduced from the Christological fact of the resurrection. Once this is unshakeably established, the course of theological thought only requires definitions and enumerations and a paraphrasing exposition of what we have listed. The consequences follow so unshakeably that one is able to renounce calmly the need for asking many questions. To mention here but a single example of that disregard of questions which keeps dogging us in the work of Barth, a disregard occasioned by his methodology, this is the case in *op. cit.*, p. 160, where the subject is the one Word and Light of God. From this point of view one could well publish a "Critical Meditations on the Church Dogmatics", though not without also in every single instance *learning positively* from Barth.

"In it there is no darkness. Indeed, outside it there is no darkness to which it is not superior in its shining, which it cannot penetrate and illumine with its shining. It is an *irrevocable* Word. There is no fault in it, nor does it contradict itself. It cannot be recalled and replaced by any other Word of God. In face of it all contradiction is ill-grounded, impotent and untenable, and therefore condemned to be silenced and removed. It is the prototype of Word—the Word which makes all others possible as such, from which they derive and to which they return, to which they approximate, which they would like to emulate but cannot, alongside which they therefore cannot range themselves. It is the declaration both of first and *original* and of last and final truth. It is the truth itself and as such. It cannot then be subjected to any criterion of truth different from itself. It is itself the criterion of all different truth. Disclosed by God it authenticates itself. If any other truth authenticates itself it does so in the power of this self-authenticating truth".

The monstrous problem of theological language, the problem which here in fact announces its presence in a way which cannot be avoided, the question of the *veritas prima*, the question of *how* the "shining through" of this one Light is to be conceived, and in *what* form the unerring truth of the one Word of God encounters us, all these are questions which are not put. But this disregard of questions is surely nothing accidental, it is legitimized, or rather nothing less than demanded, by the characteristic methodology of the work. But it was just this constructional method in the theological process of thought which Bonhoeffer, with an exaggerated polemical emphasis, but as a factual description not unfittingly, described as "revelational positivism".

Historically, Barth's whole theological thought grew out of an antithesis to neo-Protestantism, though in saying so we must not, of course, lose sight of the positive basis which it also had in the encounter with the Word of God, and this was accompanied, according to the detail given in the *Prolegomena* on Church Dogmatics (Volume I, Section I), by a further antithesis to Roman Catholicism. The resultant note sounded powerfully for the first time in the *Epistle to the Romans*. But this was too narrow a foundation on which to build, and hence the fundamental *assertion* of this theology had to be maintained throughout the whole breadth of the traditional subject matter of dogmatics. This is what was done in the *Church Dogmatics* as the work of decades. The declaratory, and therefore in the end monological, style of the work is thus to be understood in the light of its origin, according to the law which governed its appearance.[11]

Because of the comprehensive character of his *Church Dogmatics*, Karl Barth has occasionally been compared to Thomas Aquinas. In some respects the comparison is not unjust. But in respect of methodology we find in the *Summa Theologiae* the exact opposite of the style of the *Church Dogmatics*, the method of *Quaestio*. It is the *dialogical* method, which invites the objections of the partner in discussion, not without learning from him, the methodological taking seriously of the incarnation, the "incarnational method" of which theology today has need, at least now that it has found its

[11] As characteristic of the distinctive style of thought and language of the whole of Barth's theology, and as marking its connection with its historical situation, we may quote Barth's remarks at the beginning of the "Answers to Questions" which are added to the lectures on the Apostles' Creed given in Utrecht in 1935, and published with the title *Credo* (tr. Macnab, H. & S., 1936). Barth there says to his Dutch hearers, "And now this Professor has blown in from Germany and with regard to many matters has said something very *definite* in a somewhat *binding* fashion . . . Be clear about what has been happening during these last months in Germany and Bonn . . . All this has in Germany been a challenge to the Church and to theology, has been and is a challenge to each individual theologian to make a stand, to decide, to confess . . ." (pp. 174f.). But this fighting confessional style, in keeping with the situation of the time, which Barth compares to the "great times of the Church's past . . . in which Church dogma arose", has remained throughout the characteristic style of his theological statements. This is the reason for the impressive unambiguity of the man and his work. But what has to be considered is if in the meantime the situation of the Church has not taken another and a new appearance. For in history nothing stands still.

foundations again through the affirmations of Karl Barth. This is what Bonhoeffer foresaw in his somewhat blunt dissociation of himself from Barth's "revelational positivism".[12]

This factual situation which we have described is mirrored in the relation to philosophical thought which theology gives itself. In the chapter on "The Communion of Saints" we shall see more exactly how Bonhoeffer in his early writing took pains to integrate into theology secular philosophical thought about it. On the other side Karl Barth in 1960, in *Philosophie und christliche Existenz*, the *Festschrift* for his brother Heinrich Barth, wrote, *inter alia*, under the title *Philosophie und Theologie*: "The theologian cannot prescribe to him (sc. the philosopher) what he shall learn from him. Indeed, what he would have to say to him could, were he to open his black heart for just one moment, lead to the unashamed and intolerable demand that the philosopher should consider that the end of all philosophy has long been here, and that he should therefore devote himself at best to a study of its completed history, and

[12] In his controversy with Barth's anthropology (*Church Dogmatics*, III, 2) Hendrik van Oyen refers, very aptly in my opinion, to a certain inconsistency in Barth's system of dogma; "... But Barth yet finds himself compelled to speak of a generally admitted fact of human ability to be a creation of God's (pp. 224f.), that is to say, to speak of a formal *humanum*. In my opinion this is a matter of an either-or. Either one declares that it is only from faith that this position as creation becomes evident, which rules out the possibility of assuming a recognizable structure which can be *generally* admitted, or one admits a generally recognizable situation, that is to say, a formal *humanum* ... In my opinion the first has always been Barth's standpoint, but in anthropology at least ... there opens a perspective, as he admits with hesitation, to a speculative element in theology" (*Bemerkungen zu Karl Barths Anthropologie*, in *Zeitschrift für evangelische Ethik*, 7th year, Vol. 5, 1963; Quotation from p. 302).

It seems that Barth did not possess the concepts and categories which would enable him to say really and consistently what, rightly in my opinion, he would have liked to say. He would wish on the one hand to maintain a certain "illumination" of the reality of human life in its fundamental character, e.g. as social life, as something given, or better, as something taking place each time, along with that reality, but on the other hand he did not wish to surrender the Christocentric foundation of his dogmatics. One could surely do justice to this by thinking of the factual, concrete human reality as one already encountered, enfolded and interpenetrated by God in Christ, and not of some reality of a man completely untouched by God's saving grace, something which does not exist! That is to say, one would understand in terms of Christ the components of this reality as they showed themselves from time to time in events, we might say in the sense of a "supernatural existential" (on which see Chapter X below). Admittedly this presupposes that one treats with complete seriousness the ontological question about the reality of the real.

beyond that perhaps to the exposition of a formal logic"
(p. 104). But precisely the exact study of the posthumously
appearing *Erkenntnis der Existenz*,[13] the main systematic work
of Heinrich Barth, a Christian philosopher surely too little
known so far in comparison with his great significance, will
teach the theologians the measure of illuminating and fruitful
insight for theology which can be expected from attention to
philosophy. In Karl Barth by contrast the radicality of the
theological approach in one way receives its form by making
as a presupposition impossible the radicality of philosophical
questioning, necessary as that is in *the context* of theology and for
the sake of theology's own consistency.

But the method of "revelational positivism", the morphology
of which we have been endeavouring to sketch, has not been
without influence on Christian preaching. We take as an
example a sermon preached in 1957 by Eduard Thurneysen,
who must surely count as Karl Barth's closest companion on
the way from the earliest days. The text is Matthew 17: 1–13,
the passage about the transfiguration of Jesus. The following
short extracts can of course only serve to illustrate the typology;
they permit a certain characteristic kinship to be recognized,
but in no way permit the conclusion that a theological position
completely bearing the stamp of Karl Barth can result only in
exactly *this* type of preaching and in no other. The preacher
says:

> "Is then the human form in which Jesus is among us, in his
> earthly life, the life of the 'Son of Man', only something like a
> semblance of life which he took upon himself for a time and then
> shook off, in order to resume his true form? ... No, a thousand
> times, no! For Jesus this earthly life of ours on which he enters,
> in order to share it with us, in order to be with us there, is full
> reality. He did not slip hurriedly across this earth for a little like
> some ghost, then to disappear again, he entered upon this life,
> he took it upon himself with all its guilt and all its death. Yes,
> in that he shares our life with us, this life of ours is first discovered
> in all its hard reality. It is only through him that we know at all
> how dark everything here upon earth is ...
>
> Yes, this is what is happening in the life of Jesus, that here the
> One who bears in himself the whole majesty and glory of God goes

[13] Basel, 1965.

down deeper into the darkness of this world than any other, and that down there, since he has been there, sin and death are now discovered in all their horror. But the other thing, too, is discovered, the hand of the Father which reaches towards us there and snatches us away from all guilt and all death. Where were we if Jesus had only become the appearance of a man! Where were we if he had not completely become our brother, even to the deepest and loneliest hours of our life! He certainly did not need to take all this upon him, he surely could have remained where he was, in the light and radiance of God. But now the unheard of thing happens, that he lays aside all his glory and becomes poor, humbles himself, is crucified. Since then the darkness of the world is full of hope and help . . .

Jesus himself foretold to his disciples that he would be condemned. It is true that they did not understand him. Peter answered him, Why should you die, you are the Son of God! But stop, the reverse is true! Precisely because he is the Son of God he must and will die, in order that the light of God may pierce down into the depths of death. This is the mystery before which the disciples stand on the Mount of Transfiguration. They see for a moment Jesus in the light of God's radiance. But then he will go down from this mountain, into man's need and guilt, to be victor over all. The glory of God now shines on the face of Jesus and it is to become clear that God has the last word in the darkness of this world. This is the road which Jesus travels, this is the work which he accomplishes" (*Basler Predigten*, 21st year, Sept. 5, 1957, pp. 7ff.).

The claim is here maintained emphatically that the event witnessed to in the sermon is decisive for its hearers. But at the same time the articulation of the *Kerygma* appears as "revelational positivist", and in complete keeping at that with the description which Bonhoeffer gives of "revelational positivism", in that the hearer is told in magisterial style of a drama of salvation running its course on his behalf, a drama completely self-enclosed as a process, but of which it is then additionally *asserted* that it touches upon his existence. A self-enclosed spiritual picture is *added* to reality for the hearer by means of a firm *assertion*. We set beside it by way of comparison some sections from a sermon preached by Bonhoeffer in 1935 on Matthew 18: 21–33. This also is again merely an illustration and no proof that Bonhoeffer was not capable of preaching under any circumstances in the style of "revelational positivism". But the language of the sermon might be said to provide a good example of the type of preaching which must result from the use of "non-religious interpretation".

"Let us begin this sermon by asking if we know a man from our surroundings, from our family or from our friends, whom we have not forgiven the wrong that he has done to us, a man from whom we have parted in anger, perhaps not in open anger but in silent bitterness with the thought, 'I can bear it no longer, I cannot have fellowship with this man any more'.

Or can we be so thoughtless as to say that we do not know any? Are other men of so little importance to us that we do not even know properly whether we are at peace with them or not? . . .

We care so little about our fellowmen. We deaden ourselves and think that if we foster no evil thoughts against someone, that is just the same as if we had forgiven him. And we then overlook completely the fact that we are not thinking any good thoughts about him. And to forgive him means to have nothing but good thoughts about him, that we suffer him whenever we can. And this is exactly what we evade, we go on our way beside him and accustom ourselves to his silence, yes, we do not take him at all seriously. But suffering someone means exactly that we endure him in all respects, in all his difficult and inconvenient sides, and keep silence about his wrong and his sins, even the ones against ourselves— that would be approaching forgiveness . . .

It is a real torment, this question. How shall I have done enough about this man, what does tolerating him mean? Where do my rights as against him begin? Only let us always go to Jesus with this question, as Peter did. For if we went to anyone else, if we asked ourselves, we should receive but poor help, or none at all. Jesus helps, but in a quite astonishing manner. 'Not seven times, Peter, but seventy times seven', says Jesus, the answer which he knows is alone of any help. Do not count, Peter, but forgive without counting; do not torture yourself with the question, how long; forgive without end, Peter! Without end, that is to forgive —and that is grace for you, that alone makes you free!" (*Ges. Sch., IV*, pp. 400ff.).

The preacher has exactly the same Christological foundation as he speaks. But the event of salvation does not run its course far from the hearer, so that to "apply" it to his own existence the additional task of assertion and the consequent acceptance of an assertion is required. Instead, we might say, the whole event of Christ is so present that it does not need to be expressly described in detail at all. Unexpressed, it determines the whole course of the sermon. Its surpassing reality dovetails itself, as it were, into the empirical reality of the hearer. Through the mediation of the word of preaching it enters his life, unavoidably demanding and mercifully encompassing and upholding.

To complete the path our thought has taken we must still endeavour to formulate our interim conclusion with regard to non-religious interpretation. For we do believe that now, after the study of Bonhoeffer's concept of "revelational positivism", we have already a clearer insight into this question. It can also be called by him "worldly" interpretation, because it proceeds from the assumption that God has not left the world to itself. It also presupposes absolutely that God is already present in the world. He is no religious *deus ex machina* which somehow or other touches on the boundaries of the reality of the world and of humanity, to solve the problems with which man has not yet proved able to cope. He is also no "Lord of the world" whose lordship is, as it were, asserted "from outside", he has already entered upon his Lordship in the world. All of this could, and indeed must, also be said from the Barthian side. But Bonhoeffer is seeking, in *theology* for the sake of *preaching*, for a new manner of speaking which will also do methodological justice to the fundamental factual situation. His task is to discover the hidden Christ in the world, following his tracks step by step. Hence everything cannot not be said once and for all *en masse*, for then the *Kerygma* of revelation would remain, so to speak, *outside* the world at which it is aimed, that is to say, it would remain "law". The question then which must become the crucial point for everything in Bonhoeffer is that about the *manner of the real presence of Christ in the world*. Chapter Five on "The Communion of Saints" and especially on his dissertation *Sanctorum Communio* will make a further contribution to the problem of the appropriate method for pursuing this question further.

6. *Non-religious Interpretation and its Starting-point in Existentialism*

After these two demarcations which Bonhoeffer himself works out in the field of contemporary discussion, we now consider the boundaries which are set to his undertaking by its own starting-point.

Eberhard Bethge reports that Payne Best, an English companion of Bonhoeffer in his last days who had known nothing about him before, says of him, "Bonhoeffer was one of the very few men whom I have ever met for whom God was real and always near" (*Die mündige Welt, I*, p. 22). Bonhoeffer himself can write, "I believe that nothing that happens to me is meaningless" (LPP, p. 159;—German is literally "I know"— Tr.). or on another occasion:

> "... I am firmly convinced—however strange it may seem— that my life has followed a straight and unbroken course, at any rate in its outward conduct. It has been an uninterrupted enrichment of experience, for which I can only be thankful. If I were to end my life here in these conditions, that would have a meaning that I think I could understand; on the other hand, everything might be a thorough preparation for a new start and a new task when peace comes ..." (LPP, p. 149; April 11, 1944).

When Bonhoeffer so speaks about the conduct of his life and about the meaning that he thinks he understands, all this is not meant in any metaphorical sense, but as in the highest degree literal. He is reckoning with the fact that God is acting in history and in his own personal history, acting, it is true, as the Lord, surpassingly, freely and inscrutably, but acting in the most real, one might say most palpable, fashion. (On this cp. also the whole of Chapter Seven on Providence in Bonhoeffer.)

> "... Please don't ever get anxious or worried about me, but don't forget to pray for me—I'm sure you don't! I am so sure of God's guiding hand that I hope I shall always be kept in that certainty. You must never doubt that I am travelling with gratitude and cheerfulness along the road where I am being led. My past life is brim-full of God's goodness, and my sins are covered by the forgiving love of Christ crucified" (LPP, p. 215).

Bonhoeffer believes that he can trace the shape of the power of prayer and intercession.

> "I have often found it a great help to think in the evening of all those who I know are praying for me, children as well as grown-ups. I think I owe it to the prayers of others, both known

143

and unknown, that I have often been kept in safety" (LPP, p. 214; August 21, 1944).

This line of thought finds its final culmination in a passage from the letter just quoted, where he says of Jesus Christ:

"The key to everything is the 'in him'. All that we may rightly expect from God and ask him for, is to be found in Jesus Christ. The God of Jesus Christ has nothing to do with what God, as we imagine him, could do and ought to do. If we are to learn what God promises, and what he fulfils, we must persevere in quiet meditation on the life, sayings, deeds, sufferings and death of Jesus. It is certain that we may always live close to God and in the light of his presence, and that such living is an entirely new life for us, that nothing then is impossible for us, because all things are possible with God; that no earthly power can touch us without his will, and that danger and distress can only drive us closer to him. It is certain that we can claim nothing for ourselves and may yet pray for everything; it is certain that our joy is hidden in suffering and our life in death; it is certain that in all this we are in a fellowship that sustains us. In Jesus God has said Yes and Amen to it all, and that Yes and Amen is the firm ground on which we stand. In these turbulent times we repeatedly lose sight of what really makes life worth living. We think that, because this or that person is living, it makes sense for us to live too. But the truth is that if this earth was good enough for the man Jesus Christ, if such a man as Jesus lived, then and only then, has life a meaning for us" (LPP, pp. 213ff.).

Jesus Christ appears here as in a certain sense the embodiment of that nearness and "palpability" of God, the nearness and palpability of his activity in the world. But in Bonhoeffer such passages take their place immediately beside texts which speak of non-religious interpretation and the legitimate religionlessness of modern man. They stand beside utterances like the following, which, over twenty years after, shines like a beacon directly upon our Church situation today and becomes for us an urgent warning:

"I am enclosing the outline of a book that I have planned" (The outline is in LPP, the reference is to the work which he wanted to write about the theme which stimulated him in the last part of his life). ". . . I hope I shall be given the peace and strength to finish it. The Church must come out of its stagnation.

We must move out again into the open air of intellectual discussion with the world, and risk saying controversial things,
if we are to get down to the serious problems of life. I feel obliged
to tackle these questions as one who, though a 'modern' theologian,
is still aware today of the debt that he owes to liberal theology.
There will not be many of the younger men in whom these two
trends are combined" (LPP, pp. 207f.; August 3, 1944).

It is true that the Church must come out of its stagnation!
But as for its necessary entry into the open air of intellectual
discussion with the world, this is not achieved by writing books
about "Christianity and Modern Art", "Christianity and Existentialism", "Christianity and Marxism", etc. The Church, and
that means all, clergy and laymen, who wish to confess Christ
before the world, must learn a new language. A transformation
in their intellectual attitude is demanded. When one reads
today the words of leading fathers and theologians at the
Council, one gets the impression that the Church of Rome is
setting its course for such a transformation. But that the
Protestant world also is waiting for just this is shown by, for
example, the immense response accorded to Bishop Robinson's
book. But it, combining though it does Bonhoeffer's thought of
non-religious interpretation with Paul Tillich's speculative "end
of theism", can never, as has already been shown in more
detail above, do justice to what Bonhoeffer really wanted.
There is in it a misunderstanding of non-religious interpretation,
a misunderstanding which does not notice or does not understand that factual peculiarity, that harsh collocation in Bonhoeffer of two keynotes which are apparently distinct. Precisely
this collocation is characteristic of Bonhoeffer, and must be
noted by anyone who would understand non-religious interpretation.

A historian of theology might perhaps describe Bonhoeffer
as one of the "modern" theologians after the change of the
twenties, whose work is dominated by dialectical theology, but
in whose thought a strongly pietistic element is combined with
a strongly liberal one. Such a characterization, which might
in fact be built up then with subtle ramifications into an exceedingly scholarly portraiture (!), would certainly not be out
of place within the framework of its own method, and in some
ways would be "right". The one remaining question would be

where in point of fact such a method led. Must we not rather, if only to do justice to some degree to the *historical* phenomenon of Bonhoeffer (!), think out the matter along the lines of *the facts themselves*? *From the viewpoint of the facts*, what can Bonhoeffer have meant, this Bonhoeffer who brings together so much that is different? How do the lines run together in him? Has he himself shown us the answer clearly enough? Surely he has scarcely done so, otherwise misunderstandings would be less frequent than they are. This is certain, that the "palpability" of God *in Christo*, who acts personally in history, leading, judging, forgiving and healing men, hearing our prayers, making good come out of evil, is a *concretissimum* which cannot be outdated or explained away in any speculative fashion. This is no thesis set down for human reason to deal with at its free discretion; it is solid, unavoidable, "palpable" reality in our life, reality with which one collides; "God is here"! Non-religious interpretation cannot break off the point of this fact, cannot set aside this collision. Its intention and plan is not to dissolve the *concretissimum*, but to confirm it, make it appear, palpably and unavoidably and freed from all religious framework, to the man of today who can no longer think and feel "religiously". "Liberal Pietism"? What purpose can such a title, for example, serve? The question must be if it is *true*, if the undertaking can be *carried through*, if a man can so *think*, (or should it be, must so *think*?) today as a Christian and theologian, and if we can *live* by it.

Thus the project of non-religious interpretation has by its own nature boundaries set to it by its starting-point and foundation; it is bound to the *concretissimum* of certainty of God, of the presence of Christ. *This* must be said! *This* will find expression in the linguistic problem thrown up by non-religious interpretation! This frontier must not be violated.

7. *The Linguistic Problem and Secret Discipline*

But further, this linguistic problem of non-religious interpretation is no matter of old terms being replaced by new ones easier to enter into. It is a matter of the old, "traditional" concepts and words of the Bible, and of Dogmatics, coming to light anew in the context of a theological penetrativeness, and, above all, in a new and transformed engagement of the Church with the world. In this sense Bonhoeffer has more than once declared himself for the preservation of the property which we have in the old concepts. So it is, for example, when he charges Bultmann with a process of reduction and holds against him that we cannot separate from one another "God" and "miracle"; so it is when he puts on the same plane concepts like "miracle" and "ascension" on the one side, and "God" and "faith" on the other, to quote the concepts he himself chooses in LPP, p. 156, where he charges Bultmann with having allowed such concepts as "God" and "faith" simply to stand, and with having omitted to give them a non-religious interpretation! But so it is most of all in this charming passage in "Thoughts on the Baptism of D.W.R." in May 1944:

> Today you will be baptized a Christian. All these great ancient words of the Christian proclamation will be spoken over you, and the command of Jesus Christ to baptize will be carried out on you, without your knowing anything about it. But we are once again being driven right back to the beginnings of our understanding. Reconciliation and redemption, regeneration and the Holy Ghost, love of our enemies, cross and resurrection, life in Christ and Christian discipleship—all these things are so difficult and remote that we hardly venture any more to speak of them. In the traditional words and acts we suspect that there may be something quite new and revolutionary, though we cannot as yet grasp or express it. That is our own fault. Our Church which has been fighting in these years only for its self-preservation, as though that were an end in itself, is incapable of taking the word of reconciliation and redemption to mankind and the world. Our earlier words are therefore bound to lose their force and cease, and our being Christians today will be limited to two things: prayer and righteous action among men. All Christian thinking, speaking and organizing must be born anew out of this prayer and action . . . It is not for us to prophesy the day (though the day will come) when men will once more be called so to utter the word of God that the world will be changed and renewed by it. It will be a new language, perhaps quite non-religious, but liberating and redeeming—as was Jesus' language; it will shock people and yet overcome them by its power; it will be the language of a new righteousness and truth, proclaiming God's peace with men and the coming of his kingdom" (LPP, pp. 171f.).

According to Bonhoeffer the language which the Church in cross-section speaks today is incapable of achieving this. It does not change the world. Nobody is shocked by it. I might add that even where it is "non-conformist" it is so often *only that*! It remains somewhere in non-involvement. But the new language which the Church will find one day will not be formed by replacing concepts, but by helping to expression that "new and revolutionary" which we suspect is there in the traditional words and acts, "though we cannot as yet grasp or express it".

There are yet two more passages in which Bonhoeffer enumerates individual "traditional" Christian concepts requiring a worldly interpretation. In the passage we have already quoted in LPP, p. 157 he names "repentance, faith, justification, rebirth", which we are to "reinterpret . . . in the sense of the Old Testament and of John 1: 14". And then in the first outline of his book which he sent to Bethge, he speaks of the attributes of God, "omnipotence, omniscience and omnipresence". The sole "ground" of these is Jesus' "being there for others" (LPP, pp. 209f.). And then he adds, "Faith is participation in this being of Jesus (incarnation, cross and resurrection)", shortly after which there follows the note, "Interpretation of biblical concepts on this basis. (Creation, fall, atonement, repentance, faith, the new life, last things)" (LPP, p. 210). The basis is of course "Jesus' being for others", the incarnation and the cross.

But in the passage quoted above from the baptismal thoughts, when Bonhoeffer says that we are being driven back to the beginnings of our understanding and that the Church will one day find the new language, this indicates that non-religious interpretation has the character of a linguistic problem. When in the same context he says, ". . . all these things are so difficult and so remote that we hardly venture any more to speak of them", this points to what he has called *"secret discipline"*. The direction of our thoughts already led us to this concept before. It only appears expressly twice in Bonhoeffer, and both times there is a certain connection with the criticism of "revelational positivism".

"In that case Christ is no longer an object of religion, but something quite different, really the Lord of the world. But what does that mean? What is the place of worship and prayer in a religionless situation? Does the secret discipline, or alternatively the difference (which I have suggested to you before) between penultimate and ultimate take on a new importance here?" (LPP, pp. 153f.).

"There are degrees of knowledge and degrees of significance; that means that a secret discipline must be restored whereby the *mysteries* of the Christian faith are protected from profanation" (LPP, p. 157).

"Secret discipline" meant in the ancient Church the discipline laid upon the baptized person not to speak to outsiders about the *arcana* of the Christian faith. Bonhoeffer's opinion is that something of this reserve must again be accepted in our day. Today is not the time to speak of *all* dimensions of the Christian faith. To be exact we are just not in a position to do so and hence there is much that we scarcely venture to speak about, for fear of profaning the tremendous mystery of Christ. For we "suspect" what is revolutionary, we have not yet *understood* it, or at least so understood it that we can speak of it in the public vindication of the Gospel. Here "the positivism of revelation makes it too easy for itself" (LPP, p. 157), in that it thinks that it can speak today about everything, since all is "contained" in the record of revelation or can be deduced from the Christological systematic principle. It lacks the reserve, the respect for mystery and the consenting understanding that one must keep silence about what one does not yet *really* understand. It is true that the "real" understanding, to be reached each time to enable us to speak, is still in continual eschatological tension with the "greater mystery" of God, the mystery which we never adequately grasp so long as we walk by faith and not by sight.[14] To speak on what is "last", the eschatological justification of the sinner before God, is difficult (cp. here Chapter Three of Bonhoeffer's *Ethics* on "The Last Things and the Things before the Last"—E. pp. 79ff.). Perhaps for the time being we must remain at the things before the last, which are surely the manifestations of faith, the manifestations of the activity of God in everyday reality, and yet we must do so without forgetting or even doing away with the last things, but in such a way that these are preserved, sensed in silence.

---

[14] Cp. my essay, *Herméneutique et Eschatologie*, Rome, 1962, in *Archivio di Filosofia*, nn. 1 and 2, pp. 105ff.

In this concept of "secret discipline" we see the last boundary to be set to Bonhoeffer's programme of non-religious interpretation, that set by tradition. There is preserved in the tradition of the Christian community truth which cannot just simply be repeated at any time, truth which rather waits, each element for its own hour, but which none the less remains effective and powerful, though it may only be preserved in the traditional formulae of prayer and worship.[15] Greater than any awareness and understanding of truth by individual believers and single generations of believers is the latent understanding in the Christian community as such down the ages. Admittedly this thought, conceived by a convinced Protestant Christian and theologian, is very suggestive of the Catholic concept of the *depositum fidei* and the Catholic understanding of tradition. This we must openly acknowledge. And the trend can be unmistakably followed back to the early Bonhoeffer who in *Act and Being* had set a "community" principle of the recognition of revelation against the purely individualist response to the particular situation.[16] But surely to forge out of this acknowledgement a Protestant argument against his "position" would be some purely confessional action of the type no longer timely today. Surely on this point we must accept the claim made upon us by thought, the claim of the facts which we have to think about, and seek to consider Bonhoeffer's thoughts in

[15] What Bonhoeffer has in mind when he speaks of "secret discipline" has its "secular" parallel in the way in which a philosophical thinker can wait. Any thought cannot be thought at any time, and one must wait until something is ripe to be thought and expressed. Thus, for example, we notice how Martin Heidegger can often wait for years, almost decades, before he decides on the publication of some statement, and how clearly he keeps before his eyes the possibility that it might still be too early for something. His essay, for instance, *Die Sprache*, was delivered as a lecture in 1950, and then circulated in various transcripts and only published in 1959 in *Unterwegs zur Sprache*. Or *Aus der Erfahrung des Denkens* was written in 1947 and published in 1954. These long intervals are no accident, they are to be understood as arising from the nature of Heidegger's thought.

[16] On this, more in Chapter Five. The "theologico-sociological category" developed by Bonhoeffer in *Sanctorum Communio* and *Act and Being* is obviously the condition which makes possible what he called "secret discipline" in the late period of his theological creativity, and it belongs as constitutive to his project of non-religious interpretation. Here we see the close factual connection between the early and the late Bonhoeffer, the factual consistency and unity of what seem at first sight the so many different strata of his thought.

complete openness, testing them as we consider, without allowing ourselves to be inhibited by any too hastily decided confessional prejudices.[17] And then the question remains for our consideration if, after we have subtracted from Bonhoeffer this thought of "secret discipline" and the whole "Catholic" trend bound up with it, this whole undertaking of non-religious interpretation does not simply in the end coincide with Rudolf Bultmann's "demythologizing". But from this we have seen that, though recognizing the justification for its motives, he yet consciously held himself apart.

Do we find then coupled in Bonhoeffer a strong traditionalism, as far as the Christian treasury of thoughts is concerned, with a radicalism bursting all bonds in its willingness to enter into the spirit of modern times? But once again, of what assistance are such labels to us? The right course is to direct our questions at the facts themselves and to ask if it is a plan which can be carried out, that without in the least surrendering the great words and concepts of the Christian tradition, and above all of the Bible itself, we should yet interpret them in such a radically new way that they become absolutely credible and palpable to the typical man of today, to whom "God" is no longer to be taken for granted. The only answer in the meantime must be, *experiendum est*. Yet it is true that success is in God's hands, and that without the enlightenment of the Holy Spirit no interpretation will be of any avail. Bonhoeffer himself says that the day will come and that it is not for us to prophesy when . . . But that does not preclude us from going forward in sincere and dedicated work, as far as in us lies, to meet that day.

8. "Religious" Interpretation

How does one carry out non-religious interpretation? We have reserved until now the key-question for further advance on this point; what then does "religious interpretation" mean? When we know this we at least have a starting-point from which to pursue further this hermeneutical undertaking, for it is surely with this that we are dealing, a fact of methodological

[17] Secret discipline is no marginal thought but a specific constituent of Bonhoeffer's type of interpretation.

exposition, and not merely, say, some task of topical and existentialist preaching which has nothing to do with questions of method.[18] Bonhoeffer's decisive reference to the key question is as follows:

"What does it mean to 'interpret in a religious sense'?" (This question is put by Bonhoeffer immediately after he has argued against Bultmann's interpretation of Biblical concepts as inadequate!) "I think it means to speak on the one hand metaphysically and on the other hand individualistically. *Neither of these is relevant to the Bible message or to the man of today*" (Our italics). "Has not the individualistic question about personal salvation almost completely left us all? Are we not really under the impression that there are more important things than that question (perhaps not more important than the *matter* itself, but more important than the *question*!)? I know it sounds pretty monstrous to say that. But, fundamentally, is it not actually biblical? Does the question about saving one's soul appear in the Old Testament at all? Are not righteousness and the Kingdom of God on earth the focus of everything, and is it not true that Romans 3: 24ff. is not an individualistic doctrine of salvation, but the culmination of the view that God alone is righteous? It is not with the beyond that we are concerned, but with this world as created and preserved, subjected to laws, reconciled, and restored. What is above this world is, in the Gospel, intended to exist for this world; I mean that, not in the anthropocentric sense of liberal, mystic pietistic, ethical theology, but in the biblical sense of the creation and of the incarnation, crucifixion, and resurrection of Jesus Christ" (LPP, p. 156; May 5, 1944).

[18] This is the distinction made by Götz Harbsmeier in his essay, *Die "nicht-religiose Interpretation biblischer Begriffe" bei Bonhoeffer und die Entmythologisierung* (*Die mündige Welt, II*, pp. 74ff.). He tries to distinguish between the undertakings of Bonhoeffer and Bultmann as on quite different planes, Bonhoeffer not being concerned as Bultmann is with the hermeneutical task of existential interpretation, but with something much more direct, with a pastoral approach to modern "mature" man, comparable to that of the Old Testament "Wisdom". This is certainly true. But even such a venture has its hermeneutical and methodological aspect, a fact which Harbsmeier seems to me to overlook. If non-religious interpretation were not *also* a matter of method, why did Bonhoeffer occupy himself so thoroughly with it theologically, and set it as an alternative against both the "revelational positivist" method of Barth and Bultmann's demythologizing. For his disagreement with Harbsmeier, see also Gerhard Krause, *Dietrich Bonhoeffer und Rudolf Bultmann*, in *Zeit und Geschichte*, pp. 439ff. In this article Krause emphasizes very strongly that in Bonhoeffer's programme of non-religious interpretation of Biblical concepts we are dealing with a hermeneutical problem.

Immediately after this important passage there follow the decisive words in controversy with Barth's "revelational positivism". It is significant that Bonhoeffer places what he has to say in definition of his own programme between his criticisms of his two older theological contemporaries. His approach is in fact distinct from both of theirs. What he sought to do could be placed between, or rather beyond, but not without relation to, their distinctive positions.

"Metaphysical" and "individualistic" are the names Bonhoeffer gives to the "religious" way of thinking and feeling. "Metaphysical" here means that behind the "here" is concealed a "beyond", behind this world another world, that the existence of a God beyond is asserted and that man is directed away from the "here" to this "beyond", that therefore we begin to speak of God as something metaphysical, belonging to the beyond, just at that point where man reaches his "boundaries". He regards speaking of "boundaries" as a fundamentally unemployable vehicle for theological thought.

"I have come to be doubtful of talking of any human boundaries (is even death, which people now hardly fear, and is sin, which they now hardly understand, still a genuine boundary today?). It always seems to me that we are trying anxiously in this way to reserve some space for God; I should like to speak of God not on the boundaries but at the centre, not in weakness but in strength; and therefore not in death and guilt but in man's life and goodness.[19] As to the boundaries, it seems to me better to be silent and leave the insoluble unsolved. Belief in the resurrection is *not* the 'solution' of the problem of death. God's 'beyond' is not the beyond of our cognitive faculties. The transcendence of epistemological theory has nothing to do with the transcendence of God. God is beyond in the midst of our life. The Church stands, not at the boundaries where human powers give out, but in the midst of the village. That is how it is in the Old Testament, and in this sense we still read the New Testament far too little

[19] On this cp. also *Creation and Fall* on Gen. 2: 8–17 (in *Creation and Temptation*, p. 50): "For this reason the tree of life is only mentioned very simply in this passage. It was in the middle—that is all that is said about it. The life that comes forth from God is in the middle. This means that God, who gives life, is in the middle. In the middle of the world which is at Adam's disposal and over which he has been given dominion is not Adam himself but the tree of divine life. Adam's life comes from the middle which is not Adam himself but God. It constantly revolves around this middle without ever making the attempt to make this middle of existence its own possession".

in the light of the Old. How this religionless Christianity looks, what form it takes, is something that I am thinking about a great deal ..." (LPP, pp. 154f.; April 30, 1944).

Karl Barth has left behind him this type of religious thinking, and Bonhoeffer gives him credit for it. He never begins from human questions about what is "beyond" our own boundaries—that would be an unreal apologetic in Barth's eyes. Rather he begins from the sovereign position of God. Thus far, then, he does not think metaphysically. Nor is the individualistic question of salvation in any way dominating in Barth's theological thought. In him its anxiety has long since been replaced by the triumphant awareness of grace. He is therefore free from the two basic traits of the religious and would be in a position to think in terms of a non-religious theology if this methodological error of revelational positivism did not intervene.[20]

It must be said of Bultmann also that he does not think metaphysically. His subject is not the metaphysical beyond of God, but the paradoxical, eschatological presence of the Eternal in the history of this world. Faith takes place completely and entirely in this world, involved in the encounters of this world, where human historicity holds its ground. But as against this, his thought seems to me to be very deeply stamped with individualism. Luther's question, "How can I find a gracious God?", reappears in him in the form, "How can I attain, before God, to the authenticity of my own being?" And to this extent he still remains within the category of those whom Bonhoeffer calls the religious.

*

It is true that one can raise against Bonhoeffer's concept of

[20] The question has been raised (by Eberhard Bethge) if "revelational positivism" in speech is not in *effect* "religious" speech again. This position seems to me justified, for the reading of many, though certainly not all, typically "Barthian" sermons shows that the message of salvation is in them simply brought in from without as a pure assertion into the reality of man and the world, thus satisfying Bonhoeffer's concept of the religious in one of its characteristic marks. Further, there would also then be brought in the typical "religious" particularism, by which only one defined group of men, and certainly one sociologically more or less exactly identifiable, is in a position to believe the assertion, and thus the universalism of the Gospel, its fundamental universal comprehensibility, is lost.

the religious, composed as it is of these two main distinguishing marks, the question if it really is also in keeping with the phenomenon of religion as found in mankind generally. And further, if today we are entering into a religionless era, if to speak religiously no longer wins belief today, was there then ever a time when religion was a legitimate and credible possibility? Was there ever a time when the Gospel of Christ could be and ought to have been proclaimed with a *religious* interpretation? What is the position of religiousness in the Old Testament, to which Bonhoeffer so forcibly refers? These two mutually connected questions, which are raised by Ebeling in his interpretation of Bonhoeffer, are very complex.[21] Yet

---

[21] As an example Ebeling asks, "What would religion be if it could cease to be a genuine potentiality of human nature? Bonhoeffer thinks that it would now be plain that religion 'was a historically conditioned and temporary form of human self-expression'. There would then be no such thing as a religious disposition essentially belonging to human nature, a so-called 'religious *a priori*'. If we accept that for the moment we then go on to ask: what, then, was the existentialist condition that made religion possible as a passing and temporary historical form of human self-expression? What was it that sought 'expression' in the 'form' of religion and in what 'form' does it find 'expression' when religion has disappeared? The purely negative term 'non-religiousness' is manifestly insufficient the moment we are faced, as is inevitable, by the problem of providing an existentialist interpretation of religion *and* non-religiousness, i.e., by the question of the relation both bear to man's human nature. The problem of the religious *a priori* will have to be very thoroughly thought through once again before we accept the assertion that it simply does not exist" (*The Non-religious Interpretation of Biblical Concepts*, in *Word and Faith*, tr. Leitch, S.C.M., 1963, pp. 137f.). Again he later asks, "What theological category—and that surely means, what category based on and determined by the Gospel itself—is suited to define the place of religion and non-religiousness in theology?" And he comes to the conclusion, "The problem of religion (and with it of course also the phenomenon of non-religiousness!) falls under the theological category of the law" (p. 141). In support of this Ebeling quotes a thought Bonhoeffer repeatedly utters, when, referring to St. Paul's statement that circumcision is not a condition of justification, he declares that religion is not a condition of salvation (Ebeling, *op. cit.*, pp. 141ff., cp. LPP, pp. 154, 181f.). We have already dealt in greater detail with the question of the suitability of the concepts "Law" and "Gospel" in relation to this basic trait of Bonhoeffer's thought (cp. Chapter Three, Section 4). But as regards the problem of Bonhoeffer's concept of religion in particular, Ebeling in his interpretation and his questions seems to have radicalized this in a way that is foreign to Bonhoeffer. For he is obviously making an effort to force into the context of Bonhoeffer's thought the theological category of the law, a concept which, while it certainly does appear occasionally, is very far from having for him the same importance as it has in Ebeling's theology. Ebeling appears to me to overlook the fact that Bonhoeffer, when he speaks of "religion", does not have in mind *every* religious phenomenon, but one quite

Bonhoeffer himself, so far as I can see, really seems to give no thought at all to this whole complex of questions. He sees and

---

definite happening in the Christian world, which he defines exactly by the concepts "metaphysical" and "individualistic", the former again having the quite specific sense of "otherworldly", and the latter of individual salvation. One can certainly put to Bonhoeffer the questions whether religion was once a legitimate possibility for man, and what now comes in in its place, and under what inclusive category both old and new can be put. But no satisfying answer is received from him, an indication, it seems to me, that in putting these questions one is leaving the tenor of Bonhoeffer's thought. Ebeling, after putting this question, is understandably not satisfied when the only reply he receives is that religion is a historically transient and passing form of expression, and he would like to take up again against Bonhoeffer the question of the religious *a priori*. But the latter, it seems to me, is consistent throughout. "Religion", in the narrow sense in which he understands the concept, *is* in fact only a passing form of expression which in the realm of Christianity is now replaced by a new form. He is obviously not interested at all in the problem of religion in general, but in the change in form in Christianity. The one question which, to follow his own train of thought, one would have to put to him, would, I think, be if "religiousness" in the narrow form was formerly a legitimate form of expression for the *Christian* faith. To be consistent Bonhoeffer would have to reply in the affirmative. But how does this square with his statement that the individualistic question about the salvation of one's own soul was fundamentally not a Biblical one? (LPP, p. 156). Bonhoeffer still does not seem to have given enough consideration to this complex of questions. In my opinion the question is only to be resolved by our saying that we, standing in our own epoch before God, cannot penetrate into the secrets of former epochs of Church history (cp. Section 9 below).

Compelling evidence that Bonhoeffer, when he speaks about "religion", is interested, not in any general concept of religion, but exclusively in the change in the form of Christianity, is to my mind given by the following passage. "I am at present reading the quite outstanding book by W. F. Otto, the classics man at Königsberg, *Die Götter Griechenlands*. To quote from his closing words, it is about 'this world of faith, which sprang from the wealth and depth of human existence, not from its cares and longings'. Can you understand my finding something very attractive in this theme and its treatment and also—*horribile dictu*—my finding these gods, when they are so treated, less offensive than certain brands of Christianity? In fact, that I almost think I could claim these gods for Christ? The book is most helpful for my present theological reflections" (LPP, p. 183; June 21, 1944). The gods, then, of ancient Greece as portrayed by Walter F. Otto, that is to say, something which is patently a phenomenon in the history of religion, are for Bonhoeffer not some example of "religion", but on the contrary one of this-worldliness, one of the counter-concepts to "religion"! That is, a general concept of religion covers a much wider span than what Bonhoeffer calls by that name. Thus there can be no equation of the concept in Bonhoeffer with the same concept as it appears in the student of the phenomenology of religion Mircea Eliade, according to whom the *homo religiosus* experiences the reality of the world as transparent to an absolute reality. (Cp., for instance, Mircea Eliade, *Das Heilige und das Profane. Vom Wesen des Religiosen*, rowohlts deutsche enzyklopädie, 1957).

defines "religion" as an outdated and discredited possibility and manifestation of the Christian faith in our time. He thinks completely within the horizon of his, and our, epoch and his, and our, question, who Jesus Christ really is for us today, and how a man of today can be a Christian. There is no meaning then in our engaging ourselves in a discussion with Bonhoeffer on the general concept of religion and the history of the religiousness of the human race. What concerns him is much too urgent in his eyes for him to allow himself to become involved in such a general analysis. What he has to say and what he understands under the heading "religious" is nothing general but something quite definite, which he meets with in certain defined forms of Christian speech and conduct. He has no interest in surveying the ages and the epochs; he thinks concretely and "epochally", that is to say, as one bound to his own era.

9. *The Encounter of God with our Epoch and the Response of his Church*

Such "epochal" thinking sheds light on the factual situation. Something still appearing today, the religious manifestation of what is Christian, is coming to an end. It may have had its own legitimate validity in its own time, but to decide on this is not in the last resort our concern, for we have our place in *our* epoch, and of it we can only recognize that it is coming to an end. But when we look at the fact itself, that is, at Christ, we must say that it is good that it is so. God himself is sending us this. God himself encounters us essentially in a way for our epoch, he himself comes into our times. He himself compels us to live before him today *etsi deus non daretur*. What is happening today is not merely a transformation in the history of ideas, one which goes on to work out to the advantage of Christianity by its correction of a false representation of what is Christian, and by its replacement by a better understanding of a false metaphysical concept of God which then drops out. What has happened is a new epoch in the history of the divine encounter, in a certain sense *in the history of God himself*. It is surely in this sense, and if so rightly, that in his lecture,

Der Gottesgedanke und der moderne Mensch,[22] Bultmann has spoken of the "transformations of God". In addition, the thought of Martin Buber seems to me to live by a similar experience of the character of the divine encounter as one fitting the epoch. God today does not meet us as the One beyond; he meets us here and now as the thisworldly in our human encounters.[23] In these he reproves us. Here or nowhere at all is he to be found.

> "There is a tale that a man inspired by God once went out from creaturely realms into the vast waste. There he wandered until he came to the gates of the mystery. He knocked. From within came the cry, 'What do you want here?' He said, 'I have proclaimed your praise in ears of mortals, but they were deaf to me. So I come to you that you yourself may hear me and reply'. 'Turn back', came the cry from within, 'here is no ear for you. I have sunk my hearing in the deafness of mortals' " (Buber, *Dialogue*, in *Between Man and Man*, tr. Gregor Smith, S.C.M., 1947, p. 15; also Fontana).

[22] ZThK, 1963, 3, pp. 335ff., recently reprinted in *Glaube und Verstehen*, IV, Tübingen, 1965.

[23] Further earnest testimony to this experience of God by the modern Christian is given today from the most varied quarters. I should like only to quote Karl Rahner's article, *Warum und wie können wir die Heiligen verehren? Einige theologische Erwagungen zum VII. Kapitel des Konzilsdekretes "Uber die Kirche"* (Geist und Leben. Zs. für Aszese und Mystik, 1964, 5, pp. 325ff.), ". . . the subjective possibility for man today depends essentially on his experience of God and how it is ordained for him in his epoch. Something like this is true even within the one eschatological time of the Church, because the intellectual situation of the world also belongs to the moments in that time, and shares in determining its destiny and the peculiar form of its faith. But today God has become infinite, incomprehensible and 'remote' to the truly believing man himself, even if the Christian knows, in a way which can be fulfilled existentially but never taken up into a higher 'synthesis', that this remote and incomprehensible God is also, as the mystery which imparts itself freely, at the same time infinitely near. Of course man has always known and acknowledged this. But one is experiencing it today with a new and radical sharpness, because the world has become unspeakably great and at the same time secular, and God does not appear as one datum 'beside' others in its daily happenings which now include no miracles. If, for methodological reasons at least, we disregard the peculiar events of the history of salvation, God is experienced as the silent mystery of infinite ineffability and incomprehensibility, which *as* such continually increases more and more, never diminishing, the more man develops in his religious existence" (p. 328). Rahner's train of thought goes on to say that it is this same mysterious, silent God who is experienced as mediated through Jesus Christ, and precisely for this reason, precisely in him, *through our fellowmen.* The experience of his mediation through humanity belongs to this specific modern experience of the silent God.

But in Bonhoeffer's mind this "epochal" side to the divine encounter is to be satisfied, not only prophetically, but hermeneutically. Not only must we recognize before God the situation and the epoch as he shows it to us entirely in this-worldliness, but it is also relevant to give detailed work to considering the method of speaking which makes possible a credible preaching of the Gospel for us today. This speaking will be no longer religious, that is to say, it will in any event be no longer metaphysical and no longer individualistic. A third mark, which certainly does not appear in the texts we have quoted on the marks of the religious, but which is occasionally mentioned by Bonhoeffer, and without doubt is connected with these others, could be added; the Christian's being in the Church is no longer to be understood as a privileged position.[24] The Church, that is to say, the visible Church, is no longer the bosom in which, taken out of the world, the privileged waiter for salvation rests. Where the Church regards itself in this way it is no longer coming to terms with the challenge of the age. It becomes just as unworthy of belief as the man who tries to allure with Heaven and terrify with Hell, or the man who, while reminding us that we cannot know all so certainly, that our knowledge has its limits, uses metaphysical facts he claims we must believe in order to postulate a *Cosmos* beyond. To our epoch of divine encounter belongs the disappearance both of the metaphysical question and the question of an individualist salvation. Thus Bonhoeffer can say that man today scarcely any longer believes himself sinful and in existential need. Paul Tillich makes an observation completely in keeping with this when, in *The Courage to Be*,[25] he sets out in

[24] In his interpretation of Bonhoeffer, Eberhard Bethge distinguishes in him seven characteristics of the religious; 1. The "metaphysical"; 2. Individualism; 3. Partiality, i.e. what is religious is only one particular province of life; 4. The concept of the *Deus ex machina*, i.e. the intervention of the religious always just where man's knowledge goes no further; 5. The privileged character; 6. The pre-mature stage of man; 7. Dispensability, i.e. religion is dispensable, we can do without it.

For this collection I am indebted to a friendly communication from Eberhard Bethge in connection with a lecture he gave in Basel about Dietrich Bonhoeffer and the problem of non-religious interpretation.

[25] Nisbet, 1952, espec. pp. 53ff. There Tillich distinguishes between three types and three eras of anxiety; anxiety of death at the breakdown of the ancient world, anxiety of guilt at the breakdown of the Middle Ages, and anxiety of meaninglessness at the breakdown (?) of the modern world.

detail that the basic anxiety of man today is no longer, as in the
breakdown of the Middle Ages, anxiety of guilt, but anxiety
of meaninglessness. But this implies that the seat of conflict
in the Christian faith, the form which the conviction of being
lost takes, has become radically transformed. We must interpret it in this way, that there still remains the constant, that
man is a sinner, and that awareness of sin and of grace is demanded of him. And further, as we know at least since Martin
Luther, that man in his belief in grace is always man in conflict. This remains unchanged throughout the history of
Christendom. But in the course of that history, awareness of
sin, awareness of grace and conflict are all subject to a transformation in form.

It is true that one can still put these metaphysical and individualistic questions. But at bottom they no longer interest
the average man of today, or the man who is completely honest
with himself. We shall find deaf ears if we still today preach
a Christianity orientated towards these questions. What we
have to say may be accepted as knowledge with goodwill, but
it carries no sense of obligation. There is no sense of obligation
carried, in spite of all display and all emphasis, by what today
passes for pietistic evangelizing, to pass no judgement on the
great figures of the pietism of the past, or by any pietistic
form or doctrine of preaching. From this we except "pietism"
in the sense given the word by the two Blumhardts. That has
another form, and may well have another future!

But if the man of today no longer truly finds such questions
come home, does it mean that he is altogether deaf to the Gospel
of Christ? Bonhoeffer believes that the opposite is the case!

To speak of an "epochal" character of the divine encounter,
one which finds its fulfilment according to the epoch, does not
mean that as part of the theology of history we can sketch out
a plan for its whole course. The concept of "epochs" is not to be
understood historically, or in terms of a "history of salvation".
We are not in our thought the masters of bygone ages. In spite
of all the solidarity I may have with my ancestors, I no longer
know how God spoke to them in their day. It is true that as a
historian I can bring much to light, but in so doing I do not
succeed to the extent of understanding former ages from within
and piercing the mystery of how they stood before God. Hence

the most comprehensive historical knowledge does not put me in a position to survey all epochs of the history of Christendom and to understand them in their variety and their meaningful succession. I only feel and know that I in my time and in solidarity with my contemporaries am chosen and addressed by God in this way, specific for the time. This is all that "epochal encounter" means. We must resist, then, the temptation of a theology of history covering universal history just as we must avoid an interpretation of "standpoints" which knows only individuals before God, and no epochs and no solidarity in being addressed in a specific way. But is not this concept of a history of God which we presuppose here a pure projection? Can the history of God mean anything more than the history of the Church? Is what we have done here not simply to take the transformation in our understanding of the Word of God and to transfer it as a pure postulate to God himself? As against this we have to consider that it is not we who set the requirements for God but he for us. God does not simply mirror himself in our changing situation in the history of ideas, a situation which changes without his doing anything thereto. He himself while he appears to us and addresses us, also gives to us that particular situation for understanding in which he seeks to appear to us. For this reason, for a real understanding of the Word of God it is not enough to attend in a biblicist spirit to the unchanging text of canonical scripture, we must also consider what in our historical situation comes face to face with the Word of God, be it in expectation or opposition, or both together.[26]

10. Non-religious Interpretation as a Radical Theology of the Incarnation

Let us turn once again to that instructive passage where

[26] In the context of the "Presence of the Church in the World", the Second Vatican Council studies the thought that the Church ever more and more finds itself through its historical encounter with the world.

Cp. also on this question my essay, Existentiale Interpretation und anonyme Christlichkeit, in Zeit und Geschichte, pp. 367ff., in which I quote on this point Bultmann's lecture, Der Gottesgedanke und der moderne Mensch, and the thought there expressed of the "transformation of God", and also the Catholic concept of the development of dogma, as emphasized especially at the present time by Karl Rahner.

Bonhoeffer says: "What is above this world is, in the gospel, intended to exist *for* this world; I mean that, not in the anthropocentric sense of liberal ... etc., theology, but in the Biblical sense of the creation and of the incarnation, crucifixion, and resurrection of Jesus Christ" (LPP, p. 156). The rejection, then, of "metaphysical" thinking[27] by no means leads in Bonhoeffer to an immanentism of any stamp. The reality of God is not lost in the "reality" of this world. It is not dissolved. Bonhoeffer speaks throughout about "what is above this world". But this very thing is "in the gospel, intended to exist for this world". And once again he defines his position as against any anthropocentric, "liberal, mystic, pietistic, ethical theology". He is concerned with the reality of *God himself*, the living God, the "wholly Other", but concerned with him not as some asserted "beyond" but as palpably in this world. We are concerned with "this world as created and preserved, subjected to laws, reconciled, and restored". And he quotes the "incarnation, crucifixion, and resurrection of Jesus Christ". Here God, though the "wholly other", is for this world and in a certain sense in this world, no longer an asserted metaphysical "beyond", but completely thisworldly and yet completely he himself. To show this thisworldly Christ in the world is to practise non-religious interpretation. For then we have begun neither from a metaphysical assertion nor from an individualistic question of salvation, but from the fact of the revelation and of the redemption of the *world* which have taken place in Christ. Hence Bonhoeffer can also say in the same letter that he is thinking about "how we can reinterpret in a 'worldly' sense—in the sense of the Old Testament and of John 1: 14—the concepts of repentance, faith, justification, rebirth and sanctification" (LPP, p. 157).

These concepts, then, are given a worldly interpretation when, without the presupposition of an individualistic question of salvation, they are applied to a thisworldly Christ. Dogmatically, the concepts gathered together in this passage

[27] Bonhoeffer uses the word "metaphysical" in a quite definite and limited sense. We must note this here in order that misunderstanding be avoided, especially today at a time when in Protestant theology men have slipped into a horror, widely bordering upon some "tabuism" but at bottom unconsidered, of anything that is "metaphysical", and the word itself is often used only and simply as a term of abuse.

belong to the context of the *ordo salutis*, the human way of salvation as it is opened to us through Christ. They are concepts which name what man accomplishes and at the same time what happens to man, as do, for example, "rebirth" or "justification". The meaning of, for example, "faith" or "penitence" in a worldly interpretation would have to take such a form that by them a describable, concrete, demandable accomplishment of man is indicated. What was so named would not simply be something "factual", but an accomplishment, that is, a way which man has to travel. Non-religious interpretation summons him and gives him his travel directions by describing the accomplishment. The existence of man, "what he is and has to be", is not ruled out. The venture, the step of faith, is required of him. But this same step can be described in the context of this world and its phenomena. And the man who ventures upon this step of faith and penitence knows exactly what he is doing. It is not demanded of him that he surrender himself to something otherworldly which he does not know and to which he has fundamentally no understandable relation. But this same describable step is also no merely human ethical behaviour; the description of non-religious interpretation must be such that it shows man that he does not in his venture go out into the void, but that he *finds* something, namely, that the thisworldly Christ within the world waits for him and comes to meet him. The imperative is matched by an indicative.

This then would be the transitional point at which to pass on to Bonhoeffer's Christology. For it has become clear to us step by step that it is from Christology alone that the non-religious interpretation can receive an answer. In Christ, and in Christ alone, is God "worldly". But reference must first be made to the "Outline for a Book", consisting only of headings, which Bonhoeffer sent to his friend and at which he was busy to the end. It is printed in LPP, pp. 208–221. He wished in this book to work out in detail the thoughts which occupied him so much in his last days. It was to consist of three chapters, 1. A Stock-taking of Christianity, 2. The Real Meaning of Christian Faith, and 3. Conclusions. Characteristic of the sketch is the twice repeated polemical reference to Karl Barth and the Confessing Church. Obviously the exposition of this antithesis was of especial importance to Bonhoeffer for the sake of gaining clarity about his own purposes.

"... The Confessing Church: the theology of revelation; a δὸς μοί πού στῶ [28] over against the world ... Generally in the Confessing Church; standing up for the Church's 'cause', but little personal faith in Christ. 'Jesus' is disappearing from sight. Sociologically; no effect on the masses—interest confined to the upper and lower middle classes. A heavy incubus of difficult traditional ideas. The decisive factor: the Church on the defensive. No taking risks for others" (LPP, p. 209).

This we find in the first chapter, and the second is dominated by the question:

"What do we really believe? I mean, believe in such a way that we stake our lives on it? ... 'What must I believe?' is the wrong question; antiquated controversies, especially those between the different sects; the Lutheran versus Reformed, and to some extent the Roman Catholic versus Protestant, are now unreal. They may at any time be revived with passion, but they no longer carry conviction. There is no proof of this, and we must simply take it that it is so. All that we can prove is that the faith of the Bible and Christianity does not stand or fall by these issues. Karl Barth and the Confessing Church have encouraged us to entrench ourselves persistently behind the 'faith of the Church', and to evade the honest question as to what we ourselves really believe. That is why the air is not quite fresh, even in the Confessing Church" (LPP, p. 210).

Bonhoeffer then demands that we give an entirely honest and complete account of what we ourselves really believe. One's faith must be describable, and, above all, so concrete that it is made obvious from the description how far the believer "stakes his life on it". But such a making obvious is the hall-mark of what we today call the existential interpretation.[29]

[28] (Note in LPP here refers to *ibid.* p. 146, δὸς μοί πού στῶ καὶ κινήσω τὴν γῆν,, "Give me a place to stand, and I will move the earth"—Tr.).

[29] In *Existentiale Interpretation und anonyme Christlichkeit*, in *Zeit und Geschichte*, pp. 367ff., I have called this moment of reality which has to be made visible by existential interpretation, the *stirring of existence* in faith. In this concept of the stirring of existence there is implied not merely that human existence is "stirred", but that it is stirred by God in encounter with him. Real faith, then, is not merely a content of conviction but in its deepest foundation a personal encounter and a stirring of existence. For this very reason it must be said that we really believe only what "we stake our lives on".

But Bonhoeffer seeks to carry out this description, or at least to begin it, by reducing everything to the simple formula that it is a matter of "encounter with Jesus Christ" (LPP, p. 209). "Faith is participation in this being of Jesus (incarnation, cross, and resurrection)" (p. 210). "The transcendental is not infinite and unattainable tasks, but the neighbour who is within reach in any given situation" (*ibid.*). Here then, in this context, faith becomes concrete and describable.

Finally, the conclusions in the third chapter are interesting:

"The Church is the Church only when it exists for others. To make a start it should give away all its property to those in need. The clergy must live solely on the free-will offerings of their congregations, or possibly engage in some secular calling. The Church must share in the secular problems of ordinary human life, not dominating, but helping and serving. It must tell men of every calling what it means to live in Christ, to exist for others" (LPP, p. 211).

That is to say, the conclusions are of a highly practical nature, and concern the attitude, the appearance and the service of the Church.

When we set it against his great project of non-religious interpretation, this short sketch of Bonhoeffer's which we have is manifestly too incomplete both in method and in content. We could not build upon it alone if we were to try to develop his intention, and yet we should be able to obtain essential indications from it. What seems to me especially important is his postulate of the concrete describability of what our faith is, and equally with it the emphasis on "Jesus there only for others". This is the road by which faith in Christ, which for Bonhoeffer must be the foundation of everything, leads to human relations as the place of its verification and authentication. At the same time it becomes clear that non-religious interpretation must find fulfilment in a new attitude of the Church of Jesus Christ towards man who belongs to him. Thus the hermeneutical task of a new existential interpretation inevitably and from its very nature includes within itself an ecclesiological aspect, a highly practical aspect of "Church politics". And with this method of non-religious interpretation one must further compare what is said below in the chapter *The Fellowship of the Saints* on Bonhoeffer's method in *Sanctorum Communio* and on the integration of reality.

CHAPTER FOUR

JESUS CHRIST AND REALITY

1. *Reality as a Problem for the Christian Faith*

"Christian belief deduces that the reality of God is not in itself merely an idea from the fact that this reality of God has manifested and revealed itself in the midst of the real world. In Jesus Christ the reality of God entered into the reality of this world. The place where the answer is given, both to the question concerning the reality of God and to the question concerning the reality of this world, is designated solely and alone by the name Jesus Christ. In Him all things consist (Col. 1: 17). Henceforward one can speak neither of God nor of the world without speaking of Jesus Christ. All concepts of reality which do not take account of Him are abstractions" (E. p. 61).

THIS PASSAGE has a key significance as showing the basic theological *motif* of Bonhoeffer's life and work. All his life he wrestled with the question, "Who is Jesus Christ?". Thus we find his late project of non-religious interpretation dominated from the beginning by the question, "Who Christ really is for us today". The reality, the timely importance, the presence of Jesus Christ was never a question for Bonhoeffer; it was the *beginning* of his questioning. And the question "Who Christ is" busied him all the more intensively precisely because of this, precisely because at the foundation of all there lay this unquestionable fact. How can we say to ourselves and to others who Jesus Christ is and how we can find him? In his *Ethics* Bonhoeffer has finally come to this insight and equation, that Jesus Christ equals reality. But this surely implies that he is not only real, that he is not only one reality beside others, *but that he is that reality itself, which or who is the truly real in all that is real.* Wherever we come up against reality, it can be Christ encountering us unawares. *This* is what Jesus Christ is for us. This is the answer to the question about "Who he is".

This he still more is for us today, this he must become more than ever for our Christian awareness in this religionless time, the One who surrounds us, upholds us and addresses us on every side. This is true of all times. For Jesus Christ is the same yesterday, today and for ever. But it is the especial promise of this religionless epoch of ours, when the "metaphysical" transcendent divinity of God is disappearing, that Jesus Christ comes anew into sight for us in this universality and living reality of his.

The statement about the equation of Christ with reality has throughout in Bonhoeffer's work nothing like an incidental character. That same dominant question, "Who Jesus Christ really is for us today", already points to its central position. And Bonhoeffer's whole *Ethics* is centred around this affirmation, everything else becoming intelligible from it. And to the end he regarded his *Ethics* as his authentic work.

> "I sometimes feel as if my life were more or less over, and as if all I had to do now were to finish my *Ethics*. But, you know, when I feel like this, there comes over me a longing (unlike any other that I experience) not to vanish without a trace—an Old Testament rather than a New Testament wish, I suppose . . ." (LPP, p. 107; December 15, 1943).

But it is interesting that the same thought, expressed in a similar form, is already found more than a decade earlier in his lectures on *Christology* delivered in 1933 in Berlin. This view of Christ as the truly real upholding all reality is maintained throughout his work, it may be with varying nuances, but without any material break.

> ". . . the Christological question is fundamentally an onto-logical question. Its aim is to work out the ontological structure of the 'Who?', without coming to grief on the Scylla of the question 'How?' or the Charybdis of the 'fact' of revelation . . ."
> "To what extent is the Christological question the central question of scholarship? It has this significance insomuch as it alone has put the question of transcendence in the form of the question of existence, inasmuch as the ontological question has here been put as the question of the being of a Person, the person Jesus Christ. The old Logos is judged by the transcendence of the person of Christ, and learns to understand it correctly

within its necessary limitations.[1] As logology, Christology alone makes scholarship possible . . ." (Ch, p. 33).

"Only a discipline which knows itself to be within the sphere of the Church will be able to agree here that Christology is the centre of the academic world. For the rest, it remains the unknown and hidden centre of the *universitas literarum*" (Ch, p. 28).[2]

It is true that in such formulations much remains concealed or at best only hinted at. We must also take account of the fact that what we are dealing with is not an autograph, but students' notes taken by Bonhoeffer's hearers. But the fundamental trend is none the less clear. If one puts these early formulations we have quoted, and others in keeping with them from the same lectures, beside that late formulation in the *Ethics*, that "all concepts of reality which do not take account of him (sc. Christ) are abstractions", it then becomes unmistakably clear that what Bonhoeffer sought was to structure the ontology of all that is real as Christology, or in other words, to develop Christology as the ontology of all that is real. All *concepts* of reality which do not take account of Christ are

---

[1] (A literal translation of the German as quoted by Ott would be, ". . . and learns to understand its new relative rightness, its limitations and its necessity" —Tr.)

[2] Bonhoeffer in this context also speaks of the question "Who?" as the one way of questioning appropriate to this subject-matter; "The question 'Who?' is the question of transcendence. The question 'How?' is the question of immanence. Because the one who is questioned here is the Son, the immanent question cannot grasp him. Not 'How are you possible?'—that is the godless question, the serpent's question—but 'Who are you?' The question 'Who?' expresses the strangeness and otherness of the encounter and at the same time reveals itself as the question of the very existence of the enquirer himself . . . So the question of transcendence is the question of existence and the question of existence is the question of transcendence. In theological terms, man only knows who he is in the light of God" (Ch, p. 30). This emphasizing of the question "Who?" and its status as at the same time the questions of transcendence and of existence seems to me an important contribution by Bonhoeffer to the problem of the personal nature of God and man's relation to him. Essentially it is personal confrontation which, in a hard "strangeness and otherness", and yet in an unalterable uniqueness (something could be said here about the *name* of God and his "character"), comes before the eyes of the questioner, so that every other question is cut short except this single one, "*Who* is this?" But this unique confrontation is at the same time the true transcendence of man and includes within itself the whole meaning of his existence. The unique One, God in person, is at the same time the absolutely universal One, since it is he who integrates all questioning existence and answers its very questions about being. The absolutely strange is at the same time what meets the self at its deepest.

abstraction; that does not mean simply that they would be false, but that they do not express the whole, final and intrinsic nature of reality. They may have their own limited correctness; they may on occasion in certain respects express appropriately in words the reality of the real. We could think for example of philosophical concepts of reality, or of ontological concepts orientated towards scientific knowledge of phenomena of the world. But there is lacking in them the final adequacy and concreteness.

Bonhoeffer's Christological ontology or ontological Christology is no experiment in thought, no theoretical speculation, but manifestly an endeavour, undertaken with clenched fist and tautened sinew of thought, with the astonishing intellectual power which was typical of this man, really to satisfy the challenge of the existential question of faith, who Jesus Christ really is for us today. It is manifest that in this endeavour he did not reach his goal. But it would be untrue to say that he went astray in it.

Under the inescapable compulsion of faith itself, a faith which, in the utmost sincerity, has to be lived and testified to credibly in the encounter with humanity of today, Bonhoeffer is also concerned to debate both the reality of Jesus Christ, the reality of the God who encounters us in Christ, and at one and the same time the palpable reality which surrounds us and is in ourselves. At one and the same time, for there is no other possibility of debate in sincerity! God can only be conceived in this concrete life which he gives us as a prize of war, in this reality, or not at all. There arises here a terrible tension into which we as believers and thinkers are drawn, the tension between him, Jesus Christ, who speaks to us his demand and his promise, and the realities which can remain dumb for us and stare at us enigmatically. This tension it is the task of the Christian to endure, and indeed to overcome. It is his task to endure and to overcome through the activity of the Christian life, "in prayer and in doing justly among men". But parallel to that, or rather intertwined with it, it is his task to endure and to overcome in theological *thought*, in finding a concept of reality which bridges the tension, which is no longer an "abstraction" because it no longer "takes no account of Jesus Christ". Such a bridging is, it is true, no such resolution of the tension as would mean that this no longer existed thereafter. It continues to exist in the sense that time and again the act of venture is demanded of Christian existence. Rather it is in some ways the task to make the tension very visible, so that the act of venture may become understandable. But this will not happen so long as Jesus is still spoken of religiously as the fulfiller of "metaphysical" and "individualistic" needs.

2. The Ethical Point of Attack and the Universal Breadth of the Question of Reality in Bonhoeffer

Bonhoeffer is seeking to make an end of this speaking about Christ in religious terms. In saying this we are not mistakenly importing into the early context of the Christology lectures his late thought about non-religious interpretation. We are making our interpretation from the context of the subject-matter itself which was his concern. For we have already seen that in the *Ethics*, which essentially is contemporary with his prison letters, the thought of a Christological ontology, which already appears in his earlier works, has found its most crucial form. To make clear what we are saying about "Christological ontology", let us bring forward the text which Bonhoeffer quotes at the one decisive point. Col. 1: 16 runs (N.E.B.), "In him (sc. Christ) everything in heaven and on earth was created ... thrones, sovereignties, authorities and powers: the whole universe has been created through him and for him", and v. 17 continues, "and he exists before everything, and all things are held together in him". It is this universalist trend in the New Testament witness to Christ which Bonhoeffer is seeking to follow in his thought of a Christology to be developed ontologically. And the Christ who is so experienced and so thought of is no longer the religiously "transcendent" Christ or the "Jesus of the individual soul". He is the Christ in all reality. But the question now is how this thought of Bonhoeffer or rather of the New Testament itself can be worked out. How are we to think of it? How can the immanence, the "real presence of Christ" in the world be so expounded that in the end the exposition and the testimony appear more worthy of belief than any "religious" view of Christ, or for that matter

than the Christocentric principle in the system of a "revelational positivism"? Does not this undertaking in its turn
end finally as a pure assertion, one which remains extraneous
to the facts and to real life itself.

Bonhoeffer, of course, could not escape this question either.
If he did not put it in this direct and thematic way, at least
he permits us to see very clearly his approach to it, that it is
part of the complex of ethical problems. Hence its clearest
formulation is found in his equation of Christ and reality in
his *Ethics*. It is in itself astonishing, and yet characteristic of
Bonhoeffer's type of thinking, that an Ethic should in this
way find its crucial point in an ontological train of thought,
and that such fundamental ontological thoughts appear in
precisely an ethical context. This is how the chapter of "The
Concept of Reality" in his *Ethics* leads us from ethics to the
concept of reality:

> "Whoever wishes to take up the problem of a Christian ethic
> must be confronted at once with a demand which is quite without
> parallel. He must from the outset discard as irrelevant the two
> questions which alone impel him to concern himself with the
> problem of ethics. 'How can I be good?' and 'How can I do good?',
> and instead of these he must ask the utterly and totally different
> question, 'What is the will of God?'. This requirement is so
> immensely far-reaching because it presupposes a decision with
> regard to the ultimate reality; it presupposes a decision of faith.
> If the ethical problem presents itself essentially in the form of
> enquiries about one's own being good and doing good, that means
> that it has already been decided that it is the self and the world
> which are the ultimate reality. The aim of all ethical reflection is,
> then, that I myself shall be good and that the world shall become
> good through my action. But the problem of ethics at once
> assumes a new aspect if it becomes apparent that these realities,
> myself and the world, themselves lie embedded in a quite different
> ultimate reality, namely the reality of God, the Creator, Reconciler,
> and Redeemer. What is of ultimate importance is now no longer
> that I should become good, or that the condition of the world
> should be made better by my action, but that the reality of God
> should show itself everywhere to be the ultimate reality" (E, p. 55).

It is in the question of ethics, in responsible existence, in
the realm of the existentialist question, "What am I to do?",

that understanding thus dawns upon Bonhoeffer that God is the true and final reality in all realities, that all created things are in Christ and he in them all. My duty as one who exists responsibly is not to ask myself how I can effect something in the world and on the world and on myself, but to surrender myself to the fact that God is already there as the unsurpassable reality, already present in the very things which are the subject and sphere of my responsible decisions and my ethical existence in a given situation, that God is already there in the ethical situation in which a claim is made upon my responsibility, and in a sense is waiting there for me. But of course this raises the question of how we are to conceive of this *immanence* of God, or of Christ the embodiment of the divine immanence, in the situation, and that of the situation in him. This is merely a particular instance of the question already put by us in Chapter Three about the manner of the real presence of Christ in the world. But the general Christological and ontological thought of immanence obviously becomes alive for Bonhoeffer in ethics, in the immanence of God in the ethical situation. Final elucidation of either the general or the particular question he has not given us. But let us seek to follow out his beginnings.

Three things require still to be clarified here:

1. If we speak of God as the final reality to which the responsible existence of the Christian has to surrender itself, what is meant by that is not simply that beyond this reality which we know is the God who is real in a final and absolute sense. Bonhoeffer's thought is in no way "other-worldly". Rather this assertion is to be understood in a strictly *ontological* way, that God as the finally real is the true reality *in* the reality of this world which we know. And this again is not to be understood pantheistically, but in the sense of reconciliation. "The reality of God discloses itself only by setting me entirely in the reality of the world. And when I encounter the reality of the world it is always already sustained, accepted and reconciled in the reality of God" (E, p. 61). (Here incidentally, we find in the *Ethics* an exact parallel to the late thoughts about "worldliness"!) The final reality of all things is their reconciliation in the person and work of Jesus Christ. But to ask what this means, this immanence of God or Jesus Christ in the world

which is not simply "identical" but "sustaining, accepting and reconciling", is simply a particular case of the fundamental question we have already put several times.[3]

2. With this immanence in the sense of reconciliation another element is connected by its very nature. The real of which Bonhoeffer speaks is not simply the "factual". A quotation, again from the context of the ethical approach to the problem to reality, may serve as an illustration of this:

> "For the sake of avoiding a misunderstanding, there is need at this point of some further clarification of what is meant here by reality.
>
> "There is a way of basing ethics upon the concept of reality which differs entirely from the Christian way. This is the positive and empirical approach, which aims at the entire elimination from ethics of the concept of norms and standards because it regards this concept as being merely the idealization of factual and practically expedient attitudes . . . It now transpires that the concept of reality which underlies the positivistic ethic is the meretricious concept of the empirically verifiable, which implies denial of the origin of this reality in the ultimate reality, in God. Reality, understood in this inadequate sense, cannot be the source of good, because all it demands is complete surrender to the contingent, the casual, the advantageous, and the momentarily expedient, because it fails to recognize the ultimate reality and because in this way it destroys and abandons the unity of the good" (E, p. 60).

In Bonhoeffer, then, the real is not simply the factual, the

---

[3] Jürgen Moltmann, in his essay, *Die Wirklichkeit der Welt und Gottes konkretes Gebot nach Dietrich Bonhoeffer*, in *Die mündige Welt*, III, pp. 42ff., has described the essence of Bonhoeffer's thought very aptly. Thus he speaks of the "Christocratic structure of reality" (p. 57), of Bonhoeffer's peculiar insight of "an *anhypostasia* of the reality of the world in the incarnation of God" (p. 45). "The reality of which Bonhoeffer speaks has a Christological structure for him" (p. 46). "That this reality discloses itself in the word of Christ as revelation alone does not mean that it only exists in the act of recognition of revelation and in faith. Rather the whole of reality in which faith comes into existence, in which it takes part and in the history of which it becomes implicated, is before belief or unbelief the reality surrounded and accepted by God" (*ibid.*). All this is very relevant. It is also apt when (p. 53), quoting Bonhoeffer's *Ethics*, he speaks of a "movement of (sc. the world's) being accepted and becoming accepted by God in Christ". The immanence of God in the reality of the world is not something "static" or "substantial", but has the character of a movement. The nature of this movement is a matter for further enquiry.

empirically verifiable; it has in addition a new dimension of depth. "... It (sc. the Christian ethic) speaks of the reality of God as the ultimate reality without and within(!) everything that is. It speaks of the reality of the world as it is, which possesses reality solely through the reality of God" (E, p. 61). But this "in addition" as well as the "verifiable" is not to be understood merely as something added, as if first of all one had to orientate oneself completely towards the "factually" verifiable, and then, in addition, to postulate or assert something further. Rather this "in addition" is a structural component. What after all is this "factually verifiable" element? What are we really saying when we say that something is factual and verifiable? Do we know in the end what we mean? It cannot be doubted that for Bonhoeffer a concept of reality limited to the factual is an abstraction. The factual is not yet the real but something abstracted from the fullness of the real. This fullness, properly speaking, is God, the reconciliation of the world in him, his reconciling presence. But this must not remain an empty assertion, it must be an ontological structure, capable of explanation in terms of the reality of what is real in the world, though not to be derived from it alone. This still remains to be accomplished. Bonhoeffer was the first to undertake a definition, and in so doing to point to a direction. And yet, have we not really known for a long time already from our dealings with the real, that this is not simply the factual and verifiable? It is true that there is much that we can "verify", or surely it would be truer to say that the facts verify themselves to us, nailing us firmly, so to speak, to their reality from which we cannot escape. But yet at the same time the real also encounters us as the radically questionable, the meaning of which we do not understand and which yet forces upon us the question of its meaning.[4] But this questionableness itself takes us beyond the purely factual, although not yet of course containing that fullness of the concept of reality which Bonhoeffer sees in the fact of Christ. But we only receive insight into this final fullness "ethically", and not at all theoretically, that is to say, we receive it in the adventure of responsibility. In this way we gain understanding of Bonhoeffer's

---

[4] I have entered in more detail into this basic trait of the real in my *Was ist Wirklichkeit?*, in *Deutsches Pfarrerblatt*, 1964, 14, pp. 369ff.

approach to the ontological by the path that leads through the ethical.

3. But, on the other hand, it would not be in keeping with the facts to conceive of this "reality", of which Bonhoeffer speaks in the context of ethics, with which we come face to face in the ethical situation, and which finds its finality in the name of Jesus Christ, as a reality relevant only in this ethical context, so that there could be other realms of this world which are not primarily relevant ethically, and have in the first instance nothing at all to do with this one. "All things", says Bonhoeffer, "appear distorted if they are not seen and recognized in God" (E, p. 56). *All* things! And in the section in the *Ethics* following the one we have so far been discussing, he resists the temptation of "Thinking in Terms of Two Spheres": "As soon as we try to advance along this path (sc. that of equating Christ with reality), our way is blocked by the colossal obstacle of a large part of traditional Christian ethical thought" (E, p. 62). He mentions the scholastic division of reality into nature and grace, that of the post-Reformation into the kingdom of the Gospel and the kingdom of the world of autonomous laws, and that of the enthusiasts into the community of the elect and the world which is hostile to God. "In all these schemes the cause of Christ becomes a partial and provisional matter within the limits of reality. It is assumed that there are realities which lie outside the reality that is in Christ. It follows that these realities are accessible by some way of their own, and otherwise than through Christ" (E, p. 63). But the world must not be divided into a sacred and a profane realm. Against it stands universalism in our understanding of Christ. Thus we see how in Bonhoeffer the ontological exposition of Christology makes a total claim upon the whole of reality. That Christ, as the foundation which supports and establishes reality, is not to be thought of as only in one particular realm of "ethical" reality follows also from the Christology lectures of 1933, where Christ (pp. 62ff.) is thought of as the centre of human existence, as the centre of history, and finally as the centre of nature also.[5] This is what is said of nature there:

[5] In these lectures Bonhoeffer in characteristic fashion deals first with the *Christus praesens* ("Part One: The Present Christ—the '*Pro Me*' "—Ch. pp. 41ff.), and only goes on from there to the historical Christ in Part Two (Ch.

"As fallen creation, however, it is dumb, in thrall under the guilt of man. Like history, nature suffers from the loss of its meaning and freedom. It longs for a new freedom. Nature is not reconciled, like man and history, but it is redeemed for a new freedom . . .

To sum up, we must continue to stress that Christ is indeed the centre of human existence, the centre of history and now, too, the centre of nature; but these three aspects can be distinguished only in the abstract. In fact human existence is always history, always nature as well. As fulfiller of the law and liberator of creation, the mediator acts for the whole of human existence. He is the same, who is intercessor and *pro me*, and who is himself the end of the old world and the beginning of the new world of God" (Ch, pp. 66f.).

---

p. 71). "We have spoken so far of the present Christ; but this present-historical (*geschichtliche*) Christ is the same person as the historical (*historische*) Jesus of Nazareth". The "figure" (pp. 49ff.) and the "place" (pp. 61ff.) of the present Christ are discussed. The figure of Christ is a threefold one, Word, Sacrament and Community. On the place of Christ he writes, "If we look for the place of Christ, we are looking for the structure of the 'Where?' within that of the 'Who?'. We are thus remaining within the structure of the person. Everything depends on Christ being present to his Church as a person in space and time" (p. 61). The place of the present Christ is the centre of existence, of history, and of nature; "That Christ is the centre of our existence does not mean that he is the centre of our personality, our thought and our feeling. Christ is our centre even when he stands at the periphery of our consciousness; he is our centre even when Christian piety is forced to the periphery of our being. The character of the statement about his centrality is not psychological but ontologico-theological. It does not relate to our personality but to our being a person before God. The centre of the person is not demonstrable" (p. 62). These statements are particularly significant for the question about the anonymous existential knowledge of the universal Christ who penetrates and sustains all reality. Christ is "objectively" the centre of our person even where he is not accepted as such. On the "centre of history" he says, "History lies between promise and fulfilment. It bears within itself the promise, the divine promise, of becoming the womb of God's birth. The promise of a Messiah is alive everywhere in history. History lives in and from this expectation. That is its meaning, the coming of the Messiah . . . The fulfilment of this promise cannot be demonstrated in any way; it can only be proclaimed. That means that the Messiah Christ is at the same time both the destruction and the fulfilment of all the Messianic expectations of history. He is their destruction in so far as the visible Messiah does not appear but the fulfilment takes place in secret. He is their fulfilment in so far as God has really entered history and the expected one is now really there" (pp. 63f.). Here we already meet with that readiness in Bonhoeffer to approximate the concepts "meaning" and "promise", and hence the eschatological structuring of the concept of meaning, as we find it at one important point (LPP, p. 214) later. (Cp. with this our Chapter Seven, Section 6).

It is true that Bonhoeffer does not yet use the keyword "reality", but the line of thought is already the same. Finally this universalism of his, which departs from every particularism of the "ethical", can be illustrated from his letter of Advent IV, 1943, where he meditates on a Christmas hymn and reaches the thought of *Anakephalaiosis*;[6]

"... For this last week or so these lines have kept on running running through my head:

> "*Lasset fahr'n, o liebe Brüder,*
> *was euch quält, was euch fehlt;*
> *ich bring alles wieder*".

("Let go, dear brothers, every pain and every want; I will restore everything", from *Fröhlich soll mein Herze springen*, by Paul Gerhardt).

"What does this 'I will restore' mean? It means that nothing is lost, that everything is taken up in Christ, although it is transformed, made transparent, clear, and free from all selfish desire. Christ restores all this as God originally intended it to be, without the distortion resulting from our sins. The doctrine derived from Eph. I: 10—that of the restoration of all things, ἀνακεφαλαίωσις, *recapitulatio* (Irenaeus)—is a magnificent conception, full of comfort. This is how the promise 'God seeks what has been driven away' is fulfilled. And no one has expressed this so simply and artlessly as Paul Gerhardt in the words that he puts into the mouth of the Christ-child: *Ich bring alles wieder*. Perhaps this line will help you a little in the coming weeks" (LPP, p. 112).

Here this Christology of Bonhoeffer, which we were to expound ontologically, all at once receives a new eschatological aspect. Eschatology, properly speaking, drops into the background in him. But it does not drop out. If we would enquire about his approach to eschatological thought here is where we must begin. We might further ask if the tone of this hymn is not expressly "religious". Obviously it is not according to Bonhoeffer's understanding of the word. This simple "religious" meditation with its childlike note is found in a letter in the midst of the fermentation processes of the doctrine of non-religious interpretation! This eschatological aspect of the

---

[6] On this passage also cp. Chapter Seven, Section 6, "The Existential Verification of the Doctrine of Providence".

reality of Christ has its place among what are the absolute presuppositions which form the basis for non-religious interpretation, and cannot be given up as an element in it. It would surely have no meaning for the opponent of Bonhoeffer to bring into play here the concept of "myth" from Bultmann. For what Bonhoeffer expresses here as a presentiment, but at the same time is deeply in earnest about, is certainly not at all any "external" remaining myth, but the considered statement, to be explained ontologically, of the reality which is closest to us of all. If we would enter into controversy with him we must at least attempt once and for all to launch ourselves out on this way of ontological exposition.[7]

One further note! It is striking that Bonhoeffer, just as on occasion he quotes Colossians, here quotes Ephesians at materially decisive points. Are these Deutero-Pauline letters to become today decisive texts in Church history just as Romans and Galatians were at another time?

Thus we recognize that Christ is thought of as the foundation of *all* reality and the One immanent in it all. The door is barred to every particularism and "provincialism" in our Christian faith in its understanding of Christ. And yet at the same time it remains true that the road leading to the decisive equation is the ethical. If we would follow Bonhoeffer we must follow him through this gate. Εἶναι ἐν Χριστῷ is primarily to be explained in this way.

3. *Reality and Realization, Formation and Conformation*

Bonhoeffer sought to develop his *Ethics* under the main

---

[7] In my essay, *Herméneutique et Eschatologie* (*Archivio di Filosofia*, 1 e 2, Rome, 1963, pp. 105ff.), I have attempted an approach from the viewpoint of Christian eschatology to thought on the ontological structure of all reality as such. All reality, in so far as it comes into the horizon of our experience, encounters us, as far as its final significance is concerned, as something provisional looking for a fulfilment. This is to be found in Christ. And here Bonhoeffer seems to me to be thinking in a similar direction; Jesus Christ appears in him as he who " brings again", that is to say, sums up in himself and brings to view and to fulfilment the real and refined meaning of *all* reality. The thought is never pursued further by him. It appears as a theological *aperçu* which is, however, very characteristic for the whole trend of this thought, the tendency to regard Christ as the truly real in all reality.

heading "Formation", taken from Gal. 4: 9, "... that Christ may be formed in you". It is true that the work was left in a very fragmentary state. But the editor, Bethge, in his Preface to the edition of the fragments, gives us Bonhoeffer's plan. This envisaged two parts, I. The Foundations, II. The Structure (E, p. xii). One of the possible titles in mind was, "The foundations and the structure of a world which is reconciled with God". Christian Ethics is formation, οἰκοδομή. In its building, in its formation, it is orientated towards the future. Thus the first section in the first part is entitled, "Ethics as Formation". And in the edited fragments we find an important section with the title, "Conformation" (E, pp. 17ff.). Obviously the later section which we made our starting-point, that about the concept of reality (pp. 55ff.), is connected with this thought of formation.

> "The problem of Christian Ethics is the realization among God's creatures of the revelational reality of God in Christ, just as the problem of dogmatics is the truth of the revelational reality of God in Christ" (E, p. 57).
> "The place which in all other ethics is occupied by the antithesis of 'should be' and 'is', idea and accomplishment, motive and performance, is occupied in Christian ethics by the relation of reality and realization, past and present, history and event (faith), or, to replace the equivocal concept by the unambiguous name, the relation of Jesus Christ and the Holy Spirit. The question of good becomes the question of participation in the divine reality which is revealed in Christ. Good is now no longer a valuation of what is ... Good is the real itself. It is not the real in the abstract, the real which is detached from the reality of God, but the real which possesses reality only in God ... A desire to be good for its own sake, as an end in itself, so to speak, or as a vocation in life, falls victim to the irony of unreality. The genuine striving for good now becomes the self-assertiveness of the prig" (E, p. 57).

Thus Bonhoeffer characterizes the significance for Christian ethics of the concept of reality. The good is not an ideal stretched like an archway over reality, a mere ought-to-be which we have first to realize. The good is reality itself, and not "an independent theme of life" beside it, "if it were so it would be the craziest kind of quixotry" (E, p. 57f.). The good is the real God himself in all real things, the God who sustains these things and as their Redeemer purposes good for them on each occasion. In every human situation, in every involvement, in every realm of decision we may say that God also is involved as Lord and Reconciler. His countenance looks out at us at every moment from them all. And just this is the consequence of the incarnation of God in Christ. In spite of their apodeictic sound, all these statements of Bonhoeffer's, the fragmentariness and incompleteness of whose work we have to allow for, have no more than an indicative, as it were a signalling and pointing, character. He was not yet in a position to say precisely what it means that God himself is present in reality, and that the good which we should strive to achieve in our activity consists simply in him himself, the reality in all that is real. Bonhoeffer only gives us a signal, calls us to go on to finish the task, to a venture of seeing and hearing. He who does not seek to see and hear, who will not permit reality to speak to him, who does not *venture* to see and hear—he will not see and hear. He will pass by reality in ethical Pharisaism or in quixotry, even if these should call themselves by the name of Christian, and in so doing he will overlook God and, blind and deaf, deliver his essentially irrelevant censures. Bonhoeffer uses suggestion to show us, giving us indirect information which challenges us, the possibility of a truly ethical attitude in permitting ourselves to surrender ourselves to God. He seeks to open our eyes and our ears for the finger of God in all things and the voice of the Good Shepherd reaching us everywhere. That he was not yet able to describe more precisely the real presence of God in the ethical situation, that he only gave an indication of it, does not imply that nobody can go on to give a more precise intellectual description of what he saw, as a visionary so to speak, in the ethical realm.

We can also say still more about the real presence of God at any given time in the ethical situation, say it above all by a careful interpretation of Bonhoeffer's beginnings, that is, by extending his lines. In doing so, attention has to be paid to what he says about behaviour in keeping with reality. To this behaviour he often gave thought. The *Ethics* opens with a longish passage on it. But we shall have to deal with this in the next chapter. What is important for us here is that he understands the basic problem of ethics as "realization", by which he means participation in reality.

> "Christian ethics enquires about the realization in our world of this divine and cosmic reality which is given in Christ" (E, pp. 61f.).

To this extent ethics is formation or structure. "The foundations and structure of a world which is reconciled with God", runs Bonhoeffer's proposed title for his *Ethics*.[8] The foundation is God himself, Christ who is already there as the real, who is present as its basis in all that is real. But this is the same hidden reality which does not simply mean facticity; we cannot use the real presence of God in the real to soothe ourselves. Rather what this reality demands of us is realization. It demands a formation which is not an autonomous work of man, but is *con*formation.

Bonhoeffer begins the section of his *Ethics* entitled "Conformation" with an expression of mistrust in his own leading concept of formation!

> "The word 'formation' arouses our suspicion. We are sick and tired of Christian programmes and of the thoughtless and superficial slogan of what is called 'practical' Christianity as distinct from 'dogmatic' Christianity. We have seen that the formative forces in the world do not arise from Christianity at all, and that the so-called practical Christianity is at least as unavailing in the world as is the dogmatic kind. The word 'formation', therefore, must be taken in a quite different sense from that to which we are accustomed ... Their (sc. the Holy Scriptures') primary concern is not with the forming of a world by means of plans and programmes. Whenever they speak of forming they are concerned only with the one form which has overcome the world, the form of Jesus Christ. Formation can only come from this form. But here again it is not a question of applying directly to the world the teaching of Christ or what are referred to as Christian principles, so that the world might be formed in accordance with these. On the contrary, formation comes only by being drawn in into the form of Jesus Christ. It comes only as formation in His likeness, as *conformation with the unique form of Him who was made man, was crucified, and rose again*" (E, pp. 17f.).

[8] Cp. Eberhard Bethge's Preface to the *Ethics* (E, p. xii).

"Foundations" and "structures", "form" and "conformation", "reality" and "realization", these pairs of concepts are in Bonhoeffer obviously in mutual correspondence. And when in this he distinguishes what he says from any kind of Christian programme, this certainly does not imply in his case any type of Christian quietism, any renunciation of positive activity in the world, or of sharing in the task of building up the fellowship. What it does mean is that the horizon of Christian ethics dare not be limited to such a superficial view of Christian responsibility, but that here more than anywhere else something happens which is the true ethical event, something founded on the reality of Christian existence, namely that surrender of oneself to the true reality of God, that conformation with the form of Jesus Christ the truly real. This is the ethical event, as seen in the true depths of its being.

And what takes place here? First of all, not merely that *we* make efforts to "become like Jesus", but that "Christ remains the only giver of form" (E, p. 18).

> "It is not Christian men who shape the world with their ideas, but it is Christ who shapes men in conformity with Himself. But just as we misunderstand the form of Christ if we take Him to be essentially the teacher of a pious and good life, so, too, we should misunderstand the formation of man if we were to regard it as instruction in the way in which a pious and good life is to be attained. Christ is the Incarnate, Crucified and Risen One whom the Christian faith confesses . . . ." (E, p. 18).

What is still undefined in Bonhoeffer's brief but decided statement about conformation, about participation in true reality, is here defined somewhat more closely. Conformation means being drawn into the reality and form of Jesus Christ, who is the Incarnate, Crucified and Risen.[9] Incarnation, Cross and Resurrection are the three essential and constitutive components of the one reality of Jesus Christ. Jesus appears in this unchangeable, essential and irrevocable, but at the same

[9] To be drawn thus into this threefold reality might be said to find expression in the ancient prayer, "The Angels of the Lord", the German text of which is found in the *Stundengebet* of the "*Michaels-Bruderschaft*", 2nd. edn. 1949 (I have not succeeded in finding an English version—Tr.); ". . . May we learn from the mouth of the angel, that thy Son Jesus Christ has taken upon him our flesh and blood, and that we through his sufferings and cross have attained to the glory of the resurrection".

time universally significant, form. Incarnation, Cross and Resurrection are structural components of his person, but equally components of his being for others, his being for the world, and therefore components of such an "openness" that all reality, and especially all real human being, can participate in it. The reality of Jesus Christ in these very components has a cosmic, universal relevance.[10]

As has already been mentioned, it is very characteristic of Bonhoeffer's thought that in the early Christology lectures he drew his picture in two main parts, the present and the historical Christ, and that in this he deliberately treated first the present Christ. Jesus as historical concerns us and must interest us because he is the now present and real. But as such he is none other than the historical.

> "Jesus is the Christ present as the Crucified and Risen One. That is the first statement of Christology. 'Present' is to be understood in a temporal and spatial sense, *hic et nunc*. So it is part of the definition of the person ..." (Ch, p. 43; Beginning of Part One).

> "We have spoken so far of the present Christ, but this present-historical (*geschichtliche*) Christ is the same person as the historical (*historische*) Jesus of Nazareth. Were this not so, we should have to say with St. Paul that our faith is vain and an illusion. The Church would be deprived of its substance. There can be no isolation of the so-called historical (*historische*) Jesus from the Christ who is present now" (Ch, p. 71; Beginning of Part Two).

[10] The question arises of how we can regard theologically the importance of the event of Christ for the *cosmos* beyond human history. It is not enough here, of course, simply to quote again the New Testament passages which point to a cosmic theology. The question is how we can really *understand* these texts. The cosmic dimension becomes relevant for faith in Christ, or faith in Christ for the interpretation of the cosmic dimension, by a path that leads through man, for human existence cannot be thought of apart from the *cosmos*. But at this point we might continue further in the direction that the attitude of man to the *cosmos* and the manner in which it enters his experience are regarded as of Christological structure. Nature reveals its secret in so far as man lives in solidarity with it, with the world of animals, for example, where there could be an attitude analogous to that of human relations, and in so far as he shares the suffering of creation and also hopes for it. Thus the components of the Christ-event would affect nature also. This certainly does not mean that they are simply components of a subjective human attitude. They are to be understood as components of an encounter, and to this extent of reality itself. But it is true that this is no more than the indication of a direction. (Cp. further on this, Chapter Eight).

The present is the historical. In this way the road to speculation is barred. The Christological ontology of Bonhoeffer is
something completely different from speculation; it is the
exposition of Christ at the place of his most inescapable
livingness, and this is why beginning with *Christus praesens* is
successful. Incidentally it is also the reason why Bonhoeffer
was anything but a "speculative spirit" in the bad sense,
why his was no spirit which ever stood in danger of sliding
away into the uncommitting and general, and getting out of
the field of force of what is alive and binding upon us at this
moment. And this is why the entry to Bonhoeffer's ontology is
by way of ethics. And not only the methodological entry!
This was also the point at which there most of all pressed in on
him the necessity of equating Christ with reality, the point
where Christ so confronted him that he had to perceive the
shipwreck of all other ethical endeavours for reality.

4. *Incarnation, Cross and Resurrection as Structural Components of the Reality of Christ*

Where do we stand? We are asking how we can make
concrete the statement, central and constitutive for Bonhoeffer,
that Jesus Christ is the true reality in all that is real. We have
recognized that this statement extends to all reality without
any exception whatsoever. Bonhoeffer had the whole of
reality in view. But despite this universalism, to which testimony
is also given in the Christological conclusions from *Christus
praesens*, Bonhoeffer yet comes to his outlook from one quite
definite point, from the ethical situation of responsible man
in the face of inescapable reality. Here he found himself
compelled to say that God in a fundamental way was already
in reality, indeed that in fact God himself was reality, not in
any sense of *Deus sive natura* but in the sense of the immanence
of the Reconciler, and that the ethical attitude of the Christian
had to align itself to this.

But Bonhoeffer's thought goes further. He speaks of conformation with the real, with Christ, and of the three moments
of formation in their inscrutable double significance as on the
one hand components of the One and on the other universal
components.

There is more to be said on this threefold conformation. We find in them a moment which gives concreteness, and which because of that enables us to enter into Bonhoeffer's outlook with greater understanding. I should certainly say that in its first, general and still undefined form his call is already clear enough—for him that hath ears to hear—to indicate the direction he is taking, that the proclamation of Christ will not be credible today if Christ is, as it were, "preached on to" reality from without, or if he remains one particular province in the totality of the real. In the same way Christian activity will not gain its ultimate credibility if it is orientated towards any one particular ideal or duty set beside others. Here we are shown anew the inward bond between his Christology and his non-religious interpretation.

But Bonhoeffer sketches certain characters of realistic being in conformation with the real Christ in his threefold structure:

"To be conformed with the Incarnate—that is to be a real man. It is man's right and duty that he should be man. The quest for the superman, the endeavour to outgrow the man within the man, the pursuit of the heroic, the cult of the demigod, all this is not the proper concern of man, for it is untrue. The real man is not an object either for contempt or deification, but an object of the love of God. The rich and manifold variety of God's creation suffers no violence here from false uniformity or from the forcing of man into the pattern of an ideal or a type or a definite picture of the human character ... To be conformed with the incarnate is to have the right to be the man one really is. Now there is no more pretence, no more hypocrisy or self-violence, no more compulsion to be something other, better and more ideal than what one is. God loves the real man. God became a real man" (E, pp. 18f.).

"To be formed into the likeness of the Crucified—this means being a man sentenced by God. In his daily existence man carries with him God's sentence of death, the necessity of dying before God for the sake of sin. With his life he testifies that nothing can stand before God save only under God's sentence and grace. Every day man dies the death of a sinner. Humbly he bears the scars on his body and soul, the marks of the wounds which sin inflicts on him. He cannot raise himself up above any other man, or set himself before him as a model, for he knows himself to be the greatest of all sinners. He can excuse the sin of another, but never his own. He bears all the suffering imposed upon him, in the knowledge that it serves to enable him to die with his own will and to accept God's judgement upon him" (E, p. 19).

"To be conformed with the Risen One—that is to be a new man before God. In the midst of death he is in life. In the midst of sin he is righteous. In the midst of the old he is new. His secret remains hidden from the world. He lives because Christ lives, and lives in Christ alone . . . So long as the glory of Christ is hidden, so long, too, does the glory of his new life remain 'hidden with Christ in God' (Col. 3:3). But he who knows espies already here and there a gleam of what is to come. The new man lives in the world like any other man . . . Transfigured though he is in the form of the Risen One, here he bears only the sign of the cross and the judgement. By bearing it willingly he shows himself to be the one who has received the Holy Spirit and who is united with Jesus Christ in incomparable love and fellowship" (E, pp. 19f.).

This is how the existence of the man who has been conformed with Christ appears. It is a description, admittedly again very terse and abbreviated, of existence in the Holy Spirit, of being *kata pneuma*. It is the behaviour of a humanity with nothing unnatural about it, of a humble openness which has renounced every form of self-justification, a joyful confident openness towards an ineffable future. More than this can scarcely be said for the moment about these quotations from Bonhoeffer on the three components of the reality of Christ and on conformation. It seems to me important that he, with a clear insight, has set out precisely these three components as the essential ones in the encounter with Christ, and it is just at this point that the problem of the Christological structure of all reality would have to be taken up anew. For the manner in which Christ is present in him who is conformed to him points us to the manner of his presence in reality in general.

But further, this behaviour of the conformed is certainly not one particular possibility for man among others. It is something absolutely universal, that is to say, this basic attitude permits the most varied existential modifications and can assume the most varied, and according to the occasion the most individual and peculiar, concrete forms in matters of detail.

"In Christ there was re-created the form of man before God. It was not an outcome of the place or the time, of the climate or the race, of the individual or the society, or of religion or of taste, but quite simply the life of mankind as such, that mankind at this point recognized its image and its hope. What befell Christ had befallen mankind. It is a mystery, for which there is no explanation, that only a part of mankind recognizes the form of their Redeemer. The longing of the Incarnate to take form in all men is as yet still unsatisfied" (E, p. 20).

The human part, the place at which conformation has to begin and does in fact begin, is the Church. But again the Church is not something particular; what takes place in it takes place representatively for the whole of mankind. And here we meet with the basic statement of Bonhoeffer's ecclesiology, that the Church is conformed with Christ, that it is the form of Jesus Christ, though nevertheless not simply, we might say, identical with him, that it is "Christ existing as a community", and is so representatively for all humanity. When in his "Outline for a Book" on non-religious interpretation, in *Letters and Papers from Prison*, he describes the "being-therefor-others" of Jesus as his real being, with which the Church in its being has to be in keeping ("The Church is the Church only when it exists for others ... It must tell men of every calling what it means to exist in Christ, to live for others"— LPP, p. 211), then this is the precise equivalent of the thought of conformation developed in the *Ethics*.

Having now before our eyes, at least in its fundamental features, this threefold and yet unified, this universal but therefore modifiable and variable, behaviour of the man who is conformed with Christ, we have to add that it would not be in keeping with the facts to believe that this *human* behaviour simply, as it were, coincides with the reality of Christ. This would be a fatal misunderstanding of the whole of Bonhoeffer's thought. On the one hand, such behaviour is the reality of Christ become concrete in the realm of human and existential ethics, but, on the other, it is only possible because Jesus is present in person as the essential form of man, the form of the incarnate God to whom we are conformed. Conformation presupposes his form as a *prius*. Jesus Christ himself, in person, is the primary reality, to which the man who exists ethically surrenders himself in order so to become truly "real". The person of Jesus Christ is not "resolved" into some human behaviour which then men have to make their own. There is always first presupposed his being himself as the Incarnate, Crucified and Risen. Hence the Christology lectures of 1933 already emphasize that Christology, while it is regarded universally, as "logology", as the foundation of all knowledge, must yet be concerned exclusively with the question "Who?" That is to say, its unqualified presupposition is the personal presence of Jesus Christ, and then it asks *who* he is. It has not to ask how it is possible that he is (the question "How?"), or the question if he is (the question "If?"). Nor can I see any reason for assuming that in his later period Bonhoeffer retreated in any way at all from this decisive definition.

But at this point there remains the further problem, perhaps the most important in Bonhoeffer's Christology. Even though he makes it obvious how he himself thought, we have not completely removed the misunderstanding that his ethical exposition of the real presence of Christ through the threefold concept of conformation means the disappearance of the reality of Christ somehow in human behaviour. Our first problem in this connection was as to how the manner of the real presence of Christ in all reality was to be *described*. This problem is not yet solved. Bonhoeffer himself has not answered the question. But in my opinion he has made it sufficiently clear that the question must be put, and as well as this he has given us in passing a few concrete indications by means of which we can make future attempts on it. The second problem, closely connected with it, must be what the relation is of the completely universal significance of Christ to his "Who?", to his inscrutable individual person. How far is his person undeniably presupposed in all that is said in a concrete way about the significance of the real in all reality?

To me it seems obvious that both questions, that about the concrete description of the real presence of Christ, and that about the connection with his person which must be maintained of the elements which give concreteness, Incarnation, Cross and Resurrection, are fundamentally one single question. Further enquiry will be made on this in Chapter Ten.

5. *The Hiddenness of the Universal Reality of Jesus Christ*

To make clear the whole theological breadth of the universal significance, because universal reality, of Christ, let us refer finally to the following instructive passage:

> "Your summary of our theological theme is very clear and simple. The question how there can be a 'natural piety' is at the same time a question of 'unconscious Christianity', with which I am more and more concerned. Lutheran dogmatics distinguished between a *fides directa* and a *fides reflexa*. They related this to the so-called children's faith, at baptism. I wonder whether this does not raise a far-reaching problem. I hope we shall soon come back to it" (LPP, pp. 204f.).

Bonhoeffer was not to reach the point of saying more again on this subject. But it is important and significant that this passage is found among his late thoughts, the letter being dated July 27, 1944. Here we must travel further along the theologian Bonhoeffer's path. If Christ is universally real and present, one cannot bypass the question of his universal recognizability, or to be more exact, of his recognizability outside the visible Church. There is intensive thought on this question today also, and especially, on the Catholic side.[11] It must of course remain clear all the time that the *kerygma* of Christ and the Church are not to become irrelevant and superfluous. Their relevance Bonhoeffer would have been the last to deny. It is also clear that what is here called "natural piety" (and one must note the inverted commas!) has in fact a Christological stamp, that is to say, it is knowledge of Christ.

In addition to this letter, there are a few other passages

---

[11] On this cp. espec. K. Rahner, *Dogmatic Notes on Ecclesiological Piety*, in *Theological Investigations*, Vol. V, tr. Krüger, Darton, Longman and Todd, 1966, pp. 336ff., and also *The Teaching of Vatican II on the Church and the Future Reality of Christian Life*, in *The Christian of the Future*, tr. O'Hara, Burns and Oates, 1967, pp. 77ff. Further, *Anonymous Christians*, in *Theological Investigations*, Vol. VI, tr. K. H. and B. Krüger, D. L. & T., 1969, pp. 390ff. This thought as developed by Rahner I have attempted to take up in *Existentiale Interpretation und anonyme Christlichkeit*, and also in *Glaube und Bekennen* and *Die Lehre das II Vatikanischen Konzils. Ein evangelischer Kommentar*, both Basel, 1963, and in *Glaube* (*Theologie für Nicht-theologen*, 2nd. series, Stuttgart, 1964, pp. 42ff.).

in Bonhoeffer, including some very early ones in his Christology lectures, which deal with the thought of a universal self-revelation of Christ. Here, too, we can place his essay, "What is meant by 'Telling the Truth'?" (E, pp. 326ff.). Thematically, its subject is reality, but more implicitly it is also Christ; it is a matter of the real presence of Christ in the ethical situation and of the possibility of recognizing him in realistic ethical behaviour as such.

In the lectures on *Christology* Bonhoeffer also speaks of an *"incognito Christi"* in all realms of the world; we encounter Christ himself in the question, "Who art thou?", which we direct to him, for our question is only a reflection of, or even an answer to, his question which he has already put to us. Our question about Christ can appear in the widest variety of forms and in different contexts. What is important is not so much the form in which it is put as the fact that it is *put at all.*

"What does it mean when, in his world of suspicion and distrust, the worker says, 'Jesus Christ was a good man'? It means that there is no need to distrust him. But when he says 'Jesus was a good man' he is at any rate saying more than when the bourgeois says, 'Jesus is God'. God for him is something which belongs to the Church. But Jesus can be present on the factory floor as the socialist, in politics as the idealist, in the worker's own world as the good man. He fights in their ranks against the enemy, capitalism. Who are you? Are you our brother and Lord? Is the question merely evaded here? Or do they, in their own way, put it seriously? . . .
. . . Christ goes through the ages, questioned anew, missed anew, killed anew" (Ch, pp. 30f.).

There are ways then of encountering and experiencing Christ apart from the encounter with the *kerygma*. All real and essential experience becomes in this way the experience of Jesus Christ as *the* real. Even where he is "missed" and "killed", it is still *he* who is missed and killed and who therefore encounters us in his hiddenness.

CHAPTER FIVE

THE COMMUNION OF SAINTS

1. *The Place of* Communio *Generally in Bonhoeffer's Thought*

HERE we shall be concerned also, though not exclusively, with Bonhoeffer's doctoral dissertation, *Sanctorum Communio*. The thought of the *Communio Sanctorum* runs right through his whole life's work as one of the essential components which his method discovered. For this reason it is to be regarded as organically bound up with the other basic themes of his theology. For "thinking is narrowing to a single thought . . ." (Martin Heidegger).

Sanctorum Communio means the Church. But, with the choice of this concept and this title for the Church, Bonhoeffer has already indicated the special element in that Church which feeling and thought had led him to regard as the essential one. His scientific activity begins with his special interest in the Church. The roots of this in his own life would, properly speaking, still require enquiry. It would seem that early experiences and in particular his experience of Rome played an important role. And to the end of his life Bonhoeffer is thinking and writing about the Church, about its renewal and its mission. Nor did he retract in the later period of his thought the structures which he had worked out in his early days; we find clues which point to the fact that they still have for him their former validity, even if other questions and aspects are now in the foreground, having become thematic for him. Indeed in his *Ethics*, which for practical purposes is to be regarded as contemporaneous with *Letters and Papers from Prison*, an important role is played by the thought of representation, a decisive moment in the thought of *communio*. In the same direction also points the thought of Christ being formed in us (Gal. 4: 19), one which makes its mark on the whole of his *Ethics*. Here we have quite clearly an echo of the early thought of "Christ existing as a community" which completely dominates *Sanctorum Communio* and the lectures on *Christology*. Obviously it is essentially the same thought reappearing and developing new aspects of its power to make its mark. However easy it is to establish changes in the theological diction and the main direction of interest in the three phases of Bonhoeffer's life and work, it is still the continuity of a single thought which we find here, a thought which is able to last and to develop, which maintains itself the same in different forms.

Within the purpose of our interpretation of Bonhoeffer it cannot be our concern to analyse and to discuss single theses from the works of the 21- and 24-year-old graduand and inaugural lecturer on the problem of the Church, although this in itself would doubtless be a fruitful task. But our task is rather to recognize the general trend of this thinking on the reality of the Church of Christ, and to expand and to interpret its essential insights.

It is natural to ask about the background in experience of Bonhoeffer's thought of *communio*. We know that, at least at the end of his life, solidarity with his fellowmen, with his neighbours, had become a feeling of especial importance for him. Even in the loneliness of his cell he knew that he was not alone, but really, in a certain sense palpably, united with his neighbours:

"I feel myself so much a part of you all that I know that we live and bear everything in common, acting and thinking for one another, even though we have to be separated" (LPP, p. 46; May 15, 1943).

"Well, Whitsuntide is here and we are still separated; but it is in a special way a feast of fellowship. When the bells rang this morning, I longed to go to Church, but instead I did as John did on the island of Patmos, and had such a splendid service of my own, that I did not feel lonely at all, for you were all with me, every one of you, and so were the congregations in whose company I have kept Whitsuntide" (LPP, p. 55; June 14, 1943).

"It is remarkable how we think at such times (sc. the bombing of Berlin) about the people that we should not like to live without, and almost or entirely forget ourselves. It is only then that we feel how closely our own lives are bound up with other people's, and in fact how the centre of our own lives is outside ourselves, and how little we are separate entities. The 'as though it were a part of me' " (See p. 18 above—Tr.) "is perfectly true, as I have often felt after hearing that one of my colleagues or pupils had been killed. I think it is a literal fact of nature that human life extends far beyond our physical existence" (LPP, p. 65; September 5, 1943).

Once only, of course, this could be simply a beautiful figure of speech, an especially strong expression of heartfelt unity as experienced between man and man. But this is, as it were, a constant thread which runs through Bonhoeffer's thought, and we find in him so many and so strong testimonies to this way of experiencing human relations, that we must surely see in it more than a beautiful and intimate turn of speech, and rather a specific way of regarding life, obviously character-istic of Bonhoeffer, one also which was no mere theoretical figure of thought, but *a characteristic of his existential experience itself*, and therefore an essential structural component of his picture of humanity as he experienced it. Human life, he holds, the reality of the individual man's being, reaches out beyond individual existence and does so in a completely real way that is not at all to be understood metaphorically or secondarily. This reaching out belongs each time to the reality of my being, to what Heidegger calls the *Jemeinigkeit* of my existence. I this individual am in reality more than merely this individual. I am not only associated with others and co-operating with them, not merely brought together secondarily into some relation with them. I am unified with them in a much more original way. They are a part of me myself. All this, it is true, has only found as yet a very unprecise expression, meeting us not as a theory but as a type of experience which is still not thought through. But in the meantime it is important for us to establish that this genuine solidarity between men is not formulated by Bonhoeffer as a metaphor, but experienced as something structural, something essential. Thus we see here, expressed strongly and as a matter of experience, a breaking through the normal individualistic understanding of man.

Of course all this is true in human relations generally and

not only in the Church. But as against this, the factual situation with which Bonhoeffer's thought of *communio* is primarily concerned is a Christological one. And yet that other human experience is helpful for the understanding of what is in the last resort a Christological factual situation, especially as it is always a peculiarity and a tendency in Bonhoeffer that he integrates into the Christological whole human and earthly components as clarifying elements, though at the same time surely elements themselves in need of clarification.

2. *Bonhoeffer's Method in* Sanctorum Communio *and its Fundamental Significance for the Trend of his Thought*

This characteristic, this tendency towards mutual integration of theological and other viewpoints, is clearly recognizable in the plan and in the definition of the problem in *Sanctorum Communio*. There Bonhoeffer says in Chapter One:

"The sociology of religion is therefore a phenomenological study of the structural characteristics of religious communities. But to avoid misunderstanding it should be noted that the present work on the *sanctorum communio* is theological rather than sociological. Its place is within Christian dogmatics, and the insights of social philosophy and sociology are drawn into the service of dogmatics. We wish to understand the structure, from the standpoint of social philosophy and sociology, of the reality of the Church of Christ which is given in the revelation in Christ. But the nature of the Church can only be understood from within *cum ira et studio*, and never from a disinterested standpoint. Only by taking the claim of the Church seriously, without relativizing it alongside other claims or alongside one's own reason, but understanding it on the basis of the Gospel, can we hope to see it in its essential nature. So our problem has had to be attacked from two, or even from three, sides: that of dogmatics, of social philosophy, and sociology.

In the next chapter we shall show that the Christian concept of the person is real only in sociality. Then we shall show, in a social-philosophical section, how man's spiritual being is likewise possible and real only in sociality. Then in a purely sociological section we shall consider the structures of empirical communities, being by that time in a position to refute the atomist view of society. Only then, through the insight we have acquired into the nature of community, shall we be able to come near to a conceptual understanding of Christian community, of the *sanctorum communio*" (SC, pp. 20f.).

These programmatic remarks of Bonhoeffer's, prefatory to his first greater work, are from various points of view characteristic of his style of thought. They show the correlated aspects of a specific method which, in my opinion, continues right through to his late period, because it is the method which is in keeping with the most peculiar and personal trend of his whole manner of thinking. The method, then, to which we refer, is significant for the whole of his thought with its varied thematic horizons. Here it is developed with reference to one particular great subject and applied to it, and we accordingly attempt to describe it within this framework, but in the awareness of its more general significance.

Bonhoeffer, following contemporary sociologists, distinguishes in this way between social philosophy and sociology:

"Social philosophy investigates the ultimate social relations which are *prior* to all knowledge of and will for empirical community, and the 'origins' of sociality in man's spiritual life and its essential connection with it . . ." "Sociology is the science of the structures of empirical communities" (SC, p. 19).

These two realms of knowledge Bonhoeffer seeks to unite with dogmatics, with dogmatic ecclesiology, to form a type of *continuum* for putting questions. It is true that ecclesiology, the question of the nature of the specific fellowship which is called "Church" and is to be defined as the *communio sanctorum*, cannot become a sociology of religion, a "neutral" scientific analysis which examines the phenomenon of fellowship, the "Church", with *exclusively* the same sociological viewpoints and the same sociological methods which are available for the analysis of any other phenomenon of fellowship. By the *exclusive* use of this method one would not find the clue to the specific nature of this fellowship. This specific nature cannot be discerned from without, from a neutral relativism, *sine ira et studio*, that is, without involvement. The "autonomy" of theology is preserved in the sense that it cannot be absolutely dependent upon the results of a "neutral" scientific or philosophical analysis, or be resolved into such an analysis. The "reality of the Church of Christ" is "given in the revelation in Christ". It is to be studied with an orientation towards revelation, but this means in recognition of revelation, in involvement. But for this very reason the "insights of social philosophy and sociology" can and must be "drawn into the service of dogmatics". Since the Church is also a completely earthly phenomenon of history, the problem of the Church and its nature can and must be "attacked from two, or even from three, sides: that of dogmatics, of social philosophy, and sociology". Thus there takes place something like a *convergence* of the different methods of observation and examination, which certainly begin from different positions and use different methods, but have all before their eyes the same "subject", the phenomenon of the Church, and the same goal, the illumination and better understanding of the phenomenon. They converge, that is to say, they come together in seeking this goal. At the same time of course the properly theological method, the dogmatic one, has precedence. In other words, "neutrality" in *Weltanschauung*, the "lack of presuppositions" which elsewhere is, in appearance if not in fact, the presupposition of both the other methods, is deliberately ruled out for the whole process. Yet in the same whole process social philosophy and sociology still retain their significance. For the subject under study, the Church, is in fact an event of fellowship, and therefore, at least to a certain degree, comprehensible by sociological methods.[1] And it is equally meaningful and necessary to use the thought of social philosophy to relate this phenomenon of fellowship, the "Church", to human society and culture in general. The usefulness of the employment of such methods in no way depends on our presupposing a so-called absence of presuppositions in our *Weltanschauung*. Even without this our examination can be orientated phenomenologically towards the phenomenon itself. Indeed in some

---

[1] Of course the expositions of the twenty-year-old Bonhoeffer are not to be measured against the precision of sociological methods developed since his day. With different stipulations, the problem of the relation of theology to sociology has today a more open future, and surely offers a wide field for empirical research. But apart from this it seems to me that the abiding contribution, still valid today, of what Bonhoeffer attempted in *Sanctorum Communio* is (1) the general method of integration of theological and sociological approaches, and (2) the existential of the collective personality.

circumstances, including the case of the Church, "lack of pre-suppositions" can even make one blind to what is specific in the phenomenon itself!

On the other hand, failure to use this method would incur the risk of missing the worldly concreteness, and surely thereby the fullness of the phenomenon of the Church. A purely dogmatic study of it, renouncing every point of view coming from sociology and social philosophy, could not at all do justice to the complex reality of the Church, at once eschatological and historical, at once divine and social. And it is just this *concrete reality in its complexity* to which Bonhoeffer seeks to find the clue. He seeks to speak of the true Church and no phantasm, the Church of Jesus Christ, but the Church as it really is among men. If he were to give himself up to pure dogmatic abstractions he would miss the divine-human concreteness and the real Church. But if he were to give himself up to the abstractions of an analysis "without presuppositions", carried out *sine ira et studio*, he would equally miss concreteness. But the tendency of Bonhoeffer's thought from his earliest days, as we are now seeing, to his latest, as can easily be shown from the *Ethics* and from *Letters and Papers from Prison*, is precisely that *he wrestles with reality and seeks to match the articulation of his thought to its divine-human concreteness.*

But of course this does not mean that, in *Sanctorum Communio* for example but also in his thought elsewhere, two, or three, ways of thinking are simply added one to another and run parallel and unconnected side by side. In particular, nothing would be gained for knowledge of the reality of the Church, in the last resort not even for theological knowledge, if we were to explain that we had worked on the matter purely within the realm of theology, exegetically and dogmatically, but that of course there was another sociological way of thinking, the insights of which were also to be taken seriously in their own sphere. What Bonhoeffer is seeking for is a *continuity*, a mutual interpenetration, or, to use the metaphor we have previously preferred, a convergence, and a mutual fructification of the two types of knowledge. The employment of the sociological point of view and that of social philosophy should clear the way somewhat for theological understanding of the subject. Hence Bonhoeffer can also say that the nature of the Church can only be understood "from within" and "*cum ira et studio*", but that it has its value nevertheless "to understand the structure, from the standpoint of social philosophy and sociology, of the reality of the Church of Christ which is given in the revelation in Christ". But this must surely mean that approaches from social philosophy and sociology should help one to see the structures or certain structural components of the reality, the "Church". But in the last resort dogmatic ecclesiology is surely nothing other than the knowledge of the structure of the divine-human reality of the Church as given in the revelation in Christ. Thus the approaches of social philosophy and sociology assist theological study of the Church in finding the answer to its own most peculiar task in that they expound certain parts of its construction. They are therefore necessarily to be embraced in the whole process of theological illumination. Theology in the narrower sense is the more comprehensive, it gives the more comprehensive and final interpretation of the reality in question. It gives this interpretation because it thinks in the light of revelation. But in this more comprehensive framework which it has it cannot dispense with the use of "worldly" ways of thinking, for this very reason that if it did, it would inevitably miss the very structure of its subject, which is, after all, divine-*human* reality.

This integration or convergence of "purely theological" and "worldly" methods is therefore the *methodological consequence of the Incarnation*. Hence it holds true not only for the subject, the "Church", but for all that is connected with revelation, and therefore for any theological theme at all. A "purely theological" way of thinking which neglects or refuses contact, and to a certain degree co-operation, with secular thought is seen in the light of the Incarnation as a half-truth which leads to abstractions and unproved assertions.[2]

---

[2] Interesting, though at the same time somewhat obscure in places, are the following remarks of Bonhoeffer on the relation of philosophy and theology, belonging to the Winter Semester 1931–32.

". . . For the relation of philosophy and theology this means in *both* cases (sc. Heidegger and Grisebach) that philosophy precedes theology.

1. To this theology can admit,

(a) that it uses philosophical terminology and in this way submits itself to the claim to omnipotence of the "concept".

(b) that in this, even as systematic theology, it is really a positive science, subordinated to philosophy.

In addition Bonhoeffer, in the course of the programmatic prefatory remarks in which he sketches the course of the whole undertaking of the *Sanctorum Communio*, gives an example of how he pictures concretely the integration and convergence of theology and sociology (or social philosophy). A Christian understanding of the person is introduced into the illumination of the nature of human sociality. Then further, this understanding of the person is on its side developed with reference to basic ethical experiences of personality, not independently, but in a way completely determined by revelation, though by no means simply deduced from Bible texts.[3] After the phenomenon of human sociability is thus already interpreted through a Christian concept of the person, the examination turns to the properly sociological components "in a purely sociological section". Thus the sociological study is undertaken with a preliminary glance at the revealed truth, and then carried out in what is certainly a strictly sociological manner, that is to say, without the disturbing intrusion of any dogmas from without the phenomena themselves. But finally, this purely sociological section is made fruitful theologically. "Only then, through the insight we have acquired into the nature of community, shall we be able to come to a conceptual understanding of Christian community, of the *sanctorum communio*". Important here is surely also the remark that sociological insights help the theologian to a *conceptual* understanding of his ecclesiological subject. This must mean that the theologian is not in a position to forge the suitable conceptual instruments or models for asserting the reality of the Church if he does not remain in a constructive conversation with secular science. The findings that are to be obtained in sociology and social philosophy help to mark off the concepts to be employed in theology. Theology then will use to some extent concepts which

---

(c) that philosophy is bound to regard it in this way.

2. Theology cannot admit,

(a) that it recognizes its form as a servant, corresponding to the subordination of the Church to the cultural institution . . .

(b) that it recognizes its oppositeness to the concept "sight".

(c) that it recognizes the eschatological possibility of a *philosophia christiana*".

(*Ges. Sch., III*, 1960, p. 161).

[3] On Bonhoeffer's concept of the person, see Section Eight, Sociality and Personality.

are also relevant in non-theological realms of knowledge, which may indeed be even worked out in such fields. It is true that we shall have to reckon with the fact that such concepts and categories, used in the realm of theology, will undergo necessary modifications because of the peculiarity of the theological subject.

We said that theological study would not make its way without the integration of points of view from social philosophy and sociology, or, to put it more generally, from "secular" philosophy and science. This negative definition is an assured result of the early Bonhoeffer's whole undertaking, for his effort is certainly no playing with ideas. His concern, too, is not to examine, as some game or side-interest, whether sociological categories can be applied in each case to the phenomenon of the Church, without coming in conflict in so doing with the fundamental assertions of dogmatic ecclesiology. He is passionately in earnest on his subject, and both the putting of his questions and the carrying out of his work betray that he knew himself to be upon a necessary and unavoidable path of theological thought. This is shown also in his preface, written more than three years later, where he again emphasizes the primarily theological character of his essay in social philosophy and sociology:

"This study places social philosophy and sociology in the service of dogmatics. Only by this means did the structure of the Christian church as a community seem to yield itself to systematic understanding. The subject under discussion belongs to dogmatics, not to the sociology of religion. The inquiry into Christian social philosophy and sociology is a genuinely dogmatic one, since it can be answered only if our starting-point is the concept of the Church. The more theologians have considered the significance of the sociological category for theology, the more clearly the social intention of all the basic Christian concepts has emerged. Ideas such as 'person', 'primal state', 'sin', and 'revelation' are fully understandable only in relation to sociality" (SC, p. 13).

Two things are obviously emphasized here, on the one side factually, the essentially social aspect of the whole complex of theological themes, and on the other methodologically, that these will only yield to "systematic understanding" with the help

of "secular" ways of thinking. It seems to me that the same factual and methodological concern is seen again in the Bonhoeffer
of the latest period, championed with the same, or rather
with still greater, passion. It is seen in the vehement anti-
individualism of the postulate of non-religious interpretation,
as developed in *Letters and Papers from Prison*. To interpret
individualistically what is Christian is to interpret it merely
religiously and in so doing to miss its meaning. For there is a
"structure of the Christian church as a community" belonging
unalterably to its nature, a "social intention" running through
all the themes given by the revelation of God. On the other
hand, as far as the methodological side is concerned, the whole
theological programme of non-religious interpretation means
just this, that contact is sought with the reality of human
being and of the world which surrounds it, contact is sought
resolutely and systematically in the style of one's theological
thought, in the language of proclamation, but above all in the
behaviour of the Christian witness, the believer in the world.
The theme of faith must not be seen as an "ideological" superstructure of illusory religion, built over the reality of our life
in human society, a superstructure operating by means of
assertions and living on assertions about a "world beyond",
a superstructure whose one relation to reality consists in the
satisfaction of one-sided needs of a religious type, still cherished
certainly by individuals, but on the average to be presupposed
ever less and less today. Both preaching and theology, in their
attitude and even in the framing of their theological and kerygmatic language, must take in earnest to the uttermost reality
as it is lived, in order that that to which they testify may on its
side be seen as a reality to be taken in earnest, a reality which is
palpable and powerfully invasive, a reality which transforms
reality. It must be so intelligibly and credibly for all who have
ears to hear, and not as some illusion which with a good conscience can be regarded as indifferent and irrelevant. Hence
this subject-matter of theology must also be authenticated
step by step by reality.[4]

[4] There does not seem to me to be any contradiction here to what Jürgen
Moltmann, in *The Theology of Hope*, tr. Leitch, S.C.M., 1967, says about "hope's
statements" as the specific form of theological statement. For example, he
writes, "The truth of doctrinal statements is found in the fact that they can

Biographically, the urge towards such a verification of the gospel may be connected with the fact that Bonhoeffer grew up in a completely secular environment and, as the youngest of the family, made a quite personal resolve for the study of theology, to the amazement, which could easily have been distaste, of the others. This background set him at the starting-point of his own peculiar theological path, in that it gave him an urge to an apologetic which was not artificial and in the last resort away from the facts, but drove to a better understanding of the facts themselves and to verification by understanding. This drive is already in its pioneering stages in his earliest theological works, and finds expression in a thrilling way in his latest theological utterances. *Letters and Papers*

---

be shown to agree with the existing reality which we can all experience. Hope's statements of promise, however, must stand in contradiction to the reality which can at present be experienced. They do not result from experiences, but are the condition of the possibility of new experiences. They do not seek to illuminate the reality which exists, but the reality which is coming. They do not seek to make a mental picture of existing reality, but to lead existing reality towards the promised and hoped-for transformation. They do not seek to bear the train of reality, but to carry the torch for it" (p. 18). Or, "Creative activity springing from faith is impossible without new thinking and planning that springs from hope. For our knowledge and comprehension of reality, and our reflections on it, that means at least this, that in the medium of hope our theological concepts become, not judgements which nail down reality to what it is, but anticipations which show reality its prospects and its future responsibilities. Theological concepts do not give a fixed form to reality, but they are expanded by hope and anticipate future being" (pp. 35f.). With this characterization of theological speech I can completely agree. Certainly the dimension of the future belongs to the reality which faith has to articulate theologically, and does so, not as a dimension which merely forms part, but as one which determines the whole. But the hope which theology has to articulate is just the hope for *this* reality in so far as it concerns us. It has to be added further that in any case our involvement in reality does not have the character of pure facticity, pure present or past, but always of itself includes within itself the dimension of the future. Reality, in so far as it concerns us, always poses us a question which only the future can answer "creatively". In *Herméneutique et Eschatologie*, in *Archivio di Filosofia*, 1 e 2, Rome, 1963, pp. 105ff., and in *Was ist Wirklichkeit?*, in *Deutsches Pfarrerblatt*, 14, 1964, pp. 369ff., I have sought to bring out this aspect of the real. Bonhoeffer, too, becomes a witness for us here, where in LPP, p. 112 he speaks of the restoration of all things through Christ, and thereby thinks of reality as sketched in Christ. The "hope's statements" in this case will have to integrate reality as it now concerns us, without being committed thereby to a present or past aspect of reality. The verification of theological statements by reference to reality itself proves right also in that it thereby becomes clear how far faith "transforms the world", or better, "*this* world", and does not merely take steps to transform it.

from Prison and *Ethics* are one single drive towards reality, to a reality which is nobody and nothing other than Jesus Christ himself, but which at the same time is the reality which palpably surrounds us and which undeniably and unavoidably concerns us.

The motive is the same at the beginning and at the end of the road, but at the end Bonhoeffer surpasses and excels himself in face of the hard and compelling reality of the atheistic generation. Had the late and extremist project of a non-religious interpretation succeeded in a positive working out (for what we find in the prison letters is at most the beginnings of a positive working out), the methodological approach of the doctoral dissertation could most surely have been adopted for the purpose. For it was a deep-seated striving for the integration of secularly phenomenological ways of thinking in the more comprehensive phenomenology of theology, a striving for phenomenological evidence of the significance, the relevance to reality, of all that is to be said of Jesus Christ as testimony, and was this step by step, always entering into the phenomenon directly before him, directly at issue, in its divine-human form, avoiding the form of general assertions which oppose a world beyond to reality as a whole, treating reality as some lump sum which has been commuted for, or interpreting man in general in terms of his existential fallenness and weakness, in order to solve his boundary problems when it is thought that he has reached the limits of his being. Non-religious interpretation will have to show that the gospel of Christ enters step by step, aspect by aspect, into the reality lived by us, experienced by us, and given to us as our task. For this reason it cannot thrust aside any non-theological illumination of the realm of this reality, be it philosophical or scientific. In this sense *Sanctorum Communio* is already something towards the exposition of the non-religious interpretation demanded and proclaimed in *Letters and Papers from Prison*.

Again, we understand better in this context the charge of *revelational positivism* which in the interests of non-religious interpretation Bonhoeffer directed against the Barthian theology. In his view what it precisely does not do is to expound the subject of Christian theology step by step in constant contact with reality, gradually discovering the relation to reality and following out "the stages of significance"; rather it sets up a dogmatic system *en bloc*. It is clear here that "revelational positivistic" thought has no need of the integration of secular ways of thinking into dogmatics, because it is already conceptually, and not merely existentially, certain of its facts before any proof. At the same time, out of the comparison and the mutually enlightening interpretations of *Sanctorum Communio* and *Letters and Papers from Prison*, there is growing for us a positive indication for defining the relation of theology and philosophy. It is already clear in the dissertation, both in this respect and as a whole, that the theological path which Bonhoeffer is to tread is from the very beginning a different one from that of Karl Barth, in spite of all strong influence and indebtedness, and in spite of all unity in the last resort in subject-matter. And the way is already prepared in his doctoral dissertation for the final factual definition and radicalizing in Bonhoeffer's thought. The road as a whole shows such an astonishing unity.

3. *The Category of the "Collective Person"*

An essential, yes, perhaps the decisive component in the whole complex of thought about the *"communio sanctorum"* is that of the "collective person". It is somewhat difficult to place. It is certainly illustrated from theological points of view by Bonhoeffer in *Sanctorum Communio*, and yet it surely cannot be claimed as the object of purely theological knowledge. On the other hand, it cannot be demonstrated purely empirically, by bringing forward empirical statistical evidence, and therefore one could not attribute it to sociology. One could ascribe it most easily to social philosophy, to philosophical thinking about the phenomenon of human sociability, or about existence in fellowship on the basis of generally accessible empirical factual solutions.

"If the subject of sin is at once the individual and the race, what is the form of sociological unity suitable for the mankind of Adam? This reintroduces the question of the ethical personality of collective persons . . . which determines whether there is any meaning in the idea of a collective person. Is it possible to regard the collective person as an ethical person, that is, place it in the concrete situation of being addressed by a Thou? If so, then we shall have proved that it is a centre of action" (SC, p. 82).

The question, then, whether it has any meaning to employ the concept of "collective person" at all, and to develop thoughts by using this concept, is decided by a definite experience which we can call the ethical experience. Bonhoeffer, as we shall see, verifies it with examples drawn from life, from ethical existence in the light of revelation. But this is not to say that this experience is unintelligible and not to be expected beyond the realm of Christendom, not even when on the other hand the experience only receives in the light of revelation its final interpretation and confirmation.

One must have the relevant experience to understand it. This is no entity which can be empirically established and demonstrated; it can only be achieved in the undertaking of personal responsibility, in the responsible undertaking of one's own ethical existence. None the less, to have the experience is to be able to speak about it thereafter and to interpret it. On the basis of this experience, then, the concept of "collective person" can appear meaningful, can even force itself upon one.

"The meaning and reality of such a call can be comprehended only by one who, as a part of an empirical community, has experienced it. It is the Israelite concept of the people of God, which arose solely through being thus challenged by God, by the prophets, by the course of political history and by alien peoples. The call is to the collective person, and not to the individual. It is the people that is to do penance as the people of God. It was the people, and not the individuals who had sinned ... When peoples are called, God's will is seen shaping history, just as when the individual is called, he experiences his history ... God does not only have eyes for the nation; he has a purpose for every smallest community, for every friendship, every marriage, every family. And in this same sense he has a purpose for the church too. It is not only individual Germans and individual Christians who are guilty; Germany and the church are guilty too. Here the contrition and justification of individuals is of no avail; Germany and the church themselves must repent and be justified. The community which is from God to God ... stands in God's sight, and does not dissolve into the fate of the many ... It is clear that this can happen only 'in' the individual. Only thus can the hearing of the call be concretely comprehended, and yet it is not the individuals, but the collective person (*Gesamtheit*) who, in the individuals, hears, repents and believes. The centre of action lies in the collective person" (SC, pp. 82f.).

The thought which appears here could be called a crucial point for Bonhoeffer's thought. Here there meet different lines which are characteristic for his view of revelation and reality. There is first his understanding of history which begins at this point and can be understood from it. He believes, as we can clearly see, especially in his latest writings, in a divine guiding of history. For him there is a meaning and a goal, a judgement and a grace of God in world history, and these are for peoples and not only for individuals. An understanding of history and salvation with an individualistic stamp, such as we meet with in Rudolf Bultmann, and, so far as I can see, in what is called the Bultmann school to date,[5] cannot achieve this thought. This faith in a guidance and providence of God in history, which, as we have yet to see (cp. Chapter Seven), is for Bonhoeffer essential and indispensable, is obviously most closely connected with this structural component of the collective person. This picture of history, impossible on the basis of an individualistic understanding of man and the ethical, depends on the collective category. There is a God-given history for the peoples, for the greater and smaller communities, even, as Bonhoeffer says immediately after the passage just quoted, for mankind as a whole, a continuous track, meaningful in itself, of collective history, because there are collective persons with their own ethical personality.

It follows from this that what is said about collective persons is not merely an isolated statement on an individual point, but a category and a structural component which opens a pathway, or a whole area, of thought about the relevant phenomena.[6]

[5] Cp. Bultmann's important book, *History and Eschatology*, (Eng. edn., E.U.P., 1957), and especially its final chapter, "Christian Faith and History", pp. 138ff. The final passage (pp. 154f.) gives explicit witness. Only for individuals can there be a meaning to history!

[6] When here and in what follows I use the concepts "category" and "categorial", category is not meant as something opposed to "existential", as Heidegger distinguishes them in *Being and Time*. "Category" has here a more comprehensive significance, embracing both poles. Properly speaking "collective person" is an "existential category" or an "existential".

Thought is stamped by it in a certain way, and receives new prospects and possibilities. We must use both of the terms, "category" and "structural component". We are dealing with a category in the concept of the collective person, in conformity with which human phenomena are thought of, and at the same time with a structural component, which as such is one of the elements constitutive for the phenomena, and can be recognized in them. In the study of these questions, then, we must treat seriously the character of the concept of the collective person as a concept both categorial and structural, and not simply judge it by unconsidered presuppositions based on another group of categories, for example an individualistic group, the only consequence of which could be that the concept would be rejected through short-sightedness.

When Bonhoeffer says, "The community which is from God to God ... stands in God's sight, and does not dissolve into the fate of the many", perhaps the decisive assertion of the whole train of thought (!), or when he says that "God's will in shaping history" is there manifested where a call, a claim, is made upon a collective, that is to say, when he bases the concept of a "collective person" on the confrontation of that collective person by God, the question naturally arises if this concept or this category is completely dependent upon faith in God, and if it falls to the ground without this presupposition. But it is surely to be maintained that the experience of a communal responsibility and a communal guilt does not depend upon any premise, but forces itself upon us immediately as reality, and, in any case, can in itself be existentially conceived, experienced and expected. I can summon anyone to a collective responsibility or a collective sense of guilt, regardless of whether or not he believes in God. Of course I risk his declaring, "I wash my hands of the matter; I was not concerned in it!", or his replying "What has that to do with me? That is the concern of others!" But such a risk is always there in making an ethical appeal, and is not an argument against its reasonableness. And it will happen again and again that men who do not believe in God will bow to the claims of a collective responsibility or collective guilt, seeing it as a presupposition of life.

Bonhoeffer's concept of the collective person does not lead to collectivism in a bad sense of the word. For him it is clear that the collective person is only real in individuals and through individuals and comes to life in their responsibility. The individual must observe and recognize in his own existence the collective responsibility and the collective guilt. There is not beside and in addition to the individuals another, a communal, spirit with its own personality which can take away the moral duty from the individuals and absolve them of it. "And yet it is not the individuals, but the collective person who, in the individuals, hears, repents and believes. The centre of action lies in the collective person". This concept of the centre of action is for Bonhoeffer the description of the essence of the "person". Its serviceability and appropriateness would properly require further examination. But what is definite is that the individual remains involved as a free moral subject. What is equally definite on the other hand is that the individuals are involved in a way which cannot be understood if we begin from the number of individuals as the primary moral datum. The fact of collective responsibility and collective guilt is not simply a moral thought which lives in the single moral individuals and is the cause in them of moral acts. It is not a pure "ought" which is active only in the being of individual entities. The collective person is not simply an "ought" or a complex of "oughts", which in reality, that is, as an entity, is "not there". As can be shown also from the *Ethics*, the strict separation of "is" and "ought" is foreign to this thinking. The collective person has completely the character of a reality. It is an entity. But this reality is not to be thought of as a reality *beside* that of the individuals, but as one *in* them. And this "in" does not mean that the collective person is something like a "part" of the whole of the individual person, but that the moral existence of the individual as such and as a whole is determined by the claim arising from the collective person. When it is said and when it happens that "the collective person ... in the individuals, hears, repents, and believes", this is a claim which comes from the collective person and determines the existence of the individual. That individuals repent for the people means that the claim which comes from the collective guilt of the collective person determines the existence of these individuals. In itself it determines the existence of all moral individuals in the relevant collective person, but it becomes effective, and reaches its goal and its fulfilment, in the few who repent. One might possibly think that this simply implied judgement upon the many who do not repent, which would mean individualism setting itself for the last time as an obstacle in the way of this train of thought, for then the concern would in the last resort not be with the whole but with the atonement or judgement of individuals. This must not be excluded, but Bonhoeffer's thought takes another course. To him, that the few repent for the whole means that the sin of the whole, and hence also the sin of the many who do not repent, can be atoned for. Thus Bonhoeffer overcomes the last obstacle which individualism and individualistic thinking in ethics form. But what he says on this only become intelligible with the help of the thought of representation. And this is what will enable us at the same time to measure the whole depth and breadth of his thought.

For determining the relation between the collective person and the individual, that same "in", the *concept of a structural component* again offers a helpful instrument. The collective person is a structural component in the existence of the individual, though not in any sense that the existence of the individual is the exclusive place in which the component of the collective person can find life and subsist. Rather the component of the collective person marks in a certain sense an *extra nos*, a historical factual situation, in which the existence of the individual, the single person, first finds itself as such. Further, this component is also historical in the sense that on each occasion it is not only an "associated extra" to the existence of the individual with this structure, but means a historical claim upon the latter. As a historically existing individual I participate in one or more collective persons, and I exist historically as an individual only by virtue of this participation. I am a member of a family, of a people and of humanity. But this participation is not so simply personal to myself as is the colour of my eyes or the abilities of my intellect. It is given to me and laid upon me as a constant *claim*, that I should know myself and regard myself as in solidarity with the collective person, because and in so far as I begin by being in such solidarity. And yet that this is given me and laid upon me does not imply that it has the nature of a *superadditum*. Without what I have been given and have laid upon me I would not be what I am as an individual. This simply implies that its being is that of a structural component or existential. To this extent one can speak of primacy of the collective person, since it constitutes the historical being of the individual as such. On the other hand, as Bonhoeffer makes clear, the collective person is orientated towards the individual existence, since only in it is it brought to life. If we should wish to use here the old ontological concept of subsistence, the relation is not that the collective person subsists in the individual, whether as accident or as *proprium*, but neither is it that the collective person in any way subsists in itself apart from the other. As a matter of fact this double stipulation may serve as evidence that the traditional ontological formalism of substance and accidence, of substantiality and subsistence, which has put its stamp upon theology from of old, in Christology for example, is not adequate to comprehend the personal reality of existence, whether it be the existence of God and of man in the light of revelation, or whether it be quite simply existence as an everyday phenomenon. An individualistic ethic and anthropology, and a theology which consciously or unconsciously bases itself upon these, surely always thinks too substantially on this point.

4. *The Concept of Representation*

The concept of the collective person, which has such significance for Bonhoeffer's anthropology and ethics, and in consequence for his Christology also, indeed for all his dogmatic theology, could not be worked out without the concept of representation.

The governing context here is expounded by Bonhoeffer as follows:

"The 'people' is to repent, but it is not a question of the number who repent, and in practice it will never be the whole people, the whole church, but God can so regard it 'as if' the whole people has repented. 'For the sake of ten I will not destroy it' (Gen. 18: 32). He can see the whole people in a few individuals, just as he saw and reconciled the whole of mankind in one man. Here the problem of vicarious action arises . . . When the collective person is addressed ('He who has an ear, let him hear what the Spirit says to the churches'—Rev. 2 and 3), the conscience of each individual person is addressed. Each person, however, has only one conscience, which is valid for him both as a member of the collective person, and as an individual. For there are not two strata in man, one social and one private; a man is structurally a unity ... He must know himself and make decisions as an inner unity, must not therefore blindly subject himself to the concrete claims of the collective person, but struggle through to an integrated decision of the will" (SC, pp. 83f.).

The category or the existential of the collective person is dependent upon the fact that representation is possible. Were it not, a claim could be made upon individuals only on the grounds of their individual guilt or responsibility. Since of course in Bonhoeffer's presentation we do not have to think of a collective person as in any way hypostasized, there would then be only any number of individual persons with strictly limited individual responsibilities. Then one would also have to ask further at this point if the *phenomenon of responsibility*, that primary phenomenon of existence, could be suitably grasped and described on such an individualistic basis. Perhaps the very endeavour to understand the phenomenon of responsibility purely as a phenomenon drives us on to think the thought of the collective person.

In his *Ethics* Bonhoeffer also explains the necessary structural connection between the collective person, or representation, and responsibility in the following way:

"The fact that responsibility is fundamentally a matter of deputyship is demonstrated most clearly in those circumstances in which a man is directly obliged to act in the place of other men, for example as a father, as a statesman or as a teacher. The father acts for the children, working for them, caring for them, interceding, fighting and suffering for them. Thus in a real sense he is their deputy. He is not an isolated individual, but he combines in himself the selves of a number of human beings. Any attempt to live as though he were alone is a denial of the actual fact of his responsibility. He cannot evade the responsibility which is laid upon him with his paternity. This reality shatters the fiction that the subject, the performer, of all ethical conduct is the isolated individual. Not the individual in isolation but the responsible man is the subject, the agent, with whom ethical reflexion must concern itself. This principle is not affected by the extent of the responsibility assumed, whether it be for a single human being, for a community or for whole groups of communities. No man can altogether escape responsibility, and this means that no man can avoid deputyship" (E, pp. 194f.).

Responsibility, according to this, is essentially representation. If there were no existential of the collective person and representation, the individual could perhaps do something for individuals. One could not, however, adequately think how far the individual *is* responsible for others even before he does anything, so that what he does may appear as merely the fulfilment or the realization of such responsibility.

In her delightful and brilliant book, *Christ the Representative. An Essay in Theology after the Death of God*, tr. Lewis, S.C.M., 1967, Dorothée Solle, *inter alia*, opposes Bonhoeffer's concept of representation (cp. pp. 92ff.). According to her he thinks more appropriately and more personally of representation than does Karl Barth, for whom "representation" really only means "replacement", and Christ as our perfect representative is fundamentally the substitute who does not truly *represent* us but rather "forces" and "replaces" us (cp. pp. 88ff.). And yet, she says, Bonhoeffer none the less still thinks of the existential event of representation in too one-sided a way.

Frau Solle regards the complete structure of representation in this way, ". . . Dependence and responsibility—according to whether the standpoint is that of the one represented or the representative. We experience representation when we are dependent on another or on others, and when we bear responsibility for another or for others. The two aspects belong inseparably together. The moment either aspect is divorced from its dialectical correlate, both personality and temporality are in danger. An absolutized dependence can at any time involve the reduction of the person to immaturity, while a responsibility which is exclusive can become an undisguised tyranny exercised by some over others" (p. 56).

According to her Barth absolutizes in a one-sided way the dependence upon Christ the representative of the man who is represented, or in truth then "replaced". Bonhoeffer, on the contrary, absolutizes the responsibility of the man who as representative acts responsibly for others, the Church, for example, acting for the world. He only succeeds in thinking of representation as responsibility. "Dependence, its indispensable correlate, vanishes, and the ethics of responsible representation must either be given dogmatic basis—because Christ represented us, therefore our life is intended to be representation—or else it collapses into itself"

(p. 94). Representative service by the man responsible for others then threatens to become a hidden lordship, which manipulates others and respects too little their personality.

Certainly reference is rightly made to the demarcation which Bonhoeffer succeeds in making to remove the danger. "The danger that the responsible party will absolutize his own function was clearly recognized by Bonhoeffer, who therefore sought to limit responsibility in two ways. On the one hand, responsibility will be limited by the neighbour, who is or who will become capable of personal responsibility; and on the other hand it is limited by God who is the final judge of our actions and of their unforeseeable consequences . . . There is no such thing as 'absolute responsibility,' a responsibility without limits" (p. 95). Yet in my opinion Frau Solle has not taken sufficiently seriously these demarcations of Bonhoeffer's when she passes over them with this statement about them, "But is it really possible to mark off such limits—God and the neighbour—objectively?" (p. 95), and in support of this merely repeats once more the doubts she has already expressed as regards Bonhoeffer's understanding of representation. For what in the first place does "mark off objectively" mean here? The fact is that our responsibility, which structurally must be defined as representation, is limited by the responsibility of our neighbour and the responsibility of God. Bonhoeffer saw this clearly, even if in his fragmentary work it is true that it is not yet adequately worked out. We might add that in this limiting of our responsible existence we could truthfully find included that moment of "dependence" which he missed.

She also seems to me to have missed the mark when she says about the structure of representation in Bonhoeffer: "Bonhoeffer does not indeed attempt to understand this structure in anthropological terms, but explains it *a priori* in christological terms . . . The christological explanation remains obscure. It is simply taken for granted as being axiomatic. In phenomenological terms the statement would need to read: because all life demands representation, and without it hardens into a dead, replaceable thing, Christ, in meeting this demand, is in fact 'the life'. Bonhoeffer's thought does not move from below upwards, from the anthropological reality to the christological event, indeed he disqualifies such thinking as 'religious' " (pp. 93f.). But Bonhoeffer does throughout know something of representation as an anthropological phenomenon. The true factual situation as regards him seems to me rather this, that he thinks neither one-sidedly "from above" nor one-sidedly "from below", but that representation as an anthropological phenomenon and representation as a theological structural component meet as it were in the middle and mutually explain one another.

There is no doubt that Frau Sölle, in her analysis of the structure of representation, has said something worthy of the greatest consideration for the understanding of the phenomenon of "lived representation" among men. But I cannot regard the analysis so much as a criticism as rather an explanation and a closer definition of Bonhoeffer's thoughts on representation.

For *Christology*, too, this book, in which she "proposes to examine one of the oldest titles of Christ, the title of Representative" (p. 13), seems to me extraordinarily fruitful. And it is so above all in this closer definition, that representation, as a personal event, never means "replacement". The "replacement" forces himself in, and takes the place of the one replaced, but the representative on the contrary keeps the place of the represented man *open* for the time when it is needed. But the individual man is irreplaceable—and yet, it is true, representable. And he has need of a representative, for "the very fact that a man's life is not completely contained in his present success or failure, but always includes an element that is still future, means that he needs representation" (p. 102). Thus Christ is not, as a "Christocratic perfectionism" would have it, the universal replacement of all men, but their representative. "But Christ represents us only for a time, conditionally and incompletely. Christ does not substitute himself for us; he represents us for a time. And this must be mentioned in opposition to all forms of christocratic perfectionism. We remain irreplaceable precisely because we need him as a representative. He who in our place believes, hopes and lives—and who therefore does what we have failed to do—does not obliterate us in that nothing now depends on us. Christ does not replace our life, making us superfluous, not counted on by anyone any longer ... God is not content with our representative. Our representative speaks for us, but we ourselves have to learn to speak. He believes for us, but we ourselves have to learn how to believe" (pp. 103f.).

As we define more closely in this way our understanding of representation, further questions are raised in Christology. It seems to me in fact in this connection that the thought of the "complete representative" has one justified component, which does not in any way lead to that "perfectionism", and which has perhaps been overlooked by Frau Sölle. The representative Christ does not only hold a place open for us until the time comes when it is our turn. For it *is* already our turn. But yet Christ also stands in our place as the "condition of the possibility" of what we have nevertheless to do. "I live, yet not I, but Christ lives in me" (Gal. 2: 20)! Here the trinitarian character of the event of Christ comes into view. Christ embraces us, or rather, we are embraced by God through Christ. But Christ also stands with us and for us at the time, and exactly at the time, when we ourselves do what God is waiting for. Here also there arises the question of *Christus praesens*, about which Bonhoeffer was so concerned.

The further question also arises how Christ the representative represents those who have died in tragedy and immaturity. Once again we come face to face here with the theological terms, *"Christus praesens"* and "eternal life", both of which have been provided for us beforehand by tradition. Both of these theological terms, regarded by many as "objectifying" and "metaphysical", demand imperiously at this point entry into the thinking of existential interpretation, if the latter is not to become some ideological exercise. The two surely form the point at which it will be decided whether this "Theology after the 'Death of God' " which has been expounded on the subject of representation remains Christological, or whether, certainly contrary to the intention and the splendid inspiration of the authoress, it takes a wrong turning into the purely ideological. The question is if the thought of Jesus as representative for men is carried through to the end, that is, if Jesus as *Christus praesens* is a living reality for the existence of all men, or if his power in history is to be thought of as in the last resort merely that of an idea continuing to be effective in history, and reaching some men and not others.

Further, it does seem to me that in this, to which she has given what I feel to be the unfortunate title of "Death of God", what is for our epoch, clearly though it is expounded, is yet thought out too little in the finality and historicity of real epochal thinking, and too much rather in the limitedness of an artificial historical survey.

"God has changed. What happened to Moses at the burning bush belongs to an irrevocable past. What St. Francis felt and experienced is no longer open to us to experience as something immediate. Luther's anxieties can be explained by the psycho-analyst and stripped of their unconditionality ... The Christ who represents God has come into the world in such a way that his representation is now the only possible experience of God; a religious experience but not in the usual sense of one which culminates in a direct experience of the holy, of the *fascinans* and the *tremendum*" (pp. 140f.). It is true that the old, direct, "religious" experience of God still continues to live, within and without Christianity, but, she claims, it is superfluous, not obligatory (pp. 141f.). But does this not mean that we who have experienced the "death of God" are first to have really experienced Christ? But in that case are we not claiming to pass a judgement on the experience of God and Christ of past epochs in Christendom, a judgement which is not incumbent upon us? Would not then God mediated through Christ have been truly present to St. Francis also in what he experienced "religiously" in the manner of his epoch? Epochal thinking, aware of its historicity, would have to content itself with experiencing and articulating the manner in which God encounters *us* and makes himself open to experience for *us* in *our* epoch and leave to the freedom of God how he has dealt and how he will deal with men of another epoch.

Without the possibility of representation it would only be possible to charge the individual with what he had done and with what, in the narrow sector of his life and individual interest, he could and should do. Were one to direct, say, to an individual the demand that he should do something or sacrifice something for the community to which he belonged, one might well parry the complaint "Why must it be me?" with the well-known compelling question, "What would happen if all were to take up that attitude?" But the power of this question only reaches to the point where what is demanded of all is effectively the same or proportionate to their power of achievement, as for example in the payment of taxes. If the individual freely presents a special achievement of a special sacrifice, we are already on another plane. But this can only be understood meaningfully if it can be assumed that the individual acts or suffers representatively for the community.[7] It certainly is quite possible that occasionally a man, out of egoistic altruism or altruistic egoism, it may be out of that lovable disposition which makes it a joy to serve others and give joy, may freely take upon himself more than he is responsible for. But the phenomenon of great, or for that matter of small or at least inconspicuous, actions and sufferings for the community

[7] In Catholic spirituality we meet in this context with the thought of *sacrifice*. The representative sacrifice of the individual for others or for a cause still appears as meaningful when and where there is no apparent causal connection. It takes place then in a way in the "medium" of God, or in the medium of the reality of the Church, in which indeed God himself is also involved. It can, for instance, only be explained in the light of this piety that John XXIII should understand his death as a sacrifice for the Council (Cp. on this Louis Capovilla, *The Heart and Mind of John XXIII*, tr. Reilly, Corgi Books, 1966).

cannot be adequately accounted for in this way. For here the individual involves himself, not, or not primarily, because it gives him joy, but occasionally even in spite of the fact that it gives him no joy, because he knows the command of the hour. He involves himself of necessity and not as a luxury. He judges the challenge directed to the collective person as directed to himself, and the response which he makes is the response of the collective person. If there were no such representation, if it were not meaningful and in face of the phenomena necessary, to assume it, no collective person could be addressed, no collective person could reply, in other words, to speak of a collective person would be nonsense.[8]

Now it is true that in Bonhoeffer's context the thought of representation proves itself a Christological one. And in addition the meaning of representation is based upon the fact that "God can so regard the matter as if . . .". At first sight it will appear again as if it were only possible to conceive the thought of representation on the basis of a definite Christian, or at least "theistic" premise, as if then it were not recognized in the phenomenon, but planted within the phenomenon by a certain religious doctrine. But the appearance is deceptive; the thought of representation forces itself upon us everywhere out of the reality in which we live, the reality of responsible life. Representation is in point of fact interpreted by Bonhoeffer in terms of God and in the last resort Christologically. And it does permit of such an interpretation and in the last resort perhaps demands it. But in the first instance representation can be experienced directly in responsible life, and is to a certain degree, as I have already shown to be true also of the reality of the collective person, existentially discernible in experience. It is experienced, for example, when I take upon myself a challenge and a necessity which is laid upon the community to which I belong, and involve myself without seeing evidence first as to whether others are doing the same. But this means that I will not furnish merely my own proportional share of what has to be done, and will not merely be ready, freely and without neces-

[8] The sociologically examinable entity of the "mass" is distinguished from the collective person by the fact that the mass has no ethical personality and that for it no representation is possible. The mass may have an idol or a demagogue, who hypnotizes it by speaking in terms of its collective drive, a responsible representative it has not.

sity, but that I will know myself called to act for all as a representative. I will then also be able to renounce the right to expect reward or thanks for what I have done for all. Reward and thanks are a luxury. They are not necessary to compensate my special personal achievement and thus restore everything to a correct balance once more. For my deed is not in fact my special personal achievement, an extra performance of mine, on which as support I can afterwards base a claim for something as a special compensation. But it is an act for the community and thereby an act of the community. For what I do for the community none of the others is under any obligation to me. The community has already met its obligation in my person and through my representative action. Reward and thanks may follow as a recognition, but they do not belong to the essence of the matter, as anyone who acts representatively knows. In some such way we gain insight into the reality of representation. And in saying so we include, and do not exclude, the fact that its deepest, clearest and most intelligible interpretation is that which is in terms of God and Christological.

5. *Intercession and the Forgiveness of Sins as Realizations of Representation and the Collective Person*

But such representation, as an existentially experienced reality which makes possible and demands the existential of the collective person, is seen by Bonhoeffer again in a quite special way as the event taking place in the community. The Christian Church is in a special way constituted through representation. This is shown above all in the events of intercession and forgiveness of sins in the community, but also in "renunciatory, active work for our neighbour".

> "With all of them it is a question of abandoning oneself 'for' one's neighbour, for his good, but with the readiness to do and bear everything in his stead, indeed if need be to sacrifice oneself for him, to act *vicariously* for him. Even if purely vicarious action is seldom actualized, the intention to achieve it is contained in every genuine act of love" (SC, p. 130).

Intercession has a social structure and is only to be thought of in terms of representation. Bonhoeffer quotes on this point Exodus 32 : 32, where Moses seeks to be blotted out of the book of life together with his people, and the analogous text in St. Paul (Romans 9: 19), who would be accursed for the sake of his brothers. "This is a paradox of the law of God which it is hard to resolve" (SC, p. 131). We have a reference here to an experience of faith which also appears later in mysticism,[9] and for which, it appears to me, a new sensitivity is growing in the situation of modern Christendom.[10] It must strike us that the 20-year-old Bonhoeffer is already quoting these passages, for the same *motif* of an extremely anti-individualist Christianity meets us again in his latest utterances, for example where he expresses the opinion, at first sight shocking, that the question of the personal salvation of our souls had become almost completely a matter of indifference to us—and rightly so! (cp. on this Chapter Three, Section 8). Again we see here the astonishing unity in the progress of his thought. As far as the Biblical figures quoted are concerned, what he says is:

"Fundamentally this describes the kind of abyss into which the individual can be drawn by his prayer of intercession. The problem of the social structure consists in the question of how we must conceive of the relationship of those who are praying for one another, and here the universal basis must be sought in the fact that the church leads one life, and that the individual has communion with God only if he takes part in this life . . ."

"Every intercession potentially draws the one for whom it is intended into the church . . . A third person is drawn into my solitary relation with God, or rather, I move in intercession into the other man's place, when my prayer remains my own, but nevertheless springs from his distress and need; I really enter into

[9] So for example Meister Eckhart, "God gives also when he does not give,—for instance when a man knows how to renounce what he wants to receive for the sake of God's will, after the manner of the text, 'I would wish myself to be accursed by Christ for the same of my brothers' " (*Kommentar zum Johannes-Evangelium, Latein. Werke*, III, p. 67).

[10] This Karl Rahner, in *The Christian of the Future*, tr. O'Hara, Burns and Oates, 1967, in *The Teaching of Vatican II on the Church and the Future Reality of the Christian Life*, p. 93, contrasts in the following words the understanding of a former age on salvation and the Church with that of today, confirmed by the Second Vatican Council, "If Francis Xavier told his Japanese questioners that their ancestors were in hell, and they answered that they did not aim at any better lot for themselves, the story really sums up the whole problem, the progress which has been made in actual awareness of the faith since the sixteenth century, as well as the respective missionary advantages and disadvantages of both attitudes."

the other man, into his guilt and distress; I am afflicted by his sins and his infirmity" (SC, pp. 131ff.).

In the *forgiveness of sins* the same happens.

"This has brought us already to the final problem, the one giving us deepest insight into the miracle of the Church. This miracle is that one man, by the prerogative of his priesthood, can forgive sins . . . No one can forgive sins but he who takes them upon himself, bears them and cancels them; thus Christ alone can do it. But this means that the Church, as the *sanctorum communio*, can forgive sins. The individual can do it only if he is a member of the church, and as a member he should do it. He relieves the other's conscience of its guilt and lays it upon himself, but this he can do only by laying it in turn upon Christ. His action is thus possible only in the church . . .

"The church is thus able to bear the guilt that none of its members can. It can bear more guilt than all its members together. This being so it must be a spiritual reality extending beyond the sum of all individuals. Not the sum of all the individuals, but the church as a totality is in Christ, is the 'Body of Christ', is '*Christ existing as the church*' " (SC, pp. 134f.).

Here Bonhoeffer makes his decisive formulation, "*Christ existing as a community*".[11] Christ himself is the community and the community Christ, "It has itself died and risen with Christ and is now the *nova creatura* in Christ. It is not only a means to an end, but at the same time an end in itself, it is the presence of Christ himself, and that is why 'being in Christ' and 'being in the Church' are one and the same thing" (SC, p. 135). In support of what he says about the community as the place of the forgiveness of sins and the bearer of that forgiveness, about its authority to forgive sins, Bonhoeffer refers to St. Augustine, and especially Luther, ". . . as we divest ourselves of all grief and temptation and lay it upon the Church, and especially upon Christ . . . all my misfortune is now shared by Christ and the saints" (WA, II, p. 745, quoted SC, p. 135; E.T. as given there). In the forgiveness of sins as in intercession I take the place of the other. I take his guilt upon me, and I am able to do so because I am no longer I alone, but completely

---

[11] Bonhoeffer marks this expression with the words, "We thus modify Hegel's concept" (SC, p. 134), i.e., the concept "God existing as a community" as the concept of the Christian Church in Hegel's philosophy of religion.

and entirely in the community of Christ, embedded in it, and a participant in its life. So I stand as representative in place of the other, as does the community as representative in my place, and Jesus Christ himself as representative in place of the community. All my misfortune is shared, not with Christ only, but with Christ and his saints. For these are now inseparable from Christ.[12] Thus the peculiarly and quite essentially social structure of the Church, determined by representation, comes to view and is made intelligible in the light of the structural component of responsible existence which meets us empirically, can be experienced and to some degree analysed by sociology and existential analysis.

6. *"Christ Existing as a Community"*

The group of facts expressed in the formula, "Christ existing as a Community", form one of the leading elements in Dietrich Bonhoeffer's theological thought, and meet us again and again throughout his work. It is still there late, in the context of non-religious interpretation, in the statement that the specific form of existence of the Christian is to permit himself to be involved in the Messianic sufferings of Christ.[13] But the

[12] Cp. with this also this passage from the *Tesseradekas*, *"Dum ego patior, patior jam non solus, patitur mecum Christus et omnes Christiani . . . Ita onus meum portant alii, illorum virtus mea est. Fides Ecclesiae meae trepidationi succurrit, castitas aliorum meae libidinis tentationem suffert, aliorum jejunia mea lucra sunt, alterius oratio pro me sollicita est . . . Quis ergo queat desperare in peccatis? Quis non gaudeat in penis, qui sua peccata et penas jam neque portat aut si portat non solus portat, adjutus tot sanctis filiis dei, ipso denique Christo? Tanta res est communio sanctorum et Ecclesia Christi"* (WA, 6, p. 131).

(E.T., in *Reformation Writings of Martin Luther*, tr. Woolf, Lutterworth, II, 1956, p. 65; "Hence, when I suffer, I do not suffer alone; Christ and all Christians suffer with me . . . In this way others bear my burden, and the strength of others is my own. The faith of the Church succours me in my trepidation, the purity of others helps me when I am lustful, the fasts of others are my merits, another's prayer is my consolation . . . What man, then, could fall into despair if he fall into sin? What man would not rejoice in his sufferings, if he had not to bear his own sins and sufferings, or at least not alone? He is aided by the host of the saints of God, nay, by Christ himself. This shows how great a thing is the communion of saints and similarly the Church of Christ".)

[13] Cp. for example, LPP, pp. 198ff., and especially the second verse of the poem, "Christians and Pagans":
"Men go to God when he is sore bestead,
Find him poor and scorned, without shelter or bread,
Whelmed under the weight of the wicked, the weak, the dead;
Christians stand by God in his hour of grieving".

motif is also an essential one in the Christology lectures of 1933:

> "Christ is not only the head of the community but also the community itself (Cf. I Cor. 12 and the Epistle to the Ephesians). Christ is head and every member. Only in the Epistle to the Ephesians does the separation between head and members appear, it is not originally Pauline. The head means the Lordship. But the two expressions do not contradict one another" (Ch, p. 61).

Is the being of Jesus Christ resolved into the being of the community, the Church? Is the confrontation of the two abolished? What Bonhoeffer says here sounds peculiarly Catholic, and yet he disputes every destruction of this confrontation, and surely it is to this that we should have to hold fast. On the contrary he asserts that the confrontation of the community by Christ not only does not contradict the being of Christ *as* community, but, far from it, originally makes it possible. The two seemingly contradictory aspects mutually depend upon one another and are to be interpreted in the light of one another.

> "Just as Christ is present as the Word and in the Word, as the sacrament and in the sacrament, so too he is also present as community and in the community. His presence in Word and sacrament is related to his presence in the community as reality is to figure. Christ is the community by virtue of his being *pro me*. His form, indeed his only form, is the community between the ascension and the second coming. The fact that he is in heaven at the right hand of God does not contradict this; on the contrary it alone makes possible his presence in and as the community" (Ch., pp. 59f.).

One might object that this positive correlation, such a mutual illumination of the two aspects, and such an enabling relation, is a pure assertion on Bonhoeffer's part, and that the truth is that the two aspects do in fact necessarily contradict one another, and that therefore Christ exists either as opposed to the community or in and as the community. We dare not be too hasty in making such an objection. In our discussion of the interpretation we must in fairness make every effort to follow Bonhoeffer on his path. If his view can appear here as a pure assertion, that may also be connected with the fact that we have his lectures on Christology only in the form of college notes, that is, surely, in considerable abbreviation and without the fine shades and blending. One could add also that in oral lectures things are often said for the first time which the speaker has not yet thought through from every angle, but of which he is already intuitively certain.

In order to follow Bonhoeffer along this path of his, recognizing the structural unity of the two aspects, surely what we must rather first ask is what really is the meaning of this talk of "confrontation" so beloved by theologians. Perhaps "confrontation" is best defined in terms of the event of the word. Then we should first of all have to ask about this event of the word as an event in the personal and intra-personal realm, and we should have to enquire if the formation of a community is not peculiar to the nature of the word, and if something like this is not true both, to a certain extent, in the secular realm, and, as we can learn from the witness of Holy Scripture, in the realm of the divine Word of revelation.[14] In this context Bonhoeffer begins by referring to the Biblical concept of the Body:

> "The community is the body of Christ. Body here is not just a metaphor. The community *is* the body of Christ, it does not *represent* the body of Christ. Applied to the community, the concept of the body is not just a functional concept which merely refers to the members of this body; it is a comprehensive and central concept of the mode of existence of the one who is present in his exaltation and his humiliation" (Ch, p. 60).

[14] All fellowship between men, if meaningful, is due to a word, for example, the fellowship of marriage to the marriage vows. Even parenthood and childhood, which in the first instance come into being through birth without words, are taken out of the sphere of the animal and denoted as human by the word. The word dwells among those whose fellowship is constituted by it. In a certain sense it *is* this fellowship. Those who have fellowship with one another are responsible to this word. The word is not the fellowship or the fellowship the word in the sense of a plain identity, since both are in fact historical realities. *Their identity rests on the reality of responsibility.* A fellowship of men is not simply the sum of the single individuals who take part in it, but a nexus of responsibilities defined by the word, which also defines the single individuals.

In this sense it can also be said that Jesus Christ, by his very being the Word which creates the community, is also the community itself. He dwells in the community as the Word and is himself the community. But it is true that this *Logos* is himself a person, acting in the present, and thereby distinguished from every human word.

Whether other concepts and figures of the Biblical testimony could support Bonhoeffer's view of the union of the word which confronts and the immanence of fellowship, would be a matter for examination. The concept, say, of *Spirit* or that of *covenant* might.[15] He obviously so sees the factual situation that Christ is both the one who speaks and, as the community, the one who hears.

"What does it mean that Christ as *Word* is also community? It means that the *Logos* of God has extension in space and time in and as the community. Christ, the Word, is spiritually and physically present. The *Logos* is not only the weak word of human teaching, *doctrina*; he is also the powerful Word of creation. He speaks, and thus creates the form of the community. The community is therefore not only the receiver of the Word of revelation; it is itself revelation and Word of God. Only in so far as it is itself the Word of God can it understand a Word of God. Revelation can be understood only on the basis of revelation. The Word is *in* the community in so far as the community is a recipient of revelation. But the Word is also itself community in so far as the community is itself revelation and the Word wills to have the form of a created body" (Ch, p. 60).

With what justice may the community itself be called "Word"? It may be in so far as its life belongs to the proclamation of the life of the proclaimer and the showing forth of the Word of God before the world, in obedience to the word of Jesus, "Let your light so shine before men that they may see your good works and glorify your Father which is in heaven" (Matt. 5: 16). But in so entering into the form of the community and finding form in it, the Word does not cease to be word, and as living Word, as Gospel, to stand in "confrontation" before the man addressed. Rather its so taking form is a confirmation of the Word and of its livingness. The spiritual parable of this, the man who for me embodies the goodness of God, does not take away my eyes from God to himself, but through this very figure of his faith points beyond himself to God.

Properly speaking, there would also require to be added to

---

[15] Through the *covenant* two persons who stand in confrontation with one another become a new unity. The *Spirit* denotes the indwelling of the one who confronts in the "here" without the confronter ceasing thereby to be the master.

the above passage from the Christology, a necessary consideration of the nature of word and speech. In a further analysis of the facts as envisaged by Bonhoeffer one would have to start from the point that the testimony of God is only understood through God, that God is *solus idoneus de seipso testis* ("the only true witness to himself"),[16] that therefore for the understanding of the *verbum externum* there is required the *testimonium Spiritus Sancti internum*. To this extent Bonhoeffer is completely in accord with traditional Protestantism when he maintains that "revelation can be understood only on the basis of revelation". But this factual situation now receives from Bonhoeffer a peculiarly "ecclesial" dimension, that the Spirit, who gives the inward testimony to the outward word, is not merely there as an act at each point of time to individuals, but that he is promised beforehand to the community as such and is present in the community. Christ himself as the present One and the exalted One dwells through the Spirit in his community. This is his form. And this statement, as is to be shown in what follows, is no mere assertion, but points to an essential structure. Incidentally we also see here already in Bonhoeffer's early work an exact correspondence to the later thought of "conformation" as a principle of ethics.

But of course all this does not mean that the Spirit, Jesus Christ himself, the present One, dwelling in the community, now becomes being at rest and at our disposal. Bonhoeffer demarcates his position—and this brings us to the central problem of his quest on the subject of *"Act and Being"*—against defining revelation either as pure activism, as being an event on each separate occasion, or as having the nature of pure static being, and therefore being at our disposal.[17] And with his *"theologico-sociological category"* he believes that he has found a way which leads us beyond these false alternatives. This is also the point where Bonhoeffer differentiates his so "Catholic" sounding understanding of revelation from Roman Catholicism, for he defines its understanding of revelation as a static one of being.

---

[16] Cp. e.g., Heidanus, *Corp. Theol. chr.*, 1686, I, p. 7.

[17] The same tendency to a demarcation on either side is followed emphatically by Jean-Louis Leuba, in *New Testament Patterns. An Exegetical Enquiry into the "Catholic" and "Protestant" Dualism*, tr. Knight, Lutterworth, 1953.

"And so it is not in man that the continuity lies; it is supra-personally guaranteed through a community of persons. Instead of the institutional Catholic Church we have the community as the trans-subjective pledge of revelation's continuity and extrinsicality—the 'from outside' " (AB, pp. 123f.).

Or, in keepnig with this:

"The conception of revelation as an entity would have the following result for man's stock of knowledge,[18] that he could freely and constantly recur to this entity, which is there for the finding. It stands at his disposal, whether it be religious experience, the verbally inspired Bible or the Catholic Church. He knows himself assured by this entity, borne up by this entity—though this assurance can only consist in the fact that man remains by himself, since, as we have seen, the entity as such is finally given into his power" (AB, pp. 114f.).

It is true that there would have to be today a new examination of the question whether the Catholic Church, as it now understands itself, would allow itself to be based on this static understanding of revelation. But one circumstance does seem to justify Bonhoeffer at once, that he understands the power to forgive sins as a definition of the community of Christ itself, at work in its members, whereas Roman Catholic theology centres this on a certain sacramental institution. Under some circumstances Roman Catholic theology might here raise an objection, that in the sacrament of penance there is only fulfilled representatively and in the palpable form of a sacrament what belongs to the being of the community as such and therefore defines the Church as the "fundamental sacrament".[19]

[18] (I myself should translate here, ". . . would have the following result for the doctrine of man, that man could . . ."—Tr.).

[19] In his work, *The Church and the Sacraments* (*Quaestiones Disputatae*, 9), tr. O'Hara, Nelson, 1963, Karl Rahner defines the Church as the "fundamental sacrament" and the essential being of the Church as a sacramental one, that is, to put it briefly, one effective as a sign. The individual sacraments are only modifications, impresses and aspects of this fundamental sacrament in certain typical situations of Christian existence. The concept of the "Church as a fundamental sacrament" has also recently appeared in *De Ecclesia*, the doctrinal decree of the Second Vatican Council. The Church is the *sacramentum salutis totius mundi*. In addition, this modern Catholic concept of sacrament, understanding as it does its subject neither as sacramental magic nor in the first place juridically, and giving as it does the "Church as a sacrament" priority to the individual sacramental forms, seems to me to carry a considerable step further the discussion between Protestants and Catholics on the sacraments.

It is further conceivable that today Catholic theology might be prepared to accept Bonhoeffer's formula of "the community as the trans-subjective pledge of revelation's continuity and extrinsicality—the 'from outside' '', accept, that is to say, the community as a reality for which the "institutional Church" is only the outward form. Catholic theology, too, surely might well agree with the description Bonhoeffer gives in the same context as the first passage we quoted in definition:

> "If the individual as such were the hearer of the preaching, the continuity would still be endangered, but it is the Church itself which hears the Church's Word, even if "I" were heedless on such and such an occasion. Thus preaching is always heard. It is outside "me" that the gospel is proclaimed and heard, that Christ "is" in his community" (AB, p. 123).

It is important and striking how Bonhoeffer here, in the same breadth *and by the same argument*, establishes both the *extra me* of the *kerygma* and its continuity. The other possibility would indeed be conceivable, that the *extra me* was simply the descent upon me of a completely transcendent Word coming on each occasion "perpendicularly from above", while the continuity on the other hand appeared assured by a "horizontal" belonging to history and a fellowship. But Bonhoeffer establishes the *extra me* of Christ and his Word by the fact that the event of the sermon and its hearing is not merely a personal event within myself, and therefore dependent upon me, but takes place without me in the Church in which I participate. Even when my hearing of the Word is intermittent, that of the community is still not so. And this is not, say, because the Church, in a purely quantitative sense, contains a greater number of individuals, so that in the end, if there is a sufficiently great number, any intermittence in the hearing of the totality is extremely improbable, but because Christ himself is the community. The result is something like an "infallibility" of the Church; the community of Christ, because it is the form of the present Christ, cannot fall away from the hearing of the Word.

The event of the Word takes place in the *personal fellowship* of the community with Christ and among themselves. In this way the *extra me* and the continuity are guaranteed *at the same time*. The present Christ is not merely in *me* who open my ear to hear, but in *us*. God, one must draw the further conclusion, is so much *extra nos* that he also circumscribes us "from within" and in this way is *in nobis*. But this very *in nobis* of the *testimonium internum* is really an *in nobis*, an "in us", or in other words, the inner witness of the Spirit has, as we said, an ecclesial dimension. It is true that this dimension would still have to be thoroughly thought through.[20] And yet this third way for which Bonhoeffer is seeking is already in this preliminary sketch both plausible and very promising.

7. *The Relevance of the Sociological Category to Epistemology and to Ontology*

But it is something completely consistent that Bonhoeffer also seeks to define the *manner of gaining knowledge of God*, the knowledge of *Deus revelatus*, ecclesially, by using the theologico-sociological category, in contradistinction to any concept of knowledge either purely activist or based on a category of being.

In his inaugural dissertation he follows out his train of thought beginning on the level of a philosophical epistemology.[21] Important above all for the trend of our argument is the way in which Bonhoeffer applies to revelation the two types of epistemology, or the two approaches to it, the "transcendental" and the "ontological", from the contrast of which he begins. How is the reality of revelation to be expounded, by the concept of action or by that of being? That is to say, does revelation take place each time only *in actu*, "perpendicularly from above", or can revelation be "possessed" as an entity, as doctrine, as

[20] In this it must especially be remembered that man is essentially open to other men dialogically. We do not then require to conceive of the *testimonium Spiritus Sancti internum* as necessarily an event of enlightenment within the soul, which the individual has for himself alone. The Spirit can achieve his testimony to himself by the evidence for God suddenly becoming clear in discussion (in the widest sense of that word), in the mutual openness to one another of believers.

[21] Bonhoeffer develops this starting-point for putting his questions in the first section of *Act and Being*,
"PART ONE. The problem of act and being, treated as the epistemological problem in philosophy's understanding of Dasein.
I. The Transcendental Endeavour.
II. The Ontological Endeavour." (AB, pp. 17ff.).

experience, which one "has" and to which one can look back and refer, or as verbally inspired scripture or Church institution? Both expositions of the essence of revelation also involve each its own definite epistemology, but neither either reaches or exhausts the reality of revelation. A new exposition of the being of revelation must be set against both of them, against both the revelational activism of dialectical theology and every kind of theological existentialism on the one side, and on the other every objectifying of revelation into an entity at our disposal. And this again in its turn necessarily involves a definite exposition of the knowledge of revelation. Bonhoeffer sees this third possibility opened through the category of the collective person, and the concept of the community as the collective person. Here there comes into sight the ontological breadth covered by the course of his thought in sociology, social philosophy and ecclesiology:

> "Revelation, then, happens within the communion; it demands primarily a Christian sociology of its own. The difference between thinking of revelation individualistically and thinking of it in relation to community is fundamental . . . Man in reality is never *only* the single unity, not even the *one* "claimed by the Thou", but invariably finds himself in some community, whether in "Adam" or in "Christ". The Word of God is given to mankind, the gospel to the communion of Christ. When the social category is thus introduced, the problem of act and being—and also the problem of knowledge—is presented in a wholly fresh light.
> "The being of revelation does not lie in a unique occurrence of the past, in an entity which in principle is at my disposal and has no direct connection with my old or my new existence,[22] neither can the being of revelation be conceived solely as the ever-free, pure and non-objective act which at certain times impinges upon the existence of individuals. No, the being of revelation 'is' the being of the community of persons constituted and embraced by the person of Christ, wherein the individual finds himself to be already in his new existence. This ensures three considerations: 1. the being of revelation can be envisaged in continuity; 2. the existence of man is 'critically' involved; 3. it is impossible to regard the being of revelation as entity, as objective, or on the other hand as non-entity, as non-objective" (AB, pp. 122f.).

[22] This must surely mean existentially irrelevant, incapable of existential interpretation.

Bonhoeffer is obviously concerned here with putting an ontological question, with the ontology of theology, of revelation, and with the doctrine of theological knowledge which accompanies it. "The idea of revelation must therefore yield an epistemology of its own" (AB, p. 15). It is a matter of the appropriate definition of the *"mode of being of revelation"*.

"Revelation's mode of being, on the other hand, is definable only with reference to persons. 'There is' only the entity, the given. It is self-contradictory to seek a 'there is' on the farther side of entity. In the social context of the person the static ontology of 'there is' is set in motion. God 'is' in the personal reference and (? his) being is his being a person (*und das Sein ist sein Personsein*)" (AB, pp. 125f.).

In this ontological definition of the *modus essendi* of revelation justice is done to the moments of truth in both the expositions while their dangers are avoided. The legitimate moment is taken into account, in that revelation, when thought of in this way as essentially bound up with a community of persons, can no longer be thought of as something objectified and existing at our disposal. It is no longer in danger of being thought of as something resting so much in itself that its relation to existence remains purely external. There is also ruled out in the same way a "Theology of Facts of Salvation" in the bad sense, as given currency by, say, various critics of Bultmann! For here, too, revelation is interpreted as an entity which "there is".[23] The opposite may perhaps be *asserted* by these critics, but it is not *thought*. In Bonhoeffer the relation to existence, the connection with my old and my new existence, in other words, the existential relevance, is preserved and remains essential. And yet the legitimate moment in an exposition of revelation in terms of being is taken into account, in that the event of revelation and faith is not thereby dissolved into a discontinuous list of acts. Continuity belongs essentially to the reality of revelation.

". . . Only in faith does man know that the being of revelation, his own being in the Church of Christ, is independent of faith.

---

[23] (Very relevant here is the translator's note in AB, p. 125, pointing out how the German *es gibt* carries the sense of something available and manipulable more than the English "there is"—Tr.)

There is continuity of revelation, continuity of existence, only in faith, but there again in such a way that faith *qua* believing is suspended only in 'faith' *qua* 'being in the communion'. If here faith were understood wholly as an act, the continuity of being would be disrupted by the discontinuity of acts" (AB, p. 128).

By the "only in faith" the relation to existence and thus the justified concern of the activist exposition of revelation is assured. Yet it is just in faith that man experiences the being of revelation as independent of his personal faith, but independent this time not in the sense of some factual being-in-itself and externality, but in the sense and in the form of a community of persons which surpasses and embraces the existential reality of the individual, and yet in such transcendence remains none the less positively related to it. Faith as an event, as an act of the individual, discovers the prior self-existence of revelation, independent and positive, founding it and related to it. "To believe is as much as to say: to find God, his grace and the community of Christ already present. Faith encounters a being which is prior to the act; it depends on this being, because it knows itself involved in it . . ." (AB, pp. 127f.).

Thus the problem of act and being is solved. Revelation is both, act and being, and is both in strict and positive relation to one another. In the end it becomes clear at this point, which Bonhoeffer succeeds in reaching, that "act" and "being" are not concepts which can be established positively and really give light, they are not concepts which are parts of the structure of the reality itself which is our subject, they are rather expedients, mere outer skins which can then be stripped off in the light of a greater clarity and insight. Bonhoeffer does not come to any compromise between "act" and "being" or between the two forms of interpretation of the being and of the knowledge of revelation to which these two concepts lead; he puts an end to the false alternatives. And this end is no mere assertion, no merely asserted demarcation on either side which is not given any further positive content and concreteness. This type of thing, where someone says that he means neither this nor its opposite, but omits to expound positively what he *really* does mean, we know enough of in theology in particular. It is a method which can at most have the function of a provisional distinction. But Bonhoeffer rather has already, in the form of his sociological category, a basis on which can be established the solution and synthesis for which he strove. He can already take his stand upon the phenomenological premise, "The concept of the absolute individual is an abstraction with no corresponding reality. It is not merely in his general psychology but in his very existentiality that man is tied to society" (AB, p. 130).

The result of this then for Bonhoeffer is an astonishing lack of difficulty in his transition to his problem of act and being. Thus he can say, "Man as individual and man as humanity, man one in these two inseparable aspects, is but another way of saying man as act and being. He is never one alone" (AB, p. 131). This particular identification is certainly clear after what has gone before, but would be worth still further analysis. Through all his thinking Bonhoeffer certainly keeps himself clear of every form of abstraction. Man thought of as "act" alone would be just as much an abstraction as man as "being" alone, man as an individual alone just as much as man as humanity alone. What has to be done is to gain the *whole* fullness of reality, in this case of man, for one's field of vision.

Further prospects open out at this point. Here it seems to me is to be found the truly fruitful approach for overcoming the onesidedness of existentialism, and also for the further development of the basic principles of *existenz* philosophy. In point of fact we do not exist exclusively in the salient points of the great alternatives, the decisions in which we in an eminent sense "make ourselves", but equally in our disposition and situation. This situation of ours, too, is not something "sub-human"; it has meaning in itself, no less so than the moments of decision.

And now this very factual situation is brought by Bonhoeffer into this context and interpreted in this light, that as individuals we are always at the same time in "sociality". An existentialism taken to extremes draws a onesided picture of man. In the endeavour to think of the most concrete thing of all, the existence which one can never bring within the grasp of a system, to which one can only allude, it in its turn falls again into an abstraction. It overlooks one dimension of existence which, without reverting to before the beginnings of *existenz* philosophy, must be given its validity. It is what one might call the dimension of "vegetating" man, of "semi-conscious" man, a dimension which nevertheless cannot be regarded as one without meaning, but may perhaps be a dimension of the hiddenness of existence in a specific sense. Rudolf Bultmann once made to me this objection to this train of thought of mine, that even in times of a sheer mundane continuance of existence what was essential consisted in this, that existence was carrying out its decisions and thereby in the end renewing them every moment, and that therefore it was also still living in decision. We have to carry out, for example, throughout life the great decision of the marriage contract, carry it out in the daily round, often commonplace, of marriage. Certainly one can so see the matter, in fact must surely always so see it, for even the daily round and the pure conditions of one's life are not simply divorced from the realm of decisions, but are the closest neighbours to it. What I doubt is whether, for example, the phenomenon of being a man tied to a sick bed is adequately interpreted by saying that this man exists in that he, say, carries out and renews every moment the decision for patience. Not that I would regard it as in any way false to say so, but is it enough? On this we must think further, in the following direction for instance. To keep to our example, the sick man, even there where he lies half alive in weariness and helplessness, may find a meaning over and above the carrying out of his own decision given to him. Even there there takes place history, there takes place encounter. This too is to be conceived in categories of encounter, and not simply psychologically.

All this is no more than an indication. The interesting thing is that Bonhoeffer undertakes to expound this whole problem, the limits of an extreme existentialism, from the viewpoint of humanity as sociality. We could develop the thought further in this way. It is possible, for example, that a fellowship should sustain an individual, and that for him the meaning of his being should grow out of his being so sustained. Then the event of meaning, the truly historical, happens not only to the sustaining fellowship, but also to the individual who does nothing towards it, who perhaps in his own presuppositions does not make it real at all. Certainly there also come to him from the event new basic presuppositions, but they come, not merely as a possibility which *he* has first to realize, but as something already real which is presented to him.

As regards the theological situation in the narrower sense, it is not something new from Bonhoeffer, but something of which we are sufficiently aware today, that as regards revelation we have to avoid both its objectifying into an entity at our disposal and its resolution into pure activism. Was it new in Bonhoeffer's time? Was he then perhaps far in advance of his time? There may have been as great a development as that by today in the theological consciousness of the problem. On the other hand what is new and original in Bonhoeffer, and is still so for us today after thirty-five years (!), is that he seeks to find a solution to the dilemma by using the *"sociological category"*. Who would have thought of this possibility of a fundamental and really enlightening solution in the controversy between the theology of Bultmann and a "theology of the facts of salvation", a controversy in which, nevertheless, the issues are at bottom the same?[24] And who thinks of this day? This is a point where Bonhoeffer's contribution could today gain a great renewed significance. Up till now it has surely scarcely been considered from this point of view.

8. *Sociality and Personality*

Christ and the believers, the Communio Sanctorum: nothing other than this is the being of revelation. Revelation is not at our disposal as a thing, not is it sporadic and beyond our reach as an act; it is personal, existing in the personal "between", and in particular in a fellowship of persons. It is only in the act of faith that man discovers this being of revelation, but in the act of faith he discovers that he is embraced in it and contained in it. Thus "act" and "being" are reconciled.

A further aspect of Bonhoeffer's approach, that of personality, is clearly shown us. It belongs inseparably to the sociological category.

[24] Cp. on this, e.g. Friedrich Gogarten, *Demythologizing and History*, tr. Horton Smith, S.C.M., 1958.

"If the being of revelation is fixed in entity, it remains past, existentially impotent; if it is volatilized into the non-objective, its continuity is lost. And so the being of revelation must enjoy a mode of being which satisfies both claims, embodying both the continuity proper of being and the existential significance of the act. It is as such a mode of being that we understand the person and the community. Here the possibility of existential impact is bound up with genuine objectivity in the sense of a concrete standing-over-against; this lets itself be drawn[25] into the power of the I because it itself imposes a constraint on existence, because it is *the* externality" (AB, pp. 124f.).[26]

The nature, then, of the being of revelation is "the person *and* the fellowship". The connection between the two, which obviously have to count as aspects of one and the same reality, is developed by Bonhoeffer in this way:

"... Only through the person of Christ can the existence of man be affected, placed into truth and transplanted into a new manner of existing. Since moreover the person of Christ has revealed itself in the communion, the existence of man can only

[25] (But Ott's text here reads, "... does not let itself be drawn"—Tr.)

[26] This *"the* externality" as the characteristic of the personality standing face to face with me Bonhoeffer refers to as *"moral transcendence"* which is something quite different from "epistemological transcendence" (cp. SC, pp. 33ff.). "I can never become a real barrier to myself, but it is equally impossible for me to leap over the barrier to the other. My I as a form of Thou can only be experienced by the other I; my I as a form of I can only be experienced by myself. Thus in the experience of a Thou the I-form of the other is never immediately given ... So the Thou-form is to be defined as the other who places me before a moral decision. With this I-Thou relationship as the basic Christian relation we have left the epistemological subject-object relationship behind. Similarly with the concept of the Thou as the other I. Whether the other is also an I in the sense of the I-Thou relation is something I can never discover ... In other words, the person cannot know, but only acknowledge the other person, 'believe' in him" (*ibid*). This is an essential contribution to the structural analysis of personality. The concept of "moral transcendence" has more content than the purely formal one of person as "centre of action" of the acts set in motion by it. These sentences, quoted from the doctoral dissertation of the 20-year-old, also remind us of the "Outline for a Book" in the prison letters, where we read, "His (sc. Jesus') 'being-there-for others' is the experience of transcendence ... Faith is participation in the being of Jesus (incarnation, cross and resurrection). Our relation to God is not a 'religious' relationship to the highest, most powerful and best Being imaginable—that is not authentic transcendence—but our relation to God is a new life in 'existence for others', through participation in the being of Jesus. The transcendental is not infinite and unattainable tasks, but the neighbour who is within reach in any given situation, God in human form ..." (LPP, pp. 209f.).

be so affected through the communion. It is only from the person of Christ that other persons acquire for man the character of personhood. In this way they even become Christ for us in what they both demand and promise, in their existential impositions upon us from without. At the same time they become, as such, the pledges of revelation's continuity" (AB, p. 123).

Frankly, Bonhoeffer's development is not complete enough. The structural connection which is the real issue, that between sociality and personality, is not yet clearly enough brought to light.[27] This much, however, is already clear, that in both, personality and sociality, there takes place what he is essentially concerned with here, the event of the definition of existence. As an individual believer I cannot resolve the reality of revelation into something internal. It never becomes a *mere* definition of *my* existence, however much I am affected and determined by it, but remains a genuine *extra me*, in that it stands face to face with me, just as does the person of the other man, completely outside my disposal and limiting me, or the fellowship, in which I certainly participate, but which surrounds me and thus limits me and in which I find myself contained. It is here that lies the independence of revelation from my faith, and its continuity which I do not need to guarantee but which is guaranteed to me. Revelation is independent of me, of my knowledge of revelation, and of my faith, and is continuous in itself, not as a thing is, but as is a person or a fellowship which limits me.

From this point then, to conclude, there follow the consequences for the realm from which Bonhoeffer set out, the realm of knowledge:

"To the being of revelation, defined as that of the Christ-person in the community of persons called the Church, defined therefore in sociological terms, there must correspond a concept of knowledge envisaged in a sociological category" (AB, p. 137).

In point of fact the ontological definition of the *modus essendi* of revelation must have consequences for the methodological and epistemological, or hermeneutical, definition of the

[27] The fact is that personality and sociality go together. For fellowship, given its structure by responsibility, is always the responsibility of a group of persons towards one person or among themselves.

modus loquendi of theology, for the basic postulates of theological thought, both of the thought-process and of the individual theological statement. All these will now receive a sociological, and ecclesial, dimension. Bonhoeffer defines theology as the "remembrance of the Church". Theological thought "has its object in the remembered happenings of the Christian communion, the Bible, preaching and sacrament, prayer, confession, the Word of the Christ-person . . ." (AB, p. 143). I do certainly believe that in *Act and Being* he has not yet by any means fully unfolded the tremendous breadth of what lies concealed in his approach with respect to the sociological dimension of theological thought. There still remains much to be done here. The following may serve simply as a signpost for further study. There is a *communal character to thought and knowledge themselves*. Knowledge is not only the seeing of truth by an individual, who then seeks thereafter to impart it to others. Knowledge has fundamentally a dialogical character. In the accomplishment of dialogue a common certainty becomes visible, and in this very fact one comes closer to the facts. Knowledge is deposited in verbal articulation. The lonely experience and vision of the mystic themselves drive to speech. What cannot be verbally articulated is not fully known, not even according to the measure of what is possible for man. But speech, as the form which knowledge assumes, is always *locutio ad aliquem*. And hence knowledge is dialogical. To this extent the event of thought is connected with the sociological category, that insight, with which thought is concerned, is not primarily a matter of the individual, but of the fellowship which comes to being in dialogue, and in which the individual participates.

9. The Thought of Communio and the Ecumenical Dialogue

The last word on this complex factual situation of the sociological category in theology and its ontological and epistemological or hermeneutical significance, will be to use it to try to cast briefly three searchlights upon Bonhoeffer's work and upon the present position of the ecumenical debate.

1. The first concerns Bonhoeffer's concept of a *secret discipline*, which has a part to play in *Letters and Papers from*

Prison, and is always there when he is distinguishing his own project of non-religious interpretation from so-called revelational positivism. The Church cannot at all times with the same clarity and credibility expound all aspects of the truth committed to it. It must also be able at certain times to maintain a reverent silence about certain things. It must be able to wait until the particular subject presents itself to it anew. For it is not the master over its subject, but is contained with it within a history. None the less the whole tradition, and that means the whole "subject-matter" of the Church, both in all the aspects which past tradition has worked out, and, virtually, those which it has not yet worked out, remains preserved at every moment of the history of the Church, even when it remains as that about which one keeps silence. It remains as part of the community's common wealth of faith. For as a collective person the community has more in its "remembrance" than what the individual or the individual epoch can make explicit. Thus Bonhoeffer's late concept of secret discipline gains meaning from the earlier developed thought of the sociological category.

Here we are also reminded of the concept, common in Catholic theology, of the *depositum fidei.* But this concept of the "deposit of faith" must not be thought of too juridically as a kind of ability by endowment, nor yet too doctrinally with a positivist bias as a collection of doctrinal statements about the faith. At an earlier date this was the customary conception in Catholic theology, but today it is beginning to right itself. The *depositum fidei* has its parallel concept in Protestant theology in that of the *kerygma.* It as the Word of God is also more than any individual proclamation of a kerygmatic, liturgical or theological nature, and yet it is the *whole kerygma* of Christ which is given to the Church from the beginning as a claim, a commission and a content of meaning. In all that is proclaimed as *kerygma* and all theological doctrine what is expounded is yet the one *kerygma* from which and for which the community lives at all times. The *depositum fidei,* rightly understood, is surely nothing other than this *kerygma* of the revelation in Christ on which the Church is founded. The *depositum fidei* is given to the community even where it does not yet know it as something considered and developed. When it does develop it and articulate it in proclamation and doctrine, it is yet doing nothing arbitrary, but speaking from what has been given to it. On the possibility of a Protestant recasting of the Catholic concept of *depositum fidei* I have already expressed myself at greater length in *Der Begriff der fides implicita in der Sicht evangelischer Theologie* (duplicated in the Bulletin of the Collegium Canisianum, 9, 99th. year, April 1962). Materially, *fides implicita* and *depositum fidei* go together. Faith, which, even according to Calvin, is in a certain respect always an implicit faith, believes the *depositum fidei*, that is to say it gains its life from a Word which is living and which it has never adequately articulated because it surpasses all human articulation. On this fact that the Word of God is always greater than all human articulation and all human understanding Luther says, "No man at all can attain sufficiently to a single word of God's . . . It is an infinite word, to be grasped with a spirit at peace . . . Therefore come, come, dear Christians, and let my expounding and that of all teachers be but a framework for the true building, that we grasp this pure Word of God alone, that we taste it and abide by it; for God alone dwelleth in Zion . . ." (Preface to the *Kirchenpostille* of 1522, W.A., 10, I, 1). What, taking the word from Heidegger, I described in *What is Systematic Theology?* as the "unspoken" from which all speaking of the Gospel gains its life, refers to the same complex of facts (cp. *New Frontiers in Theology*, Vol. I, *The Later Heidegger and Theology*, ed. Robinson and Cobb, Harper & Row, 1963). In my answer to American contributors in the same volume of essays, I have already referred to the collective, or better, "communal", character of the participation of Christians in this "unspoken" element in the Word of God. It is to the *community* that the Gospel is primarily entrusted. (On this, cp. also, *Glaube und Bekennen. Ein Beitrag zum ökumenischen Dialog*, in *Begegnung*, Vol. 2, Basle, 1963, and *Die Lehre des II Vatikanischen Konzils. Ein evangelischer Kommentar*, in *Begegnung*, Vol. 4, 1963, also *Glaube*, in *Theologie für Nicht-Theologen*, Vol. II, Stuttgart, 1964). It seems to me necessary to bring to light more clearly theologically the unalterable communal character, even the essentially social structure, of faith. So far, this has not yet been done to an adequate degree. Perhaps in this generation of ours, which is always thinking in individualistic or a bad type of collectivistic categories, the time is not yet ripe for it. And yet in Bonhoeffer's factual correlation of social category and secret discipline we find the most remarkable beginnings.

2. To the hermeneutical prospects opened by the sociological category we find a really astonishing parallel in the Roman Catholic theologian Hans Urs v. Balthasar. In his book, *Herrlichkeit* (Vol. I, Einsiedeln, 1961), he expresses himself

in this way about the relation of the Word of God to the Church:

> "It is ... 'naïve realism' to picture the partnership of the covenant as merely setting against one another a speaking person and a hearing one, a commanding person and an obeying one, the hearing and obeying person being the people and the individual in it. God is not a partner in this limited human sense. 'God is but one' (Gal. 3: 20), and if according to St. Paul this does not yet come fully to expression in the Old Covenant, yet it does in Jesus Christ who is the very Word of God, but nevertheless in the form of a historical man. The fullness of the partnership with God is expressed exactly in the fact that the Word of God no longer stands before us and beside us, but has truly entered into us (Jer. 31: 31f.; Ezek. 36: 26f.), and that too not only in a 'second period', as the equally 'naïve realism' of Roman Catholic theologians would have it, after that 'in a first period' (*in actu primo*) God's objective acts of salvation in Christ have worked 'in themselves' and 'for us' but not yet 'in us'. Precisely this contradicts the principle of the incarnation as the Greek Fathers especially have understood it ... The Word of God seeks from the first to be fruitful in the fruitfulness of the believing man, it seeks always to include already within its form as address to man the form of man's answer to God" (*op. cit.*, pp. 516f.).

If it is a valid presupposition that Jesus Christ is himself the Word of God, the eternal Word of God, the incarnate Word of God, and therefore *the* true Word of God in all human *kerygma* about God, what v. Balthasar here formulates is nothing other than what Bonhoeffer has said with his formula, "Christ existing as a community". The hermeneutical consequences of this view are worth consideration. They can be followed out with the aid of v. Balthasar's description, and must hold true if we are right in what we have developed as the hermeneutical consequences of Bonhoeffer's beginnings, in the place in particular which he gives to the sociological category.[28]

---

[28] One hermeneutical consequence, for example, is the fact that the Word of God comes to us in the form of the human answer to God. The Psalms are an example of this, they are prayers, human replies to God, and precisely as such they become the mediation of the Word of God. The human answer is thus in a way taken up into the event of the Word of God, and the two form a functional unity. A theological exegesis of Biblical texts has to take account of this factual situation. The Psalms are only a particularly clear example, a pattern for the

When we embark upon this road we no more approach the "Catholic principle" (if indeed there is any such thing!) than did the convinced Protestant Bonhoeffer!

3. In the essay entitled "Word and Sacrament", fundamentally "A Contribution to the Study of the Difference between the Confessions" (in *The Word of God and Tradition*, tr. Hooke, Collins, 1968), Gerhard Ebeling expresses himself on the radical distinction between Reformed and Catholic Christianity, which according to him shows itself all the more clearly the more, as a result of the mutual ecumenical openness and the intensive dialogue between the confessions, the apparent differences which have long been held decisive collapse and show their mere seemingness. These very reasons make all the harder and clearer the antithesis which is abysmal and reaches down into the final depths of understanding.

Ebeling sees clearly that "according to Catholic teaching as well, the principle of *sola gratia* has an unconditional value". It is not here that lie the grounds of confessional difference. But "the Protestant *solo verbo* has its counterpart in *sola fide*" (op. cit., p. 212). This is the Reformers' conception of the grace of God as the pure event of the Word, and of the action of the recipient of grace as purely a co-responding to the Word, and in so far of a verbal nature on its side, an acceptance "in faith". And this is now in contrast to the specifically Catholic exposition of the being of revelation, which defines grace primarily as sacramental and the nature of the recipient of grace as due to *gratia infusa* and *gratia habitualis*, that is, not to response to the Word. Hence "Existence through Word and

---

interrelation of Word of God and word of man which runs through the whole Bible. The whole Bible is man's word, and yet as the answer taken up into the Word of God, it is at the same time God's Word. The Synoptic texts are words of the community. But precisely as such they are words of Christ himself. It need not be said that this general structure does not, as it were, solve all the varied exegetical problems by the turning of a handle. This is no straw to be clutched at by a conservative theological attitude which feels disturbed by historical critical exegesis. But this factual situation of the interrelation of word and answer may serve as a fruitful starting-point for an exegesis of Scripture which, starting from the points established by historical critical exegesis, seeks to know the theological dimension of depth of the individual texts. We never have a Word of God in "pure" form without the mediation of a word of man. But the word of man also, which we hear, dare not be separated from its opposite which it answers.

through Sacrament"![29] Ebeling can also quote here the view of the Catholic theologian W. H. van de Pol on the phenomenology of the confessions.[30] He sees it as a basic component of the antithesis between the confessions that, "The character of revelation for the Reformed Christian is *a revelation of the Word*, for the Catholic Christian, on the other hand, it is a *revelation of Reality*", and ". . . that, according to the Catholic Church, revelation is the breaking through of a supernatural divine *Reality in the sense of being (seinshaft)* in visible form, in the midst of our earthly reality; while according to the Reformation it means that God has spoken to men through his Word" (quoted Ebeling, p. 214). Here obviously Bonhoeffer's problem of act and being reappears.

What Ebeling sees as the deepest difference between the confessions, remaining after the false distinctions have been demolished, is fundamentally the difference between act and being, between the nature of the event of the Word as "act", and that of the indwelling sacramental grace as "being". Now it is interesting and thought-provoking to follow out how Ebeling comes into conflict with a modern trend among Catholic writers, who recognize that Catholic doctrine, beside an immense theology of the Sacraments, has as yet developed no unified theology of the Word, and who seek to make up the leeway by bringing together Word and Sacrament. Such are, for example, Karl Rahner's essay, "The Word and the Eucharist" (*Theological Investigations*, IV, tr. Kevin Smyth, D. L. & T., 1966, pp. 253ff.) and Otto Semmelroth's book, *Wirkendes Wort. Zur Theologie der Verkündigung* (1962). The endeavour of these theologians is obviously to give that sacramental element, with its nature as being, a meaning with the nature of word, to make it one with the Word and so to personalize it in its deepest essence, all this in contradistinction to van de Pol who from the Catholic side sees the difference between the confessions in exactly the same way as does Ebeling. As opposed to them, Ebeling seeks to preserve the fundamental difference between Word and Sacrament which they endeavour to overcome, for he takes trouble to show that such an overcoming on the part of

---

[29] (A literal translation of the title of Ebeling's essay—Tr.).

[30] W. H. van de Pol, *Das reformatorische Christentum in phänomenologischer Betrachtung*, 1956.

a Catholic theologian just *cannot* succeed at all. Thus, for instance, he writes on Rahner:

> "He goes on to say, 'It is perfectly legitimate and objectively perfectly justifiable to subsume the whole Sacrament under the concept of the efficacious word' (*op. cit.*, p. 330—E.T., p. 266). 'Grace is present always and everywhere from beginning to end, from the first word of preaching to the Sacrament inclusively, in the form of the Word' (p. 354—E.T., p. 286). It does not diminish the significance of such statements, but only clarifies them in terms of the theological context from which they come, when he asserts, 'the supreme realization of the efficacious Word of God . . . is the Sacrament and only the Sacrament' (p. 329—E.T., p. 265), and more specifically, 'The Eucharist is in all truth the Sacrament of the Word absolutely, the absolute call of the Word everywhere' (p. 351—E.T., p. 283). We can recognize how the road leads from a wholly unfamiliar starting-point through newly discovered territory to debouch with certainty into the explicit dogma and reality of the Catholic Church" (Ebeling, *op. cit.*, p. 217).

But one could surely take a quite different course in the interpretation of such endeavours. Thus it is striking that in this controversy Ebeling does not bring to his aid one category which would be suitable for clarifying and overcoming the antithesis between existence "from the Word" and "sacramental" existence, the sociological and personal category, although he could have found it in his teacher Bonhoeffer. Bonhoeffer overcame by thinking back to the factual origins the difference between act and being, and in so doing the difference between existence from the Word and existence from the Sacrament. Instead of insisting on that difference, it would be perfectly possible to interpret such endeavours as those of the Catholic theologians quoted, endeavours for the mutual integration of Word and Sacrament, as a theological wrestling for the recovery of what was factually original. Here then, as against Ebeling's endeavour, and, as I believe, following Dietrich Bonhoeffer, let me at least formulate the thesis: *that taken by themselves "belonging to the Word" and "belonging to the Sacrament" are nothing, but that they only gain meaning within the horizon of personal and communal encounter, only within the "between" between persons who according to Bonhoeffer's exposition, constitute in their fellowship the "being of revelation".*

This horizon of personality is often invoked in theology, but is scarcely adequately clarified each time, and this task still remains ours, a task for which we might find Bonhoeffer at the focal point with us. But this is the horizon for theological thought in which the concepts of pure "belonging to the Word" and pure "belonging to the Sacrament" are to be transcended in our thinking, in the light of which they are to be interpreted, and in which they thus attain to their most real nature in that theological thinking. Even Ebeling in his controversy stands within the problem of act and being, to the overcoming of which Bonhoeffer had set himself long before in a constructive way.

It is true that Bonhoeffer's thought on personality and sociality as the more original unity of act and being only shows us a direction. His thesis would still require to be developed and substantiated *in extenso*. Personal being is word-controlling being. For that very reason it has *the nature of a word*, but *constitutes* that word and is not constituted by it. Prior to the event of the word as such is the person who speaks the word and who receives it. But this is not true if taken to mean that the person could ever be thought of in a wordless, pre-verbal condition. Personality *always* has a verbal nature, not constituted by the word but constituting it. Of course, since it is word-controlling, it may be constituted anew by the word of another person, someone face to face with us. But this factual situation of the fundamental priority of the person before the word, yet never in isolation from the word, has, in so far as it is true of God as the personal origin of all personality, to be given a Trinitarian meaning.

Again, in personality as the being which precedes the word, and which yet as word-controlling always has a verbal nature, there is to be found the overcoming of the antithesis between "act" and "being". Personal being is always of a verbal nature, yet it is not a being which exhausts itself in the act of the word. But personality always also signifies sociality, just because it has this verbal nature and therefore is structurally non-alone.

CHAPTER SIX

THE ETHICAL PROBLEM

1. *Action as a Breakthrough to Freedom*

IN ORDER to be able to understand how Bonhoeffer, from his starting-point, the ethical problem, arrives at his radical equation of Christ and reality, we must form a picture of the particular place in his thought of the ethical event. That place is responsible action. Ethical "principles" miscarry. They are not after all able to master reality at the decisive moment. Reality, meaning what is at stake in the situation of decision, is only mastered by responsible action in the concrete situation. And yet action, too, in Bonhoeffer still has about it a certain ambiguity. It, too, still has its boundaries, and is only in keeping with reality when it is embraced by Jesus Christ and contained in him.

What is responsible action? It is a station on the road to freedom, that is to say, to the true reality. On July 21, 1944, immediately after the news arrived that the great hope, the attempt on Hitler, had failed, Bonhoeffer wrote to his friend, enclosing a poem which he had composed on the same day, "Stations on the Road to Freedom", which Bethge then, appropriately to the subject, prefaced to his edition of the fragments of Bonhoeffer's *Ethics*. The stations are, "Discipline", "Action", "Suffering" and "Death". The last three stanzas run:

Action
Daring to do what is right, not what fancy may tell you,
valiantly grasping occasions, not cravenly doubting—
freedom comes only through deeds, not through thoughts
   taking wing.
Faint not nor fear, but go out to the storm and the action
trusting in God whose commandment you faithfully follow;
freedom, exultant, will welcome your spirit with joy.

Suffering

A change has come indeed. Your hands, so strong and active,
are bound, in helplessness now you see your action
is ended; you sigh in relief, your cause committing
to stronger hands; so now you may rest contented.
Only for one blissful moment could you draw near to touch
    freedom;
then, that it might be perfected in glory, you gave it to God.

Death

Come now, thou greatest of feasts on the journey to freedom
    eternal;
death, cast aside all the burdensome chains, and demolish
the walls of our temporal body, the walls of our souls that
    are blinded,
so that at last we may see that which here remains hidden.
Freedom, how long have we sought thee in discipline, action
    and suffering;
dying, we now may behold thee revealed in the Lord.

(LPP, pp. 202f.; E, p. xv—I have cited the translation in LPP and
not that in E, purely because Ott now goes on to quote letters
from LPP of about the same time—Tr.)

In a letter of July 28, 1944, Bonhoeffer repeats again the
thought of the last stanza, "Death is the supreme festival
on the road to freedom" (LPP, p. 207). "I am certainly no
poet", is Bonhoeffer's comment on the verses quoted (LPP,
p. 203), implying that he wanted completely to recast them.
But we have them in no other shape than this first one. The
poetic form of the verse may sometimes be awkward, but as well
as being a moving confession, they are a significant and concise
expression of his thought. They mirror a final transition in
his existential attitude, one marked by the failure of July
20, the transition from "resistance" to "submission". Yet the
two are closely related; the character of freedom and the
genuineness of the action are preserved in readiness to suffer.

"To turn to a different point: not only action, but also suffering
is a way to freedom. In suffering, the deliverance consists in our
being allowed to put the matter out of our own hands into God's
hands. In this sense death is the crowning of human freedom.
Whether the human deed is a matter of faith or not depends on

247

whether we understand our suffering as an extension of our action and a completion of freedom. I think that is very important and very comforting" (LPP, p. 206; in the same letter of July 28, 1944).

Thus Bonhoeffer understands the change in his own life which came with July 20, as the development of a factual continuity and not as a reversal. The whole Bonhoeffer, his ethical thought and a central part of his understanding of life as a Christian theologian, could be said to receive light and become understandable from this crystallization point of July 20. Here are shown what "action", "responsibility" and "freedom", three of his basic concepts, mean for him.

It is true that at the same time we must accept that on this theme also Bonhoeffer speaks tersely, in a pregnant and sometimes obscure way, without any final theological polish, precision and clarity. Surely these burning points of his thought, the equation of Christ with reality and what he says about responsible action, enlighten and expound one another mutually. But this does not mean that either of the two sides is completely clear and adequately developed and capable of fully illuminating the other. Both are obscure, but they supplement one another as we seek a complete vision of his themes. But even this "vision" must be achieved as a second step. Both themes demand from us what was earlier described as the method of "extending the lines".

The two kernels, the two themes, are original to Bonhoeffer, and even if here and there one might discover in history other parallels echoing the same note, he is essentially uninfluenced in them by anyone, but has sensed and conceived them out of his own very individual situation. Further the two themes are in this way interrelated and to this extent form a factual unity, that the thought of responsible action is certainly also finally and properly a matter of reality, of apprehending the real and standing firm before it. The way of the "Stations on the Road to Freedom" is the way of the breakthrough to the real itself,—we might indeed hold that at this point freedom and reality mean fundamentally the same thing. It would then remain to be asked, and the question would be exceedingly instructive, why Bonhoeffer gives to reality the title of freedom.

"Daring to do what is right, not what fancy may tell you,
valiantly grasping occasions, not cravenly doubting—
freedom comes only through deeds, not through thoughts
taking wing".

This is the way of the breakthrough to reality in responsible
action. And the man who is "valiantly grasping occasions"
is as he does it the man who is "trusting in God whose commandment you faithfully follow". He is sustained basically by the
presence of Jesus Christ, on whom he depends in faith, the
encounter with whom in various situations becomes a concrete
commandment, who is awaiting him in all that is real. This we
shall follow up shortly when we deal with situation ethics with
a Christological stamp (see below, Section 3 of this chapter).

The same trait, action as a breakthrough into reality, is
also dominating already in Bonhoeffer's *The Cost of Discipleship*, which appeared in 1937. On this book he wrote later
(on July 21, 1944):

> "I thought I could acquire faith by trying to live a holy life,
> or something like it. I suppose I wrote *The Cost of Discipleship*
> as the end of that path. Today I can see the dangers of that book,
> though I still stand by what I wrote.
>
> I discovered later, and I am still discovering right up to this
> moment, that it is only by living completely in this world, that
> one learns to have faith . . ." (LPP, p. 201).

The reason why Bonhoeffer, after a conversion in his
thought which he himself recognized and admitted, "still
stands by what he wrote" could well be that here, too, the
basic motive of his theological thinking, wrestling with reality
(cp. Prologue and Chapter Eight), the reality of faith, and the
reality of God, finds expression, that same wrestling which
makes him complain about the invisibility of God which "gets
us down" (*Ges. Schr. I*, p. 61—in a letter to Helmut Rössler
dated October 1931).

Many of the thoughts which dominate his later utterances
are already here in *The Cost of Discipleship*, giving it their
stamp as they appear. Thus the thought of conformation
with Christ, later the "principle" of the *Ethics*, is there in the
final chapter, "The Image of Christ" (CD, pp. 269ff.). The
call to discipleship makes itself heard again in "being caught up

into the messianic sufferings of God in Jesus Christ" (LPP, p. 199). And again, non-religious interpretation has already sounded its note in such statements in *The Cost of Discipleship* as:

"When we go to church and listen to the sermon, what we want is to hear his Word—and that not merely for selfish reasons, but for the sake of the many for whom the Church and her message are foreign. We have a strange feeling that if Jesus himself— Jesus alone with his Word—could come into our midst at sermon time, we should find a quite different set of men hearing the Word, and quite a different set rejecting it . . . Of course it is our aim to preach Christ and Christ alone, but, when all is said and done, it is not the fault of our critics that they find our preaching so hard to understand, so overburdened with ideas and expressions which are hopelessly out of touch with the mental climate in which they live. It is just not true that every word of criticism directed against contemporary preaching is a deliberate rejection of Christ and proceeds from the spirit of Antichrist. So many people come to church with a genuine desire to hear what we have to say, yet they are always going back home with the uncomfortable feeling that we are making it too difficult for them to come to Jesus. Are we determined to have nothing to do with all these people? They are convinced that it is not the Word of Jesus himself that puts them off, but the superstructure of human, institutional and doctrinal elements in our preaching. Of course we know all the answers to these objections, and those answers certainly make it easy for us to slide out of our responsibilities" (CD, pp. 29f.).

The fight against "cheap grace" (CD, pp. 35ff.) is nothing else than the fight against an unreal Gospel, one floating in the air above reality, purely ideological and merely "religious".

"Cheap grace means grace as a doctrine, a principle, a system. It means forgiveness of sins proclaimed as a general truth, the love of God taught as the Christian 'conception' of God . . . Grace alone does everything, they say, and so everything can remain as it was before. 'All for sin could not atone.' The world goes on in the same old way, and we are still sinners 'even in the best life', as Luther said. Well, then, let the Christian live like the rest of the world, let him model himself on the world's standards in every sphere of life, and not presumptuously aspire to live a different life under grace from his old life under sin. That was the heresy of the enthusiasts, the Anabaptists and their kind" (CD. pp. 35ff.).

250

But the activity of the disciple, his "single-minded obedience" (cp. CD, pp. 69ff.), consists in breaking through a purely ideological Christianity to the reality of Jesus Christ himself.

Basically *The Cost of Discipleship* is the beginning of the protest against what Bonhoeffer described as the danger of "revelational positivism". "Revelational positivism" seems to him to set up a "law of faith" (LPP, p. 157). Later he realized that *The Cost of Discipleship* was at least threatened by the danger that in it a *law of works* would be set up. But for the sake of the open protest which it represented against an unreal understanding of grace, and for the sake of its testimony to the reality of Jesus Christ, he still continued to stand by his book.

2. *The Dialectic of Resistance and Submission as a Component of Responsible Activity*

As early as February 21, 1944, Bonhoeffer, in a letter which is extremely instructive for our present subject, expressed himself on the relation of resistance and submission in a passage which may have given Bethge the title of his book.[1] As early as this, at a time, that is, when he still believed in the success of the attempt on Hitler's life, he expounded with the utmost clarity the continuity between the two. This continuity between resistance and submission really lay for him, then, in the subject-matter itself. It was no expedient to give himself peace after the hope of success was itself snatched away from him. He speaks there of the

". . . 'dread' of straightforward simple actions, dread of having to make necessary decisions. I have often wondered here where we are to draw the line between necessary resistance to 'fate', and equally necessary submission. Don Quixote is the symbol of resistance carried to the point of absurdity, even lunacy; and similarly Michael Kohlhaas, insisting on his rights, puts himself in the wrong . . . in both cases resistance at last defeats its own object, and evaporates in theoretical fantasy. Sancho Panza is the type of complacent and artful accommodation to things as

[1] (The German title of LPP, *Widerstand und Ergebung*, means, literally translated, "Resistance and Submission"—Tr.)

they are. I think we must rise to the great demands that are made on us personally, and yet at the same time fulfil the commonplace and necessary tasks of daily life. We must confront fate—to me the neuter gender of the word 'fate' (*Schicksal*) is significant—as resolutely as we submit to it at the right time. One can speak of 'guidance' only on the other side of that twofold process, with God meeting us no longer as 'Thou', but also 'disguised' in the 'It'; so in the last resort my question is how we are to find the 'Thou' in this 'It' (i.e. fate), or, in other words, how does 'fate' really become 'guidance'. It is therefore impossible to define the boundary between resistance and submission on abstract principles; but both of them must exist, and both must be practised. Faith demands this elasticity of behaviour. Only so can we stand our ground in each situation as it arises, and turn it to gain" (LPP, pp. 133ff.).

Into the subject of divine guidance we shall enter in more detail in the following chapter. For Bonhoeffer this in no way belongs to, say, any "religious" way of thinking and speaking, but to the presupposed matter for interpretation, that is, the personally experienced and unquestionable reality of God and Christ itself. But this same personal guidance of God itself now becomes a problem. How is it to be thought of, how are we to speak credibly of it, how is it to be confirmed in one's own experience, while all the time the real is encountering us as "it", as a neuter, as fate? Bonhoeffer is obviously giving thought in his own situation to the attitude which finds in the "it" the "Thou", in fate guidance, in the impersonally real which presses in on us on all sides the truly real, the living God. In this attitude both resistance and submission are obviously ruling elements. In responsibly free activity which on each occasion lays hold courageously on what is then the real, in natural straightforward action, in that acceptance of necessary decisions which is the breakthrough to freedom and therefore to reality, there already rules, essentially and by the necessity of their structure, suffering, submission, surrender, the placing of one's own activity in the hands of God. What we have just learned in the poem to know as "stations" is now revealed as structure, as the interpenetration of structural moments. And it is in the light of this structure that this central subject for Bonhoeffer, free responsible action, is to be interpreted.

Further, it is clear that in the passage we have just quoted the matter at stake is again the concept of reality. Don Quixote and Sancho Panza both have an unreal attitude to reality. The former, "in theoretical fantasy", passes by reality, while the latter on the other hand accepts at once as the real what is in a pedestrian sense "given", he does not understand the dimension of depth in reality. His existential concept of reality, that is to say, the one to which his existence attains, is in a certain sense that positivist one of "pure facticity" against which, as we have already seen, Bonhoeffer demarcates his own position in a decisive passage in his *Ethics*. The man who avoids both dangers and embarks upon the situation "sustained by God's commandment and his faith alone" is the only man to find his way into the depth of reality, that is to say in the end, to come face to face with Jesus Christ.

In the manuscript already mentioned, "After Ten Years", Bonhoeffer has worked out this Don Quixote-Sancho Panza problem in a still more comprehensive and considered way. He wrote this at the turn of the year 1942–43, intending it as a Christmas present for some of his friends, and it stands at the beginning, both of his *Letters and Papers from Prison*, and, in a different form but largely with the same thoughts and in part with almost the same formulation of them, of his *Ethics*. Here he pictures his own ethical situation and that of his friends, that group of like-minded men of the same generation in the first ten years of Nazi rule. In almost apocalyptic pictures he describes the "masquerade of evil" of his time:

"Today there are once more villains and saints, and they are not hidden from the public view. Instead of the uniform greyness of the rainy day we have now the black storm-cloud and the brilliant lightning-flash. The outlines stand out with exaggerated sharpness. Reality lays itself bare. Shakespeare's characters walk in our midst. But the villain and the saint have little or nothing to do with systematic ethical studies. They emerge from primeval depths and by their appearance they tear open the infernal or the divine abyss from which they come and enable us to see for a moment into mysteries of which we had never dreamed . . ." (E, p. 3).
"If evil appears in the form of light, beneficence, loyalty and

renewal, if it conforms with historical necessity and social justice, then this, if it is understood straightforwardly, is a clear additional proof of its abysmal wickedness. But the moral theorist is blinded by it . . . " (E, p. 4; in complete agreement is LPP, pp. 26ff.; "The great masquerade of evil has played havoc with all our ethical concepts . . . etc.").

In this situation Bonhoeffer puts the question, "*Who stands firm*? Who stands by reality?" And he himself anticipates the answer: "It is not by astuteness, by knowing the tricks, but only by simple steadfastness in the truth of God, by training the eye upon this truth until it is simple and wise, that there comes the experience and the knowledge of the ethical reality" (E, p. 4).[2]

Accordingly he dismisses the various types of ethical mastery, or attempts at mastery, over reality. They none of them stand firm, they all lose heart before reality. If in more peaceful times they had their relative justification, in the time of apocalyptic storm when reality itself discloses a deeper stratum, their insufficiency, their failure to grow to match reality, stands revealed. The "reasonable" approach which thinks it can straighten out the contradictions by reason fails; every ethical fanaticism, every unqualified subscription to such and such an ethical principle fails; both the man of conscience and the man of duty fail. The former "in the end . . . is satisfied if instead of a clear conscience he has a salved one", the latter "will end by having to fulfil his obligation even to the devil" (E, p. 5). The way of private virtuousness also fails.

[2] "*Standing firm facing reality*" is what Bonhoeffer here especially fixes his eye upon as a moment in the specifically ethical individual situation. But in addition to this, believing existence in all its extension in time can certainly also be conceived as a standing firm facing reality, as a wrestling for the recognition of the Divine "Thou" in the "it" of the circumstances of life. Here incidentally we see a tension in the concept of reality which surely is characteristic of Bonhoeffer as well as belonging to the facts themselves. On the one side reality is what oppresses me and calls me in question, the evil, for instance, which discloses itself in its naked reality, and therefore that against which I have to stand firm. But on the other side reality is Jesus Christ himself, the great gift which makes me capable of standing firm. And if Bonhoeffer tells us that reality is to be given a wholly Christological meaning, this does not mean that this tension is thereby removed. Rather, experience of this tension and reflection upon it already belong to the Christological meaning of reality. This does not bring into theology any "principle of contradiction", or of "polarity". But it becomes clear that theological thought arises out of troubled Christian existence, and that it is in the same that it finds on each occasion its final task.

The man who would follow it "must be blind and deaf to the wrongs which surround him. It is only at the price of an act of self-deception that he can safeguard his private blamelessness against contamination through responsible action in the world" (E, p. 6). All these attitudes fail to contact reality. This, however, does not mean that there is nothing to be said for them. On Don Quixote, as the embodiment of failure to contact reality Bonhoeffer says in the same section, "It is all too easy to pour scorn on the weapons which we have inherited from our fathers, the weapons which served them to perform great feats but which in the present struggle can no longer be sufficient. It is the mean-spirited man who can read of what befell Don Quixote and not be stirred to sympathy" (E, pp. 6f.).

A special position among the attitudes which fail in face of reality, that is in this context, ethical reality in its final apocalyptic disclosure and pointedness, is taken by "the bold stroke of the deed which is done on one's own free responsibility". Of it Bonhoeffer says that it is "the only kind of deed which can strike at the heart of evil and overcome it" (E, p. 5). But even this attitude has its problems. Let such a man "beware lest precisely his supposed freedom may ultimately prove his undoing. He will easily consent to the bad, knowing full well that it is bad, in order to ward off what is worse, and in doing this he will no longer be able to see that precisely the worse which he is trying to avoid may still be the better. This is one of the underlying themes of tragedy" (E, pp. 5f.).

Bonhoeffer does not develop systematically the answer which he finally gives and in which he himself endeavours to live. Yet the direction which he takes and the approach which he gives to us are absolutely clear. The place at which we stand firm facing reality is surely responsible and free action. But this must receive yet one more qualification of its own. As the act of the Christian who goes out into the storm of reality "sustained only by the command of God and his faith", responsible activity is a behaviour which combines *simplicity and wisdom* ("Be ye wise as serpents and harmless as doves"—Matt. 10: 16).

"To be simple is to fix one's eyes solely on the simple truth of God at a time when all concepts are being confused, distorted and turned upside-down. It is to be single-hearted and not a man of two souls, an ἀνὴρ δίψυχος (James 1: 18)" (E, p. 7).

Such a man looks to God alone:

"He belongs simply and solely to God and to the will of God. It is precisely because he looks only to God, without any sidelong glance at the world, that he is able to look at the reality of the world freely and without prejudice. And that is how simplicity becomes wisdom. The wise man is the one who sees reality as it is, and who sees into the depths of things. That is why only that man is wise who sees reality in God. To understand reality is not the same as to know about outward events. It is to perceive the essential nature of things. The best informed man is not necessarily the wisest . . . But on the other hand knowledge of an apparently trivial detail often makes it possible to see into the depths of things . . . To look in freedom at God and at reality, which rests solely upon Him, this is to combine simplicity with wisdom. There is no true simplicity without wisdom and there is no wisdom without simplicity" (E, pp. 7f.).

In contradistinction, "existential" folly has an ethically negative quality and is not any matter of indifference. Folly is more dangerous than wickedness, as Bonhoeffer forcefully describes for us in "After Ten Years" (LPP, p. 30).

Thus the circle is completed. From the subject of responsible activity we have won our way back again to the subject of reality conceived in God, God as the depth of reality—not the same thing as the "depth of being", for it is the personal God who became flesh that is meant! As we look in freedom upon reality and in wise and honest action surrender ourselves to it, we meet with God himself in the form of Jesus Christ. God himself as reality encounters us exclusively in the situation, in the concrete life which he gives to us as a prize of war. And the implication is that theology, both dogmatics and ethics, must start from such concrete encounter with God and remain orientated towards it, if it is not to miss God himself.

Bonhoeffer gives us no recipe for responsible activity which stands firm facing reality. How could such a thing be possible! But he gives us an insight and indicates a structure, a structure of activity and passivity in one. Man acts in free alignment towards the concrete, unhampered in the last resort by principles, yielding himself in such activity at one and the same time to the judgement and to the mercy of the personal God. Thus impersonal reality becomes for him personal and the "it" the "Thou", that is to say, reality discloses to the man who acts, to him alone and not to the theorist, its depths and its essential nature.

The dialectic of resistance and submission receives its final, moving confirmation in Bonhoeffer's end as it is described under the title, "The Last Days", by Eberhard Bethge at the end of *Letters and Papers from Prison*. To the very end it seemed as if Bonhoeffer was to survive. On *Quasimodo geniti* Sunday (Low Sunday) he still preached to his fellow-prisoners on the text of the day, "and with his stripes we are healed" (Isa. 53: 5) and "Blessed be the God and Father of our Lord Jesus Christ. By his great mercy we have been born anew to a living hope through the resurrection of Jesus Christ from the dead" (I Peter 1: 3). "He spoke of the thoughts and decisions that their eventful imprisonment together had brought to them all. The prisoners detained for family reasons had planned to smuggle Bonhoeffer into their room after the service, so that they could have a service there too. But it was not long before the door was flung open, and two civilians called out: 'Prisoner Bonhoeffer, get ready to come with us' . . . He asked Payne Best to send special greetings to the Bishop of Chichester, if he succeeded in getting home again. 'This is the end—for me the beginning of life' were the last words that Best hands down to us". The resistance of hope was maintained with good reason up to the last moment. The last reversal in the dialectic of resistance and submission follows suddenly and rings out in a complete yielding in submission to God; "In the grey dawn of that Monday, April 9, there took place at Flossenbürg the execution of those who were not in any circumstances to survive. The camp doctor saw Bonhoeffer kneeling in the preparation cell and praying fervently" (LPP, pp. 232ff.).

3. *The Problem of a "Situation Ethic" (A Confrontation of Dietrich Bonhoeffer and Martin Buber)*

What happens to ethics at the collapse of "natural law" or "natural morality", as a system of pronouncements to be applied to each case as it arises? For Bonhoeffer can never conceive of "Ethics", his great subject, in any such way.[3] Instead, then, of what is called a casuistic one, do we reach what is called a "pure situation ethic"? Which form will ethics now assume?

To enter more deeply into this problem we put the trend of the Christian Dietrich Bonhoeffer's thought face to face with that of the Jew Martin Buber. The two, as we shall see, are related to one another, and the glance at Buber may help to bring more clearly before our eyes the factual importance of the basic problem of Bonhoeffer's ethic. For both thinkers the ethical problem is in the same way a living one, and in their thought as a whole there is a kinship in many respects. For both the fundamental impetus to thinking is wrestling with reality, the question about the reality of the real, and is so in such a way that faith receives a definitive place in reality, that indeed as a final result the reality of faith becomes the ontological definition of the reality of all that is real.[4]

Dietrich Bonhoeffer wrote his *Ethics* at the end of his short life. The work, which must surely count as the crown of his thought, remained, like so much of his thought, completely fragmentary and first appeared four years after his death. Characteristic of the whole work is the close affinity of ethics with ontology, to which he gives a Christological stamp. As soon as the ethical problem, "What ought we to do?", arises, there arises also the question about reality. For him the concern of ethics is in the last resort who stands firm by reality and who does what is in keeping with it. But the peculiar problem, or the difficulty to overcome which the whole endeavour strives, is that unavoidable question as to whether an ethic is possible which is neither a casuistic nor a purely situation ethic. For a situation ethic also is threatened by abstractness and formalism. Bonhoeffer endeavours to go a way which avoids both dangers. He writes:

[3] Even his early lecture, *Grundfragen einer christlichen Ethik*, (*Ges. Schr.*, III, pp. 48ff.), given in Barcelona in 1929, rejects emphatically all thinking within the rigid principles of a Christian moralism.
[4] This is factually our basic problem, within the horizon of which Bonhoeffer becomes the most importunate partner in our discussion. A second volume of *Reality and Faith* is planned to follow up the question further in discussion with, among others, Martin Buber himself.

"This leads us away from any kind of abstract ethic and towards an ethic which is entirely concrete. What can and must be said is not what is good once and for all, but *the way in which Christ takes form among us here and now.* The attempt to define that which is good once and for all has, in the nature of the case, always ended in failure. Either the proposition was asserted in such general and formal terms that it retained no significance as regards its contents, or else one tried to include in it and elaborate the whole immense range of conceivable contents, and thus to say in advance what would be good in every single conceivable case; this led to a casuistic system so unmanageable that it could satisfy the demands neither of general validity nor of concreteness. The concretely Christian ethic is beyond formalism and casuistry. Formalism and casuistry set out from the conflict between the good and the real, but the Christian ethic can take for its point of departure the reconciliation, already accomplished, of the world with God and the man Jesus Christ and the acceptance of the real man by God" (E, p. 23).

We shall also have to ask *how* Bonhoeffer travels his road and what role is played in it by the concept of reality, the whole ontological problem which already sounds its note in the posing of the question. His starting-position is clear, that the "good once for all", taken as corresponding to an unalterable *natura humana,* no longer comes into consideration as a basis for ethics. On the other hand the contentless formalism of a pure situation ethic does not seem satisfying to him. And in point of fact ethical reality, where man has to make significant decisions in significant situations, establish a meaning and take the responsibility upon himself, is the absolutely concrete. And if there is to be any such thing at all as ethical study, or thought on this exceedingly concrete reality (and why should there not be?), it seems completely inadequate that it should come to a halt at a bloodless formalism. Because ethical reality is the absolutely concrete, there rules in ethical study, still undefined, it is true, but yet powerful, the need for concreteness.

Martin Buber faces the same problem. We shall consider a short work of his where he handles the problem explicitly, some passages from *Aus einer philosophischen Rechenschaft,* printed at the end of Vol. I of his *Werke* (Kosel-Verlag, 1962), where he expresses his views in various objections raised against his philosophy. Buber writes there:

259

"Friends and enemies hold it against me that I neither recognize a traditional *corpus* of laws and ordinances as absolutely valid, nor have a system of ethics of my own to offer. In point of fact this gap is there, and it is so closely connected with my understanding as a whole that to fill it would be unthinkable. If I were to endeavour to do so, it would be a violation of the essence of my outlook. 'We expect from the teacher', a friend says, 'that he should give us instructions as to how we should travel our path. I oppose this very expectation. One should expect the direction from the teacher, but not the way in which one is to strive towards this direction; that every man must discover and gain for himself, each his own, in a work which will demand of him the best powers of his soul, but will also grant to him a treasure which will be sufficient for his being. Should this great work be taken away from him?" (*op. cit.*, p. 1116).

For Buber too, then, a casuistic system of morals is not to be considered. The value of a man's moral task, the responsible finding of his own way and going by it, carries too much weight with him. And this every casuistry would prejudice. This highest of works cannot be fulfilled by man by means of a system of rules. That is, it is precisely the most concrete, the most substantial element in ethical reality which rules out a universal and casuistic moralism. But for precisely the same reason Buber cannot remain content with the abstract assertion that therefore every man must responsibly face his own decisions. Rather, while he refuses the false and inadequate endeavour of casuistry to give concreteness to ethics, he points at the same time to another concreteness, for he has something worthy of thought to say on the analysis of the ethical situation. His way then is one of a "situation ethic", but not of an abstract and formal one.

The teacher certainly cannot take away from the individual his own journey, but he surely can and should point the direction. Buber knows no universally valid system of ethics, but he regards it as "not only natural, but also ethically sound, that everyone should accept from moral precepts what in any situation helps him to find his way" (*op. cit.*, p. 1117). This he defines as follows, "I certainly think that no moral norm has an absolute claim upon a man unless it is believed to be a gift from the Absolute" (*loc. cit.*). In this Buber conceives "belief" in a very comprehensive way. It does not require to be an explicit faith in God.

"The doctrine is also ascribed to me that no activity is of moral importance unless it is bound to God. Nothing lies further from me than to teach such doctrine: I have always had a frankly naïve sympathy for the godless, or for those who live as if they were godless; and it seems to me a fine thing when the righteous man does good with all his heart 'without thinking of God' " (*op. cit.*, pp. 1117f.).

But further, not only is the individual justified in choosing certain moral precepts as vehicles for his ethical journey, but there also seem to Buber in addition to this to be eternal, absolute commandments. These, it is true, are not simply to be recognized and used as convenient standards ready to hand, but have to be interpreted in the light of the individual path which each individual has to tread.

"May I assure my critics that I have never doubted the absolute validity of the commandment, 'Honour thy father and thy mother'; but if anyone says to me that one knows always and in all circumstances what 'honour' means and what it does not, I say of him that he does not know what he is speaking about. Man must interpret the eternal words, and interpret them with his own life" (*op. cit.*, p. 1118).

Buber, that is, gives concrete content to his situation ethics in three ways, in that the teacher points the direction, in that man seeks help for his way from ethical systems, and in that he does not in his freedom create new values out of nothing, but is an *interpreter* with his life of the *already given* eternal words, while these in turn require just such an interpretation. This last point, that the ethical contents are in need of interpretation, and that they need it given, not only by word and thought, but by human existence itself, possibly takes us a stage further in the direction of what Buber has in mind. There are such things as ethical contents. Man in his responsible existence is not set in the void. But there are not such contents divorced from situations, they do not exist somewhere in a heaven of ideas, recognizable without situations, or in the unhistorical medium of an unalterable *natura humana*. They only exist, and are only recognizable, in the medium of history. Historical situations are the exclusive ontological setting of ethical contents. Hence they must be found, or interpreted, by life itself.

The question which now becomes pressing is that of the *immanence* of these ethical contents in the historical situations. How can situations, every one of which is unique and unlike anything else, conceal ethical contents? But perhaps if we are to advance further the question must be put in another way. If it is true that we cannot overleap historicity, and if it is true that ethical contents can only be recognized *in* the situation, we must ask now about the manner or the structure of their *being discovered* in the situation. And first of all there is this decisive assertion which we have to make, that man does not arbitrarily create ethical value but that he *discovers* it, in that he meets a demand in a certain situation. And accordingly Buber writes:

> "It is asserted that I violate my own teaching on the absolute-ness of the moral demand, because I 'make the individual the sole but uncertain judge of what he should do', because I put the private decision of the individual in the place of the absolute value. Because I also recognize that sometimes in a given situation which is full of contradictions it is not possible without a serious examination of the circumstances and of one's own heart to decide what is the practical meaning of following the truth, I am therefore accused of putting in question the absolute distinction between truth and falsehood" (*op. cit.*, p. 1118).

Ethical decision then, according to Buber, is a discovery of the ethical claim of a situation and of its ethical content; it is an existential investigation into a situation and an illumination of it, in the light of what it *properly*, in *reality*, is. Thus man comes gradually into contact with the basis, with the essence. This usually happens gradually; it is a journey of discovery step by step.

> "Situations have a word to speak on their side. And the real situations, the biographically or historically real ones, are not simple and smooth like principles, they carry contradiction in themselves, they raise it before our eyes and we dare not ignore it, for reality lives in contradiction. It is not a case of 'everything or nothing'! It is a matter of realizing as much of our truth as in all the contradictions of the situation is permitted to the unprejudiced penetrating insight" (*op. cit.*, p. 1119).

And then Buber gives a concrete example of how such a discovery may take place:

"You are faced by a political decision ... and for the man I mean a political decision is also a moral one. You are impelled by a commandment to do justice, and, moved in heart by it, you look into the almost chaotic depths of a situation, there where the contradiction stares back at you. You bring everything to your mind as strongly as you possibly can, both, once again and from the foundations, what you have already known and the new features which now come within your knowledge. You do not spare yourself; you allow fearful things to afflict you from both sides; you, at once the arena and the judge, allow the battle to be fought out without restrictions. And now in the middle of the strife ... something happens. I cannot say that it always does, I can truthfully say that time and again it does. It happens that surprisingly, sometimes quite overwhelmingly you are made aware of how much of your truth and justice can be realized in this situation. And in this very moment, not always, but time and again (that is the part chance plays in your life), the powers of your soul which the moment before were disputing with one another crystallize and come into harmony" (*op. cit.*, p. 1120).

Then he adds:

"This is no universally valid answer, there is no guarantee, only just a chance, only just a venture ... Even when one seeks to do the right, one must venture" (*ibid.*).

It has been held against Buber that the ethical path which he sketches is one only for an *élite*, for those who are especially gifted. He answers with a reference to *Chassidism*:

"In my youth Chassidism taught me to value the 'simple man' who is inclined with his whole soul to the godlike, without being able to comprehend intellectually this inclination of his. I have kept my love for him. I would not of course demand of him that he should reach such wholeheartedness as truly to say 'Thou' or adopt the true direction. But must not this very thing, wholeheartedness in the situation, be seen as the constantly renewed task of that very different type of man who from his early days is dedicated to the diversity of intellectual life" (*op. cit.*, p. 1121).

There are two ways of making this journey, but in both the same thing is at stake. The completeness of the simple man consists in his immediate, unstudied inclination to the

Absolute, which allows him to find the way with certainty. The man of exceptional gifts attains to completeness in the most conscientious examination of the situation.

But wholeheartedness, this same "crystallizing and coming into harmony of one's powers", is obviously a necessary part of the discovery of what the situation contains. And further, this very wholeheartedness is a motive also found in emphatic form in the thought of Dietrich Bonhoeffer. I refer to that point where, as we have already expounded, he speaks of the unity of simplicity and wisdom as the shape of being of the man who stands firm in the ethical situation of decision, who stands firm above all before the demonic nature of evil, in face of which all moralist principles must come to nothing:

"A man can hold his own here only if he can combine simplicity with wisdom. But what is simplicity? What is wisdom? And how are the two to be combined? To be simple is to fix one's eye solely on the simple truth of God at a time when all concepts are being confused, distorted and turned upside-down. It is to be single-hearted and not a man of two souls, an ἀνὴρ δίψυχος (James i, 8). Because the simple man knows God, because God is his, he clings to the commandments, the judgements and the mercies which come from God's mouth every day afresh. Not fettered by principles, but bound by love for God, he has been set free from the problems and conflicts of ethical decision. They no longer oppress him. He belongs simply and solely to God and to the will of God. It is precisely because he looks only to God, without any side-long glance at the world, that he is able to look at the reality of the world freely and without prejudice. And that is how simplicity becomes wisdom. The wise man is the one who sees reality as it is, and who sees into the depths of things. That is why only that man is wise who sees reality only in God. To understand reality is not the same as to know about outward events. It is to perceive the essential nature of things. The best informed man is not necessarily the wisest ... To recognize the significant in the factual is wisdom ... To look in freedom at God and at reality, which rests solely upon him, this is to combine simplicity with wisdom" (E, pp. 7f.).

Here the notes of Bonhoeffer's and Buber's thought are in harmony with one another. It is not a matter of one influencing the other, but surely, I think, of material kinship in the putting of the question and in the experience of thinking.

We could thus sum up how Buber feels and thinks the factual situation. The good, what is commanded, is not arbitrarily brought by man into situations. It is not he who puts his stamp upon them. Rather, what is commanded comes face to face with him out of the situations themselves, time and again, and new each time, but none the less a real object confronting him, a claim which lays its obligation upon him. But now since it is a matter of making a new discovery each time, since each situation is again different and unique, is there nothing on which one can rely? Is there no continuity of any kind? Buber would say that there is. There is the continuity of the "eternal words" which are always already promulgated but which in the changing situations man has to interpret anew each time with his life. This surely can only be understood in the following way. The eternal words, spoken as they are to man by an eternal "Thou", are also a historical event and create a historical situation. Thus there are in a sense primary or transcendental situations "behind" and "in" the concrete situations, but they are only to be grasped in the latter. As a historical man with a claim laid upon me I always am faced by an absolute provision, which here and now appears for me, always the same but each time in a new form, but which always evades me when I try to stretch out beyond the here and now of the situation and grasp it with my hands. I cannot grasp it, I can only surrender myself to it as it appears here and now and thus interpret the eternal word with my life, with the commitment of my being.

It is no chance that it was precisely the *Ethics* which Bonhoeffer was anxious to complete (cp. the passage in *Letters and Papers from Prison*, p. 107; "I sometimes feel . . . as if all I had to do now were to finish my *Ethics*"). It is in keeping with the characteristic trend of his thought, with his urge towards concrete reality, that his thinking, as far as mere thought could, should give expression to such reality. For us perhaps the highest concreteness is found in ethical decision in which we take responsibility upon ourselves. In addition it can be understood from Bonhoeffer's own biographical situation, and especially that of the last period, why reality in its hardness and inevitability, the thing, that is, with which he was concerned from the beginning, should make itself known to him precisely in the situation of ethical decision. To support himself by an abstract ethic of any kind must have seemed to him, in face of the threatening reality of evil which was pressing upon him and in face of its challenge, absolutely unsatisfactory. Hence he sees himself, as a Christian who has to stand firm, led away from every abstract ethic to a concrete one. But how is this concrete ethic to be conceived? A casuistic ethic, which applies general moral rules to the individual case, and for all its unalterable concreteness still never quite meets it, must appear just as abstract as the formalism of a pure situation ethic which disregards every concrete existential content, and in this way so limits ethical study in favour of ethical decision *in actu* that the latter remains contentless. Both dangers of remaining in the abstract are to be avoided. Bonhoeffer adopts the way of a situation ethic which permits the situations to speak, but as he does so reflects in such a way on the nature, or structure, of the ethical existence inherent in situations, that a content is seen which is common to all situations as such. For this way describes structurally what it is which confronts man out of each situation, in a different manner each time, and thus becomes his guide. It is Jesus Christ in person.

We have tried to use the example of the ethical thought of Martin Buber, who on his side feels the claim on his thinking of the unsurpassable concreteness of the ethical situation and the ethical way, and who in addition is akin to Bonhoeffer in a variety of respects (worldliness, universalism, striving for reality, etc.), to show the facts of the pressure of the Scylla of ethical formalism and the Charybdis of casuistry as alternatives, and how avoiding both becomes a postulate which in its turn drives us towards the establishment of a concrete situation ethic, full of content.

The provisional insight which Bonhoeffer made open to us as he wrestled with the problem, for it is no more than a provisional insight any more than is that of Buber, seems to me very similar to that of the latter. Not only is it the same problem with which both men wrestled, it is the same insight towards which they were fighting their way. This, moreover, is not altogether by accident; it would have to be assumed in any case, because of other remarkable kinships in the manner of thinking of the two. We have already referred to the interest of both in the reality of the real. We have likewise noted the special function of "wholeheartedness" in recognizing the situation, a wholeheartedness and singleheartedness which, we can add, can come about in Bonhoeffer also both by an immediate comprehension and by the most thoughtful examination of the circumstances. But in addition to these both thinkers are akin in their affirmation of the world through faith, a worldliness which Buber learned from Chassidism and which Bonhoeffer, with his strong orientation towards the Old Testament, championed with passionate emphasis, above all right at the end of his life. Finally the two are materially at one in that universalist trait, that attitude which demands no definite and explicit religious confession from one's fellowmen in order to know oneself in unqualified solidarity with them. Both, Buber and Bonhoeffer, recognize an implicit faith in God.[5]

Such far-reaching affinities incline us to the assumption that there will be the same prospects as regards the problem of a non-casuistic ethic. And in point of fact Bonhoeffer on his side sees ethical decision as a recognition and a discovery of what the situation demands. Ethical activity is each time a recognition of a concrete reality, of what is real at that time. Hence wisdom plays a central role in his ethical thought, and folly in its turn is not ethically indifferent.

But he does not simply appeal to the reality of the situation with the abstract statement that everything is now concrete . . . ! Rather, for Bonhoeffer the reality of the real is a concrete person, Jesus Christ, who is always the same in all situations. But of course this statement cannot simply be left standing dogmatically in this way, it needs existential interpretation for its meaning to become visible. For Bonhoeffer the name of Jesus Christ implies the reconciliation of the world with God.

"But there is a place at which God and the cosmic reality are reconciled, a place at which God and man have become one. That and that alone is what enables man to set his eyes upon God and

[5] The concept of an "unconscious" or "anonymous" faith, a "believing dynamic of existence" without the conscious content adequately corresponding to it, is to me the final radicalizing of the traditional dogmatic concept of *fides implicita* which Catholic theology in particular knows, but which nevertheless can and must with certain reservations be recognized by Protestant theology. I have endeavoured to show this in my essay, *Der Begriff der fides implicita in der Sicht evangelischer Theologie* (so far in duplicated form in the *Korrespondenzblatt des Collegium Canisianum*, 1965, 3, pp. 5ff.)

upon the world at the same time. This place does not lie somewhere out beyond reality in the realm of ideas. It lies in the midst
of history as a divine miracle. It lies in Jesus Christ, the Reconciler
of the world. As an ideal the unity of simplicity and wisdom is
doomed to failure, just as is any other attempt to hold one's own
against reality. But if it is founded upon the reality of a world
which is at one with God in Jesus Christ, the commandment of
Jesus acquires reality and meaning. Whoever sees Jesus Christ
does indeed see God and the world in one. He can henceforward
no longer see God without the world or the world without God"
(E, p. 8).

Christ therefore, the unity of God and the world, its reconciliation, the gracious immanence of God in the world, in its
circumstances, in its ethical situations, but immanence regarded as a person, as a "Thou" whom one can address, Christ
is the material *continuum*, the trustworthy element which runs
through concrete situations and confirms them all in their very
concreteness. The knowledge of Christ is also each time a
knowledge now in the situation, and, above all, characteristically in the "ethical" situation. One could say that, according
to Bonhoeffer, the man who really knows Christ as here each
time, also knows what is real and what is to be done. Yes, we
can even go so far as to dare to say the converse, that the man
who knows each time what is real and what is to be done, by
that very fact in reality knows Christ.[6] To this extent there is
for Bonhoeffer something like an implicit knowledge of Christ
in ethical existence.

And now of course there arises the question on which every-

[6] This follows, for example, from the essay, "What is meant by Telling the
Truth?" There Bonhoeffer writes, " 'Telling the truth', therefore, is not solely
a matter of moral character; it is also a matter of correct appreciation of real
situations and of serious reflection upon them. The more complex the actual
situations of a man's life, the more responsible and the more difficult will be
his task of 'telling the truth' . . . Telling the truth therefore, is something which
must be learnt. This will sound very shocking to anyone who thinks that it must
all depend on moral character and that if this is blameless the rest is child's
play. But the simple fact is that the ethical cannot be detached from reality,
and consequently continual progress in learning to appreciate reality is a
necessary ingredient in ethical action . . . It is a question of knowing the right
word on each occasion. Finding this word is a matter of long, earnest and ever
more advanced effort on the basis of experience and knowledge of the real.
If one is to say how a thing really is, i.e., if one is to speak truthfully, one's
gaze and one's thought must be directed towards the way in which the real
exists in God and through God and for God" (E, pp. 327ff.). Then somewhat

thing depends, that concerning the manner or structure of the knowledge of Christ in the ethical situation. What is it that really happens?

On this Bonhoeffer did not succeed in reaching a final intellectual clarity. It was not given to him to follow the path of his thought to the end. But thoughts are suggested by his ethical and ontological sketch, and, especially in his late work, certain contours begin to appear.

This whole sketch of a situation ethic that is non-casuistic but not formal, that has a concrete, namely a Christological, content, has in Bonhoeffer a strong biographical determination. Behind it stands his last great decision, his entry into political life and his part in the conspiracy against Hitler. He knew that the task assigned him then was against every norm and rule, and yet, indeed for that very reason, was the complete model of

---

later Bonhoeffer again takes up this last thought; "Jesus calls Satan 'the father of the lie' (John 8: 44). The lie is primarily the denial of God as he has evidenced Himself to the world ... Consequently the lie is the denial, the negation and the conscious and deliberate destruction of the reality which is created by God and which consists in God, no matter whether this purpose is achieved by speech or by silence. The assigned purpose of our words, in unity with the word of God, is to express the real, as it exists in God; and the assigned purpose of our silence is to signify the limit which is imposed upon our words by the real as it exists in God. In our endeavours to express the real we do not encounter this as a consistent whole, but in a condition of disruption and inner contradiction which has need of reconciliation and healing. We find ourselves simultaneously embedded in various different orders of the real, and our words, which strive towards the reconciliation and healing of the real, are nevertheless repeatedly drawn in into the prevalent disunion and conflict. They can indeed fulfil their assigned purpose of expressing the real, as it is in God, only by taking up into themselves both the inner contradiction and the inner consistency of the real. If the words of men are to be true they must deny neither the Fall nor God's word of creation and reconciliation, the word in which all disunion is overcome" (E, p. 332).

But it follows from this train of thought that "telling the truth" is a matter of the right knowledge of real relations. And this is the reason why folly, which mistakes the real relations, is for Bonhoeffer not ethically neutral. But for him the knowledge of real relations is in the last resort the knowledge of the real as it "exists in God and through God and for God". It is the existential knowledge and affirmation of the unity restored by God, the reconciliation of the real with God. But this has taken place in Christ,—a statement which in itself expresses the deepest mystery of Jesus Christ.

But it would surely be misguided to think that only the confessing Christian had the ability to know real relations, or that he, just because of his explicit confession of Christ, *always* had the ability to know them. Thus it follows that whoever knows real relations in his "ethical attitude", be he a confessing Christian or not, thereby himself in a certain way knows the mystery of Jesus Christ.

ethical activity. Then when the attempt of July 20 failed, Bonhoeffer saw himself completely given up to what he had already in his activity given himself up to before, and on the selfsame evening he wrote the poem "Stations on the Road to Freedom", fulfilling existentially in his behaviour what he had already meditated upon months before (Cp. the letter of February 21, 1944; LPP, pp. 133f.; see above, pp. 251f.).

Both belong to responsible ethical activity, and it is in this same irresoluble dialectic of resistance and submission, of action and suffering that guidance is experienced, that God and Christ are discovered in the situation. After acting actively and responsibly in the conspiracy, Bonhoeffer after July 20, fulfilled existentially the other side of the dialectic. Suffering, as he understood it, is but the other side of action. The structure of responsible activity is to surrender oneself to the concretely present God. Man does what his hand finds to do and submits the judgement to God, following I Cor. 4: 3, ". . . Yea, I judge not myself . . ." Not only success and failure are submitted, to God, but even judgement itself, all in complete contrast to Jean Paul Sartre's view of man and his responsible activity as expressed in his play, *Les Mouches* ("The Flies").[7] There man in complete outward ruin retains his own judgement on his activity as his last, inalienable and finally decisive reservation. But in Bonhoeffer we find the other extreme, complete surrender to the "Thou" in responsible action, complete passivity in the greatest activity. He knows that through his action he is at fault according to the norm, but he takes the responsibility upon himself because someone must take it, and in this he is certain of the forgiveness of God. It is precisely in the breach of the norm that he is certain of God. This dialectical unity of resistance and submission, of action and surrender, is surely that very wholeheartedness which has to be achieved as *the* ethical attitude, in reality and before God on each occasion, in what is great and what is small.

4. *The Ethical Principle of "Conformation"*

It is true that Bonhoeffer also recognizes a "natural law",

---

[7] (1947; The relevant philosophy of Sartre is discussed in editor's introduction, Engl. edn.,—not translation. ed. North, Harrap, 1963—Tr.)

the maintenance of life in a variety of realms. Here he speaks occasionally of the four or five "mandates", family, work, State, Church, and occasionally, friendship. The doctrine of the "mandates" is not, however, worked out precisely, the norm not being the place where we find that complex of ethical problems which was Bonhoeffer's primary interest.[8] As we said at the beginning, it is not Bonhoeffer's aim to

[8] A situation ethic in the sense of that of Bonhoeffer is called in the language of modern Catholic moral theology, "existential ethics". On this cp. Karl Rahner's essay, "On the Question of a Formal Existential Ethics", in *Theological Investigations*, II, tr. Krüger, D. L. & T., 1963, pp. 217ff.; ". . . this positively individual element in the moral action (an action which is more than the fulfilment of the universal norm or of an abstract being; 'man') is even as such to be conceived absolutely as the object of a binding will of God. It would be absurd for a God-regulated, theological morality to think that God's binding will could only be directed to the human action in so far as the latter is simply a realization of the universal norm and of a universal nature. If the creative will of God is directly and unambiguously directed to the concrete and the individual, then this surely is not true merely in so far as this individual reality is the realization of a case of the universal—rather it is directed to the concrete as such, as it really is—to the concrete in its positive, and particularly its substantial, material uniqueness. God is interested in history not only in so far as it is the carrying out of norms, but in so far as it is a history which consists in the harmony of unique events and which precisely in this way has a meaning for eternity . . . No matter how inadequate the reasons offered in the present context, it can surely be said that there is an individual ethical reality of a positive kind which is untranslatable into a material universal ethics; there is a binding ethical uniqueness . . ." (pp. 227ff.).

What seems to me questionable in Rahner is that he does to some extent add this individual existential ethic to a general one of beings or norms. The inner relation of the two is not made clear. Is the position not rather this, that the will of God is always concrete, and that one can only speak of ethical "principles" or "norms" as at most a *special case* of this general situation of the facts, a case in quite definite circumstances and with quite definite presuppositions? One might do it perhaps in cases where the moral life has to manifest itself in juridical or quasi-juridical norms. The path of the thorough carrying out of an individual existential ethic, the path which Bonhoeffer trod, is something quite different again from that of adding existential ethics to a presupposed ethic of norms, and this is what we see in the essay of Rahner's which we quoted. One might compare further Rahner's recent essay, "Situation Ethics in an Ecumenical Perspective", in *The Christian of the Future*, tr. O'Hara, Burns & Oates, 1967, pp. 39ff. There Rahner develops the thought that from the beginning Catholic thought tended more to an "essential" or casuistic ethic, and Protestant thought more to an existential or situation one, but that because of the present situation of Christendom in the world a factual *rapprochement* is taking place. This is happening for this reason among others, that in the world of today more and more spheres of life and relations are coming into existence which are not yet covered by any norms but which are demanding creative ethical answers. In this way the world situation is demanding the ecumenical dialogue.

remain at the point of an abstract, formal situation ethic. But he seeks to gain concreteness, not from a universally valid norm, but from the analysis of the situation itself. What can and should be said is not what is good once and for all, but "how Christ is formed in us today and here" (following Gal. 4: 19). Thus the concept of *"conformation with Christ"* becomes important for him as a structural concept of responsible behaviour in the ethical situation.

"The man whom God has taken to himself, sentenced and awakened to a new life, this is Jesus Christ. In Him it is all man-kind. It is ourselves. Only the form of Jesus Christ confronts the world and defeats it. And it is from this form alone that there comes the formation of a new world, a world which is reconciled with God . . .

". . . Formation comes only by being drawn into the form of Jesus Christ. It comes only as formation in his likeness, as *con-formation* with the unique form of Him who was made man, was crucified, and rose again. This is not achieved by dint of efforts 'to become like Jesus', which is the way in which we usually interpret it. It is achieved only when the form of Jesus Christ itself works upon us in such a manner that it moulds our form in its own likeness (Gal. iv, 19). Christ remains the only giver of forms. It is not Christian men who shape the world with their ideas, but it is Christ who shapes men in conformity with Himself. But just as we misunderstand the form of Christ if we take Him to be essentially the teacher of a pious and good life, so, too, we should misunder-stand the formation of man if we were to regard it as instruction in the way in which a pious and good life is to be attained" (E, pp. 17f.).

To be conformed with Christ means to be conformed with Christ Incarnate, Crucified and Risen; with the Incarnate in unreserved openness towards one's neighbour; with the Cruci-fied in acceptance of judgement upon oneself; with the Risen in the maintenance of a hope transcending all that is foresee-able. But this does not mean for Bonhoeffer that man takes upon himself a certain "virtuousness", but simply that Christ himself "is formed" among us, in this "between" in the ethical situation.

There is yet another viewpoint from which Bonhoeffer sees the ethical situation made materially concrete, it is so through the responsibility of the one who acts for the shaping of the future, that area of the future given as our responsibility. It is an ever-recurring theme in Bonhoeffer that we must act, not from principles, but out of our responsibility for the future, and that success also is ethically not simply indifferent. He did not work out further how to link this thought to the Christological structure of ethical action—and yet we find an echo of it in what he says on the Christological *motif* of representation; the man who is responsible acts as representative also for those for whom he takes over responsibility.

There is yet another respect in which the principle of representation proves itself fruitful for overcoming a mere formalism, an empty, purely formal, situation ethic. The situation of the ethicist, and therefore of ethical study, is for its part historical. The ethicist cannot place himself and his thinking outside that historical context. Hence his studies can never take on an unhistorical character, but the study is itself a historical act, a historical decision. It has its own setting, its own special place, in the historical situation, and cannot escape from that concrete place. In that case what is *once for all* good can never be worked out by concrete study or by responsible thought; our eyes have to be turned solely towards how Christ is formed among us *here and today*. But now this *hic et nunc* refers for Bonhoeffer not merely to the individual and unrepeatable ethical situation, it extends beyond it by virtue of his category of the collective person. He works out the thought thus in his *Ethics* under the heading, "The Concrete Place":

"But the question of how Christ takes form among us here and now, or how we are conformed with His form, contains within itself still further difficult questions. What do we mean by 'among us', 'now' and 'here'? If it is impossible to establish for all times and places what is good, then the question still arises for what times and places any answer at all can be given to our enquiry. It must not remain in doubt for a single moment that any one section to which we may now turn our attention is to be regarded precisely as a section, as a part of the whole of humanity. In every section of his history man is simply and entirely the man taken upon Himself by Christ. And for this reason whatever may have to be said about this section will always refer not only to this part but also to the whole. However, we must now answer the question regarding the times and places of which we are thinking when we set out to speak of formation through the form of Christ. There are in the first place quite generally the times and places which in some way concern us, those of which we have experience and which are reality for us. They are the times and places which confront us with concrete problems, set us tasks and charge us with responsibility. The 'among us', the 'now' and 'here' is therefore the region of our decisions and encounters. This region undoubtedly varies very greatly in extent according to the individual and it might consequently be supposed that these definitions could in the end be interpreted so widely and so vaguely as to make room for unrestrained individualism. What prevents this is the fact that by our history we are set objectively in a definite nexus of experiences, responsibilities and decision from which we cannot free ourselves again except by an abstraction. We live, in fact, within this nexus, whether or not we are in every respect aware of it" (E, pp. 23f.).

There are not only individual situations in ethics, there are also "collective" situations, each with a certain extension in history, collective situations in which individuals are inescapably jointly involved. One such nexus of experience, responsibility and decision, or rather *the* one which was pressing to Bonhoeffer in his intellectual situation, is the history of the Western world. According to Bonhoeffer's presentation this is the realm in the history of mankind which up to now has been palpably stamped in an exceptional way by the event of Christ. Here Christ for the first time has begun to take form in the visible history of mankind, which of course does not mean that the eschatological event of Christ is nearer to this realm of history than to others. But yet there can be found here a certain palpable contact with historical form induced by the history of Jesus Christ upon earth, a certain historical legacy given and determined by Christ. Under the title, "Inheritance and Decay", Bonhoeffer attempts in his *Ethics* to sketch in broad contours the historical trends of development of this realm through the centuries. How far he has succeeded remains questionable. On the whole it seems to me no more than an experiment, a sketch not meant to be finally valid (Cp. the note on p. 106 above). But what is important is not these details but rather the principle underlying them of a sphere of responsibility as a principle of ethical study. In such a sphere of responsibility, in a concrete place, in a "collective situation", the ethicist is able to speak. And thus all is not received into a complete individualism which no longer permits any concrete ethical instruction with content in it. It is surely possible to say within the framework of a collective situation how Christ is able to take form among us. The ethicist then surely speaks, thinks and gives his teaching about the content of ethics, not unhistorically, once for all time, but for a definite, though more comprehensive, area. Because he thinks and speaks thus in a situation, that is, the collective situation, because he for his part speaks thus historically and bound to the situation, his speaking is responsible speaking, arising from decision. He seeks, in a certain way *representatively*, to know the nature and the demands of the collective situation, he gives his teaching representatively for his contemporaries who stand with him in the same complex of history. Here there could be found a prophetic task, a prophetic office of the Church of Christ, its theology and its thought, above all in the province of ethics. The thought of the ethicist, then, is certainly study, and it is certainly marked by content, but it is prophetic study, accepting responsibility, and to this extent concrete. He makes his decisions representatively for his contemporaries. And their answer in its turn can only be a free co-responding which accepts responsibility.

5. *Further Prospects*

Ethics, as Bonhoeffer understood that word, still constituted at the end his intense theological interest. His thought on ethical problems did not win through to a final systematic elucidation. But the unity of his basic tendency is none the less clearly recognizable to the unprejudiced view. It is so obvious that to develop further the systematic elucidation is worthwhile. I wish now, after following out the trend in its various characteristics, to close by beginning briefly to gather together the elements which in my opinion are typical of his ethical thought and which it would be worthwhile, by means of this systematic elucidation, to bring into an organic relation. In Bonhoeffer they simply stand side by side, to some extent unintegrated or only partly integrated, but their conceptual connection in the one basic thought is certainly to be felt, if it is not articulated.

The *urge to concreteness* is impressive as a basic trait ruling in Bonhoeffer's ethics, and hence a unified tendency appears in all the individual constitutive traits. It can be observed at once by the unprejudiced reader. And yet Bonhoeffer had not yet clarified conceptually this factual unity of his thinking, this unity of *motif* and trend, to give the coherence of a system. This task still remains to be done. As the position is today, to stand before Bonhoeffer's ethical study, before the sketch of his ethics, to which of course we recognize essential parallels and complements in the *Letters and Papers from Prison*, is to stand before a mighty endeavour of thought, in itself plausible, which carries us with it and challenges us. But the practical task of ethical thought is not thereby yet solved for us. We are not relieved of the individual problems of ethics as they present themselves for the theologian's ethical study, and which demand that he give a practical, pastoral instruction. We cannot at once apply to them fruitfully Bonhoeffer's principles. But this we must demand of a Christian ethic. This is the goal of ethical study, it strives for practical, evangelical instruction on details, for an instruction which will give "pastoral" significance to our situation or realm of situations, without of course thereby in any way taking away the responsibility from ourselves. If an endeavour in ethical study is to keep true to its subject, it must advance into this realm and show itself helpful here. This Bonhoeffer's *Ethics* has not yet succeeded in doing, apart, perhaps, from examples given in particular cases, as, for instance, that little essay so highly significant for his understanding of reality and responsibility, "What is meant by Telling the Truth?". But apart from this his *Ethics* has not yet travelled far enough on the path of study to reach that realm of practical, pastoral "applicability". None the less the beginnings he has made to ethical thought appear convincing, and their basic tendency has in practice already the effect of a liberation. The elucidation of what he has begun, then, must be carried further. The elements of his thought are already visible. It would be worthwhile now to put them into organic association and thus finally to catch sight of their elemental factual unity. These elements of thought are as follows:

1. As a starting-point and setting of the problem the endeavour for an ethic that is concrete, that is to say, neither

casuistic nor formalistic, and, arising from this, the commitment to the way of a *situation ethic with content*.

2. The concept of the "concrete place", a *nexus of experience and responsibility*, that is to say, a situation which on the one hand is historical but which on the other reaches out beyond the purely individual and so permits the pronouncement of common instruction.

3. *Conformation with Christ* as the chief material "principle" of this ethic, that Jesus Christ "takes form" among us and that we "are conformed" with him. Bonhoeffer's ethics as a whole is an endeavour to make this thought of conformation the principle of Christian ethics, and to work out the whole ethic on this foundation. The thought of conformation includes a strong moment of the personal; it is no longer in the last resort a matter of the realization of ideas and principles, or of abstract duties, virtues, and values, but of encounter with a concrete person, of correspondence to him and response to him. And this, according to Bonhoeffer's conception, is surely still true in the last resort for all ethical responsibility and not merely for the particular realm of Christian ethics, but it is reserved for the Christian ethic, by virtue of its "light of faith", clearly to address itself to the facts and to study them. *By such a personalizing of ethics Bonhoeffer seeks to reach that concreteness which forces itself upon ethical thought.* We have to recognize here that in ethical responsibility as such it is always structurally a matter of encounter with a person, and always with the same person. We say "structurally", which implies that the situation obviously is not that first of all what ethical responsibility is can adequately be described beforehand in its structure and its nature, and that the postscript then can simply be added that such responsibility is always shown towards the same person, the person of God. Indeed, in point of fact ethical responsibility is always also there arising where there is belief in God.[9] That is indisputable. And yet ethics

[9] Even where there is no explicit faith in God, yet the relation of man to his neighbour is still in the last resort related to God. Cp. on this Karl Rahner, ". . . What has just been said becomes clearer when we think of more concrete data of traditional theology. Theology maintains that there is a love of one's neighbour which is itself *caritas*, the 'divine virtue' whose 'formal object' is God himself, in which therefore an immediacy towards God-in-himself is achieved. This is an astonishing thesis for theology, however traditional it

must be personalized if for no other purpose than that it may be possible to grasp the structure of responsibility. And this structure, as we have seen, is a quite specific one, it is determined by the person of *Jesus Christ*.

Such a personalizing of ethics by the principle of conformation means a gain in concreteness in so far as both forms of abstract ethics, casuistry and formalism, can be overcome by it. Casuistry, which depends upon general principles, is overcome because a person is not anything general and unhistorical, but can only encounter in historical situations each time. The formalism of a pure "situation ethic" is overcome because, in that it is always the same person who encounters, establishes responsibility as such and makes possible ethical behaviour, a definite concrete content runs through all situations.

The "principle" of conformation is further the place where the concept of reality enters into Bonhoeffer's ethics; Jesus Christ who seeks to take form among us is *the* reality in all reality of the ethical situation. Becoming conformed with him then, as the content of ethical behaviour, means a behaviour in keeping with reality. That is, for Bonhoeffer ethical behaviour is on the one side behaviour in keeping with reality and on the other conformation with Christ. The two are one and the same thing. It is important, then, in the reality of each situa-

---

is. If it is taken seriously then what it says is not merely that the neighbour is loved because God so wills, because it is a commandment and therefore the breach of this other commandment would also be a contradiction of love toward him. The thesis says that the act of love of one's neighbour, as *caritas*, is already formally itself the love of God (Footnote:- It is sustained by grace, and therefore is love toward God made possible by God. But this takes place, not only here and there, but always and everywhere where the neighbour is truly loved and this love attains to its true nature. For the grace necessary for it must not, or at least need not, be so understood as if its proffering were merely an off-and-on activity of God; the grace which is proffered to make possible saving activity is rather an enduring existential of man, given in free graciousness, but always given, whether it is accepted by man to his saving justification or received in the refusal of freedom as judgement upon his guilt. Be it noted for the benefit of the theologians that in this way no justifying love without faith is asserted . . .). Hence the love of one's neighbour can be absolutely the highest value and the fulfilling of the law, hence the judge in Jesus' parable of the judgement asks only about what is done and what is not done in love of one's neighbour, and he carries out the judgement to all seeming according to atheistic norms" (*Warum und wie können wir die Heiligen verehren?* in *Geist und Leben. Zeitschrift für Aszese und Mystik*, 1964, 5, p. 336.

tion, to discover and open oneself to the sustaining reality of Christ, the Reconciler.[10]

4. A fourth element in the thought is *wholeheartedness* in opening oneself to Christ as the mode of behaviour in keeping with reality, in keeping with Christ. This is defined as a unity of simplicity and wisdom, and at the same time as a unity of resistance and submission, of responsible action and suffering, a unity which means complete surrender to God. Here what Bonhoeffer says about *conscience* would also then have its place, conscience the sign of man's sinful disunion with himself, which yet is at the same time both a goad and a summons back to the lost original unity.

"In shame man is reminded of his disunion with God and with other men; conscience is the sign of man's disunion with himself. Conscience is farther from the origin than shame, it presupposes disunion with God and with man and marks only the disunion with himself of the man who is already disunited from the origin. It is the voice of the apostate life which desires at least to remain one with itself. It is the call to unity of man with himself. This is evident already from the fact that the voice of conscience is always a prohibition. 'Thou shalt not'. 'You ought not to have'. Conscience is satisfied when the prohibition is not disobeyed. Whatever is not forbidden is permitted. For conscience life falls into two parts; what is permitted and what is forbidden. There is no positive commandment ... This means that conscience is concerned not with man's relation to God and to other men but with man's relation to himself ... Knowing of good and evil in disunion with the origin, man begins to reflect upon himself ... 'The point of decision of the specifically ethical experience is always conflict' (Spranger, *Lebensformen*, 7th. edn., p. 283). But in conflict the judge is invoked; and the judge is the knowledge of good and evil; he is man ...

Now anyone who reads the New Testament even superficially cannot but notice the complete absence of this world of disunion, conflict and ethical problems. Not man's falling apart from God, from men, from things, and from himself, but rather the rediscovered unity, reconciliation, is now the basis of the discussion and the 'point of decision of the specifically ethical experience'. The life and activity of men is not at all problematic or dark; it is self-evident, joyful, sure and clear" (E, pp. 148ff.).

[10] On this cp. also how the Christological future and in particular the existential interpretation of Christology are worked out in Chapter Ten.

The keynote, the style, the "atmosphere" of this ethical view, of Bonhoeffer's ethical thinking, is here particularly clear; man, happy and confident, is one with himself precisely because he is not self-seeking, does not torture himself with the biting of conscience, but simply does just what is the positive commandment of the moment as it becomes plain to him from the situation. Of course "conscience", as the "place of responsibility", can be understood in a quite different, wider and more positive sense than that given to it by Bonhoeffer here.

5. The moment of *formation of the historical future* belongs inalienably to Bonhoeffer's concept of ethics.

"One who will not allow any occurrence whatever to deprive him of his responsibility for the course of history—because he knows that it has been laid upon him by God—will thereafter achieve a more fruitful relation to the events of history than that of barren criticism and equally barren opportunism. To talk of going down fighting like heroes in the face of certain defeat is not really heroic at all, but merely a refusal to face the future. The ultimate question for a responsible man to ask is not how he is to extricate himself heroically from the affair, but how the coming generation is to live. It is only from this question, with its responsibility towards history, that fruitful solutions can come, even if for the time being they are very humiliating. In short, it is much easier to see a thing through from the point of view of abstract principle than from that of concrete responsibility. The rising generation will always instinctively discern which of these we make the basis of our actions, for it is their own future that is at stake" (LPP, p. 30).

As Eberhard Bethge tells us in the Preface to his edition of the *Ethics*, Bonhoeffer had arranged it in two parts, I. The Foundations, II. The Structure. For the title he had taken into consideration several formulations, such as "The foundations and structure of a world which is reconciled with God" and "The foundations and structure of a united West". The second title in no way indicates a theology based on the ideology of a "Christian West", but is connected with the fact that what Bonhoeffer held as possible was not an ethic in the form of general norms, but only one which was concrete instruction in a definite historical here and now, in a definite realm of history.

The arrangement and the two titles show that the formation, the structure of the world is a basic trait of this ethic. Characteristically Bonhoeffer could also change round the order, for he also took into consideration a third title. "The preparing of the way and the entry into possession". The formation, the structure, in the world of visible history, in the realm of the "penultimate", that is, what *we* have to do, is fundamentally preparing the way for Christ, preparation for what God alone can and will do.

6. We have already indicated that for Bonhoeffer, too, there is something like a *natural law*. In the realm of the "penultimate" there is a law of self-preservation, of "natural life".

There is a law of "preparing the way" for Christ, of making ready for him.

"For the sake of the ultimate the penultimate must be preserved. Any arbitrary destruction of the penultimate will do serious injury to the ultimate. If, for example, a human life is deprived of the conditions which are proper to it, then the justification of such a life by grace and faith, if it is not rendered impossible, is at least seriously impeded. In concrete terms, if a slave is so far prevented from making free use of his time that he can no longer hear the preaching of the word, then the word of God cannot in any case lead him to the justifying faith. From this fact it follows that it is necessary to see to it that the penultimate, too, is provided with the preaching of the ultimate word of God, the proclamation of the justification of the sinner by grace alone, lest the destruction of the penultimate should prove a hindrance to the ultimate ... The way must be made ready for the word. It is the word itself that demands it.

Preparing the way for the word: this is the purpose of everything that has been said about the things before the last. 'Prepare ye the way of the Lord, make his paths straight ...' Yet this making ready of the way is not merely an inward process; it is a formative activity on the very greatest visible scale. 'The valleys shall be exalted' (Isaiah 40: 4). That which has been cast down into the depths of human wretchedness, that which has been abased and humbled, is now to be raised up" (E, pp. 22f.).

To this context belongs Bonhoeffer's *concept of the mandates*. But (1) the mandates, properly speaking, are not norms, but rather spheres of responsibility. They are the four or five realms in which the formation of Christ is to take place in the sphere of the provisional and everyday, the sphere in which we are set. They are family, work, state, church, and on occasion as the fifth realm, friendship and recreation. (2) The mandates are not simply something like ordinances for life, built into creation as such. Rather they have a genuine relation to redemption, to the event of salvation. In them, in the fulfilment of the demands of natural law, the way is to be prepared for men to Christ, and for Christ to men. The mandates, as their name already tells us, are aspects of the *mission* of Christians to the world and for this reason viewpoints for a concrete ethic from the perspective of the Church of Jesus Christ in this world.

"The world, like all created things, is created through Christ and with Christ as its end, and consists in Christ alone (John 1: 10; Col. 1: 16). To speak of the world without speaking of Christ is empty and abstract. The world is relative to Christ, no matter whether it knows it or not. This relativity of the world to Christ assumes concrete form in certain mandates of God in the world. The scriptures name four such mandates; labour, marriage, government and the Church. We speak of divine mandates rather than of divine orders because the word mandate refers more clearly to a divinely imposed task than to a determination of being. It is God's will that there shall be labour, marriage, government and church in the world; and it is His will that all these, each in its own way, shall be through Christ, directed towards Christ, and in Christ. God has imposed all these mandates on all men. He has not merely imposed one of these mandates on each individual, but He has imposed all four on all men. This means that there can be no retreating from a 'secular' into a 'spiritual' sphere. There can only be the practice, the learning, of the Christian life under these four mandates of God" (E, p. 73).

"By the term 'mandate' we understand the concrete divine commission which has its foundation in the revelation of Christ and which is evidenced by Scripture; it is the legitimation and warrant for the execution of a definite divine commandment, the conferment of divine authority on an earthly agent. The term 'mandate' must also be taken to imply the claiming, the seizure and the formation of a definite earthly domain by the divine commandment. The bearer of the mandate acts as a deputy in the place of Him who assigns him his commission. In its proper sense the term 'institution' or 'order' might also be applied here, but this would involve the danger of directing attention rather towards the actual state of the institution than towards its foundation, which lies solely in the divine warrant, legitimation, and authorization. The consequence of this can all too easily be the assumption of a divine sanction for all existing orders and institutions in general and a romantic conservatism which is entirely at variance with the Christian doctrine of the four divine mandates" (E, p. 254).

The Christological alignment of this doctrine of the Mandates is surely to be noted! There follows from it that we have not here in Bonhoeffer, say, some new principle of ethics, some principle of "natural morality", that is to say, a system of rules drawn from an abstract natural law, appearing inconsequently beside the "principle" of conformation and the situation ethic with a Christological stamp. Here, too, Bonhoeffer is concerned rather with the development of his Christological, Christocentric foundation to ethics.[11] That at the same time he was still to some extent experimenting with his doctrine of the mandates, that he had not come to the end of his task, is shown in itself by his uncertainty about the number of these

[11] In this Bonhoeffer is not merely concerned with the working out of ethical principles; his concept of the mandates is ruled by the endeavour to understand Christologically the whole reality of the world. That is, "mandate" as a concept has in Bonhoeffer an ontological as much as an ethical relevance. To tell the truth, it seems to me open to question whether the concept is a suitable instrument for realizing this theological purpose, and I should like at this point to accept the criticism made by Karl Barth.

"It is along these lines that we certainly have to think, and we may gratefully acknowledge that Bonhoeffer does this, even though it may be asked whether the working out of his view does not still contain some arbitrary elements. Why, for instance, are there only four (or five) mandates and no others? Is it enough to say that these particular relationships of rank and degree occur with a certain regularity in the Bible, and that they can be more or less clearly related to Christ as the Lord of the world. Again, does the relation always have to be one of superiority and inferiority? In Bonhoeffer's doctrine of the mandates, is there not just a suggestion of North German patriarchalism? Is the notion of the authority of some over others really more characteristic of the ethical event than that of the freedom of even the very lowest before the very highest" (*Church Dogmatics*, tr. Bromily and Torrance, T. & T. Clark, III, 4, 1964, pp. 22f.).

But it would have to be a matter of the Christological interpretation of the *totality* of reality. The *whole* of reality is ordered Christwards and embraced by Christ. The very conception of this totality in terms of the four mandates, structured in this precise way, with above and below, seems to me, as it did to Barth, questionable.

mandates, four or five.[12] At this point Bonhoeffer's thought seems to me in exceptional measure in need of completion and elucidation.

7. Finally, there would have to be a more exact analysis of the passages where Bonhoeffer speaks of the method of knowing the reality of the situation, of proving the situation:

" 'Be ye transformed by the renewing of your mind, that ye may prove what is the will of God' (Romans 12: 2) ... It is not said at all that the will of God forces its way into the human heart without further ado, charged with the accent of uniqueness, or that it is simply obvious, and identical with whatever the heart may think ... and for this reason a man must ever anew examine what the will of God may be. The heart, the understanding, observation and experience must all collaborate in this task ...

... All will be embraced and pervaded by prayer. Particular experiences will afford correction and warning. Direct inspirations must in no case be heeded or expected ... Possibilities and consequences must be carefully assessed ... But in all this there will be no room for the torment of being confronted with insoluble conflicts, or for the arrogant notion that one can master every conflict, or even for the enthusiastic expectation and assertion of direct inspiration. There will be the belief that if a man asks God humbly, God will give him certain knowledge of His will; ...

The Christian cannot now indeed examine himself in any other way than on the basis of this possibility which is decisive for him, the possibility that Jesus Christ has entered into his life, nay more than that, that Jesus Christ lives for him and in him, and that Jesus Christ occupies within him exactly the space which was previously occupied by his own knowledge of good and evil ...

Consequently our self-examination will always consist precisely in our delivering up ourselves entirely to the judgement of Jesus Christ, not computing the reckoning ourselves, but committing it to Him of whom we know and acknowledge that He is within ourselves. This process of self-proving is not superfluous, because indeed Jesus Christ really is and desires to be in us and because

[12] In LPP, pp. 119ff., Bonhoeffer asks himself how the "area of freedom (art, education, friendship, play)" is to be brought within the system of the four mandates. He attempts to bring this sphere of reality under the heading of the mandate "Church", or alternatively to establish the concept of a fifth mandate.

Jesus Christ's being in us is not simply a mechanical operation but is an event which occurs and is verified ever anew precisely in this self-proving. 'I judge not mine own self. For I know nothing by myself; yet am I not hereby justified: but he that judgeth me is the Lord' (I Cor. 4: 3, 4)" (E, pp. 161ff.).

In this section, decisive in my opinion both for Bonhoeffer's ethical and his ontological conception, we meet again with a variety of elements which have already struck us. The responsible action of the Christian is at the same time a surrender, and is so structurally. The immanence of Jesus Christ in us, and in all reality (!),[13] is achieved in no mere "mechanical" way, but through responsibility, responsible imitation, though again it is not implied by this that it is we who create the presence of Christ by our imitation. The simplicity of straightforward holding to the truth of God, of straightforward doing the divine will, doing exactly what is commanded here and now, is at the same time *knowledge*, discovery, and as such the most discriminating wisdom and consideration of all that is implied in a complex human situation. "Therefore be ye wise as serpents and without guile as doves".

It is much to be regretted that Bonhoeffer has only formulated as a postulate, even if he has done so very lucidly, these thoughts about the discriminating proving of the situation out of the simplicity of a heart become one by being established in Christ, and that he has not really *developed* them. For it is here that the connection could be found between a situation ethic, as Bonhoeffer's ethics do seek to be in contrast to any ethic founded on principles, and the material concrete form for it demanded by its anchoring and founding on Christology. Under this heading, "Proving the Situation", there would have to be brought in, certainly not a casuistic ethic again, but surely a "teaching on methods" for ethical proving which entered into details, and which would bring back again the concreteness which seemed to have been lost by the principles of situation ethics. Something of this nature must surely

---

[13] According to this Jesus Christ is in us and at the same time in all reality. He is *the* reality. Thus the ethical situation in Bonhoeffer's view acquires a peculiar form; what happens in it is this, that "Christ in us" and the Christ in all the reality which surrounds us do in a certain sense come face to face with one another.

happen in any illuminating analysis of the phenomena of ethical situations and decisions. It would have to be possible to show, by reference as it were to the pattern, what is the structure of concrete ethical knowledge and decision.

It is only in the interplay of these seven elements of Bonhoeffer's ethical study that unity is revealed. One must become aware of the unified trend which is present ruling in them all. We already find this unity by a glance at the subject-matter itself. Bonhoeffer has set out on a definite self-consistent path. But there must be further discussion on the positions which he reached but did not connect with one another, and thereby a further quest for that unity and wholeness of ethics which he kept before his eyes.

CHAPTER SEVEN

THE PROVIDENCE OF GOD

1. *The Thought of Divine Guidance*

IN "AFTER TEN YEARS", included in *Letters and Papers from Prison*, a very personal meditation on Christian life in the ten years from 1933 to 1943, that is, in the time of Hitler's rule, Bonhoeffer wrote under the heading, "A Few Articles of Faith on the Sovereignty of God in History":

> "I believe that God can and will bring good out of the greatest evil. For that purpose he needs men who make the best use of everything. I believe that God will give us all the strength we need to help us to resist in all time of distress. But he never gives it in advance, lest we should rely on ourselves and not on him alone. A faith such as this should allay all our fears for the future. I believe that even our mistakes and shortcomings are turned to good account, and that it is no harder for God to deal with them than with our supposedly good deeds. I believe that God is no timeless fate, but that he waits for and answers sincere prayers and responsible actions" (LPP, p. 34).

These statements are formulated with a strong emphasis. They are "articles of faith". In them Bonhoeffer expresses his personal faith in his personal situation, in that of his friends to whom he dedicates the whole of this testament for a year's end, in that of his generation of Germans and of his Church. It is a confession determined by the situation, a confession made less before the world outside than before himself and a narrower circle of confidants, a confession which does not seek outwardly to demarcate and define a position but inwardly to give courage, but none the less a confession. What is its significance? What place does the "sovereignty of God in history" have in the totality of Bonhoeffer's thought? The question is of the greatest importance for the interpretation of his work, especially because this and related trains of thought are given a considerable part in the prison letters, that is, where the course of his thought reaches its culmination. He is quite flooded by the thought of the providence of God in his *personal life.*

"I am so sure of God's guiding hand that I hope I shall always be kept in that certainty. You must never doubt that I am travelling with gratitude and cheerfulness along the road where I am being led" (LPP, p. 215; letter of August 23, 1944).

"I believe that nothing that happens to me is meaningless" (LPP, p. 159).

"Continuity with one's past is a great gift, too . . . Everything seems to have taken its natural course, and to be determined necessarily and straightforwardly by a higher providence" (LPP, p. 150).

"Let us face the coming weeks in faith and in great assurance about the general future, and commit your way and all our ways to God" (LPP, p. 177; letter of June 6, 1944, the day of the Allied landing in Normandy).

This way in which he was flooded by the thought of personal guidance can even occasionally be for Bonhoeffer in his cell a testing and a trial. Thus, referring to the uncertain outcome of his trial and the uncertain duration of his imprisonment, he can write:

"I do want to convey to you somehow tomorrow that I believe my attitude to my case ought unquestionably to be one of faith, and I feel that it has become too much a matter of calculation and foresight" (LPP, p. 115).

And again on November 18, 1943, looking back on the first period of his imprisonment, he writes:

"At first I wondered a great deal whether it was really for the cause of Christ that I was causing you all such grief; but I soon put that out of my head as a temptation, as I became certain that the duty had been laid on me to hold out in this boundary situation with all its problems; I became quite content to do this, and have remained so ever since" (LPP, p. 87).

But *world-history as a whole,* too, is under God's guidance.

"Today is Ascension Day, and that means that it is a day of great joy for all who can believe that Christ rules the world and our lives" (LPP, p. 54).

"If in the middle of an air raid God sends out the gospel call to his kingdom in baptism, it will be quite clear what that kingdom is and what it means. It is a kingdom stronger than war and danger, a kingdom of power and authority, signifying eternal terror and judgement to some, and eternal joy and righteousness to others, not a kingdom of the heart, but one wide as the earth . . ." (LPP, p. 163).

But in the life-history of individuals and in the history of humanity the ways of God are manifold. "If war seems to you to mean nothing but death", Bonhoeffer writes to Bethge on the field of battle, "you are probably not doing justice to the manifold ways of God" (LPP, p. 164). Through the wisdom of God all that is entangled can be unravelled in astonishing fashion.[1]

"In view of what is coming, I am almost inclined to quote the biblical δεῖ . . . and I feel that I 'long to look', like the angels in I Peter 1: 12, to see how God is going to solve the apparently insoluble. I think that God is about to accomplish something that, even if we take part in it either outwardly or inwardly, we can only receive with the greatest wonder and awe" (LPP, p. 151; April 30, 1944, in expectation of the great turning-point of the war).

What is speaking in these statements is no thought and construction from the theology of history, seeking to decipher the plan of salvation and the plan of history, nor is there any comparison made between the present time and earlier epochs;

---

[1] The *sapientia Dei* is according to the traditional doctrine of God that property of God "*per quam novit, quibus rationibus res ab eodem producendae gloriam suam illustrare queant, ut eas convenienter suae naturae, perfectioni et gloriae vocare et velle possit* (by which he knows in what way all that is to be brought about by him may illustrate his own glory, that he may call all things into being and will them in keeping with his own nature, perfection and glory)". It is the "*moderatrix consiliorum Dei, per quam sic ad decentiam divinam gloriae suae attendit, ne veritati ordini, pulchritudini in ulla verborum vel operum eius parte desit* (the shaper of the counsels of God, by which he gives such attention to the divine fittingness of his own glory as to ensure that in no part of his words or works should there be lacking truth, order and beauty)" (J. H. Heidegger, *Corpus theologiae*, Zürich, 1700, III, p. 65). Thus the concept of God's *sapientia* and that of his *providentia* are interrelated. The *sapientia* of the divine providence so clears up the complexities which are inexplicable and insoluble to human wisdom that in the last resort everything must lead in the most beautiful way to the glory of God as the goal of all things.

what finds expression is simply the consciousness of bewilderment at the overruling event of history, the "it" in which is concealed God's "Thou", the mighty hand of God.

2. *Guidance as a Part of the Totality of Bonhoeffer's Thought*

We have already referred to such passages in the chapter on non-religious interpretation, because it follows clearly from them that Bonhoeffer's demand for a non-religious interpretation has nothing to do with a "Christian atheism", that for Bonhoeffer that kernel of Christian life and thought, personal confrontation with a personal and supra-personal God, remains always the presupposition and incentive of his personal thinking. But now we have to ask ourselves the question if this belief in providence is to be understood merely as an element in his personal Christian piety, if statements like those we have quoted are to be conceived as merely the manifestations of an "individual heart's faith", manifestations which surely we could understand in a time of personal suffering and testing, as well as of great tension and upheaval in the history of the world. Are we to interpret them as arising out of the situation? Or is it necessary to see this whole list of sayings of his in the substantial context of his thought? That such thoughts about God's providence and guidance are frequent in the prison letters in particular, needs no more than the situation to throw light upon it. But have they in addition an organic relation to other characteristic basic features of his theology?

This question having once arisen, we shall have to endeavour to see what specifically belongs to Bonhoeffer in these thoughts, to some extent to construct Bonhoeffer's doctrine of Providence, although he himself never expressed himself in detail on this subject as a dogmatic theme. Perhaps he would have done it, perhaps he would have had to do it, had he been given more time, and if in this time he had become aware in reflection of the especial importance which the concept of providence and faith in providence did in fact have in his own Christian and theological life! We must further seek to recognize how this element is related to others in his thought, or briefly, how far it is significant for the whole course of Bonhoeffer's thinking that precisely this thought of providence should play this role in it. This is all an exercise in interpretation, and only as we accomplish the interpretation will it become possible to obtain an acceptable answer to the question whether his assertions about guidance and providence have simply a personal character and do not properly belong to his theological work, or whether the work itself essentially bears its stamp, even if this aspect is not worked out. If the latter were our conclusion a new viewpoint would thereby be gained for a deeper understanding of Bonhoeffer, and in addition perhaps a starting-point for further fruitful work in the direction in which Bonhoeffer thought.

3. Bonhoeffer's Contribution to the Doctrine of Providence: God's Dialogue with Man

In Bonhoeffer, too, we must begin by presupposing the three traditional aspects of the doctrine of Providence, the dogmatic concepts of *providentia generalis*, *providentia specialis* and *providentia specialissima*, the providence and guiding of God with regard to the world as a whole, the Church and the individual life. Understandably, Bonhoeffer's reference to the whole is often, but not exclusively, emphatically from the point of view of the third. Of course these three aspects co-operate to form one whole and in this sense his thinking is along the lines of traditional dogmatics. But tradition was more successful in drawing the distinctions than in thinking more deeply on the connection of the whole, on the co-operation of the three viewpoints. Here is one of the problems of the doctrine of Providence which have not been worked out, a problem which Bonhoeffer, it is true, did not put expressly, but to which he had obviously given thought in his "existentialist reflection", which is also there in his sense of the existential situation and his elemental statements, for existence is always, as it were, already essentially an *understanding*, a "pre-ontological" moment in thought. The result is that if today we follow diligently the clues given by the thought, it may be that with the help of Bonhoeffer the sight of an original solution to the problem will be given us.

Especially important for this surely original, if not systematically developed, starting-point in Bonhoeffer's faith in providence seems to me the last of the four "articles of faith on the sovereignty of God in history": "I believe that God is no timeless fate, but that he waits for and answers sincere prayers and responsible actions". God directs every occurrence, but, as we might call it, "dialogically" and not with a blind and regardless necessity. God *waits* and God *answers*. It is not a matter without influence or importance for his piloting of all things, that he has set over against himself a responsible being. The course of all things is firmly anchored in God (*providentia generalis*); nothing takes place without His willing it. And yet there remains, as it were, in the gapless chain of Divine activity a space for the dialogical participation of his responsible creation.[2] Man, in so far as he knows himself confronted by God, can interpolate himself into the discussion and therefore into the piloting of events, for God as the Pilot of all things is no dumb God, no "timeless fate", but related, relating himself, to the *time* within which man exercises his finite responsibility.

"The past weeks have been more of a strain than anything before that. There is no changing it, only it is more difficult to adapt oneself to something that one thinks could have been prevented than to something inevitable. But when facts have taken shape, one just has to fit in with them. What I am thinking of particularly today is that you will soon be facing facts that will be very hard for you, probably even harder than for me. I now think that we ought first of all to do everything we can to change

---

[2] Is there a contradiction here? How can space be given in what is gapless? If we persevere in the question, the apparent contradiction points to the character of the answer, the specific nature of personal relations with which we are here concerned, that faithfulness and trust, love and responsive love, etc., as personal realities do not, as it were, stand beside one another in alternation, but essentially co-operate with one another. Thus God's piloting of the world can be a "gapless chain" which yet leaves room for the dialogical co-operation of man. Here we come again against the old theological problem, always persisting, and yet never adequately solved, of grace and freedom. The substantialist categories to which recourse has generally been made are not equal to this problem. This is why, for example, the Decree of Trent misunderstood the Reformation on the question of grace and freedom, and then in its turn was misunderstood by Protestantism. The personal categories which we require have certainly often been postulated, but they have not yet been so worked out that they are really able to provide an instrument for enlightening our thought.

these facts while there is still time; and then, if we have tried everything, even though it has been in vain, they will be much easier to bear. Of course, not everything that happens is simply 'God's will', and yet in the last resort nothing happens 'without your Father's will' (Matt. 10: 29), i.e. through every event, however untoward, there is access to God" (LPP, p. 109; December 18, 1943).

Here in the first instance Bonhoeffer's thought can to some extent be explained in terms of traditional dogmatic concepts. Not all that happens is God's will and yet in the last resort nothing takes place without God's will, "will" being here understood in the sense of *voluntas decernens*, more specifically, of *permissio* or *non-impeditio*. But that "in the last resort nothing happens without your Father's will" is so interpreted by Bonhoeffer that "through every event there is access to God". That is to say, what God decrees is at the same time a way for man, a way which *man* himself can go, an access which he himself can find. The divine government of all the world is at the same time a making room for man. God so exercises his rule over the world, his inescapable *gubernatio*, that precisely thereby he confers upon man his freedom. Man is not confined because determined to the last detail; he is set free by the providence of God even while he is being determined to the last detail. Of course there appears here at the same time the old problem, unsolved as yet by dogmatics, of Divine determination and human freedom. Tradition, healthy orthodoxy,[3] has at least held on to this problem by maintaining against heretical departures on either side, on the one hand the universal activity of God, and on the other the freedom, understood as personal responsibility, of man. But how the two are to be thought of together has, to tell the truth, never been adequately explained. Even Bonhoeffer does not solve the problem for us on the spot. But perhaps he opens the road to a solution, and even that would be a tremendous dogmatic achievement, by his obvious endeavour to think of the determining activity of God *as such* as "dialogical". God's rule over man is at the same

[3] There is a *"good orthodoxy"*, a sound instinct for what are the facts of the Christian faith, and a *"bad orthodoxy"* which only seeks to be correct in its beliefs, and which anxiously and distrustfully holds on to traditional statements, which are now only recited, but no longer assimilated.

time and *as such* an address to man summoning him to an answer, an answer which again on its side is, as it were, "allowed for" in God's rule.

All remains in God's hand and cannot be torn away from it. And yet God is no timeless fate but leaves, as it were, an interval for the time of decision, the time of human responsibility. God presents himself dialogically to man, waits for him and answers him, himself becomes "response-ible".[4] In this "interval" God waits for and replies to "sincere prayers and responsible actions". And yet, in that he answers, he does not permit the course of events to break loose from him. "I believe that God can and will bring good out of evil, even out of the greatest evil ... I believe that even our mistakes and shortcomings are turned to good account, and that it is no harder for God to deal with them than with our supposedly good deeds". God then permits the human answer to stand as given, and does not ignore it. But on his side he answers in such a way that his own particular purpose for man's salvation reaches its goal by it. *In that* he answers man God carries out his own particular will. Man is not ignored; the answer which he gives to God is not indifferent and without significance for the Divine activity. God does not simply act against human intentions, destroying them and countermanding them and carrying out his own work instead, replacing completely and utterly human work by his own, rather he does justice to human intentions, to sincere prayers and responsible actions, by answering them. And yet in his answer he transcends the question by transforming, as it were, the goal of the intentions and exalting it above itself.

At bottom Bonhoeffer here thinks completely along the lines of traditional dogmatics, which in the *locus de providentia* speaks of the first cause being effective through the second

---

[4] In *Theology and Preaching* tr. Knight, Lutterworth, 1965, I have spoken of a "responsibility of God" in the following sense, "Again we must speak of God's responsibility, but in a somewhat modified sense. Such language applied to God does not mean that He owes something to someone or that He is answerable to human beings for His decisions ... God's responsibility consists in His fidelity. It means that He remains ever faithful to His eternal counsels, that He 'stands by' His decisions. It is as this ever faithful that He meets us. God's own faithfulness marks out the horizon within which our own responsibility comes into play. His faithfulness is the 'salvation-bringing *a priori*' underlying the possibility of our own decisions" (p. 133).

cause.[5] But in the last resort the concept of causality is surely not appropriate here; it is "metaphysical", as Martin Heidegger uses that word, and in addition, if we must speak in the realm of the history of "causality", the form of the causality is still by no means made clear.[6] But Bonhoeffer thinks out anew the old thought, at his time inadequately formulated, by interpreting it dialogically, and this history, in which man, in spite of the universal activity of God, co-operates responsibly as a "second cause", becomes one single discussion between God and man.

4. Intercession and Action as Forms of the Divine-human Dialogue

God waits for sincere prayers and responsible actions. These are the two forms in which man can enter into dialogue with the Pilot of the world. Here we find the substance of human, Christian walking before God, as Bonhoeffer also says elsewhere in *Letters and Papers from Prison*, "Our earlier words are therefore bound to lose their force and cease, and our being Christians today will be limited to two things, *prayer* and righteous *action* among men" (LPP, p. 172; from "Thoughts on the Baptism of D.W.R.", May 1944. At this point Bonhoeffer is speaking of the present situation of the Church in a religionless world and of the Church's hope for a new outburst of the Word of God).

The two, prayer and action, are ways in which man answers God, in which he commits himself in binding fashion before God. The two must surely be viewed together. The prayer of Christians is in a manner also action, and their action in a manner also prayer.

[5] Cp. for instance Johann Heinrich Heidegger, "*Concursus s. cooperatio est operatio illa Dei, qua is cum causis secundis utpote ab eo sicut in esse ita etiam in operari dependentibus immediate ita cooperatur, ut et ad operandum illas excitet s. promoveat et una cum iisdem modo primae causae conveniente et naturae causarum secundarum accomodato operetur* (Concurrence or co-operation is that operation of God in which he so co-operates with these second causes which, both in their being and their operation, are everywhere dependent upon him, that he both excites or impels them to operation and operates at one with them in keeping with the manner of a first cause and agreeably to the nature of second causes)" (Corpus theologiae, Zürich, 1700, VII, p. 28).

[6] Cp. on this my disagreement with Rudolf Bultmann on his philosophy of history in the collected volume, *The Theology of Rudolf Bultmann*, ed. Charles W. Kegley, New York, 1966.

God waits for sincere *prayers* and answers them. Above all, the thought of intercession plays an essential role in the prison letters. Here again we see a material connection with the early writings, for in *Sanctorum Communio* Bonhoeffer defines intercession as an essential moment in the self-realization of the Church. Our intercession for another is heard by God.

> "I have often found it a great help to think in the evening of all those I know are praying for me, children as well as grown-ups. I think I owe it to the prayers of others, both known and unknown, that I have often been kept in safety" (LPP, p. 214).

Intercession is the last possible action for another. Here our action and our care for the other flows into the action and the loving care of God. Intercession is at the same time the form of the final human commitment.

> "From the moment we wake until we fall asleep we must commend other people wholly and unreservedly to God and leave them in his hands, and transform our anxiety for them into prayers on their behalf: '*Mit Sorgen und mit Grämen* . . . *lässt God sich* gar nichts *nehmen*' " (LPP, p. 117; Translator's note there;—"With cares and grief God *will not* be received", from *Befiehl du deine Wege*, by Paul Gerhardt).
>
> "But let us promise to remain faithful in interceding for each other. I shall ask that you may have strength, health, patience, and protection from conflicts and temptations. You can ask for the same things for me. And if it should be decided that we are not to meet again, let us remember each other to the end in thankfulness and forgiveness, and may God grant us that one day we may stand before his throne praying for each other and joining in praise and thankfulness" (LPP, p. 89).

In the act of intercession, commitment, action on behalf of a fellowman passes over into non-activity, into endurance, into submission—and yet it remains none the less commitment before God. In this way I hand over the neighbour, for whom at the moment I can do nothing further, into the hands of God, leaving him to work. Intercession is, as it were, the prolongation of my activity, and it is the mark that even my responsible activity as such is always ruled and embraced by that submission to God. And thus we come here to that same structure, that same dialectic, which we met already in the theme of Bonhoeffer's *Ethics*, where in the same way "resistance" and "submission", "activity" and "suffering", responsible action taking upon oneself the free decision, and on the other hand surrender to God, appeared as correlative aspects of one and the same reality. In a certain way intercession accomplishes existentially with regard to our neighbour that dialogical reversal from "resistance" to "submission", or from one's own free action to the surrender of the action and its object to God. In acting for our neighbour we are already prepared to commend him to God completely and entirely. And this becomes visible where we are able to do no more, but where our attitude, our commitment to action, lives on in the form of intercession. Then also we remain just as truly committed "in God" to our neighbour as we were in the position of mutual active responsibility. And we remain bound in the reality of the same commitment in God, even when we never meet again but only find one another again before the throne of God.

Thus prayer and action belong to one another. In the depths of their being they are one, the one answer of man to God, for which God waits and which he on his side will answer. They are the two aspects of this one existential reality. But it is the form and the distinguishing mark of this reality, that it has precisely *these* two aspects.

If now, after intercession, we have still something to say about the other aspect, about responsible *actions*, the first distinguishing mark of them has to all intents and purposes been already mentioned, that action goes together with prayer, and that its essence is completely determined by this unity. But a second thing must now be said. This very peculiarity of structure possessed by responsible activity receives its deeper meaning in the context of the doctrine of Providence. This aspect is not developed by Bonhoeffer himself in the *Ethics*, or at least only developed by implication. In this way the prison letters with their "existential reflections" on providence form an important basis for the interpretation of the *Ethics*. *For faith in God's sovereignty in history, both that of the world and that of the individual, and the specific interpretation which this faith finds in Bonhoeffer's theological thinking, is the horizon within which Bonhoeffer's conception of an ethic of responsible action*

*first becomes intelligible in its full depth, and on the other hand
this ethical conception is suitable for throwing light on the difficult
dogmatic* locus de providentia. This same characteristic dialectical structure of responsible action on the one hand, and
the "dialogical interpretation" of the providence of God on the
other, mutually require and illuminate one another. For the
meaning of the responsible action of the believer in its peculiar
dialectic and in its "character as prayer" is precisely this,
to give oneself up to the guidance of God.[7] But it is of the
nature of God's guidance that it integrates this human answer
precisely as an essential element of itself.

Above all one aspect, and with it the whole of Bonhoeffer's
Ethics, can be understood more deeply in the light of belief in
providence, that of *responsible shaping of the future*. The
divine piloting of history is so to be understood that man
shares responsibility for the course of history with it, and must
accordingly find a "fruitful relation to the events of history".
It is here that the ethical relevance of success is to be placed.
There is a sterility about an ethical thought and behaviour
which regards historical success as irrelevant; it is "unheroic"
not to venture a glance into the future.

"Although it is certainly not true that success justifies an
evil deed and shady means, it is impossible to regard success as
something which is ethically quite neutral. The fact is that
historical success creates a basis for the continuance of life,
and it is still a moot point whether it is ethically more responsible
to take the field like Don Quixote against a new age, or to admit
one's defeat, accept the new age, and agree to serve it. In the
last resort success makes history; and the ruler of history repeatedly
brings good out of evil over the heads of the history-makers.
Simply to ignore the ethical significance of success is a short-
circuit created by dogmatists who think unhistorically and
irresponsibly; and it is good for us sometimes to be compelled
to grapple seriously with the ethical problem of success ... We

[7] One must of course ask here what the position is with the structure of the
responsible action of an unbeliever who does not pray and will not surrender
himself to the thought of a divine guidance. It cannot be doubted that the
unbeliever, if we mean an explicit confessional faith, is also capable of responsible activity. But in his very responsibility, in so far as it is genuine responsibility, we may find a structural moment of surrender which is keeping with
that other giving oneself up to the Divine guidance. Here again we come to the
problem of "anonymous faith".

will not and must not be either outraged critics or opportunists, but must take our share of responsibility for the moulding of history in every situation and at every moment, whether we are the victors or the vanquished. One who will not allow any occurrence whatever to deprive him of his responsibility for the course of history—because he knows that it has been laid upon him by God—will thereafter achieve a more fruitful relation to the events of history than that of barren criticism and equally barren opportunism" (LPP, pp. 29f.).

By such a way of thinking Bonhoeffer seeks better to do justice to the *reality* of history and ethical situations than is possible for some abstract and dogmatist view which orientates itself to the ethical principle alone and consciously leaves out of account the course of history and therefore the success of ethical activity. Bonhoeffer refuses this way of thinking, a fact again characteristic for his attitude as Christian and theologian, from two mutually connected motives, a "practical" one, because this way of thinking is principle-ridden and therefore unfruitful, and a "theoretical" one, because it is abstract. Both in theory and in practice this way misses the reality with which he is concerned. That is, his intellectual wrestling with reality, his refusal of abstractions, has the deeper existential basis that in existence itself, reality, and therefore true fruitfulness, must not be missed. It is a duty of the Christian to face reality and to stand firm by it. The ethical dogmatist misses reality just as much as, for example, he who insists on continuing to interpret Christianity "religiously" and because of this does not make contact any more with real man of our time.

But from this whole factual situation the connection which we have in mind becomes clearer, the connection, that is, of the existential structure of the Christian's ethical activity with the thought of providence. With his "existential study" Bonhoeffer gives an analysis of ethical activity in keeping with reality. Or at least he virtually gives it, for even if it is not thought through scientifically, what is essential has been said. And this activity is not rigidly bound to formulable principle, it pays attention to the outcome of things, to the future. But this existential analysis of ethical behaviour in keeping with reality is also set by Bonhoeffer within the horizon of the doctrine of Providence. It is not the principles in accordance with which one acts, at least when regarded in isolation, which make history, but the success. The Pilot of history makes good come out of evil.

This is a further important thought which is also found in the *Ethics*. There is not only a history of God's dealing with individuals, his justification and forgiveness of their sins; there is also a history of larger groups, corresponding to the concept of the collective person, and what justification and the forgiveness of sins is for the individual, is for the group the gradual *"healing" of guilt*, so that out of the old guilt there can finally arise good! Although there cannot be justification and forgiveness in the proper sense of these words for the collective person, as there can be for individuals, yet we do have here also a history of the acts of the gracious God.

"The Church experiences in faith the forgiveness of all her sins and a new beginning through grace. For the nation there is only a healing of the wound, a cicatrization of guilt, in the return to order, to justice, to peace and the granting of free passage to the Church's proclamation of Jesus Christ. Thus the nations bear the inheritance of their guilt. Yet, through God's merciful governance in history, it may happen that what began as a curse may end as a blessing for them; out of power which has been wrongfully seized there may come justice and right; out of turmoil and insurrection there may come order; and out of bloodshed there may come peace ... This does not, of course, mean that the guilt is justified, or that it is removed or forgiven. The guilt continues, but the wound which it has inflicted is healed ... In the life of the Church and of the faithful all continuity with past guilt is broken through atonement and forgiveness, but in the historical life of the nations it is maintained. The only question here is whether the wounds of this past guilt are in fact healed, and at this point, even within the history of the internal and external political struggle of the nations, there is something in the nature of forgiveness, though it be only a faint shadow of the forgiveness which Jesus Christ vouchsafes to faith ... This forgiveness within history can come only when the wound of guilt is healed, when violence has become justice, lawlessness has become order, and war has become peace. If this is not achieved, if wrong still rules unhindered and still inflicts new wounds, then, of course, there can be no question of this kind of forgiveness and man's first concern must be to resist injustice and to call the offenders to account for their guilt" (E, pp. 52ff.).

Thus healing is no immanent favouring of law by history, on which one can rely, it is no legitimizing after the event of the wrong which has taken place in history. It is really a work of that forgiveness of God which is completely and entirely free from obligation, breaking in, as it were, "from outside", but, we must add, not merely reaching the individuals and remaining indifferent to the history of the peoples. The history of the peoples is no realm indifferent to God because it is no realm indifferent to forgiveness. Nor is it, as we might put it, a realm in which God works exclusively as the *Deus absconditus*, as the God of the law, and not as the gracious God, the God of the Gospel. This, in passing, seems to me an important point also with regard to my disagreement with Gerhard Ebeling and his review of Bonhoeffer.

Since the issue of events then, success, is in the hands, not of men, but of God, the Pilot of history, it is not a cowardly opportunism, but the truly fruitful relation to history, when we, whether as victors or vanquished, turn our attention to historical success and attribute ethical relevance to it. It is true that this in its turn has also to take place within our direct responsibility to God. It certainly does not mean any deification of success. In the *Ethics* Bonhoeffer has emphatically differentiated his position from any such attitude.[8] Ethical orientation towards success is rather defined as orientation towards God himself, the Pilot of history. In Bonhoeffer this means the truly fruitful relation to history, because it is God who grants all historical fruit, in that he himself is the final

[8] "When a successful figure becomes especially prominent and conspicuous, the majority give way to the idolization of success. They become blind to right and wrong, truth and untruth, fair play and foul play . . . Neither the triumph of the successful nor the bitter hatred which the successful arouse in the hearts of the unsuccessful can ultimately overcome the world. Jesus is certainly no apologist for the successful men in history, but neither does he head the insurrection of shipwrecked existences against their successful rivals. He is not concerned with success or failure but only with the willing acceptance of God's judgement. Only in this judgement is there reconciliation with God and among men. Christ confronts all thinking in terms of success and failure with the man who is under God's sentence, no matter whether he be successful or unsuccessful" (E, pp. 14f.).

"substance" of meaning in all historical events, the Reconciler who, present in all history, seeks to reconcile and will reconcile the world to himself. How far such an ethical realism, which does not degenerate into opportunism, is also conceivable when one is not thinking explicitly within the horizon of faith in providence, is a matter, it is true, which properly would require further elucidation.[9]

According to our last citation two things are remarkably closely allied. God lays upon us a share of responsibility for the course of history—and God acts over the heads of the men who make history, and creates out of evil good which they had not intended at all. Thus at the same time God acts without us and not without us. And this "without us" and "not without us" at the same time indicates the existential peculiarity of the intra-personal event.

It is precisely in our inward participation in God's piloting of the world that God nevertheless brings about, through us and apart from us, his own personal purpose. Our personal action, our answering co-operation, can thus on occasion appear precisely as *participation* in God's *individual* action.

> "We are certainly not Christ; we are not called on to redeem the world . . . and we need not try to assume such an impossible burden. We are not lords, but instruments in the hand of the Lord of history; and we can share in other people's sufferings only in a very limited degree. We are not Christ, but if we want to be Christians, we must have some share in Christ's large-heartedness by acting with responsibility and in freedom when the hour of danger comes, and by showing a real sympathy that springs, not from fear, but from the liberating and redeeming love of Christ for all who suffer" (LPP, p. 37).

For Bonhoeffer the two are most closely related, on the one side God's overmastering and unescapable individual action and our surrender to his will, and on the other our personal responsible co-operation. Precisely through his mighty hand, under which we can only bow ourselves, God seeks to open for us a place for our own responsibility.

> "The fact that the horrors of war are now coming home to us with such force will no doubt, if we survive, provide us with

[9] On this cp. n. 7 on p. 298.

the necessary basis for making it possible to reconstruct the life of the nations, both spiritually and materially, on Christian principles. So we must try to keep these experiences in our minds, use them in our work, make them bear fruit, and not just shake them off. Never have we been so plainly conscious of the wrath of God, and that is a sign of his grace: 'O that today you would hearken to his voice! Harden not your hearts' (Psalm 95: 7f.). The tasks that confront us are immense, but we must prepare ourselves for them now and be ready when they come (LPP, p. 100).

Or in surrender to God's will whatever it may be, and *precisely in this*, in expectancy of coming responsibility, Bonhoeffer can write:

"If I were to end my life here in these conditions, that would have a meaning that I think I could understand; on the other hand everything might be a thorough preparation for a new start and a new task when peace comes . . ." (LPP, p. 149).

5. *God in the Facts*

The following is a statement of immense compass:

"Whatever weaknesses, miscalculations, and guilt there is in what precedes the facts, God is in the facts themselves" (LPP, p. 118).

First of all we note that this assertion is made by Bonhoeffer in the closest connection with the dialectic of "resistance" and "submission", of acceptance of responsibility and surrender. Immediately before this he has written:

"As long as we ourselves are trying to help shape someone else's destiny, we are never quite free of the question whether what we are doing is really for the other person's benefit . . . But when all possibility of co-operating in anything is suddenly cut off, then behind any anxiety about him there is the consciousness that his life has now been placed wholly in better and stronger hands. For you, and for us, the greatest task during the coming weeks, and perhaps months, may be to entrust each other to these hands" (LPP, p. 118).

God opens an interval of time for our finite, unsuccessful, but yet earnestly responsible, co-operation in formation. But then he himself will be in the facts. Surely this immanence cannot be conceived simply as a metaphor. It does not simply mean that God in his providence has control of the facts, but really that he himself *is* in the facts which he controls.

Here the thought of providence gains a new aspect, one which is surely quite specifically Bonhoeffer's. In the statement that God is in the facts an insight is opened into the depths of reality. It is here that we find the connection between Bonhoeffer's faith in providence and the question of reality, yes, and of non-religious interpretation too; for in this it is precisely his aim to show that God's dwelling-place is not in some "world beyond", but "in the midst of life", in the everyday facts, in the pressing facts. That the Creator and Lord of the world is present in his creation, and that he permeates it with his presence, has always been recognized in the tradition of dogmatic thinking, it is the complex of facts which has been expressed in the concept of the omnipresence of God. But precisely this dimension of the tradition receives a new importance for Bonhoeffer, as indeed a dimension of thought which has already definitely been there in the past often does suddenly gain a new historical livingness; he feels it and is on the point of working it out.

Here we must see the three aspects side by side and in combination, the immanence of God in reality as the hidden main theme of Bonhoeffer's whole thought (cp. Jeremiah 45), the immanence of *Jesus Christ* in reality as the first aspect in concrete form and the basic theme of Bonhoeffer's ontology, and finally, the immanence of God in the *facts*—as the starting-point for his undeveloped doctrine of Providence. When we take account of the close connection and the mutual illumination of these three aspects we recognize their original factual unity, and from this we obtain the answer to our question if Bonhoeffer's faith in providence belongs organically to his theological thinking, or if it is merely determined by personal grounds. In point of fact this thought of providence fits in exactly into what we have earlier recognized as his peculiar theme. His Christology and his doctrine of Providence are interrelated. The immanence of God, the immanence of Jesus Christ in reality means just this, that "God is in the facts". God himself dwells in the facts which he controls. He does not, as it were, merely steer the course of the world from above; he enters into the facts "down here", comes face to face with man and answers him.[10] The facts are God's answer and new question, or we may put it, God himself in the facts is the answer and new question to man trying to justify himself. Thus in a certain sense the providential activity of the Creator of the world is transformed by the incarnation of the Word. The providence of God gains a Christological aspect; Christ is "in" reality, "in" the facts, not in any way as a substance, but in the manner of the God who pilots history by waiting for man and setting him on his way anew. *Christology bears the stamp of the doctrine of Providence, the doctrine of Providence that of Christology; the two are bracketed together by the thought of the God who deals dialogically with men.* Perhaps we must even say that the tendency in Bonhoeffer for Christology to become a universal ontology can only be carried through theologically through this connection with the doctrine of Providence. Without it we would have only obscure assertions. But the addition of the thought of providence makes known the personal and dialogical character of the immanence of Christ in all reality, the stamp which is put upon all reality by the event of Christ.

Further God is not "in the facts" in the sense that he is simply identical with them. We have already seen above (Chapter Four, 2) that Bonhoeffer's concept of reality, when he speaks of the true reality of the world as one permeated by Christ, is not confined merely to the factual (cp. E, pp. 206f.).

[10] Cp. also on this point the following reflections of his on the *continuum* of history, ". . . Is the Ranke-to-Delbrück interpretation of history as a *continuum* consisting of 'classical antiquity', 'the middle ages', and 'modern times' really valid, or is not Spengler also right with his theory of cultural phases as self-contained cycles, even though he gives too biological a twist to historical events? The idea of the historical *continuum* goes back to Hegel, who sees the whole course of history as culminating in modern times, i.e. in his own system of philosophy. That idea is therefore *idealistic* (in spite of Ranke's assertion that every moment of history is 'immediate to God'; that assertion might have supplied a corrective of the whole conception of the *continuum* of development, but it did not do so) . . ." (LPP, p. 138). Thinking in a bird's-eye view taken from the philosophy of history or the theology of the *Heilsgeschichte* is obviously foreign to Bonhoeffer. He may speak of the providence of God, but his doing so does not make God appear as the Pilot of the world overlooking all from a distance; God is present precisely as the *gubernator rerum* immediately and personally in the individual facts and developments and epochs.

God dwells in the facts "in a dialogical way", to use this concept here simply as a code and a signpost, as question, answer, and new question. The primary manner of God's indwelling in the facts and his ruling in history is *reconciliation*. But what this means, and here Bonhoeffer leaves us to it, only a discriminating existential interpretation of Christology could show.

6. *The Existential Verification of the Doctrine of Providence*

It can be foreseen that the thought of providence, as found in so modern a thinker as Bonhoeffer, will provide some difficulties for the modern reader, tied to an "implicit atheism". But the reason for this obviously lies in the reader and not in Bonhoeffer. In him, it seems to me, everything is organically connected. It would then be no good manner of interpretation if in our encounter with him we were to seek, for the sake of our own difficulties in understanding, to suppress this aspect which obviously gave no difficulty to Bonhoeffer himself. If we did so we should no longer be interpreting the matter "from within", but doing violence to it "from without". It would be better, in this same encounter with the Christian thinker Dietrich Bonhoeffer, to lay ourselves open to new possibilities and dimensions of existential interpretation of the reality experienced by us.

It would be an important step towards overcoming these existential and theoretical difficulties in understanding, if we were to succeed in indicating and making plausible an existential situation and behaviour so closely bound up with the thought of Divine providence and guidance that it cannot be thought of without these. We make it plausible by making it appear intelligible as an inherent possibility and capable of fulfilment. Perhaps the following passage from *Letters and Papers from Prison* opens the way to this:

> "It is weakness rather than wickedness that perverts a man and drags him down, and it needs profound sympathy to put up with that. But all the time God still reigns in heaven" (LPP, p. 212).

In the first place, the feeling lying behind this statement

seems to belong peculiarly to Bonhoeffer! It is so in the unsparing realism with which human phenomena are looked in the face. But the postscript also is peculiar to him, "But all the time God still reigns".[11] Now I would not regard this passage in itself as so conclusive, if the insight which it opens were not in keeping with the whole trend of Bonhoeffer's thought. What is the significance of this postscript? What has it to do with deep sympathy, and what with the weakness of man which degrades? In this we must begin from the point that man, or the human, is the truly real for Bonhoeffer. The person of the other is what stands face to face with us and over against us, hard and uncontrollable, in empirical life. But what is peculiar in the quotation just made is this, that right at the point where the truly real, man, is most utterly threatened by degrading weakness, at the point where man, so to speak, "nullifies" himself, Bonhoeffer takes comfort from the fact that God still reigns. Does not this mean that the reality of God supports the reality of man, and turns aside the "nullification" . . . ? God, and the God who "reigns", who pilots history, is so much bound up with man, with human reality, so much immersed in human reality, that in spite of the complete deficiency in human worth, empirically seen, he yet upholds this worth. Where man slips away from man, he cannot escape God. This agrees exactly with that other thought which recurs several times in Bonhoeffer, that God in his providence brings good out of the evil, the weak, the cowardly and the mean, deeds of man. It is not only the guilt, the *reatus culpae*, that is taken away from the guilty, the issue itself also becomes good, and thus the eschatological act of Divine forgiveness manifests itself as historically palpable in the "healing" of guilt within history.

Now there is a certain attitude towards man which makes allowance for this weakness, this degradation, and takes responsibility for it and stands its ground optimistically because "God still reigns", which accepts man completely in spite of all for God's sake, and accepts, not "man as such", but the concrete man on each occasion, even himself! It follows from this attitude that man cannot in the last resort "nullify"

11 (The words "in heaven" are not actually in the text of the German original as quoted by Ott—Tr.)

himself, precisely because God leaps into the gap. The reality
of God is so immersed in the reality of man, so bound up with
it, that the two can no longer be separated. This is the fruit of
the incarnation of Jesus Christ. God and man now meet as a
single *continuum* of reality, a *continuum* of constant encounter.[12]
Man is no longer in any way isolated by himself, nor can he any
longer be so regarded; "in, with, and under" human reality we
are encountered by the reality of God. Human reality, as the
"most real" in what surrounds us, thus receives a peculiar
new perspective and dimension of depth. And when this
perspective is seen, one can put up with man in his deepest
weakness, humiliation and degradation in this attitude of
"profound sympathy", an attitude which in the last resort is an
optimistic one. And perhaps one must also add that where
one takes such an attitude and puts up with man, where this
profound sympathy is alive, there is also there in every case, at
least implicitly, this perspective. Without this dimension of
depth opened up by the indwelling Divine reality, this attitude,

---

[12] This fruit of the incarnation has been described from of old by the
concept of the *unio hypostatica*. The hypostatic union does not hold for the
person of Jesus Christ in isolation, but through him for the whole *condition
humaine*. Jesus Christ, the *Logos*, has taken *"human nature"*, the reality of
man as such, into hypostatic union with himself. The hypostatic union has
"cosmic relevance" (Bultmann). The human situation as such is modified and
altered by it. This is the meaning of the concept of the *"supernatural existential"*
often employed by Karl Rahner. The *unio hypostatica* of human nature with
the divine in Jesus Christ means, and this is the universal relevance of the
event of Christ, the *unio* of the human race with God. But it is true that
in the *unio hypostatica* divine and human nature, though certainly undivided,
are also unconfused. The opposition of God and man is still kept even in the
situation of the supernatural existential. The ontological concept of "nature",
in my opinion dangerous and fundamentally inadequate, which tradition
employs at this point, leads one astray very easily into thinking in terms of a
confusion of natures, which takes away the opposition. The Chalcedonian
definition offered resistance to this, and what Bonhoeffer, too, says of the
immanence of Jesus Christ in all reality is to be given a Chalcedonian interpretation. Hence we speak of a *"continuum* of reality" as a *"continuum* of encounter"; the reality of God is "immersed" in such a way in the reality of man
that God still remains in opposition to man, and that the reality of man is
unavoidably, and hence "existentially", determined by this. Thus the opposition of God becomes an existential determination of the existence of man.
But this opposition in its turn must be interpreted *Christologically* in terms of
the Chalcedonian "undivided". God is not merely a distant, demanding
opposite to man, but the "near opposite" which completely surrounds him.
Here we can bring in the existential interpretation of the universal Christ,
with which we shall deal in greater detail in Chapter X.

which is yet really there, for we meet it and it is shown to ourselves (!), would not be possible or justified. But further, and this also belongs to the possibility and justification of that attitude, the "indwelling" of the reality of God is not in any sense an "ideal", which in that case would remain without consequences in the realm of the concretely real, except for those consequences which man makes for himself, it is the indwelling of God who rules in history, who does not only change man's fundamental outlook and forgive him his sins, but manifests this act of renewal in concrete reality also, in that he gives a good issue. Thus the thought of the providence and guidance of God is essentially involved in a certain attitude to man.

Where the most real of realities, that of man, including even ourselves, escapes us, it is recaptured and given back to us by God, but given back to us in a new and transformed way, in such a way that we can only receive it in faith. Thus it is God himself, the Reconciler of the world, Jesus Christ, who in the last resort still keeps us from losing confidence in man, in ourselves and in others. And thus our responsibility flows into the responsibility of God and in such a change receives the new form of intercession.

But for Bonhoeffer there is yet one more realm where palpable, unavoidable human reality escapes from man; it is the slipping away of the past, especially one's own past. This thought gave Bonhoeffer in prison much concern. He is movingly outspoken in the poem which he wrote after his fiancée had been allowed to speak with him for a short time. The end of the poem, "The Past", runs:

". . . Are you lost to me once more? Is it always vainly
   that I seek you,
you, my past?
I stretch my hands out,
and I pray—
and a new thing now I hear:
'The past will come to you once more,
and be your life's enduring part,
through thanks and repentance.
Feel in the past God's forgiveness and goodness,
pray him to keep you today and tomorrow' " (LPP, p. 226).

God brings back the past—this is also the theme of Bonhoeffer's famous declaration of the Fourth Sunday in Advent, 1943, which was already quoted in Chapter Four.

"... For this last week or so these lines have kept running through my head:

> *Lasset fahr'n, o liebe Brüder,*
> *was euch quält, was euch fehlt;*
> *ich bring alles wieder.*

(Translator's note in LPP—'Let go, dear brothers, every pain and want; I will restore everything' (From *Fröhlich soll mein Herze springen*, by Paul Gerhardt).) What does this 'I will restore' mean? It means that nothing is lost, that everything is taken up in Christ, although it is transformed, made transparent, clear, and free from all selfish desire. Christ restores all this as God originally intended it to be, without the distortion resulting from our sins. The doctrine derived from Eph. 1: 10—that of the restoration of all things, ἀνακεφαλαίωσις, *recapitulatio*, (Irenaeus)—is a magnificent conception, full of comfort. This is how the promise 'God seeks what has been driven away' is fulfilled. And no one has expressed this so simply and artlessly as Paul Gerhardt in the words that he puts into the mouth of the Christ-child: *Ich bring alles wieder*" (LPP, p. 112).

"... 'restoration' is spirit, not in the sense of 'spiritualization' (which is also σάρξ), but of καινὴ κτίσις through the πνεῦμα ἅγιον, a new creation through the Holy Spirit. I think this point is also very important when we have to talk to people who ask us about their relation to their dead. 'I will restore everything'—that is, we cannot and should not take it back ourselves, but allow Christ to give it back to us" (LPP, p. 113).[13]

---

[13] Cp. also on this the following in *The Cost of Discipleship*, "For the Christian the only God-given realities are those he receives from Christ ... The path, too, to the 'God-given reality' of my fellow-man or woman with whom I have to live leads through Christ, or it is a blind alley. We are separated from one another by an unbridgeable gulf of otherness and strangeness which resists all our attempts to overcome it by means of natural association or spiritual union. There is no way from one person to another ... For there are no direct relationships, not even between soul and soul. Christ stands between us, and we can only get into touch with our neighbours through him. That is why intercession is the most promising way to reach our neighbours, and corporate prayer, offered in the name of Christ, the purest form of fellowship" (CD, pp. 87f.). The special tone of this period to which *The Cost of Discipleship* belonged is unmistakable, and yet this thought of the mediation of all reality through Christ has an obvious relatedness with the Christological ontology of the *Ethics*.

As far as Bonhoeffer's writings as a whole are concerned, one may feel the eschatological note to be largely missing. Even in his late period, the period of his suffering, the expectation of the Kingdom of God has scarcely any place; everything is of this world. And yet we find here, in the margin to all appearance, and yet very significantly, the beginnings to an eschatology capable of the greatest development and at the same time in the closest proximity to the centre of his thought. Jesus Christ, the Divine Reconciler of the world, recaptures the present reality which is slipping away from us into the past, and restores it at the fulfilment of all things. Nothing is lost, all is guarded and retains its meaning, or rather wins it for the first time, wins it in the universal Christ, who restores and gathers up into himself everything. He is the universal Giver of meaning to the universe, he in person the meaning of reality. Thus God's reign in history shows itself finally as a giving of meaning in Christ, directed towards a goal, a "restoration", in which the giving of meaning becomes clear. And thus there appears once more in a clear light the kinship of Christology, the doctrine of Providence, and Eschatology.

On this concept of meaning and the final giving of meaning Bonhoeffer writes:

> "We think that, because this or that person is living, it makes sense for us to live too. But the truth is that if this earth was good enough for the man Jesus Christ, if such a man as Jesus lived, then, and only then, has life a meaning for us. If Jesus had not lived, then our life would be meaningless, in spite of all the other people whom we know and honour and love. Perhaps we now sometimes forget the meaning and purpose of our profession. But is not this the simplest way of putting it? The unbiblical idea of 'meaning' is indeed only a translation of what the Bible calls 'promise' " (LPP, p. 214).

If "meaning" and "promise" have for Bonhoeffer the same significance this must imply that the meaning of the real has an eschatological character, that its reference is to the future of Jesus Christ as something promised, that reality therefore has, as it were, its centre of gravity in that future of Jesus Christ.

PART THREE

The Future

CHAPTER EIGHT

REALITY AS BONHOEFFER'S THEME
AND OURS

WE CAN see the peculiar power, definiteness and originality in Bonhoeffer's thought in the fact that *he
gives us to think*. But the purpose and method of our
study has been from the beginning, not mere description, but
rather a discussion with Bonhoeffer, since we believed in the
first place that in the realm of history and of the knowledge of
history, or "hermeneutics", in all its dimensions, description is
in the last resort only possible at all as discussion. But now
from the character of this discussion, which has so far determined
our road, certain consequences are to be drawn. If we wish to do
justice to Bonhoeffer we have to engage ourselves with the
thoughts that his thought raises in us.

We have endeavoured to think after Bonhoeffer what he
felt and thought as Christian and thinker. Perhaps by our
definition and our underlining we have succeeded in making
more clearly understood here and there the class of question
which he raised and his theses. Perhaps now then the matter
could be carried a little further and it is time for us to join
Bonhoeffer in thought and advance with him again and again to
the frontier of still open questions. This is the position which,
together with him, we have now reached. In this dialogical
procedure the last part of this book has still a special function
to fulfil.

Bonhoeffer's thought gives us to think by opening up a
future, and into that future we must go forward. This is
meaningful and necessary even when it is not yet possible to
reach the goal. While up to this point, although already it has
always been in dialogue, we have interpreted what he has
said, in order to expound the *facts* with which he was concerned,
we shall now gradually depart from his actual text and think

further on these same facts, in the main without explicit reference to him, although always with him implicitly in mind. In such a way, perhaps, after a fruitful discussion, the partners separate at a late hour of the evening, return home and think further on what has been discussed, not everything perhaps about which they have spoken, but particularly these points which strike them as most important and most difficult. Even then the further thought will not become monological, but one will keep one's colleague before one's eyes, and in addition will take the opportunity to examine the matter and test the points of view which have resulted along with a third person in whom one has some confidence. So we also in looking at the "future" will bring in new partners in discussion, above all, Thomas Aquinas, and in connection with him Gerhard Ebeling, who, basing his arguments upon Luther, has ventured to oppose him, Pierre Teilhard de Chardin, in brief references Wolfhart Pannenberg and two Asiatic theologians, and finally also Karl Rahner, who has already given us many helpful suggestions as we dealt with Bonhoeffer, and Ernst Fuchs.

First of all, let us cast one more glance at the general appearance, the silhouette, one might say, of Bonhoeffer's theology, and establish as the abiding general impression what already at the beginning of our interpretation guided us as our first impression and our working hypothesis, that his problem in all parts of his thought is reality. This was the subject both of his life and of his theology. We find in it a "thought" of this thinker, the invisible law of the inner unity of his development, even if it is only occasionally explicitly treated. It is because of this that Bonhoeffer has forced himself upon us as the first witness and the theological authority in whose name we have raised the questions essentially implied in the title of this work, *Reality and Faith*. Belonging both as man and as theologian entirely to our century and our epoch, Bonhoeffer was the first to sense with such clarity and such passion the hidden fundamental question of our era which troubles us, the question difficult to formulate, perhaps up to now not formulated at all, yet always unavoidably and disturbingly there and concerning us as our destiny, *the question about reality*. It is alive in the philosophical thinking of our time, for example in J.P. Sartre's reductional movement to man's picture of himself as the final πoῦ στῶ, or in Heidegger's question about the technical age as the reality to which we are delivered up today, in both Martin Buber's philosophy of dialogical life and the irreducible reality of the I-Thou relation and Heinrich Barth's philosophy of manifestation as the original datum. These are only a very few examples, and yet significant examples. The basic question about reality is also the driving force of theological thinking; it is surely there behind the break through and break away of the early Karl Barth from the housings of a neo-Protestant philosophy of religion. It is there behind the drive towards hermeneutics of present-day German theology, towards the true conception of the reality of history, and behind the drive of present-day American theology towards essays in linguistic analysis, in order finally to be able to say clearly what can be said theologically, behind the Catholic *aggiornamento* which seeks to take into its sights the real man of today, and behind W. Pannenberg's endeavour to conceive the whole of reality as universal history. For all their differences and even their hostility to one another, these are ruled by a hidden brotherhood in the question at stake.

Dietrich Bonhoeffer lived and thought under the influence of this hidden, but mighty, stream. One feels that one can detect the underground current in each of his works. And now the time for *systematizing* this question in theology seems wellnigh come. Bonhoeffer's work will simply compel us to do so. And yet systematizing is no easy task, for the question is one covering many strata and affecting many theological points. It can scarcely be accurately described as a single problem. One *motif* is what we might call the increasing incomprehensibility of the real, in which the real nevertheless remains just as "real", hard and inescapable, looking at us with questioning eyes. And the question now is where faith has its place in this immense reality. Or better, *how* is faith *real*, real in such a way that its reality appears as something different from the reality of an ideology? And how is the *subject* of faith real? *Where is God?* The question about the reality of God, Gollwitzer's question about the "existence of God", is one, and perhaps the most important, aspect of this problem. But it appears under other aspects too.

Another aspect of the same question is, as we have seen, the pisteological. How is the reality of faith to be described so that is it not merely ideological, but encompasses the whole man? Further aspects are the ethical, the reality of the ethical act as an act of obedience, the eschatological, the interpretation of time as we actually experience it as eschatologically aligned, aligned, that is, in such a way that Christian words about the fullness of the time do not appear mere dressing, or the ecclesiological, the reality of the fellowship of believers which is something more than a society, and is so in reality and not merely asserted as such. Because of the many strata which go to make up this question there would be many more aspects yet. But it is always the same question. And it is the fundamental problem in theology, dogmatics and ethics, for the *theologian* of our era. And it could well at the same time be the problem for *man*, or at least Western man, of our day.

It will be evident from this to anyone who can detect the underground current in Bonhoeffer's thought that his significance for the theological thought of our era can scarcely be overvalued, although, or perhaps precisely because, his thought is fragmentary and really raises for us more problems than it solves.

*

It is difficult, and in my opinion not advisable, to seek to pass general judgements on historical epochs, and to show assurance in interpreting them as whole entities. Hegel's thought was able to do this because of its presuppositions, but to a thought which is open to the hermeneutical problem such procedure gradually becomes more and more foreign.[1] Jacob Burckhardt is nearer to us today when he writes at the beginnings of his *Reflections on History* (tr. M.D.H., Allen & Unwin, 1943), "Above all we shall have nothing to do with the philosophy of history. The philosophy of history is a centaur, a contradiction in terms, for history co-ordinates, and hence is unphilosophical, while philosophy subordinates, and hence is

[1] On this cp. H. G. Gadamer's arguments against Hegel from the viewpoint of a hermeneutical conception of the understanding of history. He sets these out in *Wahrheit und Methode*, pp. 324ff., under the heading, "The Limits of a Philosophy of Reflection".

unhistorical. To deal first with philosophy, if it grapples direct with the great riddle of life, it stands high above history, which at best pursues that goal imperfectly and indirectly . . . All the same, we are deeply indebted to the centaur, and it is a pleasure to come across him now and then on the fringe of the forest of historical study. Whatever his principles may have been, he has known some vast vistas through the forest and lent spice to history" (pp. 15ff.).

We cannot have assurance in interpreting past eras, because they are past and we can no longer approach them from within. But we cannot have assurance in interpreting the era which is present for each of us, because it is present and we cannot stand at a distance from it. The greatest danger consists in this, that a systematic assertion about the present, be it philosophical or theological, be arrived at by using historical constructions and general judgements. As a foundation these cannot bear the weight.

It is true that there are characteristic traits which keep repeating, basic traits manifested by historical eras, which call for a general interpretation. This is by no means excluded, on the contrary it is a task given to us. But on each occasion it must be done with reserve, with the consciousness of its *character as decision*, the consciousness that our general judgements on past and present phenomena are on each occasion functions of our own acceptance of our own historical present.

In full awareness of these difficulties and reservations we may perhaps venture to describe "reality" as the ruling subject and problem in the thought of Western man of our era. But I would not yet venture further to interpret this factual situation. Rather, looking from within the theological situation, and therefore seeing it in the sense of an acceptance of our own present, I believe that we can say that, in so far as it is valid for the thought of Christian theology, it means nothing else than that theology in our time is wrestling with the question of the credibility of the Christian message. The basic problem, "reality", is in the theological realm identical with the problem of credibility, the believable articulation of the Gospel. Where anyone today in theology still, or anew, protects himself against the problem of reality in its manifold aspects, and feels that he has a refuge in historical confessions or dogmatic formulae, this could be taken as a sign that he is not yet, or no longer, really in earnest about the problem of the credibility of the Gospel.

*

In Bonhoeffer the power of that question which determined his life, this very same problem of reality and credibility, is to be seen with especial emphasis in the very personal confession which he made in a letter to Helmut Rössler on October 18, 1931:

> "I should like still to visit one large land, India, to see if perhaps the solution can be found there; for otherwise it seems as if the final death of Christianity is at hand. Is our time past and is the Gospel given to another people, preached perhaps with quite other words and deeds[2] ... I am now Chaplain at the Technical College—how is one to preach of such things to those there? For who still believes them? That we cannot see gets us down! If we are unable to see in our own personal life that Christ was there, then at least we would want to see it in India, but this crazy being thrown back continually upon the invisible God himself is what no man can endure any more" (*Ges. Schr.*, I, p. 61).

Have we here words spoken in some strong emotion, without reflection, born out of some mood of the moment? So to understand the text would be to overlook precisely what is characteristic for Bonhoeffer, what concerned and drove him in his inmost heart, though he seldom gave expression to it with such openness and lack of reserve. It is not the reality of God in which the young students' chaplain has lost confidence, but the manner in which we have traditionally, and perhaps inevitably, been accustomed to speak of this reality. Is it possible that we have come to the end of our tradition? Can it be in another distant world, and in a quite other foreign form, that the same God and Lord will now have to be truly experienced and preached more credibly to humanity in the future? For Bonhoeffer this longing for India is obviously the longing for the reality of God, for the experience of him

---

[2] In the passage which is here omitted he enters into a more specific problem. But the sentences which follow show how for Bonhoeffer the whole question had an absolutely comprehensive range.

and the credible preaching of him. He did not at this time travel to India, although the possibility did on one occasion come unmistakably near to him, but remained right to the final sacrifice of his life in the limited sphere which was his by birth. Solidarity with his own German people, love for the historical here and now and self-sacrifice to it, these, too, are constitutive traits in his life, for they again on their side are precisely those which belong to that wrestling with reality.

But the question was not put without reflection, the cry of the heart that "that we cannot see gets us down!" did not come from him in an unthinking moment, nor was it followed by a later recantation and Bonhoeffer giving himself satisfied to the invisible with pacified faith. On the contrary this question always remained with him and he stood by it in thought and action right to the end. "Resistance and Surrender", "The non-religious interpretation of Biblical concepts", these are nothing other than the last and most concentrated effort, with tensed muscles, to meet with it.

It is true that not only the nagging question or the complete doubt was there. It was not doubt in God or in Christ which gave its power to the urgency of this question in Bonhoeffer, it was dissatisfaction with himself, with the Church, with Christians. In the end it was the reality of God himself which was dissatisfied. Hence the nagging question was enveloped in assurance and promise. How could we trace so passionately our own dissatisfaction with the truth of God, if God himself were not near? Without this compulsion from the nearness of God so honest a man as Bonhoeffer would in all humility have given up faith in God long before.

But because that breath, which could not be lost, of assurance and promise was always in Bonhoeffer the companion of the radical question about reality, the problem of reality, and it is each time none other than this problem, even if it is not systematically stated as such, can even gain a hopeful note, one is even tempted to say an intoxicated note; the reality of life presents itself to him, the believer, in its fullness, opens itself to the man who opens himself to it in faith. This is what happens, for instance, where Bonhoeffer, in the *Letters and Papers from Prison*, expresses the thought of the "polyphony of life":

"... There is always the danger that intense love may cause one to lose what I might call the polyphony of life. What I mean is that God wants us to love him eternally with our whole hearts —not in such a way as to injure or weaken our earthly love, but to provide a kind of *cantus firmus* to which the other melodies of life provide the counterpoint. One of these contrapuntal themes (which have their own complete independence but are yet related to the *cantus firmus*) is earthly affection. Even in the Bible we have the Song of Songs; and really one can imagine no more ardent, passionate, sensual love than is portrayed there (see 7: 6). It is a good thing that that book is in the Bible, in face of all those who believe that the restraint of passion is Christian (where is there such restraint in the Old Testament?). Where the *cantus firmus* is clear and plain, the counterpoint can be developed to its limits. The two are 'undivided and yet distinct', in the words of the Chalcedonian Definition, like Christ in his divine and human natures. May not the attraction and importance of polyphony in music consist in its being a musical reflection of this Christological fact and therefore of our *vita Christiana*?" (LPP, p. 162).

"The image of polyphony is still pursuing me. When I was rather distressed today at not being with you, I could not help thinking that pain and joy are also part of life's polyphony, and that they can exist independently side by side" (LPP, p. 164).

(Cp. also LPP, p. 174. It is astonishing and very impressive, but perhaps also characteristic, that this thought of polyphony, which appears three times in *Letters and Papers from Prison*, does so twice in connection with air-raid alarms, that is, with acute uncertainty as to one's own further life.) In this thought of polyphony the fullness of immeasurable reality is gathered together into a unity. Man, and especially the believer, must open himself to it in all its manifold dimensions. It is precisely so that the unity is preserved for him, for the presence of God in Christ remains the ruling *cantus firmus*. Here reality is thought of in its many strata and in its final unity at the same time, or it would be better to say that reality is experienced, for the formulated thought is nothing more than an aphorism. The thought of polyphony is one of the strongest evidences of the relevance of ontologically conceived Christology in Bonhoeffer.

*

In this sense "reality" is Bonhoeffer's subject and our own unavoidable subject. And "reality", then, must be the area, the point of perspective, of the questions for the future of these last chapters. We shall not be able in them to speak further about all the themes which have appeared in our discussion with Bonhoeffer. Ethics and ecclesiology, as we have just mentioned and explained, and above all the problem of providence, all are aspects of the question of reality, for it is a matter of the reality of the encounter with God in all that really happens. The "future" has surely at least begun to become visible as we completed our dialogical picture. It is true that a developed ethic or ecclesiology or doctrine of providence in the spirit of Bonhoeffer remains still to be written. But here we shall confine ourselves to two future questions which in the last resort are one, and we shall allow ourselves in this choice to be guided by a word which Karl Rahner wrote briefly with regard to the Council and its ecclesiastical reflections, in particular its doctrine of collegiality:

> "The necessary and salutary reflection of the Church about itself in Vatican II will not be the final stage of theology. Another even more important one will come, for which this Council will seem to have been simply a forerunner and indirect preparation. *The ultimate hope and truth of the Church, God and his Christ, will be expressed anew as though what in fact has always been preached were really understood for the first time"* (*The Teaching of Vatican II on the Church and the Future Reality of the Christian Life*, in *The Christian of the Future*, p. 99. Our italics).

What Rahner, looking at the contemporary development of Christendom, has in mind for that future period of theology is just what Bonhoeffer thought of when he spoke of the coming day of the Church of Christ and the new language which will be liberating and redeeming, under which the world will be transformed and in which the peace of God with man and the drawing near of his kingdom will truly be proclaimed ("Thoughts on Baptism", LPP, p. 172). According to Rahner there are two subjects which will require to be stated anew in the theology of the future as if one had understood them for the first time, God and his Christ, that is to say, the whole, the final truth which is committed to Christians, the reality of God himself.

This is no arbitrary judgement of Rahner's. It is in keeping with the position of the theological problem as it already has to be described today. On the Protestant side we stand exactly at the same point, and the necessity to learn anew how to speak of God and his Christ is before us in exactly the same way and with the same urgency. The "atheism-debate", however unsatisfactory its yield to date, points in the same direction.

There result for us then two questions for the future, (1) the future of the doctrine of God, and (2) the Christological future. It will become clear that they are not two, but that in subject-matter and method the second is merely the closer definition of the first. It is possible that in what follows a very small contribution will be made, I do not venture to say "to the solution", I shall only say "to a clearer view", of the tremendous task which will keep occupied in the future and surely for our lifetime all of us who work on the theology of Jesus Christ.

CHAPTER NINE

THE FUTURE FOR THE DOCTRINE OF GOD

W E BEGIN by listening to a voice from the theology of the present day, for Gerhard Ebeling has entered into battle with Thomas Aquinas. This is an important step. German critical theology of our day with the stamp of Bultmann, which to many of its friends and enemies seemed to be completely and entirely distinguished by specifically modern ways of putting its questions has, so to speak, made a display of turning to the scholastics of the Middle Ages, to the metaphysics and the metaphysical theology of the *doctor communis*. It is done critically, of course. And yet it represents a material widening of the horizon of discussion and as such is much to be welcomed. It is true that in this Ebeling bases himself, not on Bultmann, but on Martin Luther. From the standpoint of Luther's dialectic of Law and Gospel and of the revealed and the hidden God he attacks the thought of the proof of the existence of God as we find it in Thomas, though we must add that he does so with a deep understanding for the dimensions of this thought and for its peculiar structure and strength. If we on our side enter into controversy with Ebeling's criticism of Thomas, we discover an astonishing deep and essential kinship between the understanding of reality in Thomas and that in Dietrich Bonhoeffer. This is the first thing we shall have to demonstrate.

Thereafter, by an analysis of several pertinent texts from the beginning of the *Summa Theologiae*, texts to which Ebeling also refers, we shall have to exemplify more concretely the new-won view of the understanding of reality which we now maintain as against that of Ebeling. The peculiar factual problem will thereby be fully posed. In Thomas Aquinas, above all in the first two questions of the *Summa* where he deals with the presuppositions of theology and with the proof of God's existence, it appears as the problem of the integration of the whole of reality within our reach into faith in the living Biblical God. It must also then be our concern when we ask today about the reality of God and the credible articulation of the knowledge of this reality.

And yet again, in a third section of this "Future for the Doctrine of God", our question reaches its acutest point and gains precision on the concept of the personality of God. How is our whole experience of reality to be integrated into faith as a personal act in response to a *personal* God? How then is this "fundamental factual situation in theology" to which we made frequent reference in our first chapter, *the personal encounter of faith with the personal God, to be shown as that which encompasses and overrules all our encounter with reality, and therefore as the whole horizon of our existence altogether*? Where then in our encounter with reality do we come against the reality of God? And in this we find ourselves perforce struggling with the difficult concept of "personality". This, it is true, can only be dealt with here in the form of an indication of the problem, for its proper examination demands a second attack on the question, and therefore a second volume of our endeavour on *"Reality and Faith"*. But the putting of this question, if we keep ourselves close to Bonhoeffer, but also and above all if we follow the inward course taken by the facts themselves, leads us at the same time to the Christological future, in which the future for the doctrine of God has, so to speak, its second instalment, because God has borne witness to himself in Jesus Christ.

1. *The Soteriological Relevance of the Proof of the Existence of God*

Gerhard Ebeling's argument against Thomas Aquinas, in a lecture first given at the first meeting of the inter-confessional *Schweizerischen Theologischen Gesellschaft*, in Berne in 1964, bears the significant title, *Existenz zwischen Gott und Gott. Ein Beitrag zur Frage nach der Existenz Gottes* ("Existence between God and God. A Contribution to the Question of the Existence of God"), (ZThK 62, Jg 1965, Heft 1, pp. 86ff.). Creation, according to Thomas Aquinas, exists between God as *principium* and God as *finis*, according to Martin Luther, between *Deus absconditus* and *Deus revelatus*. So Ebeling describes the two antipodes and the difference in their understanding of man's situation before God. Where he himself stands in this question is made clear by, *inter alia*, his impressive closing sentences·

> "Man as man finds himself in a situation between what incomprehensibly withdraws itself from him and what incomprehensibly gives itself to him. The embarrassment of this situation between is the place where we speak about God. The word 'God', understood elementally, is an interjection, an interruption, the cry for God of existence between God and God. This, it is true, is an interpretation which is already due to the language *of* faith, which takes seriously the last cry of Jesus. But the reality to which this interpretation refers, the fact of the embarrassment of existence, attests the language as such" (*op. cit.*, p. 113).

Ebeling accordingly makes the existence of God his subject. In a certain sense this question is the whole of theology for him. On this point we may quote his assertions with emphatic agreement:

> "But not even the most extremely substantial loading could, as one might think, force the doctrine of God into the status of a ready-to-hand *summa* of faith. Faith itself understands itself as taking second place to nothing in its nature as faith *in* God. What faith confesses as its grounds and content is nothing else than the fulfilment of what so makes faith faith, that in truth it makes God God. Hence the assertion that God is can be championed, not only by means of the most extreme enrichment through additional explanatory statements, but also by means of the most concentrated return to the simplicity of the one necessary thing. And this assertion, when one knows what one is saying by it, is the essence of Christian preaching and Christian faith" (*op. cit.*, p. 94).

*

Exceptionally lucid is Ebeling's analysis of Thomas' procedure in his examination of the question of God's existence:

> "It (sc. the development of the proof) is divided into five approaches which run parallel to one another and have the same

structure. Each time three steps, or rather three leaps, are repeated.

On each occasion a beginning is made by the assertion of elementary experience of the world, as it underlies all experience of reality as the primary model. Encounter with an existent raises the question about its connection with others. The basic experience of an existent has the character of a demand to pursue the existent to the point of what is lacking in it. No existent meeting us in a secular manner is complete and independent, but all are connected with all. Thus encounter with an existent leads beyond it ... We encounter the unquestionable reality of the world as questionable reality. The palpable, impressing itself upon us as real, indisputable and obvious, is not, as it were, discussed away. The world is treated seriously as the world. But in this acceptance man himself is so accepted into the world that its reality is experienced as questionableness. The world shows itself as the world in that it gives man to think without limit.

But at this point there now arises a sudden break through the argument that a *procedure ad infinitum* is impossible. There must be a halt at a first or a last which rules, otherwise there obviously could be nothing derivative either. The movement of thought and question into which experience of the world brings man must come to rest somewhere.

The purpose of the proof of God's existence is obviously to deliver man up to an experience of the world to which, precisely because he must recognize it as true, he must yet finally say 'No' in protest. The world is not to hold me *in infinitum*, so that it appears in the place of God. I contradict the contradiction that the finite can cause me to be engulfed in an infinite questioning. Nor do I permit myself to force my way into the place of God and to condemn myself to the role of a *procedere in infinitum*. I permit myself to be bounded by the *infinitum*, to come to a halt at the *infinitum*, which I have to accept, and not to master in a *procedere*. The denial of the being of the absolutely first, the absolutely necessary and perfect, would be a disputing of the being of the world, and therefore of my own existence. Hence the demand to address the *infinitum* as an *ens infinitum* equally arises out of experience of the world. For however questionable the experience may be it is still experience of being. That the world, although in the whirlpool of destruction of being, is yet there as finitude contained in the infinite is an invitation to address the *infinitum* as being speaking to being, as *ens infinitum*, and to give up the suicidal *procedure in infinitum*.

But there follows yet a third leap, which in a stereotyped fashion brings to an end each of the five *viae* with a brief final new turn. Up to this point the subject was never God, only a *primum movens*, a *causa efficiens*, an *ens per se necessarium*, a *maxime ens*, a *summum intelligens ens*. What has this to do with God? The answer is that when God is spoken of the whole world is meant. This is not, shall we say, the *conclusio* of a process of proof, it is a *metabasis* which one cannot prove but must accomplish, the leap into the language of faith" (*op. cit.*, pp. 98ff.).

Ebeling now sets this way of expressing the question about the existence of God against the thought which Luther develops in *De servo arbitrio*, the distinction between *Deus absconditus* and *Deus revelatus*, regarding this latter as a way more in keeping with the situation of faith in our time and the situation of absolute questionableness in which human existence today finds itself. By Thomas the proof of God is carried out in a soteriologically neutral forecourt.

"From this there follows a central difference. In traditional dogma the knowledge of the existence of God is the positive starting-point from which, through the doctrine of the completenesses of his being, the door is opened to a more comprehensive doctrine of his nature. The knowledge of the existence of God is the soteriologically neutral basis on which the revealed knowledge of God is built. For Luther, on the contrary, no bridge is required from the knowledge that God is, embracing both God and idol, to the knowledge what or who God is" (*op. cit.*, p. 110).

According to Ebeling, then, the metaphysical thinking which is operative in the *quinque viae* goes astray in expressing the being-in-himself of God analogously to the being-in-itself of an entity of this world, ignoring relation to existence. Awareness of God is treated here analogously to awareness of the thisworldly. The metaphysical understanding of the world, he would claim, which forms the basis of his proof of God in Thomas, is no longer attainable. And careful interpretation of metaphysical texts would thus show as its result that forgetting this situation was the weakness of metaphysical thinking. Of course the critical rebellion which Ebeling would seek to carry out against such traditional doctrines of God could only be maintained with the help of a doctrine of the distinction between *Deus absconditus* and *Deus revelatus*. He would say that the scholastic doctrine of God sets out from a neutral undisturbed relation to God, while Luther, on the contrary, begins from the salvationless situation of man.

In Ebeling's view, therefore, to travel by way of Thomas' proofs to the awareness that God exists is a way which does not take seriously enough the radical questionableness of existence, indeed which rather leaves out every relation to existence and argues only from the reality of material, non-existential and worldly entities, incapable of being. To him there can be opposed as a pattern of thought more credible for us Luther, in whom it is no longer possible to trace any "neutral basis" for theology. There is no more trace of a possibility of first settling the question of the existence of God before at all making our subject human existence and its salvation. Rather, through the concept of *Deus absconditus*, through the concept of the enigmatic, fearful God, concealing himself in the incomprehensibilities of being, man is seen from the very beginning in his radical questionableness before God. This is the view with which Ebeling identifies himself.

> "It remains to be asked, however, if a silent *adorare* of the *mysteria divinitatis* can be theologically maintained without also becoming explicit in a doctrine of God, which accordingly must be a doctrine of the distinction between the *Deus absconditus* and the *Deus praedicatus*, between the *Deus maiestatis* and the *Deus humanus*, between God himself and the Word of God. Otherwise we are threatened with the reduction of God to some dear God, whose love is incomprehensible precisely because it can be taken for granted. Then we make God something to be added to reality to make it complete, instead of the mystery of all reality, the Almighty who renders us speechless, not merely the potential Almighty, but he who is so in actuality. God is not merely the known and trusted God of the Church and of Sundays. He is also Auschwitz and Hiroshima, is also the prosaic reality of everyday, and therefore godlessness also in every form it takes . . .
>
> God therefore is not only the present, he is also the absent God. Or to be more exact, the *Deus absconditus*, the absent God, however much he is the Divine God, is yet at the same time, for we must speak right away in such fearful contradictions, the

godless God; however much he is the God who is active and living in all things he is yet at the same time the dead God, the God who is absolutely absent and yet present precisely in his absence. If our approach to the doctrine of God is such that to speak of the being of God is not made neutral to his being known or unknown, then atheism belongs to the doctrine of God as an experience of the *Deus absconditus*" (*op. cit.*, pp. 108f.).

It certainly remains to be asked if one can commit Luther to this. In *De servo arbitrio*, the work in which Luther expounds the distinction between the *Deus absconditus* and the *Deus revelatus*, we do also find a final resolution from an eschatological viewpoint of the tension between the two concepts. We can read of this at the end of the work (Ch. XIV, WA 18, p. 785).[1] For Luther the tension is resolved in the *eschaton*, in the *lumen gloriae*, an *eschaton now already* envisaged and addressed in his thought, for him an element and subject of theology.

Further, while we dare not weaken in any respect the radical questionableness, as it becomes the problem of modern man and especially the believer, and as it finds expression in this impressive way in Ebeling, while it is a fact that this is part of the doctrine of God today, yet it still remains to be asked about Thomas Aquinas' method of thought whether we dare define it merely in the questionable terms of a neutrality which has not yet faced trial, and whether on this very point we cannot find in him another, more positive relation than that defined for him by Ebeling. Is every relation to existence and every relation to soteriology really lacking in Thomas' proofs of God?

It would seem to me that Ebeling's view of Aquinas' position and its intellectual possibilities is too one-sided and narrow. To start from the position that it is possible today to introduce into, or to explicate from, Thomas' interpretation the dimension of the hermeneutical, and to understand the reality out of which his proof arises as a reality already permeated by God, is to obtain a picture of his doctrine of God which does not at all any longer make this appear existentially and soteriologically neutral. Rather the act in which the thinker gives himself to reality as understood by him in this way, the courage to commit

---

[1] (E.T., *The Bondage of the Will*, tr. Packer and Johnston, James Clarke & Co., 1957, pp. 316f.).

oneself at all to the goal of a proof of the existence of God, is already an act of believing decision. An appearance of neutrality, indeed, must arise from the fact that in such commitment of himself to reality the thinker does not break off contact with the unbeliever but allows himself to be accompanied by him and develops his proof in such company. That is to say, the development of his proof is not merely an "egoistic" expression of faith, it is a continual discussion about reality by faith with the unbeliever, with this as its goal, to show that this reality is to be understood as the reality of *God*.

But with the hermeneutical and Christological interpretation of Thomas' proof which we thus set against Ebeling's view of him, there comes to light a *factual* counterposition to that which Ebeling, in opposing Thomas and Luther, develops as his own. Ebeling sees man primarily in the radical questionableness which results from his being delivered up to the *Deus absconditus*, to the hidden absent, "dead" God. This is his primary reality, that of the "law". I do not deny this questionableness. If we allow it to pass out of our sight in simple Christian optimism, how are we still to succeed in speaking credibly to our generation? But it seems to me that faith, in undertaking the proof of God's existence, is already putting that questionableness behind it in trust in the Christ present in all reality. And thus with a "hermeneutically" understood Thomas Aquinas we set against Ebeling's *theologia crucis* a *theologia resurrectionis*.

Certainly we have to remember as we say this that the Resurrection in every case presupposes the Cross. I would not wish to dispute without qualification the rightness of Ebeling's *theologia crucis*. But I think that it must be relativized and balanced against this other view, which surely might also be the view of Bonhoeffer! In theology it is always the case that there should not be left standing at the end a closed system of positions, by which any truth at all is to be denied to other positions, but that a variety of ways is possible, each of which has its own specific justification, and which mutually relativize one another and remain alternately related to one another in their reference to the common centre, the subject-matter of all theology.

The next task is to endeavour still further to establish as valid Dietrich Bonhoeffer's understanding of reality as against that in which Ebeling uses Luther as a means of opposing the proofs of Thomas.

We must begin from the point that Jesus Christ is already present in this created reality as it comes into contact with man, and in the immediate evidence of its reality. God is not merely a "beyond", a metaphysical superstructure over evident reality, who must then be deduced from reality purely secondarily, through a purely intellectual process of conclusion. We must at this point listen carefully to the words in Bonhoeffer's late work against "otherworldliness", against the purely otherworldly God, against God as a "stopgap". The whole earnest theological discussion of today about the existence of God is deeply permeated by this consciousness, that the otherworldly, purely "metaphysical" God can today be no longer preached credibly. But what lies behind this is nothing other than the consciousness, or rather the sense, in the meantime surely not differentiated enough, that the reality of God is "wholly other", that it is greater than what could be expressed in this other system of thought in which God is of "another world". Here, as in the early dialectical theology, it is once more a matter of God as the "wholly other". Perhaps the present-day consciousness of the problem of theological discussion, often no more than a sense of that problem, is a step which continues further the impetus of the first outbreak of dialectical theology, whereas it itself often seems to have fallen back into a purely traditionalist orthodoxy. Certainly a theological error is committed when one attempts to give up as an objectifying metaphor the personality, the being-in-himself, and therefore in the end the genuine confrontation of God, and in place of it to speak of the "depths of being", of the "whence of my concern", or the like. In so doing one both overshoots the mark and actually falls short of one's own, perhaps legitimate, meaning and purpose. *Then* to our thought God is precisely not the "wholly other", he is no longer "other", but is conceived according to man's own ability. He has then become a mere principle such as men have from time to time sketched to round off their own limited view of the world. And it is no longer "honest to God" to think that one has found the "wholly other" God in this principle, when in reality one is only dealing with that thing

333

common from of old, a pantheistic and speculative intellectual activity.

As against this we might understand the later Bonhoeffer's process of thought, and in spite of all perhaps in *intention* at least that of his present imperfect imitators, as a continuation of the original impetus of dialectical theology, a striving to express honestly and credibly in speech the reality of the "wholly other" God.

When Bonhoeffer denied the otherworldliness of God, when he preached the thisworldliness of the Christian faith, world-liness in a world become godless, the acceptance of the situation *etsi deus non daretur*, he, as we have seen, by no means excluded personal *encounter with God*, but proclaimed this other, this freely encountering God as him who is already approaching near, who is present in worldly and creaturely reality. But this present God, completely near to us in our creaturely sphere and to this extent the "thisworldly" God, is God *in Christo*.

God the "completely other", the real, is not merely the otherworldly, he is already the thisworldly. *Etsi deus non daretur* does not mean an exclusion of God, it means that God completely permeates this world. Only when so under-stood is God truly addressed as the "wholly other". The purely otherworldly God beyond is not yet the "wholly other", but a "transcendentalist", and therefore in Bonhoeffer's sense "reli-gious", principle, just as at the other extreme "the depths of one's being" threatens to establish a more immanentist principle.

The legitimate "proof of God", then, does not take us over into a world beyond and exclude a thisworldly world. Its aim is not to complete with God a world in the meantime "godless", it begins from thisworldly reality, from "manifest" reality, that is, as a reality already secretly permeated by God. But now, according to Bonhoeffer, the God who completely per-meates reality is God *in Christo*. Thus the legitimate proof of God begins from Jesus Christ. It is Christologically determined, "mounting up" it is true, from the thisworldly, but no longer from the godless thisworldly, but from that already permeated by Christ. Fundamentally it is nothing other than a way, a process of thought, which confirms the presence of God in the manifest reality of this world.

And now accordingly, though all that we can do here is to indicate this as a programme, our task must be to endeavour to understand Christologically the reality with which on each occasion the proof engages itself. A Christological reinterpretation must be sought for each of the *quinque viae*. The reality, to the infinite questionableness of which the development of the proof surrenders itself, is, according to the knowledge of the problem which Bonhoeffer has helped us to discover, the reality already permeated by God in Christ. And from this point there then also becomes visible for the first time the inner rightness of the two "leaps" which follow, the turning away from a *processus in infinitum* and the leap into the language of faith. Such Christological reinterpretation would certainly, as has already been indicated, demand that we bring in something new, a dimension which Thomas did not yet know, or at least did not have so explicitly before his eyes as does the theology of our time, the *dimension of the hermeneutical*, the dimension of intelligible meaning. According to it, all that is real is meaningful, or at least permits us to assume and enquire for a meaning. It raises this question of meaning for us.

It is true that it remains to be asked if this is Thomist, if we are being true to the thinking of Thomas when we interpret his thought in retrospect in this way, and complete it by this dimension which was not made explicit by him. And yet it is to be maintained as a fundamental rule that the dialogical situation, which is what the situation of the interpreter always is, especially permits, or rather demands, the possibility of such a completion. The Thomist Renaissance, too, in the neo-scholastic theology of our century, has "completed" Thomas by the dimension of the transcendental which it learned from Kant and which we do not yet meet in this form in Thomas himself. But those who think in this direction believe that in this way they gain a more elemental understanding of Thomas and make more clear the actual claim of his thought upon the thinking of our time. In passing, in the course of the same Thomist Renaissance, something similar has been sought for, not only in Kant, but also in Heidegger. But its thinkers, J. Maréchal, J. B. Lotz, Karl Rahner, Gustav Siewerth, etc., are of the opinion that for this disclosure of theirs of a new horizon of thought for the interpretation of Thomas an adequate basis can be found in Thomas himself. And now we should have to examine whether an adequate basis could be found in Thomas himself for our introducing the dimension of the hermeneutical. I think that this is probable, and such a surmise may be confirmed by the review in the following section.

Within such a hermeneutical horizon, for instance, one could, in dealing with the proof of God *e possibili et necessario*, begin from the constant questionableness of meaning in all that is real, from the universal remaining in the balance of the meaning of the real, just as Thomas began from the contingency of all that is real, that it can always either be or not be. But the complete exposition of such a hermeneutical and Christological reinterpretation of the *quinque viae* would require a detailed examination.

Then it might also become clear that the proof of the existence of God, because it committed itself to a reality already determined Christologically, was an intellectual operation of *faith*. And the same would have to be said of the proof of God in Thomas as Karl Barth has shown to be true for the proof of God in Anselm of Canterbury.

The proof of God as an intellectual operation of faith seems to me to be further envisaged in Karl Rahner's words about the one proof of God's existence as a *transcendental basic experience* of man which only permits itself to be differentiated secondarily into the various proofs of God (of which there would surely then be as a consequence more than the five of Thomas), and which as an experience is caused by grace, and is no longer to be distinguished sharply from the "flight of faith". Thus the experiential and intellectual operation of the proof of God is an operation "in the light" of grace and faith.[2] In the proof man confirms for himself that he already stands in a reality of grace, or that the whole of reality in which he stands is already a reality caught up in grace. That is to say, it is a reality permeated by God *in Christo*, for, seen fundamentally, grace is always the grace of Christ. It is only when man stands in the reality of grace, or when through grace the reality in

[2] Cp. Karl Rahner and Herbert Vorgrimler, *Concise Theological Dictionary*, tr. Strachan, Burns and Oates, 1965, Proof of the Existence of God, pp. 381ff., *Praeambula Fidei*, pp. 368ff.

which he stands can be experienced as a reality of grace, that the operation of the proof of God's existence can be carried out. This operation, to use Ebeling's words, is an operation "between God and God", an operation of thought borne by faith from Christ to Christ.

It is true that the proof of God's existence always and essentially has the argumentative component also, that of discussion with the unbeliever. This must by no means be allowed to drop out if we are also to speak of an intellectual operation of faith. For if this side fell out then the interpretation of Thomas for which the expression is used would certainly be untrue. But this aspect is maintained, it is found in the fact that the intellectual operation of faith aims at an integration of the reality in which the unbeliever also lives. This operation of integration, which is peculiar to the development of theological proof, is the realm for discussion, for the reality which it seeks to integrate is the meeting-point of faith with unbelief.

2. The Integration into Faith in God of the Reality of the World (Understanding of Theology and Proof of God in Thomas Aquinas)

The proof of the existence of God begins in no neutral realm, no forecourt to faith. Just as it is the task of theology in general to describe intellectually the prior existential understanding of faith, so the proof of God's existence, as we now seek to understand it, as an element in a genuine theology of faith, describes after the event a certain aspect of faith, that of the integration of reality. The proof of God is an intellectual operation of gradual enlightenment, a gradual bringing to light of the understanding of reality implicit in that faith which itself is lived. Before reflection, and therefore before theology, faith has its specific understanding of reality; it is present in all reality of God. It understands all reality as permeated by God, as pregnant with God. It cannot place outside the frontiers of God's realm any sector of the reality with which it is concerned. It binds itself to this insight against the temptation which seeks to talk it into the absence of God from certain areas, and therefore very soon from all areas.

In "simple faith" in all its naïveté and spontaneity there is always already found this aspect of totality. Faith as faith integrates the whole of reality into the *"milieu divin"*, as Teilhard de Chardin calls it. The proof of God reflects this integrative character of faith.[3] in that it begins with the reality in which we men all live, and shows that this very reality, just as it is, is already marked with the stamp of God, open to God, and claimed by God. It is clear that the proof of God does this in discussion with the unbeliever, that it seeks to convince the unbelieving. For it starts by thinking on that reality in which believer and unbelieving dwell side by side. It is quite meaningless to say that the proof of God is still no genuine exposition of faith, and therefore no theology in the strict sense, because it turns to the unbeliever and tries to convince him of that of which the believer has already been long convinced, and which for him is absolutely the basis of all his "doctrine". For faith does not live in an empty space but in reality, which means that it lives together with unbelief. Its living in reality implies *de facto* its living together with unbelief. This, it is true, must be experienced. Thomas Aquinas experienced it in the great cultural and political threat to Christendom in his day, and we again experience it today in a specific way. But the proof of God, as a later intellectual demonstration of that operation of integration which faith itself already fundamentally is, is accordingly not merely doing something preliminary in relation to the proper and essential discipline of theology, it is something like an embodiment of theology, in that what it accomplishes is precisely what corresponds to the situation of faith in the midst of reality.

This character of theological thought in general, and of the proof of the existence of God in particular, as an integration in reflection of reality corresponding to the existential integration of reality which is faith itself, we shall now seek to exemplify briefly from Thomas Aquinas' teaching on theology (*sacra doctrina*) and from the existence of God as he expounds it in his *Summa Theologiae*. A short comment on several articles from his First Question, *"De sacra Doctrina, qualis sit et ad quae se extendat* (On what sort of teaching Christian theology is and

---

[3] I have expressed myself with somewhat greater fullness on the integrative character of faith in my article, *"La structure de l'acte de foi"*, in *Archivio di Filosofia*, Rome, 1966.

what it covers)"[4] and his Second Question, *"De Deo, an Deus sit* (On God, whether there is a God)", may confirm the thesis which in the first section we put forward against Gerhard Ebeling's attack on Thomas, the thesis that the proof of God's existence, as Thomas understood it, is founded on a reality which faith conceives as permeated and accepted by the living, that is, the Biblical, God. It would be going too far to assert that the acceptance of the world by Christ, as Bonhoeffer thinks of it in expanding the compass of the event of Christ to its necessary universality, has already in these first questions of the *Summa* become the explicit presupposition of thought on which Aquinas consciously reflected. This Christological presupposition of the proof of God is, to use the language of Martin Heidegger, still the "unthought" in Thomas. But it lies directly behind the threshold, and as far as the facts are concerned can soon be discovered. There is no doubt that already in these questions Thomas had no other God in view, and wished to think of no other God, than the Father of Jesus Christ, the God who has revealed himself and wills to be known in the gift of faith. And thus, as far as the facts are concerned, it is only a further reaching development of what in point of fact has already been set out when we say that the proof of God, arising out of the reality which can be experienced, in fact already presupposes a certain *understanding* of reality, and that this is none other than that of faith in the God revealed in Christ, and is therefore a Christological presupposition.

Apart from Thomas' proofs of God we shall refer also to the basic theological presuppositions which he first developed, because there the same character of thought as integration is clear, and is described systematically, to receive its first working out thereafter in the proof of God's existence.[5]

*

In the first question generally the subject is the basic presuppositions of theology. I would only throw up here, and not

---

[4] (Throughout this section I have added to the Latin quotations, and used in what are obviously translated quotations, the E.T. given in the Blackfriars translation, E. & S., Vol. I, tr. Gilbey, Vol. II, tr. McDonnell, 1964—Tr.)

[5] The following notes, to be fully understood, must be read in conjunction with the text of the *Summa Theologiae*.

pursue further, the question how far it might seem significant that this fundamental question of theology appears in the framework of the actual *doctrine of God*.

In the *first article*, *"Utrum sit necessarium praeter philosophicas disciplinas aliam doctrinam haberi* (Is another teaching required apart from philosophical studies?)", we are dealing with the necessity and possibility of a *sacra doctrina*. Is not theology something superfluous in face of philosophy? Does not philosophical thought already embrace everything? And is not man prevented by the creatureliness of his reason from carrying thought beyond the horizon of reason? These are the two objections which Thomas, following the method of his *articuli*, first makes himself with his formula *"videtur quod . . ."*. The aim then is to relate the totality of reality which concerns us, as well as the reason to which this reality becomes clearer for man as percipient, to a knowledge which goes beyond this universal horizon of being and knowing. The problem posed here then is that of "Theology and Reality", in the words of the title of Gerhard Ebeling's installation lecture at Zürich (*Word and Faith*, pp. 194ff.)! Thomas' answer takes the direction that the revelation of God which lays hold of man in faith is necessary for the salvation of man. But this personal revelation of salvation leads man to think a second time, from a new viewpoint, about the whole reality of the world, so that both philosophy and theology have the same subject-matter.

*

In the *second article*, *"Utrum sacra doctrina sit scientia* (Is Christian theology a science?)", we are dealing with an aspect of that fundamental question of theology which is most intensively occupying us precisely at this time, the question about the *scientific nature of theology*. What does Thomas understand by a science? How far is the understanding of science which he makes his basis to be equated with our understanding of the same word? It seems to me that the effective principle in the second *"videtur quod . . ."* and its refutation, "a science is not concerned with individual cases", gives a certain difference from the understanding which would be demanded today, as far, at least, as a hermeneutical science like theology is concerned, for it is precisely the single case which is the subject-matter of hermeneutics. But this difference does not go so far as to make the whole article irrelevant for our factual question about the subject-matter itself. Especially significant seems the kernel of the first objection and the answer to it. "Not all have faith", says Thomas, quoting 2 Thess. 3: 2. And thus there arises the problem which also occupies us today. How can there be a science of something which is not recognizable to everyone, of something which is only a subject at all for a defined group of men.

In his answer Thomas, using the analogy of the relation between a higher and a lower science among the thisworldly sciences, as for example the relation of arithmetic to music and of geometry to optics, postulates a new type of "science", a knowledge absolutely transcending all that is earthly and its foundation, or a superior science of theology, God's knowledge and that of the blessed. Its insights become the basic principles of earthly theology.

In regard to this two questions arise. (1) What is the nature of the insights of this highest knowledge which then become the "basic principles" of theology? (2) How do they, or the knowledge of them, come to man, and why are they not generally recognizable instead of only to a minority?

These questions, arising necessarily from the facts, Thomas in his description has only answered by implication, and yet in my opinion the answers could be formulated with reasonable certainty out of what he says as follows. On the first, we are dealing in this absolutely higher knowledge, this chief of sciences, not with formulable statements but with a higher clearness and perspicuity, with an immediate awareness, with the light of God himself and the clarity of his knowledge. God does not know discursively but intuitively, that is to say, all at once. Comparable is the knowledge of the blessed who have become sharers in the *visio Dei beatifica*, a knowledge approximating to the knowledge of God.

On the second, this higher knowledge is not completely foreign to man *in statu viae*, but he does not necessarily share in it, and a part in it is not among his *a priori* gifts, nor yet does he attain to it *a posteriori* in the ordinary sense, that is to say, like some fact of experience which can be tested by all in the same way. The higher wisdom of God and of the blessed comes to man and can become in him the foundation of *sacra doctrina* through an act, through a venture, through a submission of man, Man submits his reason to the higher clarity of the knowledge of God and the blessed. But this takes place in faith.

But a connection appears here also with the trend of thought in the first article. There also it was a matter of *subordinating the realm of reason in its totality to a higher viewpoint, that of God speaking and of the destining of man for a supernatural goal.*

(Here we could also bring in the far-reaching question whether in the basic theological presuppositions which Thomas begins to develop in these articles we are not dealing with a strict "theology of revelation". But how can this understanding of theology be prefixed to the train of thought which in Questions 2ff. appears on the contrary a "natural" theology? What then is the relation of "theology of revelation" to "natural" theology in Thomas?)

What then is achieved by the conception of the second article as a whole? It is an endeavour to overcome the *appearance of irrationality* in theology, that appearance which in the first place results from the fact that theology is not recognizable to all men. According to Thomas this "irrationality" rests, not on arbitrariness, but on a higher rationality. But the way to reach this higher rationality is by an upward movement of obedient hearing. The rationality of the *lumen naturale rationis* ("innate light of intelligence") is *integrated* as a whole into a higher rationality through an act of venture. But the truth is that this venture is not made by every man.

*

In the *third article* the question, "*Utrum sacra doctrina sit una scientia* (Is Christian theology a single science?)", is concerned with the *unity of theology*. Here the objections which are first raised possess an especially obvious significance for the path which his thought is to take and the content of his solution. It is only after the "*videtur quod . . .*" that a formulation of the answer becomes possible. Its content is that, even if *to begin with* there are before us various *material objects*, namely varied objects of knowledge through experience and faith, yet theology has a unified *formal object*, a unified "matter in hand", its *ratio formalis obiecti* ("formal objective meaning"), that is to say, a viewpoint under which it sees everything, namely, regard for God and his revelation. Thomas' solution is really an *answer* to a justified question and to an assumption of the opposite which is not without reason. It is only through this question that the essential solution becomes possible.

What does this solution signify? What does it achieve? We must again ask this here also. For again there appears a close kinship of thought with the first two articles; here again everything leads to this, that the *whole* knowledge of the world is brought under one viewpoint, the unified "matter in hand", the revelation of the Divine person. In a certain sense it is the whole knowledge of the world which is accepted and integrated into the sacred teaching, by coming under this final and fundamental viewpoint. But the meaning of this must surely be that it is precisely so, in a higher "light", that the final reality and truth of all things appears.

*

The *fourth article*, "*Utrum sacra doctrina sit scientia practica* (Is Christian theology a practical science?)", enters into controversy with an objection which, if it were justified, would lead to a certain particularizing of *sacra doctrina*. According to it theology would rather be merely a practical science, a certain way of life which went on to think about itself and describe itself, a consideration of the right way to live. It would then certainly still be a science, but a science which, in spite of the high goal which it set, did not integrate *everything*.

We find a certain parallel today to this problematical situation in, say, the way in which the early Heidegger in *Being and Time* (tr. MacQuarrie and Robinson, S.C.M., 1962, Section 3) defines theology as in its essence one positive science beside others, one which, like all others, has its own ontology, which, however, is based on the fundamental ontology as systematized in *Being and Time*. As against this we must maintain that theology itself is the true fundamental ontology.

In the fourth article, then, of the first question what is at stake is the *universality of theology* as a science, gathering together comprehensively *all* realms under one viewpoint. Into this, of course, is also integrated practical wisdom for life. Theology embraces dogmatics and ethics.

*

In the fifth article, *"Utrum sacra doctrina sit dignior aliis scientiis* (Is Christian theology more valuable than the other sciences?)"*, the objections are again important for our understanding. It is only with these in mind that we can understand what the concept "more valuable" in the title means.

Two thoughts are important in Thomas' answer. 1. Theology is not of less but of *"higher certitude"* than the other sciences. But this certitude is a certitude *sui generis*, to be distinguished from the certitude of all other sciences. Thomas, it is quite clear, distinguishes a "subjective" and an "objective" certitude. Admittedly, as far as subjective certitude is concerned, the truth which is learned in theology is less certain, but this is the result of the incompleteness and finitude of human understanding. In spite of it the truth learned in theology is "in itself", objectively, the most certain of all.

A fact, then, can be certain in itself, but not so in the same measure for us. What does this mean? It is obvious that Thomas has a different concept of certitude from us. For to us the concept "certitude" from its very nature essentially includes the subjective moment. In our understanding there is really only subjective certitude and nothing else. And thus the task is laid upon us to ask and examine whether the double understanding of certitude in Thomas contributes anything positive to our own concept, to the certitude of faith, for example. And this in fact does seem to be the case as soon as we consider more deeply the personal character of the act of faith.

The way may first be prepared by an example from human relations. Here, it is true, an indication must suffice. Faith means trust, and trust has its place in a "between" between two persons. If one could regard as separate from one another the two persons so bound together, which would be an isolation exactly contradicting the essence of personal phenomena, we should have to say that there was uncertainty in the one subject but certitude in the other. In a journey by night the child is uncertain about the way home and, if alone, would be afraid, but it trusts that the father is certain of the way and

what Germans call *Objekt* can be named by him both *subiectum* and *obiectum*.[6] *Subiectum* means the real subject-matter, the phenomenon itself, the reality which encounters, with which knowledge really has to deal. *Obiectum* means the *systematized* subject-matter, the encountering reality in one definite regard, the formal object.

The subject-matter of theology is God and he alone. Everything else which is given thought in theology is thought of *with reference to him* and represents no second subject-matter beside him. This thought is natural to us today for we understand faith as a personal relation. Theology is the science of this personal relation, its illumination of itself. Hence theology also can have only one subject-matter, the person of the God who encounters in faith. This is the formal object of theology, with which, like faith, it always deals.

It is true that this one subject-matter is not definable *a priori*. Theology is no deductive science in the sense that something is deduced from leading principles which have first been stated in the form of clear definitions. Rather, theology begins from experience. Thomas says that in our thought we reach God from the *effects* of God. To this extent theology is an *a posteriori* science. But again it is not this in the sense of the other empirical sciences. The "facts" from which theology begins, experiences, effects, or data, are, one might say, transparent; God shows himself in them. But must not this mean that theology thinks in another *lumen* in which the effects of God appear from the beginning as the effects *of God*? How else would the "step" be possible from the effects to the cause? There is here no mere theoretical drawing of conclusions from an effect to a *distant* cause which cannot be experienced, as, for example, the existence of an invisible planet has been concluded from the observed movements of other planets, but in the "effects" God is shown as their "cause", *near to them and experienced together with them.*

*

In the eighth article, *"Utrum haec doctrina sit argumentativa*

---

[6] (In English, of course the German *Objekt* sometimes must be translated "subject", though the distinction is hardly the same as that given here between *subiectum* and *obiectum*—Tr.)

(Is this teaching probative?)", we are dealing with the *methods* of theology. These are discursive, drawing conclusions. For indeed there is no other form of thought available to man, even when he busies himself with divine things. Two things require to be said:

1. Inferential thought in theology surely means, not that the articles of faith are deduced, but that conclusions are drawn from them.

2. The inferential thought of philosophical studies can be integrated into the context of theology according to the principle, *gratia naturam non tollit, sed perficit* ("grace does not scrap nature but brings it to perfection"). It is true that philosophical processes of thought are accepted *non . . . ad probandum fidem, sed ad manifestandum aliqua alia quae traduntur in hac doctrina* . . . ("not with which to prove the faith . . . but to make manifest some implications of its message"), that is to say, not for proof, but for clearer portrayal. Philosophy can learn in its own "light". Its insights are not necessarily false merely because they were not gained in the light of revelation. But they cannot be the foundation and grounds of faith, but enter meaningfully in other ways into the context of theology.

The *common trait* in these articles of the first question with which we have dealt consists in this, that the relation of the two horizons, the horizon of personal faith in God the Revealer, and the horizon of comprehensive knowledge of the reality of the world through reason, are considered, and that the latter is integrated into the former as the more comprehensive.

*

In the *second question, "De Deo, an Deus sit* (Whether there is a God)", Thomas begins by speaking of God as the *principium et finis* ("beginning and end"), of all reality. The specific reference which is marked by these two concepts points to the essential historicity of the relation to God of all that is real. All that is real is related to God, and is so in a history, it comes from God and leads back again to God. God holds reality "behind and before" within his embrace, and this not merely in the sense of a naked, shall we say "mechanistic", causality and finality, but in the sense of a process of meaning. God is the origin and the goal of meaning, and all that is real is meaningful, and as a meaningful process is thus encompassed between origin and goal. This is the process essentially adopted by the meaningful structure of the real as such.

In the *first article, "Utrum Deus esse sit per se notum* (Is it self-evident that there is a God?)", very pointed forms of Anselm's argument and Bultmann's are discussed side by side. Bultmann's "question about God", the presupposition of the man asking about God, is still no knowledge of God. It is at most a vague turning towards God as the final benefactor. Man strives for "happiness". It is not misleading to translate this assertion thus within the horizon of present-day terminology, that man asks and strives for his own self-realization. For the "happiness" of which Thomas speaks is not merely a feeling of happiness, but "objective happiness", which man as man has as his aim. This vague turning of man towards God is certainly a constitutive factual situation anthropologically, but it is still blind. It has not yet the "eyes of faith" which alone are capable of seeing God. This turning towards God, peculiar "by nature" to man, which constitutes him a man, must not yet be called the knowledge of God. Significant here is the simple example which Thomas gives in his answer to the first *"videtur quod . . .", "*any more than to be aware of someone approaching is to be aware of Peter, even should it be Peter approaching". What is properly "meeting with Peter" has not yet taken place when I see in the distance a man coming towards me whose face I cannot yet recognize. The moment of otherness, of newness, and therefore of the reality of true personal encounter only then enters when Peter stands before me. In the same way, and this is to be said in favour of the conception of Thomas, as also that of Rudolf Bultmann, as against possible objections from the "right", nothing is lost of the eschatological newness, complete otherness and foreignness, and therefore of the reality of God, the *novitas Dei* in true personal encounter with God, when we speak of a turning towards God by man, one to be described existentially, as constitutive anthropologically.

Parallel in some ways with the first objection is the third, that man always knows that there is truth, and that God himself is the truth, and that therefore man knows of himself *a priori* about the existence of God. In point of fact there is always

349

in the act of knowing, or rather already in the demand to know, the assumption that there is something like truth, given with knowledge as the transcendental condition of its possibility. But this factual situation is the description of a vague direction of our looking, and not of a vision of the "fundamental" and highest concrete truth which is God himself. Of course a continuity of all truth with the final, or primal, truth which is God himself does exist "objectively" and "in itself". All truth is seen in the light of the primal truth of God, and man, in learning about the things of this world, is moving within this *continuum*. But he does not yet thereby know God. For to "see" God, to know him truly, means to look him in the face. That is to say, it implies concrete personal encounter.

The answer to the middle *"videtur quod . . ."* in this article is directed against Anselm's famous "ontological" proof of God. Thomas here argues that we cannot begin from a clear, transparent concept of God, from a definition of God. We cannot think about God deductively "from above". And even if we had within our understanding the appropriate concept of God, yet this would only be a concept *in our understanding*. And it cannot at all be deduced from this point that there must also be something in reality corresponding to this concept. In essence, this means that we cannot take God into our intellect or embrace him within it. Or if we do it nevertheless, we are yet only dealing with a content of consciousness and no longer with God *himself*. We only reach God when in the activity of faith we become aware that God completely and entirely circumscribes us, understanding and all, and when we surrender ourselves, understanding and all, in faith to him who circumscribes.

With his argument, then, Thomas sets down a testimony to the sovereignty of God, to the absolutely circumscribing character of the Divine reality. On the other side, it is true, there can be seen in Anselm's train of thought, according to Karl Barth's famous interpretation, a description of the act of faith as testimony to the glory of God.

*

In the *second article*, *"Utrum Deum esse sit demonstrabile* (Can it be made evident?)"*, Thomas distinguishes between two forms of proof, the proof *"propter quid* (why)" and the proof *"quia* (that)". Appropriate theological discussion of the existence of God is only concerned with the latter. In it Thomas again points to what already found expression in the first article, *the specific situation of our thought before God.* In our thought we cannot have God in our control; we cannot speak about him deductively, but only "rising to him from below". Hence proof proceeds from the effects to the original cause. But in the "effects" are to be reckoned the whole meaningful reality of creation.

Our thought must permit itself to be circumscribed by God. Yet what it is able to think "on this side of the boundary", within its own proper sphere and in the light of nature, is not simply in a state of discontinuity with God. For God is no Marcionite God who has nothing to do with creation, he is the Creator of reality, and hence reality stands in a relation to God, a relation described by Thomas by means of the concepts *"causa"* and *"effectus".* In this, however, we are not simply to think of causality in any modern scientific sense, Newtonian or Kantian. But this relation to the Creator in which the reality which surrounds us stands admits of intellectual expression. And this is what the legitimate proof of God does, proceeding from the effect to the cause. But we must add, it does not reach in this way a true and complete, much less perfect, knowledge of God (cp. the answer to the third objection). It reaches true knowledge of God only in the encounter of faith. Hence the proofs of God are only called *"praeambula fidei",* precursors, a preparation for faith.

The question of course remains if we can demonstrate this preparation for faith, the proof of God, if we do not already stand in the light of revelation. In my opinion it is only then that we can think about the structuring of the real upon God.[7] Here also there is importance in the factual situation that in Q.1 Thomas presupposes for this study of the existence of God a theological foundation based upon revelation and faith.

[7] Thus modern Catholic theologians like Karl Rahner and Herbert Vorgrimler speak about the preamble to faith as "this interior experience, which integrates the discrete plurality of the individual external elements . . .". This "can then no longer be clearly distinguished from the interior light of the grace of faith . . ." (*Concise Theological Dictionary,* tr. Strachan, Burns & Oates, 1965, pp. 369f.).

According to Thomas, whoever does not understand the proof can also simply accept the existence of God as something to be believed (cp. the answer to the first objection!). This, according to our interpretation so far, means that there is a simple faith which is straightforward trust and nothing else and does nor require any theological vindication and verification of faith in God in its manifold relations to reality.

*

For the right understanding and the right orientation of the five proofs of God in the *third article*, "*Utrum Deus sit* (Is there a God?)*"*, it is again important to pay attention to the objections and the answers to them. The *first objection* raises the question of theodicy; does not the fact of evil contradict the existence of God? The answer, that God is so almighty and good that he can make good come even out of evil, points to the living God acting in history. It is precisely the same thought, that God has the power to make good out of evil, which we met in Dietrich Bonhoeffer's "Articles of Faith on the Sovereignty of God in History": "I believe that God can and will bring good out of evil, even out of the greatest evil" (LPP, p. 34). And it is just this living power and providence of God which *is presupposed in the concept of God* with which we are dealing in Thomas. It is towards this God that the proof is directed. And this could also be brought forward against Ebeling's thesis on the proofs of God in Thomas, that these are carried out in a forecourt of soteriological neutrality.

That God is mighty to bring out of evil is the mark of a living God, acting in history. When Thomas then says that this very thing belongs to the infinite goodness of God, this signifies that to begin with God is thought of as just such a living historical God.

In the "*sed contra*" Thomas refers to the name of God according to the interpretation of Exodus 3: 14. Of course it will have to be noted that Exodus 3: 14 is expounded here in the light of a Greek concept of being. But yet, can we not still catch, even in Thomas, the echoes of the original historical mystery of the name of God. This would at least accord well with his answer to the first objection.

The *second objection* brings us into battle with the problem of reality. How can the assertion of the existence of God stand before our experience of reality? Reality is divided into two realms, that of the natural, and that of what happens "on purpose" (*a proposito*). And what follows is not a denial with grounds of the existence of God, but rather the viewpoint that the assertion of his existence is an unnecessary assumption, an irrelevant dressing up of reality as experienced by us. What is naturally real is sufficiently explained by the laws of nature, and the reality which lies in the realm of human freedom sufficiently by purpose. Once again we find ourselves reminded of Bonhoeffer; we can do without the hypothesis of "God".

Against this Thomas makes the point that God is already presupposed in the reality which we can experience, as the *causa prima* which is active in the *causae secundae* of the various realms of reality. According to him we do not have to begin from a godless reality as a very presupposition.

When we now pass to the *quinque viae* the first necessity is a preliminary consideration of method. Here we are struck by the stereotyped conclusion to the five proofs of God, "... *et hoc omnes intelligunt Deum* (and this is what everybody understands by God)" or " ... *quam omnes Deum nominant* (to which everyone gives the name God)", etc. But this stereotyped conclusion must surely mean that anyone who has had the experience described in the relevant *via* has come face to face with a final reality. And this final reality is none other than he whom all, all Christians that is, call "God". That is to say, the final reality which is so experienced, to which the proof sets its sights, is none other than that of God. It is not a mere illusion, something which "in reality" is not there, nor is it a second form of reality beside or under God. It is true that factually it can often be experienced anonymously, without the name. But Christians know the name of God and call this reality "God."

When we so see the matter the presupposition always is that the proof of God is later intellectual reflection upon an *experience*. And as such it is not simply mere theory. This presupposition is in keeping with the insight of Karl Rahner, according to whom the proof of God is a "transcendental basic experience" which man does not have without the activity of Divine grace, a coming face to face with the final reality which encounters him in his being. This single proof of God, which in its substance is first of all an experience and not a mere thought, can subsequently be articulated intellectually in different ways and partitioned out into the different proofs of God.[8]

Thus we have a viewpoint for the interpretation of the five *viae*. Their foundation lies in a basic experience which from time to time men have and in which they can understand one another, because they all stand at one before the reality of being and of the world. When they have this basic experience, which admittedly cannot be taken for granted, they come face to face with a final reality. The Christian, too, has this experience, for he, too, stands at one with all men before reality. When he has it he can speak about it, understand and recognize it again in others and speak to these others about it. He recognizes the final reality experienced in this way as the reality of God, the God who makes himself known personally and by name in his revelation to Israel and in Jesus Christ and sends into the world as his witnesses those who recognize him.

Thus the five *viae* all are the intellectual expression of experiences with reality, experiences which meet with God as the final reality. That such experience *takes place* depends upon grace, and that the experience is *recognized* as encounter with God, the Father of Jesus Christ, takes place in faith. But from the viewpoint of faith it can be said of such experiences, "to which everyone gives the name God".

The *first via, "ex parte motus* (based on change)"*, experiences reality as a complex of illimitable movement. When Thomas says, "Some things in this world are certainly in process of change; this we plainly see", he appeals in saying it to the immediate obviousness of the real.

The *second via, "ex ratione causae efficientis* (based on the nature of causation)"*, speaks of the effective causes and in so doing draws attention to a certain order to the process of movement in the real.

The *third via, "ex possibili et necessario* (based on what need not be and what must be)"*, begins from the experience of the contingency of the real, that it is factual and is not "not", although it would also be possible for it not to be.

---

[8] Cp. Rahner and Vorgrimler, *Concise Theological Dictionary*, Art. "Proof of the Existence of God", pp. 381ff.

As regards the first three *viae* there arises the common question as to why exactly the regress *ad infinitum* is rejected. Ebeling has rightly pointed to the fact that this rejection is a component of the proof of God. Here already we find a presupposition, namely that man is not content with reality as a mere fact, that for him rather reality remains an open question, and in such openness becomes transparent and demands a final controlledness. But is this presupposition as *experienced* not already a beginning to that opening of oneself which we call "faith"? Surely the other possibility is open to man, that of stolidly remaining simply with the facts and reducing to silence within himself that gently spoken question with which all that is real meets him.

The *fourth via, "ex gradibus qui in rebus inveniuntur* (based on the gradations we observe in things)", is conceived in terms of the Aristotelian exposition or being, that "truest" equals "noblest" which equals "most in being". But what basic experience of the real is behind this? It is the experience of the *differentiation* of the *cosmos*, of reality. It is the experience of the fullness of reality, of "value", which radiates out of what is real to meet every man. The experience of reality which is here effective senses behind the real which encounters us an origin to which such radiation points back. But this means that the thinker, open towards God, is already venturing into reality in its fullness of meaning as the reality belonging to God. Reality which is so experienced becomes a problem for him. It points to an origin which as yet cannot be named. Here again what takes place is that reality becomes transparent. And this goes hand in hand with that opening of himself towards God by man which is effected by grace. In itself it is indeed again possible that reality simply remains dumb towards man, that he hardens his heart before it, that he simply accepts it without question as pure factuality, or that he affirms as the last word the insolubility of the questions. As against this it is an act of the grace of God when reality becomes transparent for man. For in the reality that is transparent God himself encounters man and makes him open to himself.

The *fifth via, "ex gubernatione rerum* (based on the guidedness of nature)", rests first of all upon a teleological exposition of the world, one such as we can no longer carry out directly

355

since in all our description of natural phenomena and research into them we have learned to ask about their foundations in purely causal terms in the first place, and to exclude all that is anthropomorphic. And yet in a certain sense the experience which forms the basis of the fifth *via* can be our experience, too, for there are realms which in the first instance have for us nothing to do with meaning and purpose, but behind which we nevertheless sense something like a meaning and a purpose. The experience of which the fifth *via* is a deposit would then be that of the question of meaning as regards non-human spheres, the question of the "historicity of what is outside history".

*

This brief and cursory interpretation of several important articles in the *Summa Theologiae* may perhaps show clearly enough an inner consistency and natural sequence of data in its theological thought. Taking a fundamental question as his example, Thomas carries through in Q.2 exactly the programme of integration of reality which in Q.1 he had developed as the programme of theology as a whole. An ascension is made from reality as it can be experienced in the world, in so far as this is experienced as reality belonging to God, to describe the human becoming aware of the reality of God, that reality of God which has revealed itself and is recognized in faith. But this is now thought of *apart from* revelation and faith, as the final reality as experienced *de facto* by the believer also, or better, as it may be experienced again and again through the hidden grace of God. The proof of God, then, is a chapter in the dialogue of faith with unbelief about reality. But all theology has to be this dialogue, step by step. Where it becomes a monologue of faith with itself, it becomes sterile and loses its missionary and light-bringing dimension.

It is true that to all this one may object that in this interpreting and paraphrasing review there takes place a reinterpretation of the original thought, since Thomas, thinking from a Greek conception of being, did not yet possess these categories which we have employed of a historical conception of being.[9]

---

[9] In this connection, for how far it is permissible to speak of "categories", see Section 3.

Without venturing on the complex philosophical problems which this raises, we would only point here to the rules which we noted in Chapter Two on the hermeneutical phenomenon of discussion. One thing is certain, that Thomas sought to think in terms of the Biblical God, and in so far as we seek the same, becomes relevant for us as soon as we enter into discussion with him about the possibility, and the theological duty, of thinking in terms of the Biblical God. But what he says when we are in discussion with him has to be made relative by us to the common *subject-matter*. And that we really *listen* to Thomas in discussion must have the effect of what he says showing itself fruitful for our own need to think on the common subject-matter. But precisely this is extremely true of the first two questions of the *Summa Theologiae*.

3. *The Personality of God as a Horizon for Integration*

The God into whose realm faith integrates all reality is understood as a person in both Testaments of Holy Scripture. The strongest evidence for this is prayer, which belongs to the history of faith. In the Bible men pray to God in thanksgiving, petition, intercession, etc., and believe that God hears and will answer.

This aspect is not really emphasized by Thomas in his process of theological integration, as he ascends from reality which can be experienced to the assurance of the reality of God. To him it is to be taken for granted. His ". . . *quod omnes dicunt Deum*" presupposes without question the personal God with whom Christians are concerned. The verification of the reality of this God through the reality of the world which can be experienced—and this is what the proof of God is, though by our interpretation "verification" is not to be understood as compelling, but as the evidence of an experience—only shows the extent to which man in his being in the world comes against its frontiers, in the guise of which there comes face to face with him the one whom Christians in prayer and faith name "God." That the one who comes face to face is a *person* is not really thought out. On this point surely our questions today must be more radical, and we must take a step further than Thomas, a step which we must take precisely in the

357

direction of that verifying process of integration in which Thomas himself is already moving.

One could of course object to this that the proof of God is by its very nature incomplete, that it does not mediate to us a full knowledge of God such as we rather share in through revelation alone, that it is only in the light of revelation, and not in any light of a "natural theology's" proof of God, that God becomes recognizable as a person. But such an argument would still be thinking within the two stages of that well-known Catholic scheme, the two stages of "natural" and "revealed" knowledge of God, and the rigidity of this scheme is precisely what a modern Roman Catholic understanding of the proof of God seeks to overcome by seeing it as the systematization of a human experience which in the last resort is effected by grace. As and when we make this understanding ours, and interpret the proof of God in Thomas as the demonstration of the reality of God through the reality of the world as already understood in advance by faith, we are in our proof of God by that very fact dealing with no mere "God of the philosophers and scholars" but with the living God of the Bible. And for Thomas himself this last point is unambiguously true. But if in our proof of God we are concerned with this and no other God, then surely his *being a person* would also have to be the subject of verification through our proof from the reality of the world as understood in advance by faith.

We are seeking here to elucidate from the thought of Bonhoeffer, and especially from his thought of the reality of the world being accepted by God, the "future for the doctrine of God". On the grounds of numerous and important indications we have believed that we could assume a similar understanding of reality to be at the foundations in the theological presuppositions and the proofs of the existence of God in Thomas. God, the Father of Jesus Christ, already dwells in all the reality which we encounter. It belongs to him. There is set then for the theological doctrine of God, if we are to travel further on Bonhoeffer's road, the task of verifying from the reality of the world as understood in advance by faith the being and reality of the *personal* God, as he becomes partner to man in Jesus Christ. That God is a person, supra-personal perhaps but certainly not sub-personal, must become visible in the path taken by theological thought on the integration into faith in God of the reality of the world, an integration already achieved in advance in the existential understanding of reality by faith. In all this of course the existential understanding of reality by faith is already presupposed. But how is this to be verified. The question arises if in the last resort there is not after all asserted here a no longer verifiable axiom. The fact is that the *existential* understanding of reality by faith is verified in its being *maintained* in the midst of the reality of this world, in questions and decisions, actions and sufferings, in all encounters with men, animals and things. Faith, wherever it goes and stands in the world, understands the world there as God's world, and will not allow itself to be dissuaded from this. It remains everywhere expectant of God. And all that theology can do is to describe this subsequently. That faith can maintain the totality of its *existential* understanding of reality is shown for the questioner and thinker by the fact that theology can maintain the totality of its *explicit* understanding of reality. But what this means is that it "proves" the reality of God from the world understood beforehand in a certain way, not that it does so against the evidence of the phenomena.

It is only when one understands the proof of God as an operation of faith that one can demand and expect that the personal nature of God should also be part of what is proved.

Even a modern theologian like Karl Rahner seems still today to stand in this Thomist tradition of excluding from the proof of God the question of personality. In his essay, "On the Theology of the Incarnation" (*Theological Investigations*, IV, tr. Kevin Smith, D.L. & T., 1966, pp. 105ff.), he uses in passing the important expression, ". . . if indeed God's way of owning the world is that the world is not only his work, a work distinct from him, but becomes his own reality (as the 'nature' which he has assumed (sc. the human nature of Christ) or the '*milieu*' necessarily adjoined to that nature) . . ." (pp. 106f.). Here he is speaking of a certain understanding of the event of Christ which in its turn implies a certain understanding of reality, that of the acceptance of the reality of the world as God's own reality (our theme in Chapter Ten). Rahner here obviously comes very close to Bonhoeffer's ontological Christology. But there remains unanswered the question as to how this thought of a reality of the world accepted as God's own reality is still distinguished from a pantheist understanding of the world.

Rahner, like Thomas, does not find the same necessity and urgency to consider this, for he thinks, if I understand him rightly, in the opposite direction. In his essay, "Thoughts on the Possibility of Belief Today" (*Theological Investigations*, V, tr. Krüger, 1966, pp. 3f.), he takes examples in considering the question how one can be a Christian today, and begins from his own personal Christianity, "I begin with the fact that I have —quite simply—always been a believer and that I have met with no reason which would force or cause me not to believe any more. I was born a Catholic because I was born and baptized in a believing environment" (p. 4). In this point of commencement personal relations with a personal God are already presupposed without question. But Rahner goes on to show that this same presupposition, which belongs to the theme of his being a Christian by inheritance, is at the same time the all-embracing, absolutely transcendental horizon, the mystery of all mysteries. For example, "You have, therefore, the right and the duty to hear Christianity as the universal message of truth which nothing can confine and which says 'no' only to the negations, but not to the genuine affirmations, of life. Give ear to Christianity as the universal message, as the one which 'gathers up' ('*aufhebt*') and thus preserves everything else. Listen to Christianity as the message which does not forbid anything except man's shutting himself off in his own finite nature . . ." (p. 10). The trend of his thought, then, leads from personality to the transcendental, and corresponds to Aquinas' ". . . *quod omnes dicunt Deum*".

But the reverse direction of thinking, and asking questions, that from the transcendental to personality, is also possible and in some circumstances necessary. But this is the question as to how far the all-embracing horizon, surpassing all that is given, the horizon within which what is real appears *as* real, is the personal God, the God in three Persons. In the present position of discussion, at least in Protestant theology, this direction of the question seems to me the urgent one.

This way of putting the question embraces in the last resort the whole dogmatic doctrine of God, for it deals with the verification of the reality of the personal, triune, omni-present, omnipotent and omniscient God. In the "proof of God" so understood, then, the whole traditional doctrine of the Trinity and doctrine of the properties of God must find a place, but must do so thought out anew and perhaps with very different concepts. In the short indication of the problem which is all that we are able to give here, we would simply emphasize especially one more especial difficulty of the whole question, the problem of the concept *"personality"*.

*

This problem is fundamentally the issue between Herbert Braun and Helmut Gollwitzer. It consists in this, that appear-ances suggest that "personality" is a certain category of our thinking, and that there results from its application to God a picture of God which is limited and confined by time. In his essay, *Die Frage nach Gott* (in *Evangelischer Theologie*, April-May 1965, 25 Jg., pp. 238ff.), Wolfhart Pannenberg has intervened to very good purpose in the debate between Brown and Gollwitzer, and in so doing has also raised this specific question. He concedes, referring to J. G. Fichte and the dispute about atheism, that a concept of personality gained from the fact that man is a person includes in it "the finitude of man as a constitutive element" and therefore remains un-serviceable "for the description of the infinite power which determines all reality", but then comes to the conclusion that the concept of personality is not primarily gained from man at all, but in an underived religious experience (cp. pp. 258ff.).

"Such considerations urge upon one the assumption that in personality we are dealing with an original category of the phenomenology of religion. As such it is characterized by the *undefinability* of the power which yet at the same time, in that event which constitutes religious experience, lays a concrete *claim* upon man" (p. 259).

On one point above all I agree with Pannenberg:

". . . that the personal nature of man is itself by no means to be taken for granted. What our humanist tradition describes as the inviolable personal value of man is obviously not so formed that one cannot depart from it. The individual man can also be treated as a thing. Has his value as a person not more the character of a statement of faith than that of some item of the findings of anthropology which can be demonstrated on its own?" (pp. 258f.).

As a point of fact the humanist conception of the value of the person is an idea and has as such its defined place in the history of ideas. Pannenberg is right when he makes this defined place explicit and endeavours to pass beyond this concept. But he still remains himself in the limited world of the historian, of the history of ideas, when he uses the phenomenology of religion and has recourse to primeval religious experiences, which it may be are so much no longer our experiences today that what is learned from them may also become questionable, at least in its historical limitations.

In this question about the "category of personality" we must surely take one further step beyond Pannenberg, a step to the statement that *in fact "personality" is not a category at all, but an original datum, an original experience of man.* The truth is that "personality", though a concept which for a long time has kept reappearing again and again in philosophical and theological discussion, is usually a catchword, perhaps a necessary catchword; at the best it is, as with Martin Buber, a reference to *a reality which has certainly always been felt, but for long has been insufficiently thought out.*

Pannenberg is right in seeking to avoid narrowing to a humanist interpretation this concept, necessary for the doctrine of God, of personality. Yet what he puts in the place of it, personality as a category of the phenomenology of religion, also fails to give an adequately precise meaning. There is lacking for instance in Pannenberg, beside the two moments of the phenomenon which he rightly names, the indefinability of the strange power and the fact of one's own confrontation by it, what is in my opinion an equally constitutive moment, that peculiar reciprocity of sympathy. "Torture not a beast for sport, for it feels like you the hurt", already makes our relation to the beast in a certain way personal. For Martin Buber, for example, the animals live already on the threshold of language.

To be precise, personality is still not a tractable and clear category, although philosophical and theological thought have already been working long at its clarification. For a long time "personality" did not win the instrumental power in thought possessed by, for example, the categories of "substantiality" and "causality". And yet there can scarcely be a man who does not *de facto* know, because he has felt it, what personality is. But, as against Pannenberg, we have this original sense of personality in the first place and for the most part in our encounter with *men*. It is here and not through primeval religious experiences which are no longer ours, that the phenomenon of personality becomes evident. Hence when we speak of the personal God we are not transferring to God some *category* which we can use as a concept; we are bringing God and our standing before God into relation with our *original sense* of personality. If we say "God" at all, in the sense in which the Bible says "God", this can only mean that we have as close and as historical a dealing with God as with our neighbours, though we must add, as the doctrine of the Triune God reminds us, that it is *at the same time completely different*. All, however, that the complex reality of the phenomenon "personality" includes as structural moments has not yet been elucidated philosophically. And how we are to define the peculiarity of the supra-personal God, as opposed to those human personal relations which we experience, has not yet been elucidated theologically. What is established existentially and irrefutably is that if we venture at all to say "God" in the sense of the Bible and to believe in God, we face God in our attitudes and in our expectations as a person and not as a thing. The only question then is on what we base our venture to treat this God, so understood, as a reality. Of course there can never be given here a proof in the strict sense, but surely it must be possible to give a basis for the venture of faith, a venture which consists not merely in accepting and placing a "God" in the midst of or "above" reality, but in a definite attitude to *reality as a whole*.

There is no other way than this of agreeing with the Bible in our understanding of this God, and in spite of all the difference in other respects between historical strata in the Biblical evidence, there is on this one point agreement without exception between all the Biblical witnesses. But in order to be able to speak relevantly of this God, who in spite of this is not "any-where" but integrates the whole of the reality with which we are concerned, we in fact require in the first place a real *category* of personality. This has to be worked out. *Beginnings*, in the meantime only scattered, if to some extent altogether fruitful, are to be found in the more recent trends of thought of a "personalist" philosophy and theology. But the categories in which we look intellectually at phenomena are surely won in encounter with the phenomena themselves. They are not established *a priori* in human intellect. The categories, for example, which Kant develops in his *Critique of Reason* are the *a priori* of a definite historical conception of reality, but not the *a priori* of all human understanding of reality altogether. As the categories, then, of an ontology of substance and essence, those which were derived from Aristotle and ruled powerfully in Thomas, but also in Descartes and right up to the thought of our day, have been obtained from the pattern of objective phenomena, not the completely lifeless, but vegetative entities and the products of handcrafts, so the category or categories, the existentials, of personality must be obtained from the pattern of human, historical, meaningful encounters. Heidegger, in his existential analysis of *Dasein* in *Being and Time*, has taken some steps in this direction. It is true that this, too, remains only a pattern, yet in this very respect we are pointed to creaturely patterns because we walk by faith and not by sight and our thinking is a thinking of faith, in the midst of creatureliness, and not a thinking of sight. And yet with the categories obtained from the creaturely pattern of encounter we should surely be in a position to think just as precisely and consistently of the story of God's relation with man as the scholasticism of the Middle Ages was able to do with its categories of objective ontology, but now in a more relevant way than it. In particular, the problem of Divine grace and human freedom, an insoluble difficulty for the ontology of substance, could surely become more transparent. Bonhoeffer's scattered thoughts about God's providence are only a hint in this direction.

Now as far as the pattern of human encounter is concerned, what Pannenberg says is certainly true, that the personal value of man is by no means axiomatic, that man can also treat man as a thing, and in point of fact has done and does so time and again. But the "value of the person" is not identical with the phenomenon of personality itself; it is rather the, surely appropriate, ethical interpretation of it. Even where the value of the person is disregarded, say, in the cruelty of someone seeking revenge, personality is still presupposed. It is precisely the awareness that the other person exists, that he feels, that constitutes the cruelty as such. Yes, even if it goes so far that the knowledge that the other is a person is suppressed and the cruel person seems to be no longer aware of his own cruelty, as did take place in some cases in Hitler's concentration camps, apart from the quite conscious cruelty which was surely the general rule there, we can still in principle wait for and appeal to a subsequent awakening conscience and the making itself heard again of the suppressed knowledge. At the other extreme, amid all the sociological and cultural variations of humanity, the fact of the Good Samaritan is yet surely a human phenomenon which can appear and in fact keeps reappearing, probably most often as a matter of fact in *breach* of the conventions as in Luke 10, but one might say as a constant, *always* and *everywhere*.

But one must add that the pattern of encounter on the human level, against which the category of personality can be seen, is surely incomparably more complex than this simple basic knowledge that the other is a person.

*

Bonhoeffer writes in a footnote to his *Ethics*:

"In the first picture of his dance of Death, which represents the Creation, Hans Holbein personifies the sun, the moon and the wind. In this way he gives expression in a naïve form to the fact that reality consists ultimately in the personal. In this respect there is an element of truth in primitive animism" (E, p. 198).

This is a note added to the following claim:

"In action which is genuinely in accordance with reality there is an indissoluble link between the acknowledgement and the contradiction of the factual. The reason for this is that reality is first and last not lifeless; but it is the *real* man, the

incarnate God. It is from the real man, whose name is Jesus
Christ, that all factual reality derives its ultimate foundation
and its ultimate annulment, its justification and its ultimate
contradiction, its ultimate affirmation and its ultimate negation.
To attempt to understand reality without the real man is to
live in an abstraction to which the responsible man must never fall
victim" (*ibid.*).

*Bonhoeffer here, from his ontological Christology, arrives at a
personal interpretation of reality as such.* It is true that this is a
thought which he did not follow out elsewhere, at least not so
far as is visible in his works, but yet it is obviously a thought
which belongs to the continuation of his conception of
Christology, a path which can, and perhaps must, be followed
up from this point. The verification of the reality of God as the
personal God will presumably be achieved in face of the necessity
of pointing to the personal weft in *all* that is real. In addition
to this Bonhoeffer's note gives us the hint that the verification
from the reality which can be experienced of the reality of the
personal God must also include within it Christology. In this
sense, to judge from Bonhoeffer, the future of Christology is
for us a continuation of the future of the doctrine of God. We
cannot think of the personal God who is present in all that is
real in any other way than as the God who has imparted his
nearness to us in Jesus Christ. Thus as soon as we take this
small step beyond Thomas, the subject of Christology must at
once appear, and, as it were, enter into the proof of God's
existence.

The question of the *personal nature* of God surely becomes
strongly urgent for us in our present-day theological situation
for this reason, that it is fundamentally here that lies the one
decisive point of our cultural controversy with the atheism of
our time. But we shall have to meet this atheism under the
banner of Jesus Christ. The *intellectual* preliminary work to
this lies in working out the category of personality, which will
then surely show itself as at the same time the fundamental
hermeneutical category. This work would do well to enter into
dialogue with those thinkers who have made most progress in
this question, above all with Martin Buber, who has devoted his
life's work to proving the reality of the personal, with Martin
Heidegger, who in his *Being and Time* has taken some essential

and accurate steps towards obtaining a categoriality, or "existentiality" of *Dasein*, and also with Heinrich Barth, who has interpreted reality as manifestation for existence. But this must be the subject of a new venture and a new book.

CHAPTER TEN

THE FUTURE FOR CHRISTOLOGY

IN THE last resort the subject of the doctrine of God can only be interpreted existentially and exhibited in its relation to reality, and therefore the integration of the reality of the world into faith in God can only be achieved, when that doctrine is interpreted Christologically. Let this be our provisional thesis. But it is only in the working out of the problem that the truth of this thesis becomes manifest for theological thought. But this again, as we said, is in keeping with the fact of the revelation of God in Jesus Christ, which tells us that *God is manifest in Christ*. In order, then, to demonstrate the evidence for God, it is necessary to give thought to Christ. Thus in fact and method to speak of the future of Christology is to continue speaking of the future of the doctrine of God.

First of all, by a glance at the thought of Bonhoeffer as a whole, we shall briefly bring to mind once more the place which Christology occupies in his thinking. It will become clear that, understood as an intellectual expression of a living relation to Christ, and at the same time and in this very fact as a universal ontology, Christology was at all stages of his pilgrimage the inward law of his thinking, the definitive thought. Then through the confrontation of Bonhoeffer with a contemporary with whom he was not acquainted, one whose immense spiritual influence, like his own, first began to have its effect posthumously, with Teilhard de Chardin, the problem of a universalist Christology in its "objective" necessity will begin to become clear, that it is not merely a personal theological problem of Bonhoeffer's, but a question in essence given to our era. A glance at the task of proclaiming Christ in our time will confirm this insight, and finally our journeying with Bonhoeffer will be broken off for the time with a description of the existential interpretation of Christology as a theological method, as that method, indeed, which alone can accomplish the task of a universalist Christology.

1. *The Place of Christology in Bonhoeffer's Thought*

The question about Christology in Bonhoeffer is the question of the whole significance of his work. In our attempt to hear and to reproduce the man we have laid especial stress on his Christological thought. According to both the fragments of the *Ethics*, coming from the years 1940 to 1943, and the *Lectures on Christology* of 1933, Bonhoeffer's Christology represents an ontology embracing all that is real. For Jesus Christ, not as an isolated person it is true, but in the reality of his activity as Mediator and Reconciler, is *the* real in all that is real, and a Christology which meets the facts has to think of him just as *such*.

Now the question arises as to what significance for his thought as a whole we are to give to this understanding of Christ. Are we dealing here with an isolated thought, which appeared at a certain stage in Bonhoeffer's thinking, and played its part until it disappeared before a changed viewpoint and a theological interest which was directed elsewhere, without really ever being recalled? Or is it a thought which, even if it appeared more clearly at individual stages than at others, yet possessed a validity for his whole pilgrimage? Has the *motif* of an ontologically understood Christology a peripheral or a central significance in Bonhoeffer?

If we can accept, then, that sufficient evidence has been given that it is one and the same *motif* which appears as dominating in the lectures on Christology and then again in the *Ethics*, and it is of course clear that many of Bonhoeffer's concepts and horizons had changed between the two, we can assume that in the time between, at the time of the *Cost of Discipleship* and *Life Together*, (1937 and 1939), he still held to this thought and was orientated towards it, even if another group of subjects had captured his precise interest.

That means that we have to ask about from 1933 backwards and from 1943 forwards. For the first question we can surely be content to let ourselves be led by Bonhoeffer's own understanding of himself, which he expressed in this way in a letter of April 22, 1944:

> "When you say that my time here will be very important for my practical work, and that you are very much looking forward to what I shall have to tell you later, and to what I have written, you must not indulge in any illusions about me. I have certainly learnt a great deal, but I don't think I have changed very much. There are people who change, and others who can hardly change at all. I don't think I have ever changed very much, except perhaps at the time of my first impressions abroad under the first conscious influence of Father's personality. *It was then that I turned from phraseology to reality* . . . Continuity with one's own past is a great gift, too . . . Everything seems to have taken its natural course and to be determined necessarily and straightforwardly by a higher providence" (LPP, pp. 149f.— Our italics).

According to this the "turn from phraseology to reality" is for Bonhoeffer the one real change in his life, the conversion which thereafter determined the purpose and subject of his whole thought as a constant turning towards the real! Hence, according to his own understanding of himself, a decisive alteration could not also have taken place between the beginnings of his theology and 1933, The "turn from phraseology to reality" was for him from the beginning bound up with the name of Jesus Christ, and the *motif* of the Christological structure of all that is real is a note already sounded in, for instance, his doctoral dissertation, in the Christological foundation for the existentials, universal and general for humanity, of "representation" and the "collective person" (see Chapter Five above).

Is the same consciousness of essential continuity valid also for what followed after the period of the *Ethics*? Or did Bonhoeffer on this point deceive himself about himself? For it is obvious that in the letter quoted he is emphasizing the continuity of his own personal and theological development precisely because of Bethge's interest in what he had recently written in prison. And eight days later, on April 30, there followed the decisive first letter on non-religious interpretation!

Now one could take the view that, contrary to Bonhoeffer's own understanding of himself, a radical conversion in his thought did take place once again right at the end of his life. Not only Hanfried Müller, but other interpreters, too, appear to see things so. What in point of fact is the relation to the onto-logical Christology of the *Ethics* of the following much-quoted sentences from *Letters and Papers from Prison*?

"God lets himself be pushed out of the world on to the Cross. He is weak and powerless in the world, and that is precisely the way, the only way, in which he is with us and helps us ... Man's religiosity makes him look in his distress to the power of God in the world; God is the *deus ex machina*. The Bible directs man to God's powerlessness and suffering: only the suffering God can help. To that extent we may say that the development towards the world's coming of age outlined above, which has done away with a false conception of God, opens up a way of seeing the God of the Bible, who wins power and space in the world by his weakness. This will probably be the starting point for our 'secular interpretation' " (LPP, pp. 196f.—July 16, 1944).

In our section "The Change to a Cross-theology", we already pointed to this. Did not a second conversion take place here after all, and take place precisely in his under-standing of Christ? What is the relation of this "Cross-theology" to the "triumphalism" apparent in an ontological Christology, one which sees Jesus Christ as *the* true real in all reality, as him who embraces and holds together equally existence, history and nature?

One could also put the question in another way. If Bonhoeffer had survived to the end of the war and found the opportunity to unfold his thoughts in untroubled theological work, would he have taken up again the *motif* of his *Ethics*, that of onto-logical Christology? Or did the turn of 1944 to a theology of the Cross combined with the postulate of non-religious interpre-tation mark a final departure from all this?

The *exegetical* thesis which so far has run through all our thoughts on Bonhoeffer has been and is that he was right in his understanding of an "essential continuity" in himself, both as regards his own intellectual development and also, indissolubly bound up therewith, as regards the facts themselves. The turn to a Cross-theology does not bring to an end Christo-logical ontology and ontological Christology! His understanding of Christ gives a new dimension, or, it would be better to say, a dimension which is already there gains a new emphasis and a new light, but no essential change takes place.

Factually, our *exegetical* thesis could imply that the *aggiornamento,* to quote John XXIII, of the Church of Jesus Christ, which was a fundamental concern of Bonhoeffer in his postulate of non-religious interpretation, demands a universalist understanding of the reality of Jesus Christ. But this implies an ontological understanding and one that has been *worked out* as such and not merely asserted. In this last chapter we are essentially concerned with the demonstration of this factual connection.

If then this is so, Bonhoeffer never departed from the Christology of the *Ethics.* The "coming-of-age of the world", man's being thrown upon a "powerless God", can never mean for him that man is now left to his own resources without *Christus praesens!* The thought of the "powerlessness of God" could never mean for him a theological denial of Divine providence and guidance! The numerous examples which we have adduced in Chapter Seven of the providence of God in Bonhoeffer precisely at the last period of his thinking may surely serve as a sufficient confirmation of this. If the objection should be made that on this very point Bonhoeffer had not followed his own thoughts through to the end sufficiently radically and consistently, anyone so interpreting must be warned against replacing the diversity of the facts as exegesis finds them by a deductive logic which is really simplification.

The thought of God's providence is really a connecting link which permits us to see more clearly the inner continuity in Bonhoeffer's thinking, just as, as far as his works are concerned, the *Ethics* represents a connecting link between his Christological outlook as it comes to light in the lectures on Christology and that in the thisworldliness of the *Letters and Papers from Prison.* Perhaps at first sight it may appear difficult to discover the inner unity between the lectures and the letters, but in the *Ethics* we find the two *motives* unmistakably together, mutually interpenetrating and qualifying one another. In the same way it is precisely his faith in providence which shows us that for Bonhoeffer there is obviously no contradiction between, on the one side, the lordship of God over the world and the sovereign omnipresence of the Lord

Jesus Christ as the centre of existence, history and nature, and, on the other, the affirmation of worldliness and an autonomous humanity. The God who allows himself to be forced out of the world on to the Cross, who is powerless and weak in the world, is by no means a God who has ceased to rule the world with a strong right arm. If we find a contradiction here we are obviously seeing and feeling things with less discrimination than did Bonhoeffer.

But what then is the meaning of the assertion of the powerlessness of God in the world? The Messianic suffering of Christ, the suffering of God in the world, is obviously for Bonhoeffer a deep dimension of the omnipresence of Christ, and, moreover, the specific present-day one. This is the experience of him which God has granted to us in our day. It is true that we are saying this, not from the viewpoint of God, but from that of our own existence, the only viewpoint which is ours, that from which we affirm what is actually our concern. We experience God as the one who conceals himself from us and withdraws himself from us into silence. No longer do all things speak to us about God. They do not point us to God, as they did in the tenth book of St. Augustine's *Confessions*. They remain wordless and look at us silent and questioning. Of course one can also explain these changes in sociological and economic terms. But the content of meaning in the experience itself cannot be charged to the sociological and economic data. We could call it a God-given destiny. It does not depend upon us and upon "circumstances", it depends upon God himself that we can no longer, at least in the first instance, experience him as the helper of our need, or as the highest good above all goods, or as the ruler of worlds, but instead as concealed and in a certain sense mundane. It is not that God the all-present, who interpenetrates and governs all things, has fallen victim to an a-theistic *Weltanschauung*; rather, the nature of the nearness of this very God and the manner of our experience of his nearness have been transformed. This is the meaning of the statement about the "powerlessness and weakness of God in the world"!

Further, a theology which accepts this, a theology which one could link with Bonhoeffer's expressions and call a *theologia crucis*, does not lack "triumphal" notes, and that this is so is based completely on the facts themselves. In the tale we have already quoted from Martin Buber's *Dialogue* (E.T. p. 15, cp. p. 158 above) the voice of God says, " . . . I have sunk my hearing in the deafness of mortals". We saw in this an expression of the experience of God granted to us. But the implication of this is exactly that in the deafness of mortals God *is there*! We can also think here of the triumphant note which is sounded in Bonhoeffer's "Thoughts on the Baptism of D. W. R.", where he speaks of the coming day "when men will once more be called so to utter the word of God that the world will be changed and renewed by it" (LPP, p. 172).

In summing up, it can be said that the understanding of Christ which Bonhoeffer articulated to a Christian ontology is and remains the valid fundamental experience of his whole thought. But we must add that this determining *motif* would be understood in a most dangerous way if the Christological ontology were conceived as a system of static components, as a systematizing insurance against the uncontrollability of reality. To speak of Jesus Christ as the real in all reality will have precisely the effect of opening our eyes to the unplumbable depths in the real.

2. *The Universal Christ in Dietrich Bonhoeffer and in Pierre Teilhard de Chardin*

Bonhoeffer does not stand alone in his testimony to the universal Christ who is "reality" itself. Here we do not merely think of the numerous theologians by whom this Christological thought has been taken up and is being taken up, in our time, here and there, in this form or that. In fact the *motif* is contained in the facts themselves, it is already part of the original *Kerygma* of the New Testament in the most varied places, and as such it has never completely disappeared again from Christian theology since the time of the apologists with their concept of the *Logos Spermatikos*. We are thinking of that Christian witness of our century who, one might say, corresponds to Bonhoeffer although the two did not know one another, of Pierre Teilhard de Chardin for whom this understanding of Christ which is occupying our thoughts, Christ in all reality, has in becoming the basic *motif* of his thinking shown the same power to set its seal upon everything, with the result that a whole list of astonishing agreements follow.

We may promise ourselves especially good results from a comparison and contrast of these two thinkers precisely because they are so unlike and yet in their unlikeness so akin. It is precisely against the background of this unlikeness, an unlikeness of upbringing, of way of life, of manner of acting and thinking, of spiritual horizons, of confession, of concepts employed, that there shines out the more clearly the kinship, and with it the fact itself, the common theological subject, the common area with which they were concerned. The *inner necessity of the facts themselves* is made clear, it is obvious that in spite of all differences of context, there must follow analogous consequences from the same fundamental *motif*.

Bonhoeffer wrote his most important and visionary theological assertions in the narrowness of the prison cell, Teilhard in the vastness of the central Asian desert, though he was later to confirm them.[1] The former wrote in the decision-fraught time of the Second World War, the latter in the period between the wars and then later in the post-war period, in face of the historical *novum* of a horizon of humanity which was widening spatially to the planetary and the universal. For Bonhoeffer the basic experience of reality was that of humanity, for Teilhard that of the universe. Each of these two men of faith, within his own of these two horizons, felt and reflected upon the reality of God. And for each in his own way God was a near and living, one could say palpable, God. A doctrinal relation to God was equally far from both. As regards the way we encounter him in our existence, God is primarily not the content and principle of a doctrine, but a reality which can be experienced in everyday life.

The difference in ruling horizons within which the reality of God can be experienced, humanity in the one and the universe in the other, naturally finds expression in the style of thought of the two theologians. In Bonhoeffer the relation to

[1] Shortly before his death Teilhard expressly confessed again the faith of these two writings on which we rely here, *Le Milieu Divin* and *Hymne de l'Univers*. Cp. the editor's note at the end of *Le Milieu Divin*.

(The English translations from which quotations are here made are *Le Milieu Divin*, Collins, 1960, and *The Hymn of the Universe*, tr. Bartholomew, Collins, 1965.—Tr.)

God appears more as a personal confrontation, stamped by the mark of responsible decision. In Teilhard it appears rather as a mystical relation, the activity and the suffering of men are stage by stage a union with God. Yet in my opinion there is no final contradiction here. It is only a matter of a very clear difference of emphasis. But it also becomes clear in Teilhard that the relation to God must remain a personal one.

"Blazing Spirit, Fire, personal, super-substantial, the consummation of a union so immeasurably more lovely and more desirable than that destructive fusion of which the pantheists dream; be pleased once again to come down and breathe a soul into the newly formed fragile film of matter with which this day the world is to be freshly clothed. I know we cannot forestall, still less dictate to you, even the smallest of your actions, from you alone comes all initiative—and this applies in the first place to my prayer" (*Hymn of the Universe*, p. 22).

"At this moment when your life has just poured out with superabundant vigour into the sacrament of the world, I shall savour with heightened consciousness the intense yet tranquil rapture of a vision whose coherence and harmonies I can never exhaust.

"What I experience as I stand in face of—and in the very depths of—this world which your flesh has assimilated, this world which has become your flesh, my God, is not the absorption of the monist who yearns to be dissolved into the unity of things, nor the emotion felt by the pagan as he lies prostrate before a tangible divinity, nor yet the passive self-abandonment of the quietest tossed hither and thither at the mercy of mystical impulses.

"... Like the monist I plunge into the all-inclusive One, but the One is so perfect that as it receives me and I lose myself in it I can find in it the ultimate perfection of my own individuality" (*ibid.*, pp. 26f.).

We should not allow the elements of a mystical pantheist terminology which we find in Teilhard to deter us before we begin from considering the facts which as a Christian he has experienced and seeks to say. On the other hand everything that concerns us as Protestant theologians under the heading of personal confrontation and the personality of God is still far from being made so thoroughly clear that we can refer to it as a settled "position" as against the appearance of a pantheist tendency. But it is surely conceivable that what is mystical pantheism in appearance only will help us precisely in understanding better the peculiar nature of this personal confrontation with *God* . . . Biblical theism also, because it is determined by the same unique factual situation, contains "pantheist" elements, as for example Acts 17: 28, "For in him we live and move and have our being". The 139th Psalm also, and the word of Jesus which says that the Heavenly Father is in advance of our prayers and knows what we have need of before we ask him, are indications that the personal confrontation of man by God, if we are to think of it appropriately, must be thought of as at the same time a *"being in God"*.

But just as in Teilhard we find the personality of God undeniably maintained as against a pantheist mysticism, so do we find in Bonhoeffer also the aspect of a "mystical" unity between God and man, in "Christ existing as a community", or in "Christ obtaining form in us". Both thinkers are thus moving in their outlook towards that uniqueness, which still has to be thought out, of personal relationship with God.

Both thinkers are concerned with the presence of the God who is completely other in the reality with which we meet. For Bonhoeffer the thematic place for the presence of God is ethical situations. In the complex situations of our responsible existence God himself is present in Jesus Christ. For Teilhard the place of his presence is "matter",[2] though of course not it alone, but also the spiritual and ethical existence of man. God assimilates matter to himself. The two horizons and assertions are not necessarily mutually exclusive, perhaps they even include another. It is true that in Bonhoeffer the manner of the presence of God is reconciliation, that Jesus Christ is present in all reality as the Reconciler of the world, while in Teilhard it is sacramental indwelling. This distinction would appear fundamental. And yet, in the last resort, what are both saying? It would be illusory to think that we already know this definitely. We by no means know it, for this reason, that in theology, and in preaching, we have not yet the ability to say adequately what it means that God is inconceivably near to us as a person, and yet near in such a different way from any

---

[2] We have to note here, of course, the specific sense in which Teilhard speaks of "matter" as something *animated*.

human personal partner. "Sacramental Indwelling" and "Reconciliation" are only titles which point out a direction for further thought. Whether they are paths which lead away from one another or to the same place we shall only know when we have travelled them. But it does appear important to me that both thinkers, each within the horizon in thought and feeling of his own faith, are coming to think of the presence of God in the hardest, most unavoidable, concrete and palpable part of our everyday reality, in matter and in the ethical situation. Just as we come in contact with matter, just as we ourselves are matter, in the same way we cannot avoid the ethical situations either, we must see them through.

In two respects there can be recognized the common basic *motif*, the relation in impetus to thought, the correspondence in the fundamental experience underlying that thought, which is perhaps of greater weight than all the unmistakable differences. Bonhoeffer speaks of all reality being determined by Jesus Christ. "In Jesus Christ the reality of God has entered into the reality of this world . . . All concepts of reality which do not take account of him are abstractions" (E, p. 61). What Teilhard has to say is:

"Is the Christ of the Gospels, imagined and loved within the dimensions of a Mediterranean world, capable of still embracing and still forming the centre of our prodigiously expanded universe? Is the world not in the process of becoming more vast, more close, more dazzling, than Jehovah? Will it not burst religion asunder? Eclipse our God?

Without daring, perhaps, to admit this anxiety yet, there are many (as I know from having come across them all over the world) who nevertheless feel it deep within them. It is for those that I am writing" (*Le Milieu Divin*, p. 14).

And again Teilhard speaks of the "mystical or universal Christ". In both theologians, then, there appears under the influence of what is surely a specifically modern experience, though we must agree that the emphasis is different in the two,[3] the necessity of thinking of the form of Jesus Christ as

---

[3] The experience is specifically "modern" because it is given to man of today to feel anew and to ponder anew on the one hand the giddying breadth of the universe and on the other the giddying questionableness of his here and now.

universal (cp. the Deutero-Paulines). In *Le Milieu Divin* Teilhard seeks to show how the two halves of our concrete life which we can feel, our activity and our suffering, and with them the *whole* of our reality, are completely filled by God. The "divine realm", *Le Milieu Divin*, is the absolutely universal realm which embraces all things.[4]

> "This done—that is, having shown that the two halves of our lives, and consequently the whole of our world, are full of God—it will remain for us to make an inventory of the wonderful properties of this *milieu* which is all around us (and which is nevertheless beyond and underlying everything), the only one in which from now onwards we are equipped to breathe freely" (*op. cit.*, p. 16).

Teilhard published this work, *Le Milieu Divin*, as an "Essay on the Interior Life", that is, as an ascetic writing, an "exercise in Christianity", the purpose of which is to show how in the present generation one can be a Christian in an elemental and essential sense, how Christian existence is possible today. According to Teilhard Christian existence is absolutely the truly human existence, and not merely some form of religious particularism. In the same way Bonhoeffer, when he considers the possibility of being a Christian in practice, in ethical decisions, reaches the theological vision of the universal Christ sustaining and governing all reality, and his ethics open the way to Christological ontology as their basis.

The other basic theological *motif* in Teilhard, or, if we prefer it, the other aspect of the same *motif*, is the thought of the concrete "palpability" of God.

> "In each (sc. in doing and undergoing) we shall find at the outset that in accordance with his promise, God truly waits for us in things, unless indeed he advances to meet us" (*op. cit.*, p. 16).
>
> "God, in all that is most living and incarnate in him, is not far away from us, altogether apart from the world we see, touch, hear, smell and taste about us. Rather he awaits us in every instant in our action, in the work of the moment. There is a sense in which he is at the tip of my pen, my spade, my brush, my needle—of my heart and of my thought" (*ibid.*, pp. 36f.).

[4] The whole reality of the world is the realm, the *milieu* of God. This is the meaning of the book's title.

God is palpably near, his is the *concretissimum* in all that is our concrete concern. This tendency also we find in Bonhoeffer. We have to think here, for instance, of that word of Jeremiah 45 that was so fascinating for him (cp. our Prologue), "But I will give you your life as a prize of war . . ." In what is man's prize of war, his concrete life, he is reached by what is decisive, God himself.

*

With such a surprising kinship in the two interwoven basic tendencies as a basis, it should now be possible to carry through a more comprehensive comparison of the thought of Teilhard and Bonhoeffer. Again and again, in spite of all obvious differences, we must surely be confronted by unmistakable affinities. One could go so far as to draw up a synopsis of analogies between the two theologians. And this would be no mere pastime which found pleasure in chance similarities. Rather in this way our eyes would be opened to the fact with which both thinkers were concerned, Christ as he gives himself to experience in our time. For in truth the detailed analogies are presumably components of this one fact. Where in spite of all differences, and surely in some respects these could scarcely be imagined as greater than they are, resemblances keep appearing, the cause of it must surely lie in the facts themselves. If there was an analogous basic experience in the two thinkers, it is also interpreted, made concrete and has its components clarified by such analogies in the details.

A very comprehensive catalogue of such analogies would be possible. In making it we should have from time to time to point to the differences of *nuance* and background which certainly would have to be recorded in each individual case, but at the same time we should also have to point to the essential, and not accidental, relation which nevertheless existed. Here we shall occupy ourselves briefly with a few more points from this list.

The thought of the *worldliness of Christianity* is equally characteristic and unalterable in the two. In Bonhoeffer we have to think especially, but not exclusively, here of the prison letters, of his relation to the Old Testament, of his concept of thisworldliness, of his sympathy for the worldly, the man "come of age", even the "godless" man, of his refusal of all narrowness in the name of Christianity of outlook and cultural horizon. The following quotations are evidence of Teilhard's feeling and outlook:

"Nothing is more certain, dogmatically, than that human action can be sanctified. 'Whatever you do', says St. Paul, 'do it in the name of our Lord Jesus Christ'. And the dearest of Christian traditions has always been to interpret these words to mean: in intimate union with our Lord Jesus Christ. St. Paul himself, after calling upon us to 'put on Christ', goes on to forge the famous series of words, *collaborare, compati, commori, con-resuscitare*, giving them the fullest possible meaning, a literal meaning even, and expressing the conviction that every human life must—in some sort—become a life in common with the life of Christ. The actions of life, of which Paul is speaking here, should not, as everyone knows, be understood solely in the sense of religious and devotional 'works' ... It is the whole of human life, down to its most 'natural' zones, which, the Church teaches, can be sanctified. 'Whether you eat or whether you drink', St. Paul says" (*Milieu*, p. 20).

"Try to realize that heaven itself smiles upon you and, through your works, draws you to itself; then, as you leave Church for the noisy streets, you will remain with only one feeling, that of continuing to immerse yourself in God" (*ibid.*, pp. 38f.).

"By virtue of the Creation, and still more, of the Incarnation, *nothing* here below *is profane* for those who know how to see" (*ibid.*, p. 38).

Teilhard meets with every understanding the distrust of Christians felt by the world come of age, the "suspicion that our religion makes its followers inhuman" (*op. cit.*, p. 41).

" 'Christianity', so some of the best of the Gentiles are inclined to think, 'is bad or inferior because it does not lead its followers to levels of attainment beyond ordinary human powers; rather it withdraws them from the ordinary ways of humankind and sets them on other paths. It isolates them instead of merging them with the mass. Instead of harnessing them to the common task, it causes them to lose interest in it. Hence, far from raising them to a higher level, it diminishes them and makes them false to their nature ... Christianity nourishes deserters and false friends: that is what we cannot forgive' " (*ibid.*, p. 41).

He finds this objection "deadly if it were true". But it is not true of Christianity as such, but at the most of a splinter form.

"How could we be deserters, or sceptical about the future of the tangible world? How could we be repelled by human labour? How little you know us! You suspect us of not sharing your concern and your hopes and your excitement as you penetrate the mysteries and conquer the forces of nature. 'Feelings of this kind', you say, 'can only be shared by men struggling side by side for existence; whereas you Christians profess to be saved already'.[5] As though for us as for you, indeed far more than for you, it were not a matter of life and death that the earth should flourish to the uttermost of its natural powers. As far as you are concerned (and it is here that you are not yet human enough, you do not *go to the limits* of your humanity), it is simply a matter of the success or failure of a reality which remains vague and precarious even when conceived in the form of some super-humanity. For us it is a question in a true sense of achieving the victory of no less than a God. One thing is infinitely disappointing, I grant you: far too many Christians are insufficiently conscious of the 'divine' responsibilities of their lives, and live like other men, giving only half of themselves, never experiencing the spur or the intoxication of advancing God's kingdom in every domain of mankind. But do not blame anything but our weakness: our faith imposes upon us the right and the duty to throw ourselves into the things of the earth ... You are men, you say? *Plus et ego*" (*ibid.*, pp. 42ff.).

We could adduce as a parallel to this in Bonhoeffer the same passage which Ebeling quotes more than once to show by it, *inter alia*, that Bonhoeffer's Protestant position is in complete contradistinction to the Catholic!

"I remember a conversation that I had in A.[6] thirteen years ago with a young French pastor. We were asking ourselves quite simply what we wanted to do with our lives. He said he would like to become a saint (and I think it is quite likely that he did become one). At the time I was very impressed, but I disagreed with him, and said, in effect, that I should like to learn to have

---

[5] One could compare with this the passage already quoted from *Letters and Papers from Prison*, "Has not the individualistic question about personal salvation almost completely left us all? etc." (LPP, p. 156).

[6] (Translator's note in LPP—"America"—Tr.)

THE FUTURE FOR CHRISTOLOGY

faith. For a long time I did not realize the depth of the contrast. I thought I could acquire faith by trying to live a holy life, or something like it . . . I discovered later, and I am still discovering right up to this moment, that it is only by living completely in this world that one learns to have faith. One must completely abandon any attempt to make something of oneself, whether it be a saint, or a converted sinner, or a churchman (a so-called priestly type!), a righteous man or an unrighteous one, a sick man or a healthy one. By thisworldliness I mean living unreservedly in life's duties, problems, successes and failures, experiences and perplexities. In so doing we throw ourselves completely into the arms of God, taking seriously, not our own sufferings, but those of God in the world—watching with Christ in Gethsemane. That, I think, is faith, that is *metanoia*; and that is how one becomes a man and a Christian (Cf. Jeremiah 45!)" (LPP, pp. 201f.).

Bonhoeffer recognizes that for the Christian it is in the last resort only a matter of being a *man* and of learning to believe while in the depths of the thisworldliness of being.[7]

To this experience of Christ as the absolutely universal, the experience of both Bonhoeffer and Teilhard, each in his own specific way, there obviously belongs unavoidably an attitude to the world of Christian thisworldliness and affirmation

[7] Teilhard's controversy with those who misunderstand Christianity as a despising of humanity recalls also the section of Bonhoeffer's *Ethics* entitled "Christ and Good People", where we read, " 'Blessed are they which are persecuted for righteousness' sake: for theirs is the kingdom of Heaven' (Matt. 5: 10). This does not refer to the righteousness of God: it does not refer to persecution for Jesus' sake. It is the beatification of those who are persecuted for the sake of a just cause, and, as we may now add, for the sake of a true, good and human cause . . . This beatitude puts those Christians entirely in the wrong who, in their mistaken anxiety to act rightly, seek to avoid any suffering for the sake of a just, true and good cause, because, as they maintain, they could with a clear conscience suffer only for an explicit profession of faith in Christ: it rebukes them for their ungenerousness and narrowness which looks with suspicion on all suffering for a just cause and keeps its distance from it. Jesus gives his support to those who suffer for the sake of a just cause, even if this cause is not precisely the confession of his name; He takes them under his protection, He accepts responsibility for them and he lays claim to them . . . In times of established order, when the law rules supreme and the transgressor of the law is disgraced and ostracized, it is in relation to the tax-gatherer and the prostitute that the Gospel of Jesus Christ discloses itself most clearly to men. 'The publicans and the harlots go into the kingdom of heaven before you' (Matt. 21: 31). In times which are out of joint, in times when lawlessness and wickedness triumph in complete unrestraint, it is rather in relation to the few remaining just, truthful and human men that the gospel will make itself known" (E. pp. 181f.).

of the earthly. And surely the obverse is true, that where this attitude to the world is found today, Jesus Christ cannot be thought of or experienced in faith in any other way than this. We are further given to think by Teilhard's concept of "human" in the full sense. According to him the human is understood precisely by the Christian, where there is one in the real sense of the word. The enemies of Christianity, however right they may be in part, are not yet human enough. For that concept includes a dimension of depth, a profundity, a perspective towards God. We have already discovered this very same understanding of the human in Bonhoeffer, for whom the human is absolutely the real.[8] The human is not conceived in its concreteness, its depth and its fullness, when it is thought of apart from God.

But in addition there would be numerous other resemblances to mention, and all of them surely would be founded on the essential kinship which was there behind all differences. What Bonhoeffer in his *Ethics* calls the *one* reality of the world reconciled to God through Christ meets us in Teilhard also, as for example when statements about the concrete unity of nature and grace declare exactly the theme of his thought.

"Nor should the fact arouse concern that the action of grace is not referred to or invoked more explicitly. The subject under consideration is actual, concrete, 'supernaturalized' man . . . So there was no need to distinguish explicitly between natural and supernatural, between divine influence and human operation . . . Not only as a theoretically admitted entity, but rather as a living reality, the notion of grace impregnates the whole atmosphere of my book" (*op. cit.*, p. 12).

This realm where grace, where "supernature", which always means the reality of Christ, permeates nature is really the province in which "in accordance with his promise, God truly waits for us in things, unless indeed he advances to meet us" (*Milieu*, p. 16). To see this God encountering us everywhere requires, it is true, a "way of teaching how to see" (*ibid.*, p. 15). Bonhoeffer, too, speaks of the "nothing achieved" by those

---

[8] Cp. for instance LPP, pp. 212f., "In the long run, human relationships are the most important thing in life; the modern "efficient" man can do nothing to change this . . . For many today man is just a part of the world of things, because the experience of the human simply eludes them."

who are only "reasonable" and with the best intentions naïvely mistake reality (LPP, p. 26). These do not recognize the hidden Christological depths of reality which can be recognized only by the man who "is called to obedient and responsible action in faith and in exclusive allegiance to God" (LPP, p. 28), and who in this is the man who "stands fast".

But for the man who is able to see it is true that "by virtue of the Creation, and, still more, of the Incarnation, *nothing* here below *is profane* for those who know how to see" (*Milieu*, p. 38). For he affirms being in its thisworldliness, in its secularity, in its "profaneness" just because there is nothing at all profane for him, because for him "Thinking in Terms of Two Spheres" has come to an end.

Even that tendency in Teilhard which has often been censured, that in him the sin of man appears to fall into the background or even to disappear altogether, has its telling parallel in Bonhoeffer. On this Teilhard says:

"The reader need not, therefore, be surprised at the apparently small space allotted to moral evil and sin; the soul with which we are dealing is assumed to have already turned away from the path of error" (*op. cit.*, p. 12).

If this is formulated in a traditional Roman Catholic manner which does not appear to appreciate the dialectical content of the *simul peccator—simul iustus*, yet in the context of Teilhard's thought it must imply that he who has been captured by the operation of grace, that is, of Christ, who stands in the "concrete unity of nature and supernature", and therefore in forgiveness, has in a certain sense his sins "behind him". We find the same tendency in Bonhoeffer who, precisely because he seeks to speak of Christ, refuses to recognize the continual remembrance of sins, which he calls "methodist", as a necessary moment in the proclamation of Christ.

"I think it is infrequent here, because people are not primarily concerned here, either subjectively or objectively, about 'sin'. You may perhaps have noticed that in the prayers I sent you the request for forgiveness of sins does not occupy the central place; I should consider it a complete mistake, both from a pastoral and from a practical point of view, to proceed on 'methodist' lines here. We must talk about that some day" (LPP, p. 132).

N   385

"This being caught up into the messianic suffering of God in Jesus Christ takes a variety of forms in the New Testament. It appears in the call to discipleship, in Jesus' table-fellowship with sinners, in 'conversions' in the narrower sense of the word (e.g. Zacchaeus), in the act of the woman who was a sinner (Luke 7)—an act that she performed without any confession of sin—in the healing of the sick (Matt. 8: 17; see above), in Jesus' acceptance of children. The shepherds, like the wise men from the East, stand at the crib, not as 'converted sinners', but simply because they are drawn by the star to the crib just as they are. The centurion of Capernaum (who makes no confession of sin) is held up as a model of faith (Cf. Jairus). Jesus 'loved' the rich young man. The eunuch (Acts 8) and Cornelius (Acts 10) are not standing at the edge of an abyss" (LPP, p. 199).

*

The fundamental experience which forms the basis for both thinkers, Bonhoeffer and Teilhard, is in the first instance without doubt the fact of theology as such, that Jesus Christ is a person. But we add that there also belongs here, as the basis of the considerable similarity between the two, the specifically modern angle of view, or in other words, the manner in which Jesus Christ shows himself and gives himself to experience precisely today, in the context of the life of our epoch. In what consists this specific moment of modernity which unites the two thinkers is, to tell the truth, hard to say. Perhaps it is still completely impossible for us today, because we ourselves still stand too much under its immediate claim, to which we have to conform without at the same time being able to define it from an adequate distance.

We must now add, in order not to be misunderstood, that in what has been said up to now, and in all that could be further said on the subject by continuing the comparison, we are not concerned with bringing two static positions closer together, or even declaring them to be in the last resort one and the same. Rather it is a matter of opening a dialogue, one which as far as the facts are concerned has already begun, and of showing the common point of perspective of two very distinct lines. The same fact works as the motive power of thought in different horizons. The perspective, "Christ and Nature" is laid down in Bonhoeffer (cp. the lectures on

Christology). Had it been worked out, something for which Bonhoeffer surely lacked not only the time but also the specific experience and the urge, it could well have taken a similar form to the vision which we do in fact find in Teilhard. At least from the viewpoint of the facts it could well have done so, while from that of his personal position and individuality it seems characteristic that he did not further work out precisely this dimension. To this extent the confrontation of these two so different thinkers obtains the significance of a mutual enrichment as regards the facts themselves.

For the rest it seems to me that it is not absolutely necessary to be completely comprehensive in this confrontation and to include Teilhard's viewpoints, to some extent theologically dangerous, on theological cosmology and cosmological eschatology. It is sufficient to refer to the two books, *Le Milieu Divin* and *Hymne de l'Univers*, in which the Father has actually expressed his fundamental experience. Certainly these two writings are only a part, a fragment of his work. Yet in discussion it often happens that suddenly, by a fragment of what is said, light is thrown on what is common in the subject-matter with which the two partners are concerned. Nor must we begin in discussion by putting on the same level all that one of the partners says. What we have to do in the first place is to take note of the centres of energy of his assertions, in other words of what is his primary concern, and not to catch him out on his individual words. (Cp. on this what is said in Chapter Two).

Teilhard died at Easter 1955. This was his unspoken wish, for to him Christ was primarily the Risen one who permeates with his presence all things and leads all reality to face the future of his kingdom. Bonhoeffer's experience of Christ at the end of his life was that of the Crucified; Christ is God, who suffers at the hands of his world, and in whose suffering we as his community ought to share. To us is given the task of noting the message of these two great Christian witnesses of our century, of meditating upon their thoughts, akin in their remoteness, and thus of recognizing the one Christ, crucified and risen, as he gives himself today for recognition to his community and his humanity.

3. The Universality of the Office of Christ as Mediator and the Task of the Proclamation of Christ

(a) The Theological Problem of the Title "Mediator"

The fundamental and comprehensive theological statement which outlines the whole situation to be examined here is to be found in I Timothy, 2: 4–6, ". . . (God's) will it is that all men should find salvation and come to know the truth. For there is *one* God, and also *one* mediator between God and men, Christ Jesus, himself man, who sacrificed himself to win freedom for all mankind, so providing, at the fitting time, proof of the divine purpose . . ." (N.E.B.).

In the title μεσίτης, *mediator*, the Christological foundation which underlies all Christian theology is expressed comprehensively and pregnantly. Christ is the one and only Mediator between God and man, who completely and finally restores their relation. To understand this title, "Mediator", is to understand completely the whole of Christology, for all that Christology has to say can be said in the exposition of it.[9]

---

[9] The New Testament concept of μεσίτης, deriving from Rabbinic thought, originally has a juridical aspect. It describes the agent, the intermediary. Thus the part, for instance, played by Moses in the history of salvation was thought of through the picture of a mediator. But in the New Testament this concept, though only met rarely, becomes an expression of the universalist theme of a theology orientated towards Jesus Christ. Cp. on this, say, the article μεσίτης in Kittel's *Theological Dictionary of the New Testament* (E.T. ed. Bromily, Eerdman's, IV, 1967, p. 610): "The fact that the term does not occur on the lips of Jesus, but arises only in the community raises the question whether the concept . . . is not a later contribution of the community. Much depends on this, and it is a basic problem of N.T. theology. The answer is that the mediator concept is original. It clothes itself increasingly in forms which lie ready to hand, but it maintains its N.T. individuality".

In more recent theology the concept of Mediator has been made the leading thematic concept of Christology by Emil Brunner. Cp. E. Brunner, *The Mediator, A Study of the Central Doctrine of the Christian Faith*, tr. Wyon, Lutterworth, 1934. For Brunner the emphasis falls on the *articulus stantis et cadentis Ecclesiae*, the article on Justification by Faith alone. The concept of Mediator corresponds to this as a comprehensive expression for the subject-matter of Christology, "He who needs no Mediator needs also no mercy. He is not really willing to receive righteousness as a free gift. Rather he wishes to find it in the depth of his own soul. The Mediator is the judgement on all immanental possibilities. He is the Word which humbles us, since he makes all self-defence impossible for us . . . Just as the Word of God is fulfilled in the Word made flesh, so faith is fulfilled through faith in the Mediator. Here alone (and not till this point has been attained) is there a possibility of deciding between being 'offended' and the attitude of faith" (*op. cit.*, p. 231).

In theology we must always make it our endeavour to make all that is to be studied appear in the last analysis as simple as possible, and to reduce it to a single denominator. For in the last resort theology has only one single simple theme. We cannot expect the men to whom in theology we are seeking to make ourselves understood to believe a variety of completely unconnected statements on our faith. And further, this is true, not merely because of the weakness of their ability to believe, but because of the nature of faith itself. Indeed, our understanding might well be able to grasp a diversified system of statements, but for faith this is incomprehensible. For primarily and fundamentally faith is not a matter of the understanding but one of the whole human person, and therefore, while perhaps more complex as regards its aspects, is in its final being a more simple, unified act. In order to do justice to this demand for comprehensibility arising out of the nature of faith itself, a theological train of thought, in spite of all the complexity which as responsible and circumspect consideration we grant it must have, must make the subject dealt within it appear as a single matter which permits itself to be expressed by a single concept and reduced to a single common donominator. The title and concept of Mediator offers itself as such a comprehensive concept in what especially concerns the Christological subject-matter.

It is true that this does not mean that one could not perhaps do otherwise, that Christology is bound to this concept and does not have the freedom to think through the whole of its subject-matter in terms of another concept also. The discipline of theology does not consist in finding and following on each occasion the single way which alone for all time can be travelled, but in finding and travelling by intellectual exposition of its subject the way which satisfies the unyieldingness and inevitability of the demand for understanding which comes precisely in the present. What may have been comprehensible once in earlier times, within the horizon of thought of a bygone epoch, is not necessarily so for the present also, even if the elements of what was once thought still in all probability essentially retain a certain, even a great, fruitfulness, for later times also. Nevertheless it is not strict theological study to give the answers of yesterday to the questions of today.

A theologian from Reformed Orthodoxy, Polanus, defined in the following way the concept of Mediator:

> "*Mediator reconciliationis inter Deum et homines lapsos est persona, quae media inter Deum peccatis irascentem et homines peccatores intervenit, ut a Deo hominibus merito et satisfactione sua impetret et iisdem efficaciter conferat gratiam, remissionem peccatorum et omnia ad salutem necessaria adeoque ipsam aeternam salutem*" (*Syntagma theologiae Christianae*, 1624, VI, p. 27).

("The mediator of reconciliation between God and fallen men is a person who intervenes between God angry at sins and sinful men in order that by his own merit and satisfaction he may obtain from God for men and efficaciously confer on them grace, remission of sins, all that is necessary for salvation and hence eternal salvation itself.")

Two things in this definition are as characteristic as they are questionable. 1. The point of departure is defined in moralist terms; we begin from sin. Sin in its turn is understood primarily as a *moralist and juridical factual relation* between two persons; man is in some way in debt to God, and for this reason his moral qualifications are negative. The Mediator enters into this moralist and juridical relation, pays the debt, and thus restores the relation again. 2. Connected with this, while the Mediator is indeed a person, as he has to be, he is not as Mediator interesting and relevant because of himself, because of the person he is, but only by virtue of his position as Mediator in the moralist and juridical *relation* between two other persons. The "substance" of his being as Mediator thus in a certain sense exhausts itself in this relation.

There would appear to be in this a *twofold problem* for theological thought in our present situation.

1. On the one hand it is questionable whether men of today are still able to think of God and our relation to him in these moralist and juridical categories, whether God becomes credible or intelligible, whether he becomes visible to us as God at all, when we picture him in such terms. Are these moralist and juridical categories sufficient when we are concerned with the ground of our being and of all reality in the world? Are they sufficiently comprehensive and discriminating to make an assertion about reality itself and about reality as a whole. Here, among other things we should have to enquire if there

are not worlds of Christian thought, for example in the Christianity of the East, in which these moralist and juridical categories are far from playing the same dominating role as they do in our customary and traditional understanding of what is Christian, and if theological thought in such categories is not a legacy of Western Christendom, the Reformation included. It was the dispute about a question of juridical practice and of the theology of penance in the Roman Church which was the provocation of the Reformation. To this extent Protestantism remains stamped by Roman thought.

In our time many a firmly rooted traditional system of values has begun to totter. We feel the incomprehensibility of the real, the incomprehensibility in particular of human reality, in a spiritual revolution analogous perhaps to that which the Renaissance experience of the world, for instance Giordano Bruno's experience of infinity, meant for the picture of Nature. We feel the almost unlimited historical and sociological variability of human life, the differentiation to an infinite degree, the indeterminacy and uncertainty of human existence. Every concept which seeks to capture man in a firm picture with firm co-ordinates of value soon proves to be too undifferentiated, too primitive. Consciously or unconsciously, the literature and art of our time are largely a mirror of this specifically modern sense, for which reality withdraws into questionableness, yet without ceasing to be the thing which man cannot escape.

But what we say about God, also, and about man's relation to God, and about the Mediator between God and man, must take account of this sense. Of course we shall never in theological thought be able to dispense with "ethical" categories such as guilt, pardon, or above all, responsibility.[10] But we require concepts which are wider, which certainly integrate the ethical but are not exhausted in it. It will not suffice today to develop in purely moralist categories the basis of Christian recognition of the truth, the words about one Mediator between God and man, the man Jesus Christ. The Mediator is more than a mere repairer of our transgression of God's declaration of his will,

[10] In addition, as is shown by Heidegger's analysis in *Being and Time*, such concepts have an ontological relevance extending beyond the essentially ethical.

understood in a moralist way. This leads us to the other half of
our problem.

2. It is questionable if it is enough to understand the being
of Jesus Christ the Mediator in terms of the relation between
God and man, as if we knew exactly in advance what these
two concepts mean. It could well rather be that both the reality
of man and the reality of God first really become visible in
terms of this centre, the Mediator.[11] *Jesus* shows us the face
of God and in this he is the Mediator. "He that hath seen me
hath seen the Father also"; in this Johannine statement the
Mediatorship is exactly expressed. It is from the event of Christ
in Incarnation, Cross, Resurrection, Ascension and Second
Coming, and from what after his exaltation was testified to by
the community as his Word that we must read off what God
is for us.

We attempt to give a provisional answer to this twofold
problem, to the insufficiency of purely moralist categories for
the understanding of the reality of the Mediator Jesus Christ,
and to the insufficiency of the purely relational representation.

It is that the Mediator does not only create a new harmony
in an already given system of persons with moralist obligations
to one another, but also constitutes the true determining
reality, the reality of the encounter of God and man.

But this is the point at which Dietrich Bonhoeffer's basic
Christological thought reveals its whole compass for the
Christological problem of the present day. It is the thought
that as Mediator, as Reconciler between God and man, Christ
is the true reality and that every other understanding of reality
apart from him is an abstraction. This does not of course mean
that there could be no other reality apart from a Christ in any
way limited and isolated, but rather that all that is real is
sustained as the real by the reality of this One. But it is at the
same time the thought that the components of the event of
Christ, for Bonhoeffer the Incarnation, Cross and Resurrection,

---

[11] We could surely enter into a discussion about God with someone who
does not know Christ without passing in advance the judgement upon him,
that because he does not know Christ he could in no way speak about God,
but was by presupposition speaking about something else. But for us as
theologians of the Church of Christ there is absolutely no legitimate possibility
of ourselves speaking about God without Jesus.

are the final ontological components of all that is reality at all, that the reality which we experience is in all its complexity, differentiation and incomprehensibility permeated and determined by Christ. The reality which is Christ himself is the reality of the *world* reconciled with God, the reality of *God* who encounters in the world and is reconciled with the world. Christ the Mediator is not merely a "functionary" in a predetermined system of relations. He is something in himself, as a person. He himself creates through himself a universal reality, the reality of God and man, the reality of the world reconciled by God, accepted by God and indwelt by God, the reality of the grace before the face of God in which man and world always already stand. This reality is a sphere of encounter. In it, and in it alone, God encounters. It is only at the first glance that it can appear as if the being of Christ the Mediator can in its new definition still nevertheless be explained with the help of an already given relation between God and man. The truth is given by John 14: 6, "I am the way, the truth and the life. No man cometh to the Father but by me". This is the being of the Mediator, he is truth itself and life itself. The Giver of the gift of God is himself the gift. The Revealer of the Word of God is himself the Word which he speaks. He is the reality in which we live, in which we have found ourselves since our birth, the reality that God looks graciously upon us and upon all his creatures.

So understood, the Mediator is not merely someone who takes his part in the play, even if it were the most important part of all. One might say that he himself is the stage on which we all play the parts of our life before the face of God.

It is only so that today we can do justice to the statement, made necessary by the New Testament, that there is one Mediator between God and man, today when there no longer holds sway the awareness and the general picture still presupposed in the *Corpus Christianum*, that there is a God and that there are men, and that between the two there is a relation of moralist obligation, a picture, we must add, in which it was then easy to insert Jesus Christ as Mediator.

Certainly it appears much more difficult in comparison to work out concretely in our thought the definition of the Mediator as constituting a new and universal reality, and the reality, moreover, in which we already live. Bonhoeffer also, as we have seen, has not gone further on his journey than the first few steps. And yet this task remains the one set for us and cannot be bypassed. For it is not possible today in any other way to be obedient to the claim of the New Testament and to think of and to proclaim Jesus Christ as the only Mediator.

We can travel no longer today, for instance, the way of that classic foundation of Western Christology, *"Cur Deus Homo?"*, that is, the way of presupposing as known and axiomatic the opposition of God and man, in order then to construct from these premises given as our axioms Jesus Christ the Mediator. This way is no longer open for this reason, that today the majority of our "Christian" contemporaries certainly long for God and wait on God, but no longer count it a firm presupposition that God is. One certainly can and must speak to them also about God. But one will have to speak to them about the existence of God by speaking to them about the Mediator Jesus Christ. If anything at all is to them the proof of God it is Jesus Christ the Mediator . . . And for all these reasons one will no longer be able to speak about that Mediator in categories which are derived from the presupposition as an axiom of the existence of God.[12]

(b) *The Christological Existential*

The direction taken by more recent Roman Catholic theology in the thought which appears in Karl Rahner of a "supernatural existential" runs on clearly parallel lines to this examination we have just made. The "supernatural existential" is a component of existence, that is to say, something which marks and stamps the composition of man's being as such. But it is not a component which enters being *in any natural manner*; it enters by virtue of the grace of God which has appeared in Jesus Christ and which has yet always already laid hold of all men and determined them in the deepest parts of their situation before God. But in that case the supernatural existential, which is factually, that is not by creation and nature but *factually*, a universal determinant of the existence of *all* men, must now,

[12] Cp. with this my essay on *"Anselms Versöhnungslehre"*, ThZs, Basle May-June 1957.

because the grace of God *really* takes place and makes itself known in Christ, be understood as a Christological existential.

In fact, to speak of a Christological existential means that the being of all men is laid hold of, changed, reconstituted and founded anew by the event of Christ, that all human existence is accompanied by the offer of Christ's grace, and that existence is determined by its being so accompanied. Thus the "kindness of God towards man" (Titus 3: 4) which has been made known in Christ is not merely a content of the consciousness of Christians but a real determinant of the existence of non-Christians also.[13] In the story of Jesus Christ we are not merely dealing with a historical fact, a fact in the history of salvation, or at least in the "historical account of salvation", which happened once and of which we simply have to take approving notice. What happened there and then has a "cosmic dimension" and a cosmic relevance. His present reaches out towards us and brings us into relation with him.

We are led, both by Bonhoeffer's statement that Christ is reality and by the concept of the supernatural, and in the end Christological, existential, to the dictum that *Jesus Christ the Mediator is not to be understood relationally, but as constituting reality*. He constitutes the reality in which we exist before God and in which God encounters us. Hence one can no longer speak theologically of Christ today on the basis of established and undisputed presuppositions. One cannot speak of him without asking in complete frankness what reality is and about the structure of the real. Christology must begin anew *ab ovo*. Theological wrestling with the right articulation of the message of Christ and the specifically modern and existential wrestling with reality meet with one another.

(c) *The Situation for Preaching*

In this case too, one will not be surprised at the fact that the difficult and far-reaching dogmatic questions here envisaged are most highly relevant for the concrete proclamation of

---

[13] This does not mean that the character of faith as decision is eliminated, even if it is an "anonymous faith". Rather, the "supernatural existential" means precisely that man is set in the position of decision by God's will for his salvation and by the offer of salvation that is given in Jesus Christ, and that throughout his whole way he is always accompanied by this question of decision.

Christ and for the attitude of the Church of Jesus Christ in the world. Everything, indeed, in dogmatics must have a significance for Christian preaching.[14]

How are we to preach about Christ? Or, to put the question more correctly, how are we to preach Christ? We can be sure that our proclamation of Christ must not be particularist, say, in the manner of, "We Christians have the special and infallible recipe and draw your attention to it who stand outside", or, "We call to our own remembrance that we have this recipe". In many modern forms of pietist preaching, but not only in them, Christ is commended in some such way as this. The scheme for the affirmation of Christ in the sermon then appears something like this, "There are problems, difficult problems of life. These you also have. But they are only soluble through Jesus Christ. Therefore you must accept Christ, give your heart to him, surrender yourself completely to him, etc." Or elsewhere, saying very much the same it runs, "Everything has happened for you in Jesus Christ. You have only to allow it to be said to you. You have only to allow it to seem good to you, etc." But this appeal usually remains without the addition of that concreteness which would be necessary to enable it to win belief. It is not made clear in what consists this "give your heart to him" or "allow it to be said to you".

This form of the preaching of Christ, unable to win belief but frequent, is dogmatically ruled out by the trend of our thought about the Mediator. It is here that we find the concrete repercussions in the *Kerygma* of the path of thought on which we have set out. Nor may one preach of Christ in such a way that one is simply asserting that he is the chief figure in the great drama of the *Heilsgeschichte*. Then the question is perhaps "Whither Christ?" And in reply the story is expounded, God and man standing face to face, the mishap of sin, the "nevertheless" of the love of God, and the necessity for the Mediator. That is, the customary method of preaching Christ is still strongly determined by *"Cur Deus Homo?"* But then, however emphatically one asserts the Christological dogmas, however

---

[14] This factual situation, that every dogmatic statement only then has a justification and a real basis when there is a kerygmatic significance belonging to it, forms the theme of my book, *Theology and Preaching*, tr. Knight, Lutterworth, 1965. Cp. also in addition, *Verkündigung und Existenz*, Zürich, 1956.

one casts light on them by dramatic illustrations, the facts still do not win belief.

In this way the content of preaching still remains a "Christological drama", which is certainly self-consistent, but which runs its course remote from us. It is still only *asserted* that we are brought into the drama. This is the preaching of many Churches today. And perhaps this is the reason why many Christians, who in every way still wish to remain Christians, absent themselves from their Church, because they no longer believe the Church in these fables. They wait for God, for God's own approach, that he may speak his word for their lives, but they receive stories given in an authoritative vein. Hence we do not speak seriously today about the Mediator, and because there is only *one* Mediator between God and man, we do not speak seriously about God.

The grandfather by his stove in Tolstoy's story, "Quench the Fire while it is but a Spark", speaks more seriously when he admonishes his family who are living in dispute with their neighbours, "He strikes you on one ear, you strike him on two. He lodges a complaint against you with the police, you lodge one against him with the judge . . . Is that what our Lord has taught us? . . ." He speaks from existential seriousness and intimacy with Christ. He speaks from Christ as the Divine truth which is for him the final obligation.

We must seek to preach not so much *about* Christ as *from* Christ. Our task is not to portray the necessity for the Mediator in a Christological middle part of our sermon dealing with our relation to him, but so to speak about man before God that from what we say there can be traced the reality, irrevocably founded on Christ, of the world reconciled and accepted by God, of the nearness of God pledged once for all in him.

Christological dogma remains true as the obedient decision of the Church, the decision accepting the truth of the revelation of God. But precisely for the sake of the truth of these great traditional doctrines we must not make any fable out of them, we must not pass them on uninterpreted, otherwise we do not do justice to the claim of their truth. Jesus Christ is a person and no idea, not even the idea of a person. The story of Christ is not a myth but a real event. But it is an event *sui generis* or else we would have no right to say that this single event concerns us all and is significant and decisive for us all.

Hence our task is to define ontologically and to interpret existentially the story of Jesus Christ, the event of Christ in Incarnation, Cross and Resurrection. But how is this to be taught and learned with the sermon in view if it is not at the same time an exercise in theology, if indeed theology does exactly the opposite? For the sake, therefore, of the proclamation of Christ, the existential interpretation of the event of Christ is the most pressing task in Christology.

(d) *The Beginnings in Traditional Theology: The "Logos Incarnandus"*

The thought of the universal reality and activity of Christ the Mediator is already foreshadowed in traditional theology. Thus Johann Heinrich Heidegger writes:

> "*Officium mediatoris Christi commune est omni statui ecclesiae post peccatum. Nam Christus Iesus heri et hodie idem est et in secula* (Hebr. xiii, 8). *Sed aliter tamen mediator fuit ante incarnationem, aliter post eam. Ante incarnationem mediator fuit tum futuro merito ceu agnus mactatus a iacto mundi fundamento* (Apoc. xiii, 8), *tum efficacia meriti futuri semper praesente utpote per et propter quam etiam patres ante Christum redempti salvati sunt . . .*" (*Corpus theologiae*, Zürich, 1700, XIX, p. 26).
>
> ("The office of Christ as Mediator is a common gift to every state of the Church since the appearance of sin. For Jesus Christ is the same yesterday, today and for ever (Hebr. 13: 8). But he was Mediator in one way before the Incarnation and in another way after it. Before the Incarnation he was Mediator, firstly, by his future merit as the lamb slain from the foundation of the world (Rev. 13: 8), and, secondly, by the ever present effectiveness of that future merit, by means of which and by virtue of which the fathers also who were redeemed before Christ were saved . . .")

And Amandus Polanus writes:

> "*. . . Christus ante assumtam humanam naturam fuit mediator secundum utramque naturam, quia tum mediator hominum fuit quatenus incarnandus . . .*" (Syntagma theologiae christianae, 1624, VI, p. 27.)

("... Christ before the assumption of human nature was Mediator by both natures, because he was then Mediator of man as he who has to be incarnate ...")

According to this conception, God before the Incarnation regards the Divine and human natures as already united in Christ, for he is above time and past, present and future are for him on the same plane. Obviously there appears here the need to extend the Mediatorship of Jesus Christ backward beyond the time of his earthly appearance. Christ is not only pre-existent as the *Logos*, the second Person of the Trinity, his office as Mediator is also effective in advance. For should not the pious of the Old Testament, for instance, also be regarded as saved? Or are they to be saved without a Mediator, or with another Mediator than Christ? Both suggestions seem unthinkable and thus we cannot escape the consequence which follows. Here we find in the thought of traditional theology an essential step, and one recognized quite clearly as necessary, in the direction of a universalist exposition of the event of Christ. But this is exactly a step in the same direction in which we have already set out with our exposition so far of the title "Mediator". If Christ exercised his office as Mediator already before his Incarnation, before the "time was fulfilled" at a particular point in history, it follows that the effectiveness of his Mediatorship is not absolutely dependent on the event of Christ becoming a content of consciousness. The fathers of the Old Testament did not yet know explicitly of Christ[15] and yet were already saved through his Mediatorship,

In present-day theology this thought has received a new life, and it may be that the hour is now here when it must be thought through in all its radicalness. In the *Constitutio de Ecclesia* of the Second Vatican Council the foundation chapter *De Ecclesiae mysterio* begins with an affirmation about the *Ecclesia universalis*:

"*Aeternus Pater, liberrimo et arcano sapientiae ac bonitatis suae consilio, mundum universum creavit, homines ad participandam*

---

[15] Thomas Aquinas, in the *Summa Theologiae*, in the tractate "Concerning Faith", comes to the conclusion that the Old Testament fathers believed implicitly in the Incarnation and in the Trinity, and therefore in Christ (Cp. S. Th., II, ii, 9, 2; Blackfriars Tr., Vol. XXXII—not yet published).

vitam suam divinam elevare decrevit, eosque lapsos in Adamo non dereliquit, semper eis auxilia ad salutem praebens, intuitu Christi, Redemptoris, 'qui est imago Dei invisibilis, primogenitus omnius creaturae' (Col. i, 15) *... Tunc autem, sicut apud sanctos Patres legitur, omnes iusti inde ab Adam, 'ab Abel iusto usque ad ultimum electum' in Ecclesia universali apud Patrem congregabuntur"* (*op. cit.,* Chs. 1, 2).

("The Eternal Father, by a free and hidden plan of his own wisdom and goodness, created the whole world. His plan was to raise men to a participation of the divine life. Fallen in Adam, men were not left to themselves by God the Father, but they are ceaselessly offered helps to salvation, in view of Christ, the Redeemer, 'who is the image of the invisible God, the firstborn of every creature' . . . when, as is read in the Fathers, all the just, from Adam and 'from Abel the just one to the last of the elect' will be gathered together with the Father in the universal Church" —E.T. in Rynne, *The Third Session,* Faber & Faber, 1964, p. 297).

For our problem the expression *"intuitu Christi Redemptoris"* is decisive. It means that all the just, even before Christ, were saved in view of Christ. How this *"intuitu"* is to be interpreted remains a question; the text of the *Constitutio* does not here go into detail. The Reformed Orthodox theologians, Polan and Heidegger, as we have seen, made use here of the concept of time, that God is above time, and stands beyond the opposition of its dimensions. Hence for him the merit of Christ which lies in the future is already present, and he permits it to become effective even before Christ for the present of that time. But the question must arise here if what in the Reformed Orthodox thinkers is thought of as real and effective from the viewpoint of God would not have to be shown also as having the same reality and effectiveness from the viewpoint of the world, of men. The argument of Reformed Orthodoxy is foreign to us today and scarcely a model for the fulfilment of our task, because it argues from the viewpoint of God which we can never make our own. Hence when we seek to portray the same facts with which we share the concern of these Orthodox theologians, and now obviously of the Vatican Council also, we must set out on that other path and begin from men. We could do this in so far as we showed how and how far man as he stands before God is already *before* Christ determined by Christ. But those are also to be regarded as existing *ante Christum* for whom for legitimate reasons it has not been possible for Christ to become the content of consciousness and confession. In other words the task is set us of an existential interpretation of Christology. In this, of course, it must be made clear that this "beginning from man" instead of from God refers only to the possible range of the course of our thought, and not to the starting-point, in so far as that means the foundation. The foundation, and to this extent the starting-point, of our speaking about Christ remains in every case Christ himself, the deed of God which was done in him, and not any form of anthropology which we might be able to sketch independently of Christ. But we cannot put ourselves in the place of God, the insight which results from the recognition of the historicity of revelation and faith tells us, and hence it is not sufficient to explain the effective Mediatorship of the *Logos Incarnandus* by saying that God from the very beginning foresaw the Incarnation and the whole event of Christ. This again would be a thought in juridical categories, corresponding to what we call the retrospective validity of a law. If we wish to join with the old orthodox theologians in speaking of the effective Mediatorship of the *Logos incarnandus*, we can no longer do so today without showing the specific matter of effectiveness, already determined by Christ, of the saving grace of God at that point where it appears. Hence, not the foundation it is true, but surely the horizon of exposition of our affirmation, is the reality of *man*.

A much discussed point of approach for such an existential interpretation of Christology is the *Christological exposition of the Old Testament*. To our understanding of the Old Testament the statement about the uniqueness of the Mediator Jesus Christ must be meaningfully and consistently applied. Hence Christ is not to be found in it in the sense of an unhistorical eisegesis, but surely he is in the sense of the demonstration of a structure determined by his Mediatorship to the meeting of men with God in its pages. The way has already long been prepared for such an undertaking in the fact that the Church has at all times used the Psalms in worship while meditating on Christ, its Lord.

(e) *The Universalism of Modern Asiatic Christology*

It is interesting at this point to examine the beginnings to a

Christology which are arising in a world of theological thought not stamped by that fate of Western Christology to date, the juridical and moralist categories, I mean those beginnings which are found in the theologians of the young Churches in areas of non-Christian spheres of history and humanity, in Asia and Africa. Certainly all here is in the process of development, in embryo, and yet there can be seen a clear trend towards a universalist view of the reality of Jesus Christ. Surely we must expect in the future from this world of Eastern thought another essential contribution to our posing of the problems of Christology. The era of dialogue with such distant worlds has only just begun. Nor is it only that the openness of a world which in hearing the word is not stamped by Western Christian tradition is a help in our own situation, in our dismay before the difficulty of the problem of Christology as it puts itself to us as soon as we leave the old established lines of a relational definition of the Mediator, and the perplexity which is ours at once if without these figures of thought we are to speak credibly and clearly in proclamation and theology about the reality of the story of Jesus Christ. This openness is also at the same time in keeping with the command of the Master himself, who remains the same yesterday, today and for ever, from whom, through whom and for whom are all things, and who sends us to all peoples, yes, to all creation, and who therefore does not permit himself to be finally and exclusively contained in one definite intellectual horizon such as the Western, or in certain habits of thinking. It is just in the present-day situation of worldwide dialogue, or that beginning today, that we begin to experience existentially what it is that passes beyond all boundaries in the reality of the Mediator, something which before was only known to us in believing hearing based on Scripture. This, in passing, is surely often what has happened in the history of Christian existence and Christian thought, that we confess something obediently with a sense that it is true, and that only thereafter, in the course of the journey that we make with God, we experience it in its truth, in keeping with the words of Jesus in John 13: 7. "What I do, you do not know now; but you will experience it hereafter".

Let us choose two examples, and first the statement of an

Indian theologian, S. J. Samartha, Professor in Bangalore. Among other things he writes this:[16]

"An excessive concern with the nature of Christ has often obscured *the social consequences of his life and work in history.* Cross and Resurrection go forward to have an abiding influence on the life of men. Through Jesus Christ, the crucified and risen Lord, the power of God continues to work in the world, healing the broken life, reconciling estranged men to one another, making all that is separated from God and man strive for unification and setting free creative energies for a life in social responsibility. Faith in him helps the individual to renew his life and to take part in the task of rebuilding the fellowship" (p. 147).

The trend can be quite clearly traced here, though it is true that a final precision in formulation has not yet been reached; not only is the being of Jesus Christ, and Jesus Christ in person, to be theologically defined by the description of the event in *Heilsgeschichte* which took place then and there, but also, and indeed, primarily, the reality of Jesus Christ is to be thought of as a power which in the present works to save and heal in individual men and in human fellowship. In the quoted passage, as in the whole essay, one can clearly trace the endeavour to establish the relevance of the message of Christ for the social and political problems of a modern Asiatic nation like India, and to do so not merely as an assertion (for what ice would it cut in a non-Christian environment simply to *assert*, "Christ solves your problems"?), but in such a way that everything said points to and compels the conclusion that the theologian must know how to expound this concrete social significance.

But we are not dealing merely with the subsequent *applicatio* to live problems of our world today of a "message of Christ", that is, one based on a being of Christ already beforehand explicable and explained. The "Christology in India" which Samartha seeks to "think to the situation" seeks to understand the very being of Christ and message of Christ from a very concrete definition of its effectiveness and reality in the world of today, the world approachable by us and pressing in upon

[16] *"Einer Christologie in Indien entgegen"*, Lecture on the 150th anniversary of the Basel Mission, *Evangelisches Missions-Magazin*, 109th. Jg., 3/1965, pp. 135ff.

us. Either we understand Christ from here, how he works upon the individual man and on the community today, or we do not understand at all who Christ is for us and who he is in reality. The universalist point of this Christological trend is made completely clear in a quotation from P. D. Devanandan towards the end of Samartha's lecture:[17]

"Secondly, the claim for the uniqueness of Christ, far from being 'exclusive', in reality includes in itself the assertion that the Gospel is universal. The late Devanandan, who found himself continually in dialogue with the Hindu brotherhoods, stressed this repeatedly. He makes the following exposition of this point.

'Christians believe that with the coming of Christ, God Almighty identified Himself for a while with all man's struggles for perfection and the realization of his true nature. Such identification initiates a new era in creation. It marked the beginning of a redemptive movement which takes in humanity in its entirety, that is, the whole community of mankind inclusive of all peoples, whatever their beliefs, language or race. So that far from wanting to shut others out from participation (which would be being exclusive), the Christian wants the world of men to share his faith in this all-inclusive cosmic process of new creation.'

In a land which has to lead so many religions to find their being and which has bid welcome so many religions from beyond its frontiers, it is necessary to avoid the impression of being exclusive. But it is necessary in the same way to avoid an all too easy recognition of a general similarity between the religions. In so far as the Church of India enters into serious dialogue with men of another faith, all Christological formulations ought to be characterized by a deep understanding of the human need which men of every faith have in common, by an openness towards the awakening world which surrounds us, by a freedom to search out new approaches to life and thought, but at the same time by an essential loyalty to Jesus Christ who is wisdom (*jnana*) and the power of God (*sakti*) for all who seek him and while they seek him have already found him" (Samartha, *op. cit.*, pp. 150f.).

Existential loyalty to Jesus Christ as a unique and unambiguous person and manifestation is presupposed without question as a foundation of theology.

[17] *Preparation for Dialogue*, Christian Institute for the Study of Religion and Society, Bangalore, 1964, pp. 137ff. (Devanandan's own original English quoted—Tr.).

"Such an assertion (sc. that of the uniqueness of the claim of Christ) can only be made 'from faith to faith'. Without a committed surrender there can be no true religion. Hence this claim must be taken out of the context of the science of comparative religion and inserted into the structure of the commitment of the Church to Jesus Christ as its Lord" (*ibid.*, p. 150).

But the train of thought which begins from this "existential loyalty", the theological exposition of this unique and unambiguous personal content, must think of the reality of Christ as a universal "reconciliation movement", as a "cosmic process of the new creation including all things", in which at bottom all men are to participate regardless of their faith, as well as regardless of their language or race. According to this view the reality of Christ goes out in its world-reconciling and world-forming power, and therefore in respect of the possibility of real participation in it, beyond any explicit belonging to the confession of Christ.

In our wrestling with the Christological problem of the present, as it is posed for us today for the sake of the proclamation of Christ, we do well, if we are not to close the door to the *novitas Jesu Christi*, to listen to such voices from worlds to which Christ comes as someone new, and not someone out of the depths of their own tradition in the history of culture. We will then be protected, in the best case from taking our stand on old traditional and now barely conscious systems of thought and thus thinking too narrowly of the reality of Jesus Christ, and in the worst case from betraying this "essential loyalty" to Jesus Christ itself in the turmoil caused through these accustomed ways of thought becoming questionable.

*

Our second example comes from the world of Japanese thought, from the "Theology of the Pain of God" of the Japanese theologian Kazo Kitamori, who, according to the verdict of Keiji Ogawa, the one Japanese theologian so far to write for German speakers about the situation and problem of Christian theology in Japan, has undertaken the first venture, not merely to take over the *Kerygma* of Christ in its Western form, but to appropriate it in thought originally, that is to say, with native Japanese presuppositions as a basis.[18]

Kitamori's basic concept for the whole of theology is that of "the pain of God". From this foundation the whole of theological subject-matter becomes for him meaningful; from this point he can so appreciate the whole body of theological *loci* that all individual themes are held together by this one concept. In this he quotes the passage in Jeremiah 31: 20: "Is not Ephraim a precious son unto me? Is he a child of delight? For as often as I speak against him, I do earnestly remember him still. Therefore my heart yearneth for him. I will surely have compassion on him, saith the Lord."[19] Kitamori meditates on the Hebrew verb *"hamah"* which Jeremiah uses of God and which Buber renders *"zuwallen des Herzens"* or *"des Eingeweids"* ("my heart yearneth"). Certainly the word in the prophet implies an emotion, one might almost say an "emotional disturbance", in God. But this seemingly anthropomorphic manner of speaking now becomes for Kitamori the cardinal point for the peculiar dialectic which determines his whole theology. Following up the assertion of this verse, it is the dialectic of *pain* and *love*.

It is this same dialectic which in Ogawa's judgement constitutes what is peculiarly Japanese in this theology, this form given to the Gospel of Christ. The Japanese, he continues, has a special sensitivity for this collocation. Through his peculiar manner of thinking, strengthened by his most recent experiences in the downfall of Japan in the Second World War, he has a special opportunity to understand the "pain of God". And this does in fact appear a new and fruitful viewpoint, for the Western tradition in Dogmatics had understood the inmost being of God as impassive eternal *beatitudo*.

---

[18] Cp. for the following, Keiji Ogawa, *Die Aufgabe der neueren evangelischen Theologie in Japan*, Bd. 8 of the ecumenical series, *Begegnung*, Basel, Friedrich Reinhardt-Verlag, 1965; Kazo Kitamori, *Theology of the Pain of God*, tr. Bratcher, S.C.M., 1966. (Ott's note here explains that for quotation from Kitamori he is dependent on Ogawa as Kitamori's work is not yet translated into German, but English readers have this translation of Kitamori's own work—Tr.)

[19] Following the translation of Martin Buber in *Werke*, III, p. 342 (*Die Erzählungen der Chassidim: Levi Jizchak von Berditschew*). (I have quoted E.T. of the same, *Tales of the Hasidim, The Early Masters*, tr. Marx, Thames & Hudson, 1956, p. 223. For Kitamori on Jeremiah 31: 20, see E.T., Kitamori, *op. cit.*, pp. 151ff.—Tr.)

"When the peoples are the subject which seeks insight into the being of God, it is a matter of the heart of the people concerned. And this heart is neither thought nor theory, but spirit and feeling . . . In what is this heart of a people expressed? Without doubt in its literature, and in the literature of the masses, not that of the educated. The typical example of this literature is the stage drama . . . During the war emphasis was placed on what is called the 'Japanese spirit'. It is the spirit of triumph with a purely one-sided positiveness. But the Japanese heart also lives in a negative side, in the traditional tragedy . . . The essence of the traditional tragic feeling is 'Tsurasa'[20] . . . Kitamori goes on to say, 'Japanese tragedies are strikingly different in character from those of other countries. Whereas the latter are for the most part tragedies of incident and character, Japanese tragedy can be called the tragedy of personal relationships'.[21] The activation of feeling known as 'Tsurasa' takes place just where someone finds himself in an insoluble contradiction, for example where he must kill himself or give over to death someone whom he loves, in order to preserve the life of another. In one play, *'Terakoya'* ('The Nursery School'), a striking example is found . . . The hero, Matsuomaru, knows that enemies are making an attempt on the life of the son of their feudal lord. He and his wife then send their own son to 'Terakoya', the school, to let him die in his place. When Matsuomaru learns that his own son has died a substitutionary death and that the son of his lord has escaped from the hands of his enemies, he weeps quietly together with his wife and says to her, 'Rejoice, my dear; our son has been of service to our lord'.[22] This joy through suffering is for Kitamori a fitting illustration for the concept of the pain of God. In the old plays of the traditional Japanese theatre, *Kabuki*, there can be found many other examples of such activation of feeling. Behind them, as their foundation, there lies feudal morals. But apart from these morals the activation of feeling is very remarkable. It is not straightforward, but tortuous and even dialectical. In its complex nature one can surely with justice find an East Asian trait of character . . .

The pain of God has discovered an entirely new moment in the concept of God. It explains the concept of God in his relation to men. The concept of God in the pain of God is a relational concept . . . The concept of God in the pain of God is neither objective

[20] ("pain"—Translator's note, Kitamori, E.T., p. 177—Tr.)
[21] (Kitamori, E.T., p. 134. For Kitamori on Tragedy see E.T., pp. 134ff. and translator's note, p. 177—Tr.)
[22] (Kitamori, E.T., p. 134—Tr.)

nor subjective but a relational concept. This is the new momen
which the Japanese heart has found in the concept of God"
(Ogawa, *op. cit.*, pp. 104ff.).

Kitamori is doubtless being too rigidly systematic when he
thinks that the Greek concept of God is purely objective, that
the Lutheran Germanic is subjective, and that the "Japanese
heart" has gone beyond them in discovering what is relational
in the concept of God. Nevertheless, the thought of the pain of
God as a "relational concept" is a contribution, to be taken
seriously, to the doctrine of God and to Christology, and above
all to the problem of the personality of God, since it breaks
through the long-enduring but basically a-personal tradition,
which has ruled the Western doctrine of God, that the conception be of an imperturbable *beatitudo* and impassivity as his
inmost being. What today is emphasized repeatedly in Western
theology also, that personal encounter with men "affects"
God himself, that, for example, he does not simply remain
unmoved by sin, is here set out expressly in the basic principle
of a dogmatic system. But the thought has, of course, its own
peculiar foundation in Christology.

> "The 'pain of God' is different from the 'love of God'. That is,
> the 'pain of God' reflects his love towards those turning against
> it. The pain of God enfolds within itself his immediate love work-
> ing as a medium which must be rejected because of human sin.
> It is therefore on a higher plane than his 'love' and witnesses to
> the 'love of the Cross'. The 'love of the Cross' is poured upon those
> turning against God's immediate love which functions as law.
> The 'pain of God'—the Gospel—is love which is witnessed to, yet
> revealed, outside of the law. Both the 'pain of God' and the 'love
> of the Cross' reflect love which is poured upon us by cancelling
> our sin of rejecting God's love—it is the absolutely affirmative
> love shown in these double negatives. Man can turn against the
> immediate 'love of God', but not against the 'pain of God', the
> love of the Cross.
> ... The complete victory of 'God's pain' over sinners takes
> place at that time. Christ's complete victory—the resurrection—
> takes place in sinners when they can no longer turn against the
> love of his Cross. The victory of 'God's pain' is his love which has
> pierced through the pain—that is, 'love rooted in the pain of God'.
> The resurrection of Christ which conquers death on the cross is
> his victory ... Just as the other side of Christ's death is his

resurrection, the other side of God's 'pain' is his love" (Kitamori, *op. cit.*, p. 156).

Kitamori is a Lutheran. His theology of the pain of God is a *theologia crucis* of a Lutheran stamp. In the basic image of his theological thought he features the categories "law" and "Gospel", a Lutheran moment which stands in a congenial relation with that dialectic of pain and love which obviously expounds the intuition and existential experience of the Japanese theologian. In the history of theology the background is Luther, philosophically it is a school of philosophy found in the old imperial University of Kyoto, represented by such names as Nishida, Tanabe and Nishitani, a mystical outlook based on the dialectic of existence which, derived from the thought of Zen-Buddhism, had come under the influence of Kierkegaard's dialectic of existence (Cp. Ogawa, *op. cit.*, pp. 25–30). Using the words merely as a title, an indication of the trend, and in full consciousness of the great difficulty for us in following in our minds such an East Asian train of thought, one could perhaps describe the character of this thought as a *"mystical experience of non-immediacy"*. The "immediate" experience of reality itself, as that which is presupposed by all thought, the same pre-logical apperception of reality as such, is, it would seem, marked by a non-immediacy, a "dialectic" in the very act of experiencing reality. How far the description here attempted, and it is only the beginning of a description, meets the facts intended and prepares the way for dialogue, a Japanese must judge. Should it prove that dialogue is possible, perhaps we shall have something to learn both philosophically and theologically from this peculiar relation to reality of the Japanese thinker.

The dialectic which has been experienced, and developed in the Kyoto school into a form of thought, is worked out by Kitamori as the dialectic of pain and love. It is precisely the love of God, which is the reality of God itself and "concerns us immediately" before all thought, which can only be experienced by us in the non-immediacy of pain. It is precisely the pre-theological "immediate", the love which enters our lives as the reality of the *Deus pro nobis*, which is not immediate but "in itself mediated". This very non-immediacy is the manner of the encounter in which the reality of God meets us. In it God is thought of as strictly personal, as a person who stands face to face with us, and feels love and pain and both in their interrelation. But the whole complex of facts is interpreted Christologically, or, to state the converse, serves to interpret the event of Christ. At the same time the history of Christ is accepted as reality, that is to say, Jesus Christ by no means becomes a symbolical figure for the dialectic of pain and love, any more than, say, in this way the concept of God as an indication of the "personal basic facts" of theology would disappear, and only something like an impersonal existential event of pain and love remain. But surely the dialectic of pain and love signifies the dialectic of Cross and Resurrection and teaches us to understand it. And certainly Kitamori, with singular power and lucidity, has succeeded in using the presentiment of his own feeling and thought to *think* the victory, the unsurpassable and irrevocable triumph of the love of God made manifest in the Resurrection of Jesus Christ from the dead. And precisely this, it seems to me, is a point which we can use as a foundation and begin to ask ourselves if Christ is not just as near to the "Japanese heart" and the Japanese understanding as he is to ours. This is something which we should have known for a long time and which surely we have recognized from time to time. But now we begin to experience it in concrete form through the peculiar foreignness and kinship at the same time, through that convincing luminosity which marks one frontier of our own understanding up till now and at the same time opens new possibilities of understanding, in which our Lord encounters us in the articulation of the theology of a foreign land. We begin to experience how what is most peculiar in our own confession of Christ promises to become still more intelligible in the forms of foreign confession to the same Christ.

We must call the Christology of the "pain of God" universalist in so far as in it also Jesus Christ is not an isolated figure, the dominating role in the drama of the *Heilsgeschichte*. Rather the universal range of the Divine-human encounter, the dialectic of human being before the God of love, finds expression in it, without thereby Jesus Christ being any other than M. Kähler's "historical, Biblical Christ".

Thus apart from the command which comes to us out of our own situation, and apart from our commission for the proclamation of Christ in our own sphere, the beginnings of encounter with the faith in Christ and the language of faith of other worlds are a renewed impetus to *think* the universality of the office of Christ as Mediator. But we can only co-respond to this claim by taking the path of an existential interpretation of Christology; we must think of the historical reality of human being and show how far Jesus Christ as the victorious presence of God already in fact finds being in every man, judging and reconciling, promising and renewing.

4. *The Necessity for an Existential Interpretation of Christology*

(a) *The Doctrine of the Threefold Office and our Consideration of Method*

What is our starting-point to be if we wish to approach more closely to the Christological structure of man's standing before God? To define this point of entry correctly, we must first of all examine two possibilities, both of which, in my opinion, can finally be shown not to come into consideration methodologically, that beginning from the situation of man in isolation, and that beginning from an affirmation of revelation in isolation.

This can be made clear by using a traditional *theologumenon* of Christology, the Doctrine of the Threefold Office of Christ as Prophet, Priest and King.[23]

---

[23] The old Reformation doctrine of the Threefold Office of Christ, of which, we must add, traces are already found in the Fathers of the Church, has been taken up again, above all by Karl Barth, in more recent theology. Barth has made it into a principle of sub-division for the doctrine of Reconciliation in his Church Dogmatics (Vols. IV/1, 2 and 3), though he does so with a striking change in order, for in him the prophetic office of Christ comes at the end. God's saving activity in Christ has for Barth essentially this threefold aspect. Thus by his division into three of the doctrine of Reconciliation, and of its foundation, Christology, he unites the doctrine of the Threefold Office with the two other traditional Christological *theologumena*, the doctrine of the Two Natures, and that of the Two States (*exinanitio* and *exaltatio*, "condescension" and "exaltation"). He regards the traditional juxtaposition of these three doctrines or viewpoints as artificial and inappropriate to the facts, and endeavours to conceive them as one, just as he regards as theologically untenable the separate treatment of the Person of Christ and the Work of Christ.

As *Prophet* Christ reveals the truth of the Divine will. The proclamation of the earthly Jesus, his *prophetia imme-diata*, is continued in the *prophetia mediata* of the exalted Christ by the mediation of his community.

By contrast, in the more recent Christology of W. Pannenberg (*Jesus, God and Man*, tr. Wilkins and Priebe, S.C.M., 1968), the doctrine of the *Munus Triplex* is given no constitutive significance. The viewpoint from which Pannenberg briefly examines this doctrine (*op. cit.*, pp. 212–225) is character-istically, and certainly first of all rightly from the purely historical point of view, that of the connection of the coming of Jesus with Old Testament tradition. Is Jesus, as the doctrine sees him, the fulfiller of the Old Testament offices of prophet, priest and king? His conclusion is, "The typological pattern of the Threefold Office represents more a symbol for the relation of Jesus' activity to Israel's traditions than a showing of the real context in tradition in which Jesus' activity became possible. The real line of connection is in the apocalyptic transformation of prophetic tradition. Because of the significance of his activity and fate, the figure of Jesus attracted to itself all of Israel's traditions. Here resides the truth of the typological pattern of his threefold office" (*op. cit.*, p. 225).

What Pannenberg does not take into account, although this is already obvious in Barth, is the possibility of an understanding of the doctrine which sees in it the beginning of an existential description of the event of Christ as one whole with three indissolubly connected aspects. It could be that from such a viewpoint this *theologumenon* may one day gain such a fundamental importance for the living task of an existential description of theology as has, for instance, the doctrine of the Two Natures and the *unio hypostatica* in the Christology of Karl Rahner, about which more will yet have to be said. We find in Fritz Buri's *Dogmatik als Selbstverständnis des christlichen Glaubens* (II, 1962, pp. 375ff.), an attempt to fructify the doctrine of the Threefold Office for existential interpretation. For Buri the "self-understanding of the Christian faith" is the chief methodological concept of the whole of dogmatics. Theological articulations are to be understood as an expression of this self-understanding, and, in keeping with this, so also is the doctrine of the Three-fold Office of Christ. And the self-understanding of faith, and therefore the Christian understanding of existence, is the place where this doctrine comes alive for us. Thus, for example, Buri, following tradition and against Karl Barth, gives first place to the prophetic work of salvation and prophetic office of Christ. This first place is an expression of the fact "that in the whole doctrine of the work of salvation what is at stake is a message for faith, and that the event of salvation declared in it never takes place anywhere else than in the achievement of this self-understanding of faith related to the message . . ." (*op. cit.*, p. 387). Or on the priestly work of Christ, what he has to say on *oboedentia activa* is, "The believer understands himself as condemned by God because of his sin and at the same time accepted by God in the acknowledgment of this condemnation by faith. The dogma of the substitutionary fulfilment of the law by Jesus is to be understood in no other way than as a conceptual objectifying of the reconciliation which takes place in the ruptured personality of the sinner by his appropriating the message" (*op. cit.*, p. 405). Or on *oboedentia passiva*, "The substitutionary character of the atonement of Christ does not consist in the replacement of the atonement of the believer by the atonement of Christ, but in this, that in the fellowship of atonement there comes in the

As *Priest* Christ offers himself as sacrifice for his own in substitutionary *satisfactio* and as the Exalted makes his priestly prayer on their behalf in *intercessio* to the Father, appealing thereby to the merit of his substitutionary sacrificial death. Thus he is at the same time priestly Mediator and offering for his people. In both aspects of his priestly work there is expressed his priestly *solidarity* with the people who are his own. This is the basic trait, the structure, of his priesthood. Traditional dogmatics certainly has not so far employed

place of an unreconciled self-understanding which does not recognize its guilt and is therefore incapable of atonement, a self-understanding which avails itself of the opportunity to achieve atonement by appropriating the suffering obedience of Christ" (*op. cit.*, p. 411).

Obviously Buri, too, cannot and will not speak of the threefold work of salvation by Christ except in the context of existence. In that I am at one with him. What seems to me questionable is whether one can so limit speaking of Christ and his work to the realm of the "message for faith", that is to say, to the realm of self-understanding within the believing community, where the message of Christ is accepted with the ear and responded to in the inexpressible activity of believing self-understanding. As against this, the "prior understanding" and the "wider understanding" of the reality of Christ must be given validity.

Hence, as against Buri, I should prefer to *expound the Threefold Office of Christ in terms of the Christological existential rather than of the self-understanding of the Christian faith*. Christ is the Mediator between God and man, and it is the whole of human reality, and not merely the self-understanding of the Christian faith within the community with the stamp of a certain tradition, which is determined before God through his Mediatorship. Hence it is not in my opinion sufficient to describe the reality of Jesus Christ by describing the structure of self-understanding within the community. Very much, and much that is essential, can be said in the description of this understanding, but we are not entitled to begin by limiting our theological horizon of thought in such a way.

The doctrine of the Threefold Office of Christ would then be a foundation for the existential interpretation of Christology if one were to succeed in describing, under three aspects which showed their strong connection with one another and formed a whole, the whole event of Christ in its reality and significance for every man. According to it Christ would be for every man the One who called to understand the truth and gave light (prophet), the One who in final solidarity sustained being over the abyss of nothingness because he reconciled (priest), and the One who led the way to the final consummation and fulfilment (king). And he would be these in such a way that on each occasion the one aspect necessarily included the two others, so that from it the unity of the work of Christ would be recognizable.

I regard such a course, following the track of this venerable *theologumenon*, as full of promise within the framework of an existential interpretation of Christology. But it would require a separate dogmatic work of its own. Here this scheme, in itself full of promise, requires only a brief glance to show how both approaches which arise from the twofold traditional foundation cannot be considered for a description which interprets existentially, and what third way may in consequence show itself.

the concept of solidarity in this context, but in point of fact it seems an appropriate one in respect of both aspects, *satisfactio* and *intercessio*. One would then have to consider if the traditional doctrine of satisfaction, which is completely rejected by, for instance, Bultmann, as it already was by the Socinians, as a pure *mythologumenon*, and, objectively regarded, quite un-ethical, does not gain from the concept of solidarity a genuine existentialist, that is, existentially describable, meaning and claim. For this, of course, the concept "solidarity" must be understood as an existential component. The preliminary work which has made most progress for such an understanding we find in Dietrich Bonhoeffer (Cp. Chapter Five). If we begin from an existential of solidarity, if man is essentially understood as primarily not merely an individual, but equally originally as a community being also, the old doctrine of satis-faction becomes existentially clear and a genuine *theologumenon*, which in precisely this essential respect is not to be "demytholo-gized" but to be preached just as it is as a claim on man. And thus Jesus Christ, the High Priest, is the archetype, the origin, the successful, gracious fulfilment of the solidarity which belongs to the true being of man, and in precisely this way is also the new Adam, the archetype of the new, the true man.

Finally the *Kingship* of Jesus Christ in the old Protestant tradition has three dimensions. This concept on the one hand indicates the Lordship which the Exalted *Kyrios* Jesus exer-cises over his people, his Church, through his Word and his Spirit. Non-church institutions do rule the Church, but first and last it is the Exalted himself. He distributes the *charismata* among his people. He defends the Church against its enemies, against the powers of darkness, he protects it from downfall and leads it to its goal. But according to the traditional under-standing the Kingship of Christ reaches out beyond the sphere of the Church. Outside the *regnum gratiae*, the especial rule of Christ over those who in the time of grace recognize this grace in faith, that is the Church, traditional doctrine also speaks of a *regnum potentiae* and means by this Christ's taking part in the sovereignty of the Father over the world. If one takes seriously this concept of *regnum potentiae* and interprets it further, one is brought by compulsion to the point of accepting a gracious and Christological trait in the event of Divine providence, yes, perhaps of regarding it as precisely its constitutive trait. Here again we are very close to Bonhoeffer whose Christological concept of reality must certainly be combined with the thought of providence as it comes so strongly to the fore in *Letters and Papers from Prison*. If one asks about the manner of the *regnum potentiae*, the three elements which tradition has detailed in respect of the *regnum gratiae* may help us further, holding good here also *mutatis mutandis*. They are, distribution of gifts, protection and defence, and leading to the goal. Should not the activity of Christ the King, his gracious rule, hold good in these three respects also *extra muros ecclesiae*? At least the old Christology with its concept of the *regnum potentiae* has given us a hint in this direction. In addition, consideration of the connection between the *regnum gratiae* and the *regnum potentiae* of Christ is ecclesiologically extremely relevant, for here is to be found the foundation of all assertions about the relation of the Church to the world! Finally, they spoke of the *regnum gloriae*, meaning by that the obvious Lordship of Christ, visible to all eyes, in the *consummatio* at the end of time, a consummation of the world as well as of the Church.

But however fruitful would be a more detailed, and that would necessarily mean an existential, exposition of this *theologumenon*, triadic and yet aligned towards the conception of a single whole, an exposition at which in the digression above we have only hinted, we must renounce this here. Instead we ask about the foundation for it. How was this doctrine of the Threefold Office of Christ ever reached at all? The original foundation is that which comes from the title "Christ". Thus Calvin, in the Geneva Catechism of 1545, writes in Questions 34f.:

"*Quid deinde valet nomen Christi?—Hoc epitheto melius etiamnum exprimitur eius officium. Significat enim unctum esse a patre in regem, sacerdotem ac prophetam.*
Qui scis istud? Quoniam ad hos tres usus scriptura unctionem accommodat. Deinde haec tria, quae diximus, saepe Christo tribuit."
("What, then, does the name of Christ stand for?—By this title his office is still better described. For it signifies that he has been anointed by the Father to be king, priest and prophet.
How do you know this?—Because scripture applies anointing

to these three uses. Hence it often assigns to Christ these three which we have named.")

And Johannes Heinrich Heidegger writes:

"Cum ergo antiquae unctionis veritas in Christo quaerenda sit, sicut prophetae, sacerdotes et reges externis unctionibus muneri suo consecrati sunt; ita Christus a Deo ipso unctus propheta, sacerdos et rex existere debuit." (*Corpus theologiae*, Zürich, 1700, XIX, p. 27).

("Since, therefore, the truth of ancient anointing, as when prophets, priests and kings were consecrated by outward anointings for their office, is to be sought in Christ; so it is fitting that Christ himself should be anointed prophet, priest and king by God himself".).

But this foundation on the historical fact, or on the factual situation actually testified to in Scripture, did not seem to be completely sufficient, for in the Old Covenant prophets, priests and kings were actually anointed, but "Christ" is called "the anointed" and *is* so in the deepest sense. And so Heidegger adds:

"Accedit nativa hominis peccato corrupti conditio et indigentia, cui sublevandae Christus mediator factus est. Nam natura homo et ignorantia rerum spiritualium tenebris immersus et a Deo alienatus et ad eundem redeundi plane impos est . . ." (*op. cit.*).

("We add the innate condition and need of man corrupted by sin, for the relief of which Christ was made Mediator. For man plunged in darkness by his nature and his ignorance of spiritual things is both alienated from God and obviously incapable of returning to him.")

Against the threefold *miseria* of man a threefold *medela* (remedy) is now set up; against ignorance in spiritual things prophecy, against estrangement from God the office of priest, against the inability to travel back the road to God the office of king. Thus from the *conditio* of man there follows a threefold office of his Redeemer, and a triadic understanding of the human existential situation thus forms the basis of the Christological triad.

In this latter foundation there is expressed a justified dissatisfaction with the purely "positivist" deduction of this important Christological *theologumenon* from the Biblical title "Christ". From the "revelational positivism", by no means given up, of the original Biblical basis, one takes a further step to a kind of "existential interpretation" of the threefold office. But it remains questionable nevertheless whether it is permissible to begin in this way simply at man, at his situation, at his sin, in order to make intelligible the reality of Jesus Christ. Is the "natural" man, under the power of original sin, in himself recognizable with such essential depth and such authoritative finality that one may venture to found Christology upon him? Must not rather the reality of man's situation first of all be demonstrated in its essential depths by beginning from Christ.

Both starting-points, both foundations, seem to be insufficient. We cannot begin from the reality of man isolated in the first instance from the event of Christ and explained anthropologically, if we are to understand what has taken place in *Christus pro nobis*; we cannot do so for the reason that the event of Christ itself demands so to be understood that only from it there becomes intelligible in all its depths what man is in reality. Barth's placing of Christology before all other aspects of the doctrine of Reconciliation, Hamartiology, Soteriology, Ecclesiology and Pisteology, here finds its foundation and its justification. But on the other side neither can we begin by setting down a merely Christological "that", unrelated in the first place, such as that proclaimed in the title "Christ", a "that" which serves as an axiom and from which any existential relation is subsequently established. And finally, it is also not sufficient to say that the two foundations, that on the title "Christ" and that on the threefold need of man, the "revelational positivist" and the "anthropological" bases, must be mutually complementary, that they must converge upon one another. For they cannot come together at all unless they are thought of from the beginning in their original correlation. The mere setting down together of different aspects is a frequently practised method in theology, but never a satisfactory one, because the subject-matter of theology is always a single one and there must therefore always be shown in its different aspects their inner, structural relation.

Of course it may be objected that to begin from an original presumption is precisely in keeping with the nature of theology. For it is a science which begins with the authority of the

Word of God and is grounded upon it. Hence theology in all its departments must begin from axioms. But the *Credo* with which theology begins, and in the realm of which it remains throughout its travels, is something different from an intellectual presumption of axioms from which we go on to derive a system of knowledge. Primarily and essentially, the *Credo* is a being overcome by the Word and an obedient response to it, that is to say, a process of our existence. This, however, as a phenomenon can be described, systematized and demonstrated in its components. It can be explained by words and thoughts. Thus it is the sphere of an existential accomplishment, but at the same time that of a secondary intellectual one. As against this the mere laying down of a premise or axiom is a *point* without extension, from which nothing can be further *described*, nothing explained intellectually, a first fixed point from which only *consequences* can be drawn.

And nothing of this character as a point is altered when the axioms are Christological in content. We must surely then begin with Christ in our theological thinking, but not by simply setting down a system of Christological premises, but by showing how in faith we are overcome by the Gospel of Christ and respond to it in obedience. It is then no empty presumption, but the living encounter of Word and faith itself, which is the beginning and the foundation of theology.

But as to what concerns Christology in particular, the beginning of Christology is the Gospel of Christ, the message of the Person and work of Christ. But the "what" of this foundation is not adequately represented when it is simply asserted as a naked "that" and laid down as an assertion at the beginning, but only when it is expounded in relation to the "how". But this means that if the subject of Jesus Christ is to be properly dealt with it must be shown *how* he meets us and determines our reality.

I cannot begin by setting down Christ isolated, as it were in empty space, and then secondarily create for myself any thoughts about this "how". However many and fruitful the consequences which follow from this premise, yet in such procedure it itself as such does not win belief, and therefore the system is unstable which rests upon it.

If I begin by setting down Christ as an isolated fact and put in the second place, as a mere conclusion from the premise, the "how" of our being met by him, then fundamentally I have not yet spoken of Christ at all. For Christ has his being as Revealer, as *Logos* become flesh, not without his being-for-me, his being-for-us, or to be still more exact, his being-with-us. Thus in Christology we must begin with Jesus Christ himself, with his Person and his work, but we must so do this that from the very beginning we speak of him in no other way than in the context of our human being, our reality which we can experience and grasp, which presses in upon us, our being into which he himself has entered in order to be in reality *for us* in just this way. In other words, *the existential interpretation of Christology is the exact methodological consequence of the incarnation. The decisive Christological event of our epoch lies in this, that this epoch, while it deprives us of the axiomatic validity of fundamental premises, the "God-man co-ordinates" of tradition, compels us to draw the consequences which were already there in the facts.*

How then could one begin today from the basic Christological complex of facts understood in isolation, unless possibly one were to do so in a Biblicist and fundamentalist way, and this would imply, a way which today could not be believed and followed?

Thus the course of our thought has led us to the point where we must recognize that we cannot speak of Jesus Christ, the beginning and foundation of our being, in any other way than within the horizon and through the medium of his significance, and cannot do so because outside these he is not who he is by virtue of his Incarnation for us.

To look then for a last time at our example, the threefold office and work of salvation of Jesus Christ, we cannot begin from the threefold need of man in the sense of that old foundation, nor can we begin from "Christ" in an isolated sense, but in our Christological examination Jesus Christ, the event of Christ, the "Christological complex of facts" on the one side, and the situation of man, his "need" and also his "new vocation" on the other, must interpenetrate one another as closely as possible. We cannot, in order to understand Christology, begin from a self-enclosed anthropology, even if it were a "theological anthropology". For without Christ, the Mediator between God and man, we do not in reality and in the last resort know what man is. But neither is it possible to begin from Jesus Christ alone, thought of in an isolated manner, and from this point to draw subsequent conclusions about the real man, for this reason, that Jesus Christ is not the Mediator without man. One must never think of Jesus Christ in isolation, not even as a starting-point for a list of conclusions! If we attempt to speak about Christ in isolation, then, just because he is the *Mediator*, we have at bottom not yet spoken of him at all.

We have to speak then, as it were *in one single breath of thought*, of the Mediatorship of Jesus Christ, of Jesus Christ the Mediator, and of man existing before God through this Mediatorship.

(b) *The Doctrine of the Two Natures and our Approach to the Facts*

How is this to be done? In order to make progress in this question we turn to another traditional *theologumenon* of Christology, to the *Doctrine of the Two Natures*, and to the doctrine which gives it closer definition, that of the *unio hypostatica*. These fundamental thoughts, which have remained until this day definitive for dogmatic reflection, owe their origin to dogmatic controversies in the ancient Church. The Dogma of Chalcedon, in which these diputes reached a provisional peace, protected the *Mysterium Christi*, in which the Godhead of God dwells, from heretical alienation. In this way again and again in the course of its development theology fulfils the *function of a safeguard* and a conservation; by its limiting and defining functions it has to preserve the mystery of revelation from both surrender and superficiality. But theology, nevertheless, has another *second task and function, that of exposition*. In its exposition it has to make intelligible the mystery of the truth revealed by God, on each occasion according to the measure of what is possible at a given time, not to solve its problems with its explanations, which is impossible, but to bring its own contemporaries into relation with its light. The Dogma of Chalcedon has for centuries fulfilled its function as safeguard for the mystery of the reality of Jesus Christ, and thus it remains a canon of Christology. Today, when the task of a universalist understanding of Christ demands an existential interpretation of Christology, the time may have gradually become ripe for its exposition, an exposition for which Bonhoeffer's whole thought on Jesus Christ forms a powerful beginning. In this context it would seem characteristic that in his Christology lectures of 1933 he begins with the present Christ before the historical.

We turn to the doctrine of the Two Natures and that of the *unio hypostatica*, the doctrine of the concrete unity of Divine and human reality in the person of Jesus Christ the Mediator, because it is precisely here that that con-crete ("grown together") collocation of Jesus Christ and human reality can best be studied, that collocation which we recognized as the one possible starting-point for an existential interpretation of Christology.

Bonhoeffer's poem "Who am I" gives us a clue,

"Who am I? They often tell me
I would step from my cell's confinement
calmly, cheerfully, firmly,
like a squire from his country house.

Who am I? They often tell me
I would talk to my warders
freely and friendly and clearly
as though it were mine to command.

Who am I? They also tell me
I would bear the days of misfortune
equably, smilingly, proudly,
like one accustomed to win.

Am I then really all that which other men tell of?
Or am I only what I know of myself,
restless and longing and sick, like a bird in a cage,
struggling for breath, as though hands were compressing my throat,
yearning for colours, for flowers, for the voices of birds,
thirsting for words of kindness, for neighbourliness,
tossing in expectation of great events,
powerlessly trembling for friends at an infinite distance,
weary and empty at praying, at thinking, at making,
faint, and ready to say farewell to it all?

Who am I? This or the other?
Am I one person today and tomorrow another?
Am I both at once? A hypocrite before others,

and before myself a contemptibly woebegone weakling?
Or is something within me still like a beaten army,
fleeing in disorder from victory already achieved?

Who am I? They mock me, these lonely questions of mine.
Whoever I am, thou knowest, O God, I am thine" (LPP, pp. 197f.).

Certainly a different interpretation, such as the one on the surface, would be conceivable for this poem, which is really a prayer. But yet, if we understand it in depth, the depths, that is, of the existential emotion which expresses itself in such a prayer, it still seems to say this. Who I really am cannot be determined at all from myself alone. Neither I myself, who surely ought to know myself best, nor others know it. Who I really am is with God. He knows me and I am his. This means that my true being and my true being myself are taken away from my own sight and grasp and laid up with him, and yet not laid up in such a way that I myself am not capable of realizing anything of them or others of encountering them.

That who this certain man really is cannot be determined from the present, concrete man gains obviously here a meaning which says more than the well-known statement, that what a man is cannot be determined for the reason that it belongs essentially to the nature of man always to be in the balance, always in decision, and therefore at no moment to be determined, or as J. P. Sartre puts it, *"L'homme n'est pas, il se fait"*. Certainly something phenomenologically essential for the phenomenon of existence is expressed in this continual crisis-character given to it. But the affirmation of Bonhoeffer's poem says more, it goes further phenomenologically into the existential phenomenon which I myself, this certain person, am in my selfhood. For that *God* sees and knows me says something different, too, from what, for example, Sartre says about the *"regard d'autrui"* ("the look of others"), that this slays, in that it determines me and thus robs me of my essential freedom.[24] The look of God, by contrast, his knowing and recognizing me, precisely sets me free, opens to me the sphere of real freedom to be myself.

[24] Cp. for instance, Sartre, *The Reprieve*, tr. Sutton, Hamilton, 1947, p. 362, "You saw me; in your eyes I was solid and predictable; my acts and mood were the *actual consequences of a definite entity*".

Nor is it sufficient simply to attribute to the fact of the ambiguity of all that is historical our ignorance as to who the concrete man really is, although there is certainly a connection with this. The historical is ambiguous, because, as Bultmann puts it, "its future belongs to it", because it is interpreted anew in new encounters and new classifications in history, and therefore interpreted as something new, and because as it is understood more deeply new aspects are disclosed of the reality of its being. This fact of ambiguity is likewise an essential phenomenological trait in the phenomenon belonging to history. But Bonhoeffer's poem seems to say more. It leaves, provisionally at least, the viewpoint of the future unsettled; it does not say, "Who I really am can only be shown in the future because of the ambiguity of history". What it does say is, "Whoever I am, thou knowest, O God, I am thine".

Bonhoeffer did not ponder over these differentiations in the facts which we are now exploring, but he addressed himself to them in prayer, and in so doing opened up to us perspectives for a subsequent intellectual interpretation of what was already completed in prayer and faith. And indeed theology as a process of thought is always founded on, and continues, a process of praying faith. It sees the reality which is its subject with the "eyes of faith",[25] but it *sees* with the eyes of faith. It *sees* in the light of God the phenomena which encounter us and press in upon us. Originally, properly speaking, praying faith itself sees, and theology is merely the later, or rather the accompanying, completion in thought of its seeing. What praying faith "sees", then, is not uncontrollable, not completely inaccessible to *ratio*, but verifiable step by step in an intellectual process of theology.[26]

If, then, we seek to complete the process and the affirmation in Bonhoeffer's prayer, we shall discover that, although Christ is not explicitly mentioned, we are dealing in it with a *Christological text* of the greatest compass. For there is expressed in it a factual situation of anthropology which defines human

[25] Cp. on this, for instance, the important study by Pierre Rousselot, *Les yeux de la Foi*, Recherches de Science Religieuse, 1910. Tr. into German, 1963, *Die Augen des Glaubens*, Johannes Verlag, Einsiedeln.
[26] The underlying theological problem of the relation of faith to theological thought, which we have only touched upon, cannot of course be here pursued further.

reality in this way, that *man cannot of himself be himself*. And as he reflects upon himself he will become aware of this. Nor do we now say, "He can . . .", but "He will . . .", for, when he becomes aware, it is a gift to him. But the gift of grace, whatever the name under which it comes, or even if it comes nameless, is not an unrelated "perpendicular-from-above", but the light of grace makes known what *is* the truth. For this reason, then, though what it makes known is certainly not capable of proof, examination in the dialogue of thought is not made impossible. But to return, man of himself cannot be himself and even his indeterminacy is not given into his own hands. It is not he in the last resort who has determined who he will be.

And when man discovers in the process of praying faith (and whether or not this prayer finds words is not the primary question) that neither can he say who he really is, nor is the matter of the determination of his being given over to his own sole freedom, nor, for we must also think of this, is it given over to meaninglessness, for the question about meaning remains live in him and will not allow itself to be reduced to dumbness if he is not to surrender his own understanding existence, then he will conclude, and concluding *discover*, that he cannot be himself without the other. Being human, in its proper sense, is only possible as receiving oneself as a gift from the other. If a man seeks finally to decide about himself, he ends in emptiness.

But the word "gift" already points to this, that man who "cannot of himself be himself" has no claim to be himself. It is necessary for him to receive himself as a gift, but he cannot claim it. Both facts belong to his human being. Now the other, from whom I receive myself as a gift, can in moments of grace be the other man, and to our happiness it is so time and again. But there is a realm which the power of the other man to give cannot reach, and this realm covers and coincides with the whole of my existence. We think here, not only of that loneliness in the face of death, but also of a final loneliness of the individual in life, in which perhaps death has already found being. If the power of the other to give yet lays hold upon me here, it happens through a grace that is stronger than the power of the other to give, for he in himself is still also in the last resort a solitary one. Indeed one must surely say that this grace is always the condition for the possibility of that "power of the other to give"![27]

The affirmation of Bonhoeffer's prayer thinks of man as completely given into the hands of God. He thinks of *this* man, for the reflection which discovers this can only be carried through in the *hic et nunc*. And yet it remains a pattern for the human situation in general. "Whoever I am, thou knowest, O God, I am thine". In God alone it is determined who man is, and who each *"this man"* really is. The true human self is in God; God alone knows him, and this knowing must at the same time imply a complete assignment of himself by man to God. "I am thine"; God knows man in that he is God's. Who man is he cannot himself say, nor can other men say it to him in any finally valid way. For he can withdraw himself from them. Or they remain helpless before his final loneliness. Or he can withdraw himself from them with complete justice, because in fact they do determine him with their looks. Sartre *can* be absolutely right on this point. But because the true self of man is with God he can only receive it as a gift from God. He is directed to it, but on the other hand he cannot claim it. And it is in this very tension, of being directed and not being able to claim, that man *exists*, exists before God.

But although he can raise no claim for it, yet he already knows in faith that he is God's and that God knows him, and that therefore his true self is waiting in God for him. This God is, so to speak, the determination of human existence. But the "determination" here is the Determiner, the Lord.

Here now is the point at which we learn to *perceive* that God is the Lord and Jesus Christ is the Lord. Now "anthropology", the dis-covering of the phenomenon "Man", from which we began, becomes Kyriology. And it is here that there becomes completely apparent the Christological relevance of the text

[27] In *Urdistanz und Beziehung* Martin Buber has described impressively this power of the other to give. "It is otherwise with man; separated from the realm of natural species for the venture of his lonely category, with the storm of a chaos born with him raging around him, he looks secretly and shyly for an affirmation of the possibility of his being, which for him can only come from human person to human person; men pass one to another the heavenly bread of being oneself" (*Werke*, I, p. 423). Here Buber certainly appears to describe a reciprocity between men. But that this does not remain an illusion, two blind men leading one another, but is existential reality and fulfilment, is grace which does not come from men.

which we have made our basis. God, who as *Kyrios* is the "determination of my existence", is the God who in Jesus Christ has taken upon himself human nature, and taken it up into the unity of his Divine Person in the *unio hypostatica*.

The decisive statement here is that we have no claim on this, that we ourselves receive it as the gift of him who alone can give it to us, but that we none the less know in faith and prayer that God knows us and that we are God's. Thus it does not belong to "human nature", and "human nature" can make no claim for it, that God assumes this human nature. But since the Incarnation has in fact taken place, it, as the assumption of human nature, has in fact validity for all men. God is through Jesus Christ "the determination of the existence" of all men; whether they know it or not the reality of their being is determined by the reality of the Mediator between God and man.

By virtue of this factual situation they exist on the one side in the tension of being directed to God without being able to make a claim, but on the other this tension is nevertheless modified by the fact that the gift of their true self is already given to them and that they can know this in faith and prayer. But they also at the same time remain in the tension. For they exist in decisions and crises. They do not yet know who they are, nor do others know it. The structure, therefore, of the actual being of man before God is fourfold. 1. Man is directed to God since of himself he cannot be himself. 2. But in so being directed he has no claim upon God for the gift of his being. 3. But in fact he receives his being as a gift from God. 4. Yet even so he has not the mastery of himself, and thus he remains with God in the history in which he has to realize himself before God. These four aspects form one single structure.

We must now enquire further about the nature of this remaining "tension", in order that the *"Christological factual situation of all human reality"*, this same "supernatural existential" of Rahner's, may be made still more clearly visible.

*

So far we have recognized, expressing it in the form of keywords, that the *unio hypostatica*, that con-crete, or grown together, unity of Divine and human "nature" in the Person of Jesus Christ the Mediator, which was the subject of our enquiry, is not to be understood as a "thing", as the old concept of "nature" could mislead us into doing, but personally, as an inward association, which yet does not exclude, but includes, "tension", continual being in a state of crisis.

The *unio hypostatica*, then, means an *intertwining into one another of Divine and human reality*, which is determined and structured by the person of the one Mediator Jesus Christ. There is no other way in which Divine reality, no other way in which human reality encounters us than in such intertwining. This factual situation, which we have called Christological, is also true, also determines reality and the way in which it meets us, when one knows nothing about it. The intertwining, therefore, to quote the formula of Chalcedon, is "undivided". But it is also marked by the "unconfused" of the same formula, for there is no fusion of "substances", but the confrontation of I and Thou is still retained. Human and Divine reality remain in their indissoluble intertwining into one reality of Jesus Christ the Reconciler, and yet as "I" and "Thou" existing in confrontation.

But, conversely, how is this intertwining to be conceived, if the confrontation is nevertheless still to be retained? We have recognized that the intertwining has taken place and continues to take place in such a way that the Divine reality has become a structural moment in *human reality*. And thus here also, under the heading no longer of the protective function of theology, but of the expository function, the formula of Chalcedon is to be maintained on both of its sides. The "undivided" also is here just as valid as is the "unconfused". The latter is preserved by the maintenance of the personal "tension". But on the other hand the former is preserved by the statement that through the event of Christ God becomes a structural moment of human existence.

The "undivided" is represented in the concept "structural moment", for this concept implies that the existent in question, which has this structure, is what it is *not without* this structural moment in question. In our case the concept means that human existence is what it is *not without God*. This is not true "by nature" or "necessarily", but it is in fact true by virtue of the Word becoming flesh. The *Logos* has taken flesh upon him, and Divine and human "nature", that is to say, Divine and human reality, are united. They are "indivisibly" united since Divine reality has become a structural moment of human reality, they are "unconfusedly" united, since God and man stand face to face as persons.

It is true that they are united in the person of the Mediator. But this is no miraculous special case, for he has his significance in the fact that through him, through the *unio hypostatica* achieved in him, human "nature", that is, human reality *as a whole and generally*, is united with the Divine reality in a specific way, namely, it is structurally intertwined. But just as in the story of the Mediator himself a praying confrontation with the Father appears, right up to Gethsemane and Golgotha, as a completely unavoidable and essential trait in the story, so the concrete relation of every man to God remains a story full of tension and passion, precisely in and because of the structural intertwining of Divine and human reality.

Thus far we have followed the tracks of the doctrine of the Two Natures. If now, not in the facts but in our explicit formulation, we leave it, it must at least be noticed that even such subtle concepts as that of the *communio naturarum* or that of the *communicatio idiomatum* can and must be thought out anew in terms of the personalist definition and exposition of the doctrine.

(c) *The Person of Jesus Christ as a Structural Moment of Existence*

It is true that it is possible to misunderstand the statement that through Christ the reality of God becomes the structural moment of human reality. The concept of structure itself can lead to misunderstanding and must accordingly be clarified. This statement could be misunderstood in the sense that now God was "something in man", an anthropological definition, an accident or a property. To guard against this, we have already spoken of God the "determination of existence" as the Determiner, and of the transformation of "anthropology" into "Kyriology".

I prefer to keep to the concept of "structure" for solving the problem of an existential interpretation of Christology, because, without at the moment being able to establish more definitely what would require a separate examination,[28] I regard it as an outstandingly useful conceptual instrument for the understanding of historical and meaningful reality. But we shall only obtain a concept of structure which can be used in our context when we do not simply think of "structure" as "something in" a reality, neuter or personal, which exists for itself, as a determination "added to" a "substance" which exists for itself, but when we so widen the concept that, for example, a person can also be a "structural moment". For example, one person is a structural moment in the reality of another person, or to express it otherwise, a structural moment in the "between", which discloses itself through the personal relation of persons, but which of course can nevertheless not be hypostatized apart from the persons taking part.

This use of the concept of structure is in our case also suggested by the fact that human being must not be thought of in terms of an isolated *individuum* which only secondarily enters into *commercium* with other *individua*. It is not the isolated personal "substances" which are original but the "between". When the structural components of this reality are our subject, it must surely rather be the structural components of the "between". In this sense, then, we say that the person of Jesus Christ is *the* determining structural moment of the person of every man, or *the* determining structural moment of the "between" which forms part of all human history. But this is not to be understood exclusively and we have not by any means thereby ruled out the significance of Jesus for the reality of the *cosmos*.

It must be maintained as we say so, in keeping with the *unio hypostatica* defined by *anhypostasia* and *enhypostasia*, that it is the *person* of Jesus Christ which becomes a structural moment of human existence. If, to look back once more, we have only used here also in establishing this the aims and subject-matter of traditional doctrine, yet it has nevertheless its significant existential sense. Not only is human reality, by

---

[28] I have expressed myself in somewhat more detail on the problem of the concept of structure in the essay, *La structure de l'acte de foi* (*Archivio di Filosofia*, Rome, 1966).

virtue of the event of Christ, immersed in a Divine "medium", but the *person* of Jesus Christ is present to all human being, just as in the *unio hypostatica* human reality subsists in the very *person* of the *Logos* become flesh.

Now of course there must arise the further question as to *the way in which* the person of Jesus Christ is present to all men as a structural component of their existence. One may first of all ask if this can be said of human relations also, that one person is a structural moment in the existence of another. It would seem that this is so. It is not only secondarily in fact, after what I am is first established, that I am affected by my fellowmen; I am what I am or who I am through them on each occasion, through the essential human relations in which I stand. Thus fellowmen become structural components of my concrete existence. This claim further agrees with observations of psychology, with regard, for instance, to the forming and the function of the Super-Ego, into which we find introduced the early relations of the child with others, with, say, the authority of its parents. For the facts here envisaged an outstanding example is found in marriage. Essentially and basically this human relation is more comprehensive than any other. Thus basically being married is not merely a fact but an existential, a component of being. And this is so, not of being married as such and in general, but of being married to this concrete human being. But this means that the person of the partner in marriage becomes a structural component of one's own existence. In this way, by virtue of the personal "between", my fellowmen who stand face to face with me are at the same time something "in me myself", they share in determining my own being and nature.

Now when one confronts the statement that the person of Jesus Christ is a structural moment in the existence of all men with the other statement that a fellowman, if important, can also be a structural moment in my existence, the question then arises about the difference between these two relations. It is surely a twofold difference which we have to consider. To be sure, what its significance is can only become finally clear as our thinking proceeds. The fact that human existence is structured by the person of Jesus Christ "surpasses" the fact that it is structured by our fellowmen in two ways: 1. in that it is more comprehensive, in fact total,[29] and 2. in that it is also included, and still a determining factor, in the fact that our existence is structured by our fellowmen. The structuring of existence by a fellowman can in the end be dissolved. A definite obligation to parents can disappear, even a marriage can be dissolved or damaged, and so on. Existence remains fundamentally capable of altering and passing beyond all these particular components. But by contrast the structuring of human existence by the person of Jesus Christ cannot be recalled or damaged. It accompanies man's journey through every change and shows its presence and validity in every change, always anew, always in a new form. And on the second point, the structuring of existence by the person of Christ, the "Christological factual situation", is again *in concreto* a structural moment of the structuring of existence by the persons of certain fellowmen. Indeed in the factual position of man *post Christum*, it is to a certain extent a condition of the possibility of these individual relations with our fellowmen. My relation to another is to some extent "mediated" by Christ. He, the Mediator between God and man, is at the same time the mediator between man and man. In my relations, necessary for my being, with my parents, with my marriage-partner, with my children, with my friends and my enemies, etc., Christ is included and in a hidden way present every time. To demonstrate this inclusion plausibly is one of the essential tasks of the existential interpretation of Christology.

In this we are all the time speaking of the *factual* position of man, of humanity in general, *"post Christum"*. That this is also the position where a man does not consciously know and confess Jesus Christ follows naturally from all that we have said. But the question could now arise whether God could not also *ante Christum*, apart from the event of Christ, already be the determining structural moment of human existence. Nevertheless

---

[29] On this cp. also Rudolf Bultmann, *"Grace and Freedom"* (in *Essays, Philosophical and Theological*, tr. Greig, S.C.M. 1955); "Such happenings between man and man are a pattern of what happens between God and man. But what happens between man and man never embraces the whole of our existence. A friend can only forgive his friend the *particular* guilt through which he has become guilty in relation to him personally. But the relationship to God does embrace human existence as a whole, and his forgiving grace bestows purity and newness without more ado" (*op. cit.*, p. 179).

this is not a question which can legitimately be put. This is not because Jesus Christ now belongs to the "nature" of man. Grace remains unconditional, it always remains grace and never becomes "nature". It cannot be put because we who are *post Christum* must begin our thoughts from the *factual nature of the event of Christ*. Since he is the one Mediator between God and man, we cannot think immediately about God's relation to men. This, in my opinion, is the answer to the question, discussed in Catholic theology, about what is called the *natura pura*, that is, a human "nature" apart from the factual overtaking of it by grace in Christ.

(d) *Two Examples from Contemporary Theology*

We have already begun to answer the question which is still before us as much as ever, that of the "How" of the structuring of human existence by the person of Jesus Christ, of the "How" of the presence of Christ in all human beings, by taking as an example for our consideration the poem and prayer of Dietrich Bonhoeffer, "Who am I?". Our so using it already means something of verification by reference to experience, to what a man may experience or what he may be expected to. There is contained in what the prayer expresses an awareness of the "Christological factual situation".

Before we travel further on this path, let us confirm the tenability of our train of thought so far from the parallel trains of two contemporary theologians, Karl Rahner and Ernst Fuchs.

In his essay, "On the Theology of the Incarnation" (*Theological Investigations*, IV, tr. Kevin Smyth, pp. 105ff.), Karl Rahner writes:

". . . God has taken on a human nature, because it is essentially ready and adoptable, because it alone, in contrast to what is definable without transcendence, can exist in total dispossession of itself, and comes therein to the fulfilment of its own incomprehensible meaning. Man has ultimately no choice. He understands himself as a mere void, which one can encompass only to note with the cynical laughter of the damned that there is nothing behind it. Or—since he is not the fullness which can repose contentedly in itself—he is found by the infinite and so becomes what he is; one who never succeeds in encompassing himself because the finite can only be surpassed by moving out into the unfathomable fullness of God.

"But if this is the essence of man, he attains his supreme fulfilment, the gratuitous fulfilment of his essence to which through his own ways of perfection he is always tending, only when he adoringly believes that somewhere there is a being whose existence steps so much out of itself that it *is* just the question about the mystery utterly given over to the mystery. He must believe that there is a being who is the question which has become unquestioning, because it has been accepted as his own answer by him who answers" (pp. 110f).

Here Rahner, in his endeavour to interpret the doctrine of the Incarnation of God, has thought in terms of that interrelation of human and Divine reality, that very intertwining and con-cretion on which man has no claim, but which is factual and touches *all* human existence, therefore human "nature" as such. But this is the concrete reality of man, that in himself, taken by himself, he is nothing, the ghastly emptiness of the damned, of which one can only become aware with cynical laughter, but that now, since the infinite fullness has found him, he himself can be filled by this fullness. Here Rahner achieves an essential piece of existential, and for that reason universalist, interpretation of Christology.

In his essay, *Über die Möglichkeit, Gott zu erfahren* (*Glaube und Erfahrung, Gesammelte Aufsätze*, III, 1965, pp. 174ff.), Ernst Fuchs writes about God's being *extra nos*:

"*Extra nos* must not mean being *extra nos* in the sense of being 'really' outside us, or divorced and independent from us. It can also mean acting, thinking and caring from outside us precisely *for* us, and so by presupposition being present with us and certainly seeking to be not without us, just as the housewife out in the kitchen is busy for us. I assume that Karl Barth at least means just this last thing which we have said. At all events, I interpret the '*extra nos*' in this way . . . When God occupies himself with us, his Word indicates that he addresses us as what we 'are' not without this Word, that he therefore invades *us* by his Word in a 'no longer' and a 'not yet' of our being (Romans 4: 17). That is, God's Word, as Bultmann knows, creates a *new* situation, that situation which is called by our tradition the forgiveness of sins, and by Paul the grace of our Lord Jesus Christ. This new situation becomes the content of the faith which Paul as an

Apostle defends. It is marked through and through by the fact that in it we are no longer left to ourselves, but, having been brought into the question 'in Jesus Christ', are made one with the activity of God, the 'Spirit'. For this reason the content of the Word of God is not simply God, nor yet is it simply man; it is God's *activity on behalf of* man, an event in which faith is each time already there, because man is brought into this event through faith" (p. 188).

In spite of the different words and concepts, in spite even of the different path which he certainly takes, this important theological contemporary yet seems to me to be marching parallel, forced by the facts themselves, in the same direction. Ernst Fuchs also thinks in terms of the interrelation of God and man which is given with the event of Christ. Not "God" and not "man", each thought of in isolation or only put secondarily in relation to one another, is the content of the Word of God, but *"God's activity on behalf of man"*. The *extra nos* of the reality of God does not mean a being of God unrelated and without us in the first place. The *extra nos* is the "with us" *at the same time* in the strict sense of these words. This "at the same time" is the very mark of the "new situation", the "event in which faith is already there", into which man is "brought in" through faith. It is not faith then, but God, who establishes this new situation. This event, this new situation, is the very reality of Christ. Through the *extra nos*, which at the same time is a "with us", both aspects of the one event, the one reality of Christ, the "unconfused" and the "undivided" are preserved. Thus Fuchs also is seeking to speak of the one con-cretion of human and Divine reality which has come into being through Jesus Christ. Whether indeed he can expect for this from Karl Barth the methodological and "categorical" help which we as theologians in this position and before this task would count necessary, may well appear questionable in view of what Bonhoeffer has surely aptly expressed under the caption "revelational positivism".

Both Rahner and Fuchs think on parallel lines. Fuchs tends to treat the existential interpretation of Christology as a postulate, though he does postulate it appositely, while Rahner to a certain extent carries it out. Yet there seems to me to be a fruitful beginning to a positive further development in the remark in the passage of Fuchs which we have quoted, that God "addresses us as what we 'are' not without this Word ..." Here the essence of the personal "between" is fittingly thought of through the concept of the Word as that which has being as the inseparable intertwining of Divine and human reality through Jesus Christ. Rahner goes a further step *in the direction* of defining the "How" of the intertwining. Man, human nature or human reality, is, and may be experienced as, the emptiness which experiences its unearned filling through the fullness of the Divine mystery.[30]

But, in addition to what has been said here by Rahner and Fuchs, the existential interpretation of Christology demands still further definition.

(e) *The Question of Structure and Concrete Speaking in the Proclamation of Christ*

Here we take up again our question about the "How" of the presence of the Person of Jesus Christ in the existence of every man and as a structural moment of this existence. We are exactly putting the question about an existential interpretation of Christology.

To see more clearly we ask once more, *"What purpose is served* by putting this question?" The purpose which has followed from our consideration is the working out of a universalist understanding of Christ. That the story of Christ is valid for all men, that his reality is significant for all men, must seem some pure assertion brought in from without,

---

[30] It would be completely to short-circuit the question to seek here to construct an antithesis between a "Protestant" and a "Catholic" principle, a "theology of the Word" in Fuchs, and a "theology of the inflowing mystery" in Rahner! It is true that "mystery" is a concept more familiar in Catholic theology. But yet there is no doubt that Rahner is thinking personally in what he says of the emptiness of man and the fullness of God. And the approach by the "Word" is also to be integrated within the personal horizon. (Cp. what has been said in Chapter Five, 9 in controversy with Gerhard Ebeling). Perhaps, after thinking out Rahner's definition, one could develop it further thus on the basis of Fuchs' formulation. The fullness of the Divine mystery fills the emptiness of man *in that* God's Word, which must not exclusively mean the *Kerygma* preached in Church, "invades" this "empty" man "in the 'not yet' of his being". This combination of the two approaches even seems exceptionally fruitful. We do not here explicitly pursue it further. But in all that is still to be said it must be kept in mind.

if *how* Jesus is present to all human being cannot be said and shown. Nor is it of course sufficient to fall back on the statement that Jesus Christ is present in Christian existence in that Christians believe in him and obey him. If no more could be said than this, then Christ would appear in the last resort as one content of consciousness and feeling along with others as a purely ideological reality.

But for this reason the putting of this question in the end serves the proclamation of Christ itself. Its motive, like the motive for every essential raising of questions in dogmatics, is a kerygmatic one. In the proclamation of Christ, Christ is "brought by word into" concrete situations. This demands from the preacher a *concrete* speech and an *evangelical* speech. With the general, abstract, contentless statement, "You are a sinner and have to accept this verdict!" or "You are as a sinner redeemed by Christ and must believe this!", we are not proclaiming the Gospel but setting up a religious law. We are demanding from our hearer a religious achievement, and in return for it promising him something, but something which for the most part we cannot demonstrate to him. It is only when we speak concretely that we proclaim the Gospel, that is to say, only when we can show plausibly with regard to each existential situation how far Christ the Mediator is already present in *it*, standing at the door and knocking. What we have to preach is not "must accept Christ", for how could one accept a Christ whom at the time one does not know at all, who at the time is only an empty name? That would only be law. Rather we have to preach to the people that Christ is already there. That alone is Gospel.[31] To preach the Gospel means to demonstrate the *testimony to Christ* in every human situation. But testimony to Christ, that is surely testimony to God! It is simply not the case, as many think when Christ is preached to them in a legalist spirit, that the statement "God is", is as a "higher being" above us, still possesses a

---

[31] If I also use here the concepts "law" and "Gospel", I do not use them in the same sense as Gerhard Ebeling, but, as I believe, in that of Bonhoeffer. The word "law" does not mean here the condition of understanding the Gospel, to which the latter must always remain related; it means what must be overcome in order that the Gospel may be heard. Cp. on this my argument in Chapter Three, 4 against Gerhard Ebeling. Or in other words, "law", as we here use it, means fundamentally a Gospel perverted into a law.

certain assurance of plausibility even for a cross-section of modern man, while the same modern man can no longer make anything of the mythological representation of a God become man. Rather it is precisely in Jesus Christ that the nearness of God and therefore God himself is evident. John 14: 9, "He who sees me sees the Father", holds good with a new urgency and clarity in an era which no longer presupposes the existence of God as an axiom. With the extreme simplicity which is demanded today we could say that Christendom has no other message than this to declare to man of this generation, *that God is*. In this statement, when rightly understood, all is included and decided. But we cannot declare this very message in any other way than by preaching Jesus of Nazareth, the Christ, in whom the nearness of God to man is evident.[32]

It is true that the testimony to God in Christ is testimony of a particular kind. It is *testimony for the man in action,* and not for the mere spectator, for him who sees in his action and who acts in his seeing. It is only in the commitment of discipleship to Christ that we can read the Christological depths of the phenomena of human reality. The existential interpretation of Christology is therefore a *completion in thought,* which does not prove anything to the uninterested spectator, *but which demonstrates by itself bringing the man who becomes aware to the way that he must go.*

But it is in the proclamation that this bringing to a way,

---

[32] This was brought impressively to my notice the other day in a discussion which I had with scholars of the Benedictine University of St. Anselm in Rome. In a lecture I had made the emphatic statement that today for the Church of Christ everything depended upon being able to say to man *that God is*, that where this is *really* said everything else is implicitly said along with it. A Benedictine put the counter-question if it did not much rather depend on testifying to the people about Jesus of Nazareth. In a strange way positions were reversed! The reason surely lies in the fact that the Catholic theologian thought in a counter-reaction to his own background, an active "monotheistic" tendency in Catholic thought, as in the encyclical, *Ecclesiam Suam*, and to the danger perhaps implicit in this of a "God without Christ", while by contrast I as a Protestant reacted against my background, the active Protestant tendency or danger of a "Christ without God", as in the "Death of God" theology! And thus it suddenly became clear to me that from opposite positions we had reached the heart of the matter. "That God is" is not to be proclaimed without Jesus of Nazareth—and vice versa. The mystery of the Trinity, the expression in the ancient Church of the original mystery of God experienced in faith, dawns upon the theology of our epoch as if something new.

this concrete and evangelical speaking, *really* does take place. An existential interpretation of Christology is achieved everywhere where the Gospel of Jesus Christ is really proclaimed. This is always the case where it is said as something which can be believed, and not merely asserted in a legalist and "religious" spirit as something which has to be believed, that God in Christ is there for us. It is always the case, too, then, when Christian pastoral concern for men is an event in the proclamation. But when this is the case, what has theological analysis, the completion in reflection of the existential interpretation, still to contribute?

The existential interpretation of Christology is *implicitly* contained in true, concrete, evangelical preaching of Christ, where the preacher speaks to the situation sincerely, believingly, obediently, and therefore in a way which can be believed. This implicit existential interpretation can be made explicit. This is the task of theology. Under some circumstances the preacher himself is not in a position to do so. In speaking obediently, sincerely, and to the situation he has already done what is required of him. And yet theologically exposition is worthwhile. Especially because our obedience, our sincerity and our meeting the situation are things which we have to achieve each time, but which we are not able to take into account in advance, it is to be recommended that we prepare ourselves by explicit theological thinking, by the intellectual clarification of all implicit relations, by existential interpretation of the office of preacher as a whole, and of the individual sermon.

If one analyses into its details a complex *preaching situation*, including the congregation, the Biblical text, the preacher, the circumstances of the time, etc., and makes the implicit relations clear, and if one sets this analysis of the concrete situation face to face with the analysis of the sermon given in this situation, which need not necessarily be a word from the pulpit, one will recognize with some certainty whether one has rightly preached or whether one has merely done some talking with this as a starting-point. It is true that the theological analyst does not work with criteria of mathematical exactness but must share in the preacher's commitment. Fundamentally it is conceivable that verbally the same sermon would be in one preaching situation a true witness to Christ, and in another by contrast mere religious talk.[33]

In spite of all this, of course, there are limits to theological work. These are based on the historicity and finitude of theology as such. The one limit lies in the fact that all theological thinking cannot take away from the preacher his concrete obedience, the sincerity and the relevance to the situation which are demanded of him, and the venture bound up with these. Seen in this way, theology only enters *post festum*. The other limit consists in this, that even where theological exposition shows that one has preached rightly by human standards, it is precisely the obedient man who knows that faith does not come into being by preaching alone, but only there where God wills. Faith can also be maintained, nourished and awakened by the witness of the unconsidered and irresponsibly treated sermon—and this does happen, God be praised! For which of us *Verbi Divini ministri* would not be proved an unprofitable servant, who, in comparison with the task, fails more frequently than not, and still fails even in his occasional success? But this does not exempt us from serious care about speaking what is right.

But with the reservation of these two limits it may be said that the work of theological reflection at least serves the preaching of the Gospel in that it prepares the preacher for concrete speaking, in that it teaches him to vindicate himself responsibly. One can dispute admirably with words, but it is precisely the task of concreteness which demands the discipline of *thought*!

This then is the contribution of the theology which is the subject of enquiry, in our case the explicit and considered existential interpretation of Christology, that it trains and prepares the preacher who has to proclaim Christ to recognize Jesus Christ in the real situations in which he has to preach.

[33] For this reason printed sermons are usually something of a problem. Nevertheless it can often be discerned from a printed sermon, the situation of the preaching of which is scarcely any longer recognizable, discerned from its mere language, whether the preacher took pains and exercised himself to speak concretely. The strict practice of concrete speech is the most important task in the training of Christian preachers. Unfortunately it is neglected at the moment in our training institutions in a way bordering upon the irresponsible. Here is one of the points at which the so necessary Protestant *aggiornamento* will have to begin.

For he is only preaching the Gospel where in concrete situations, and there are no others, he can say *believably*, that is to say, can *demonstrate*, "See, Jesus Christ is already there". Mere assertion by contrast establishes the law. True saying, in fact, as Martin Heidegger saw,[34] is everywhere, and more than ever here, a *demonstration*.

(f) *Ontology Issuing into Ethics*

Theological thinking is concerned with the tracks of Jesus Christ. It will never overtake his reality. Closest to him follows the "office which preaches the reconciliation which has taken place in him", the kerygmatic speaking and demonstration which says, "See, here". Theological thinking and speaking can only be an exercise in finding the tracks, in concrete speaking and in demonstration. Following the tracks, in so far as it takes place in theological reflection, may also be called a *"Theology of the Holy Spirit"*, for it is the Spirit who makes Christ present to us.

How does this exercise take place? One thing which we cannot avoid is that it always tends towards the concrete situation, and thus the existential interpretation of Christology must itself *really* take place in this concrete situation. But there it would suddenly find itself no longer only theology, but at the same time sermon and pastoral exhortation. Even authoritative exhortation should not be without thought but should be able to say to a man responsibly, and therefore thinking and seeing, "See, there is Christ in your life! There he stands before your door and knocks! Open to him! Depend upon him!". Where this is done unconsideredly, which surely means tactlessly, the doors remain closed to the preacher, Christianity becomes an ideology which seeks to overmaster.

It cannot be doubted that there is also a theology of the individual situation, a kind of theological searching of conscience, a *theologia specialissima* which looks, not at the individual conscience alone, but in the first place at God's already being there in one's own life or in the life of certain closely

---

[34] Cp., for instance, *"Der Weg zur Sprache"*, Heidegger's essay in *Unterwegs zur Sprache*, 1959, pp. 241ff., "The essence of speech is saying as demonstration. Its demonstration is not based on any sign, but all signs spring from a demonstration in the realm of which and for the purposes of which they can be signs" (p. 254).

related men, a theology therefore with thought out and completely theological affirmations which in the first place are valid for only precisely this case. But the final concreteness which is the real realm of existential theology is scarcely reached by this. Where it is approached, man sets out on his journey. He begins to pray, to see, and to act.

But we always remain short of the final concreteness, even in our knowledge of ourselves and our knowledge of the task given to us. For the final concreteness, that is, reality itself, is Jesus Christ, the Mediator between God and men. *We* still move in our thought and behaviour, even where it concerns our personal existence itself, in conventional ways. Even the sermon still unavoidably possesses a measure of generalness and abstractness, since a plurality of men hear it. Yet there is solidarity between men, we feel in solidarity with others. This justifies the continuing abstractness of preaching, and of theology which leads on to preaching. In this sense it is permissible, too, to reckon with recurring situations and structures. On these is built the existential interpretation of Christianity, asking as it does about the recurring situations of human reality and the Christological structures of the same. In so doing it finds its life in the confidence that at bottom it can be demonstrated in every real situation that Christ is already there; and with this confidence it inspires and instructs the proclamation of the Church. There is no situation, whether in the traditional Christian sphere or in any realm of history, in which Christ is not already present. If he were only one particular reality, then one could withdraw from him into other situations for which he no longer has any significance. But theology and the proclamation find their life in the confidence that there are no such situations.

These recurring situations in which existential interpretation demonstrates the presence of Christ as already there will therefore always be merely *pattern* cases, but just the type of *pattern* cases the analysis of which will give courage to look for Christ again and again in new situations also. Existential interpretation deals with pattern cases and not with principles of a general and abstract nature.

*

Now we begin to understand more deeply why Dietrich Bonhoeffer has to write precisely an *Ethics* as his planned main work. In his sincerity and his refusal of every mere assertion and every particularism precisely this theological affirmation was the right one for him, that Jesus Christ is everywhere the true reality, the determining structural component of all that is real. But the Christological ontology which seeks to understand reality as such by endeavouring to discover Jesus Christ as its essence must necessarily become ethics, and further, as we have seen in Chapter Six, must become *a Christologically determined situation ethic*. And, conversely, we understand why this ethic must at the same time put the ontological question about reality. From the concrete situations of his life man receives the light of Jesus Christ the real. When he sees him he knows what he should do, and, on the other side, it is in activity that he sees him. Seeing and action become one.[35] *In every situation whatever in which a man finds himself, there is for him a judgement, a forgiving, a meaning, a promise, a future, and something to do. To demonstrate this to him is the proclamation of the Gospel. And in theology it means "ethics" or "ontology" or "the existential interpretation of Christology". All these are in fact one and the same concern of demonstration by words.* Bonhoeffer glances at this when he speaks of the "ruling of God in history", and when he says that "God is in the facts". That God should thus be in the facts of our life and of history is not something merely factual; it has the character of judgement and reconciliation, of question and answer. Nor is it the case that "external facts", because God dwells in them, simply overmaster our "inner man"; God can be in the facts in just such a way that, through the indwelling in us of Christ who has overcome the world, he can cause us to stand fast by them.

*

[35] On this cp. also Heinrich Barth, *Erkenntnis der Existenz*, Basle, 1965, and especially his second chapter, *"Existentielle Erkenntnis"*. "But 'decision' cannot degenerate into the meaningless self-sufficiency of an existence which is based upon itself and tied to the moment on each occasion. Arbitrariness is to sink into the chaos of remoteness from understanding. But decision as the actualizing of knowledge is a meaningful act. It is an act which is supported by committing knowledge, or rather, it exists in such knowledge. As opposed to it 'decisionism' is one of the possibilities favoured today precisely for the purpose of avoiding decision" (p. 138).

Because then the existential interpretation of Christology deals in such a way with pattern cases, it is not a science based on principles, which applies these to individual cases and explains the individual cases by them. There is no Christological "systematic principle" which one could always apply; the task is rather to discover Jesus Christ anew in every individual or collective situation. Thus theology and proclamation remain wayfarers in history as *praedicatio et theologia viatorum*. *Here theology reveals itself in its deepest being as a method, as a continual wayfaring, and not as a system.* A theologia viatorum *is no system, even if again and again it has to make affirmations which are "systematic", that is to say, coherent in themselves.*

Here we surely see the deepest difference from Karl Barth's understanding of theology. In Barth theology is understood as a system and not as a method. This is the explanation of his refusal of all the methodological considerations of present-day theology. The symbol of his theology is not the journey, the discovery step by step, but the survey, the seeking to comprehend the whole within the system. It is just this difference which brought for him from Bonhoeffer, whose theological thinking followed a fundamentally different pattern, the charge of revelational positivism.

This character as a method, of course, does not mean any atomizing of theological thought, least of all in Christology,[36] and therefore means no impossibility of making fundamental Christological affirmations. What it surely does mean is a certain essential freedom from self-containedness in theological thinking, a freedom which we must also first take account of in our method of describing the course of theological thought. By fundamental Christological affirmations we mean, for example, the classical Christological dogmas and *theologumena*, such as the doctrines of the Two Natures and the Threefold Office. These are to be compared less to mountain look-out posts from which to survey the vista of the landscape, than to signposts on the road to Christological knowledge, after which we can no longer go back. They remain open to the future and demand further and ever new interpretation. The possibility of such fundamental Christological affirmations or viewpoints

---

[36] But here, according to our development of the subject hitherto, Christology appears as in a certain sense the whole of our theology.

in no way contradicts that characteristic course of the existential interpretation of Christology which looks towards concrete situations and would reach fulfilment in a *"theologia specialissima"* of the existence of the individual. Rather, the fundamental Christological affirmations free the way to just this process of thought.

Nor, further, does it contradict this course when Christological questions are asked which reach out far beyond the concrete individual situations, provided of course that there are always kept in mind questions such as, for example, that how the crucified Christ is present in human suffering, or that about the possibility of speaking meaningfully about the Resurrection of Christ. Such reaching beyond the concrete existential situation of the individual, which constitutes the peculiar subject-matter of ethics, is made possible for theological thinking and kerygmatic speaking by that solidarity which is at the basis of all human fellowship. Thus men in suffering, however different and inexchangeable may be their destinies, are in one respect in solidarity with one another, and it is possible to speak in theology and in preaching about the presence of Christ in the suffering of man and not merely of his presence in the suffering of one particular individual. To speak about what is common, to reflect upon what is common, is more simple. And yet this common element always remains open towards the individual. To speak of the presence of Jesus Christ in a way which demonstrates can, and fundamentally will, be carried on further right to a *Christologia specialissima*. Thus at any time reflective thought issues into and loses itself in the *concretissimum* of reality itself. It passes over into Bonhoeffer's "prayer and action among men of the just". It cannot of course be said in advance up to what limits reflective thought which illuminates is possible and useful in this or that case. This point of transition, this variable frontier, would itself be the subject of an engrossing research of its own. Thus the position for the thinker has in our case the form of a *pyramid*; from the fundamental structural components as "summit", thought reaches out more and more into the vastness of the immense variety of history itself, with its ethical situations no one of which is like the other.

For the very reason, then, that Jesus Christ as Mediator is

present everywhere and is the final structural component in all reality, Christology must, in achieving existential interpretation, be pushed forward into the concrete and be modified so far as is demanded and is possible on each occasion. It is not sufficient to stand still at general statements on Christology. That this is so can also be made clear from the fact that Christ is no general truth but a concrete person, yet a person not to be set apart by himself but of decisive significance for all other persons. Hence in this case we can neither utter a general truth nor describe an individual, both of which could essentially be done with a limited number of statements. In an immense number of statements, that is, in the fulfilment of a never ending task, we have to declare the significance of this one person for all.

In this unending task of the consideration of reality, there are, it is true, thanks to the person of the Mediator and to the solidarity of the men who are determined by him, those recurring *situations* and *structures* of which we have already spoken. These form the supports for the existential interpretation of Christology.

*

The true collection of examples, showing us the recurring experiences of human life, setting them in the light of God the Father of Jesus Christ, and thus teaching us wisdom, is Holy Scripture. The Biblical examples, in so far as they are patterns for the life of men before God, are at the same time patterns by means of which Christological and existential interpretation is to be carried out. Thus certain standard situations and attitudes are to be analysed, the attitude of an Apostle to a community of Christians to whom he writes, the lot of a faithful man of the Old Testament, the attitude of a praying man, or men, in a certain Psalm. Here, as we have already seen, is the place of the Christological exposition of the Old Testament. This cannot be anything other than the existential interpretation of Christology.[37] For in the Old Testament men exist before the living God without their knowing the name of Jesus Christ.

[37] Any other Christological interpretation of the Old Testament seems to me impossible.

Yet their being before God can be none other than that mediated through Jesus Christ, the one Mediator.

Not only the existence of the Israelite faithful of the Old Testament, who consciously walk before the face of JHWH, but also the existence and the situation of any faithful man in any religion, yes, even the existence and the situation of every impious despiser of religion, is to be understood as determined by Christ, as overtaken by Christ, and capable of demonstration as so determined. Outside Holy Scripture, too, recurring human situations offer themselves as patterns for existential interpretation. Thus, for example, we may quote the periods of life with their typical traits, or relationships like marriage, parenthood, the relation of children to parents, love of home—for that matter why not even the relation of a man to an animal? Or our attitude to time, to the past and to the future, can be the structure of ethical decision in certain cases.[38] We could continue specifying ever further these and many other things. A Christian and Protestant ethic in Bonhoeffer's sense would then consist, not in proclaiming the law and formulating general rules, but in pointing to the presence of Christ and the promise thereby spoken to men in all pattern cases which can be felt and seen concretely enough. Bonhoeffer himself, with his doctrine of the Mandates, has in this regard stopped at what are only the beginnings.

Thus the book of the Bible and the book of life give us examples enough and exercises enough for us to show in them the nearness of God to men. Protestant ethics, within which then the Christological ontology of all that is real can be classed, is conscious that it never reduces it and never can reduce it to a system. For history, the reality itself in which God acts, is riches. The system is always an impoverishment. And yet consideration of the subject retains a scientific character. As far as the facts are concerned it aims at the concrete

---

[38] I see a beginning towards this in Karl Rahner's theological meditations, *Everyday Things*, tr. Heelan, Sheed & Ward, 1965. There Rahner, setting himself the goal of a "theology of everyday things", makes everyday and general human situations and complexes of facts into the subject of theological interpretation. Thus he writes "on work, on getting about, on sitting down, on seeing, on laughter, on eating, on sleep". Such situations, belonging to reality which we experience, but with a concealed theological relevance, could, of course, be added to *ad infinitum*.

and must have a horror of *abstracta*. But in its method it requires the most subtle abstraction for the very purpose of not missing concreteness, and correspondingly being able at every step to give account of what it is doing. For it must always guard against those generalizations of ordinary intelligibility which conceal the true concreteness of the facts themselves. Generalizations are as a rule easy to understand, in the sense of common intelligibility, but they are as a rule false. This is the reason why theology is difficult to make intelligible. But this does not discharge it from the duty, often disregarded, of speaking as simply as is at all *possible* on each occasion.

*

With all this watchfulness, theology, now understood as the existential interpretation of Christology (though what theme in the whole of theology would not find its place under this heading?), seeks to guard the mystery of the nearness of God in Christ. In all its parts it seeks to guard against any concealment of that dimension of depth in all reality which is given by Jesus Christ. Hence there is no need for the fear that here conceptual analysis will here take the place of Martin Kähler's "historical, Biblical Christ". That Christ as the one Mediator between God and man is universal in no way implies that he is not a concrete person but rather a "Christological principle".

What is peculiar in the manifesting of Jesus Christ and his reality is just this, that he is at the same time *concrete* and *universal*. To demonstrate the universality of this concrete person requires, as we saw, a special strictness of thought, above all in a time when the danger of religious particularism, and through it of lack of credibility between Christians and non-Christians, is so present. And the reverse also holds, that to show the concrete and personal uniqueness of this complex of facts requires a special strictness of thought. Indeed, both forms of strictness are fundamentally the same theological problem. Nevertheless there is surely no need for the fear that the universality of the Christological facts might conceal the uniqueness of the Person of the Redeemer. For his sheep know his voice (John 10). The voice of him who said "Love your enemies!" or "Be not anxious about tomorrow!" has an unmistakable note, which is not lost when such words, in keeping

447

with their authority and compass, are interpreted existentially to show their significance for the existence of *every* man.
When one hears this voice, and Christological thinking begins
by hearing it, one does not need to be anxious lest in place of
the Person of Jesus Christ a Christological principle might
appear each time in our thinking. The subject-matter of
Christology is given us in advance by words which are not
ours. The *eph'hapax* of Christ itself already maintains itself by
the uniqueness of this tone, and Christ remains himself, this
One, even when he looks at us, as Matthew 25: 31–46 puts it,
out of the eyes of every man.

In making all that is real its subject, the Christological
ontology of all reality does not become a system; rather as a
theological process it maintains its *contingent and exegetical*
character, and is still always a matter of exegesis, of the understanding of the words of One who on each occasion is the first
to speak—and who speaks again and again. We shall require
to be exegetes of his words in the text of the Bible and in the
text of reality as itself lived, always with reference to his
presence as the speaker and actor, and in such a way that one
text becomes the basis of interpretation for the other. Theological thought, then, is a continued hearing his voice, for this
reason it never leaves hearing behind, and for this reason it
remains in its final essence exegetical.

The trend towards the universal certainly has this effect,
that our reflection upon the presence of Jesus Christ in all
reality shows not only certain recurring situations of human
existence but also certain recurring structural components of
the presence of Christ. It is towards these that existential interpretation directs its aim. But even these it will not be possible
to include in a complete catalogue and thus bring into a system.
The recognition of these structural components, which one
might call "Christological existentials", not of course in the
sense that they always and everywhere belong to human being
as *such*, but rather in the sense that they do *in fact* belong to the
being which has been captured by Christ, rather has a significance related to the day; they prepare us beforehand for the
discovery and the theological demonstration of the presence
of Christ in ever new existential situations.

*

The doctrines of the Two Natures and the Threefold Office have surely as existential components a universal significance concerning the whole of the reality of Christ, but have it, as we have already seen, not in any exclusive but rather in an inclusive sense; they set free one's glance for a further and more refined structural description of this reality. The structure of "emptiness and fullness" which Rahner expounds is a new structural moment making concrete existentially the doctrine of the Two Natures. In quite a number of existential situations the presence of Jesus Christ would have to be thought of just thus, that the man involved in them exists on each occasion, and in a particular way on each occasion, as Rahner's "poor state of exile", as the emptiness, but yet as the man whom there comes to meet, *in* just this situation concerned and in a way especially designed for it, the fullness of Jesus Christ in whom dwells the *Pleroma* of God. Thus one will be able to say intelligibly to man what the presence of Christ in his life implies for him, what it means that he is laid hold of by Christ and can live from his fullness.

In our study of Bonhoeffer's poem we encountered that Christological structure of the nearness and indispensability of God,[39] that *our true self is known by God* and that we are, as it were, only on a journey towards this true self. In many situations surely what will demonstrate to a man this nearness to Christ in a way which can be believed will be to say to him, "See, who you are does not depend upon you alone". We were pointed by Ernst Fuchs to that structure of the Word, as the nearness and activity of God *in Christo*, that this Word "invades" our "not yet" and "no longer". What happens to us when we are so "invaded"? The man who can say what happens in a particular case, that is, demonstrate it, proclaims Christ.

The "supernatural" Christological existential as a structural intertwining, as an interlacing of Divine and human reality, may be further made comprehensible by the analogy of

---

[39] Cp. also on this Heinrich Schlier's *Kommentar zum Epheserbrief*, Dusseldorf, 4th edn., 1963. "Christ assigns the 'place' at which one is near to God. Christ is himself the 'sphere' of God's nearness. But 'in Christ Jesus' those who were formerly far off have come near to God . . . " (p. 122; on Eph. 2: 13).

discussion as an intra-personal event. In this, it is true, the word "personality" is always only an auxiliary concept, for precisely what "personality" is surely in the last resort requires clarification from Christology. And yet surely this trait can be observed in the daily phenomenon of discussion that here there is an interlacing of the persons who take part. The precise feature of this is that in a discussion where the one ceases and the other begins can no longer be ascertained. What is said cannot legitimately be divided out between the two partners but belongs to both, for the fact which has taken possession of both of them unites the two.[40] It is in a completely different way yet that God and man are one in Jesus Christ; for here we are dealing with a discussion which decides existence and interpenetrates every other discussion. Possibly light will dawn once again from this point on the old theological question of grace and freedom.

Christological structural components of existence are *events* and not ever-enduring data. They are personal "manners of behaviour" of God, appearing on each occasion in conjunction with a certain behaviour of man. The Christological structuring of human reality and history consists in this, that God *waits* for men. And we have to proclaim to men the presence of Christ by saying and demonstrating to them that God *in Christo* waits for them on each occasion in a particular way. Two things are bound up with the concept of the "waiting of God": (1) that God waits for *us* to do something definite, for the existential interpretation of Christology will always imply the thought of an essential act of discipleship to Christ, and (2) that God is already there, already *real*, precisely as he who waits, and that therefore the act of man does not merely realize a "pure possibility".

Here is the point to be maintained, for it is only a Protestant ethic developed as a Christological ontology which is capable of taking the next step. The thinking of existential interpretation teaches us to see the Christological structural components of reality, and therefore the present Christ himself before whom we

---

[40] This trait finds expression in a particularly beautiful way in Martin Heidegger, is discussion with the Japanese (*Unterwegs zur Sprache*, 1959, pp. 83ff.). The form used here is that on each occasion a partner in discussion takes up the uncompleted sentence of the other and brings it to an end.

then stand in worship. But this "seeing", which throughout remains something provisional and intra-temporal, confers on us the freedom and the authority to call to our contemporaries, *"Behold your God"* (Isaiah 40: 9).

INDEX